International Criminal Justice Series

Volume 4

Series Information

The *International Criminal Justice Series* aims to create a platform for publications in the whole field of international criminal justice. It, therefore, deals with issues relating, among others, to:

- the work of international criminal courts and tribunals;
- transitional justice approaches in different countries;
- international anti-corruption and anti-money laundering initiatives;
- the history of international criminal law.

The series concentrates on themes pertinent to developing countries. It is peer-reviewed and seeks to publish high-quality works emanating from excellent scholars, in particular from African countries.

Editorial Office

Prof. Dr. Gerhard Werle
Humboldt-Universität zu Berlin
Faculty of Law
Unter den Linden 6,
10099 Berlin, Germany
gerhard.werle@rewi.hu-berlin.de
moritz.vormbaum@rewi.hu-berlin.de

More information about this series at http://www.springer.com/series/13470

Petra Viebig

Illicitly Obtained Evidence at the International Criminal Court

ASSER PRESS

Springer

Petra Viebig
Public Prosecutor's Office
Staatsanwaltschaft Hamburg
Hamburg
Germany

ISSN 2352-6718 ISSN 2352-6726 (electronic)
International Criminal Justice Series
ISBN 978-94-6265-092-3 ISBN 978-94-6265-093-0 (eBook)
DOI 10.1007/978-94-6265-093-0

Library of Congress Control Number: 2015951393

Published by T.M.C. ASSER PRESS, The Hague, The Netherlands www.asserpress.nl
Produced and distributed for T.M.C. ASSER PRESS by Springer-Verlag Berlin Heidelberg

Printed on acid-free paper

Springer Science+Business Media B.V. Dordrecht is part of Springer Science+Business Media
(www.springer.com)

Acknowledgments

The research for this book was conducted under the supervision of Prof. Dr. Werle of the Humboldt University, Berlin, and I first and foremost thank him for guiding me through the whole process, from the first draft to the present book. I would also like to thank Prof. Dr. René Blattmann, a former Judge at the International Criminal Court, who was so kind to take the time to discuss parts of this book and to provide his expertise. The FAZIT Foundation has earned my gratitude for their financial support.

The first idea for this book was born during a stay at the International Criminal Court in 2010. A great number of people there inspired me to do this work, both with their advice and with enthusiasm and commitment for their work. In that respect I am especially indebted to Judge Hans-Peter Kaul, who unfortunately passed away in 2014, and to Eleni Chaitidou and Gilbert Bitti, who provided very helpful advice at an early stage of the book. I would also like to thank the many colleagues and friends at the ICC, especially Kari Pannacione and Julia Koschyk, whom I first met at the ICC and who helped me with their comments and support throughout my research.

Finally, I thank my family and friends for their enduring help and support. My special thanks go to my parents and my brother, Thomas Viebig, without whose support in so many ways this book would not exist. But most importantly, I would like to thank Martin Ehlert, who has encouraged me to start this work and whose love still encourages me every day.

Contents

Abbreviations

ACHR	American Convention of Human Rights
ACHPR	African Charter on Human and Peoples Rights
BGH	Bundesgerichtshof (German Federal Supreme Court)
Cr.App.R	Criminal Appeals Reports
Crim. L.R	Criminal Law Review
ECCC	Extraordinary Chambers in the Courts of Cambodia
ECHR	European Convention on Human Rights
ECtHR	European Court of Human Rights
EWCA	England and Wales Court of Appeal
GA	General Assembly
IACtHR	Inter-American Court of Human Rights
ICC	International Criminal Court
ICCPR	International Covenant on Civil and Political Rights
ICJ	International Court of Justice
ICTR	International Criminal Tribunal for Rwanda
ICTY	International Criminal Tribunal for the former Yugoslavia
OLG	Oberlandesgericht (German Higher Regional Court)
OTP	Office of the Prosecutor
PACE	Police and Criminal Evidence Act
para.	Paragraph
Q.B.	Queen's Bench
RPE	Rules of Procedure and Evidence
S.C.R.	Supreme Court Reports
StPO	Strafprozessordnung (German Code of Criminal Procedure)
U.S.	United States
UKHL	United Kingdom House of Lords
UN	United Nations
UNCAT	United Nations Convention against Torture
v.	Versus
VCLT	Vienna Convention on the Law of Treaties
WL	Westlaw

Chapter 1
Introduction

Abstract At the level of domestic law of criminal procedure, the admissibility of illicitly obtained evidence has always been a very prominent topic. The reason is that the way a court of law deals with tainted evidence pertains to a key aspect of procedural fairness. This question concerns the balancing of the rights of individuals to a fair trial with the interest of society in the effective enforcement of criminal law. At the level of international criminal proceedings however, the subject has not yet been discussed in detail. The present work is to fill this gap. This first chapter provides a brief introduction into the different points of view of the main democratic legal systems today and sheds light on the significance of the issue for an international criminal court. It briefly outlines the state of research, as well as of the jurisprudence of the ICC existing so far. Furthermore, it depicts the scope of the present work, as well as its comparative approach.

Keywords Evidence · Exclusion · Scope of research · Comparative approach · Balancing of rights

Contents

1.1 Introduction

At the core of the present research is a problem that all modern systems of criminal procedure must face: What is the price that a society is willing to pay to punish those who have violated its core norms and rules? Or to put it another way: what are the values a society is unwilling to give up to reach this end? Restricting a person's freedom by prosecuting, trying and possibly convicting her may be justified by the right of society to protect itself against the commission of crimes. However,

P. Viebig, *Illicitly Obtained Evidence at the International Criminal Court*,
International Criminal Justice Series 4, DOI 10.1007/978-94-6265-093-0_1

modern criminal justice systems accept the idea that not all means of investigation are acceptable. As individuals, those affected by a criminal investigation are endowed with fundamental rights that cannot be violated in order to reach even the most justified conviction.

Today, it is widely agreed that this places restraints on the measures that are legally available to investigators but also that it limits the sort of evidence that may be used in court. This opinion has not always prevailed. For a long time, domestic courts in both common and civil law systems did not look at the manner in which evidence was obtained, as long as it served the discovery of substantive truth. Even though criminal trials in common law systems tend to be governed by an extensive set of evidentiary rules, traditional common law did not initially look at the origin of a piece of evidence. The only relevant question was whether evidence was accurate and reliable.

Civil law systems in turn have always granted a great deal of discretion to judges with respect to evidentiary issues. In light of the so-called principle of the freedom of proof ('liberté de la preuve'), civil law systems, for a long time, were resistant to the idea of withdrawing cogent evidence from a judge's disposal.[1] The requirements of the rule of law however have led modern criminal law systems to place more emphasis on values other than merely the establishment of truth. As a consequence, these systems have regularly adopted some version of what has been termed the exclusionary rule.

In essence, this rule allows the removal from trial of evidence collected by means that are considered illegal or unfair. The exclusionary rule's scope of application varies throughout the different legal systems and remains a matter of heated debate, regardless of which system one looks at. In principle, the critique against the rule is understandable. To use a regularly cited quote, there is, in fact, reason enough to be at unease with the idea that "*the criminal goes free because the constable has blundered*".[2] Where serious crimes are concerned, it seems particularly disproportionate to exclude reliable evidence and possibly even to prevent a conviction because investigators have not followed the correct procedures. As a consequence, even the strongest supporters of the exclusionary rule must admit that there is a tension between conflicting values, namely the protection of individual rights on the one hand and the need for an effective prosecution of crimes on the other. Every criminal law system must deal with this antagonism in order to find its own middle ground, embodied in its own version of the exclusionary rule.

As we will see, the particular choices made by different systems depend to a large degree on how each system justifies the exclusion of illicitly obtained evidence. Different rationales for exclusion have usually been supported in the respective domestic debates. These rationales also influence the rule's implementation. A system in which excluding tainted evidence serves as a way to vindicate

[1] Altogether, Jackson and Summers 2012, p. 153.

[2] See *People v. Defore*, Court of Appeals of New York, decision of 15 May 1926, Opinion Judge Cordozo.

the violation of individual rights will not necessarily come to the same results as one in which it is meant to deter investigators from committing offences in the future. And in contrast to both of these systems, judges may decide differently in a system that strives primarily to preserve the legitimacy of its courts.

The exclusionary rule will be the focus of the present research. This book will not, however, be yet another contribution to the debate within a domestic system. It will instead treat the applicability of the exclusionary rule to the proceedings of the first permanent international criminal institution, the International Criminal Court (ICC). The legal norm that will be central to this analysis is Article 69(7) of the ICC Statute.[3] Under certain conditions, this provision allows the exclusion from trial of evidence that has been collected through means that have violated either the ICC Statute or "*internationally recognized human rights*". The fact that the ICC Statute includes such an explicit rule almost amounts to an excessive degree of regulation when compared to many domestic legal systems which have no written rule at all. The exact terms of this provision, however, remain vague. We will see in particular that it cannot give an easy answer to the position of the ICC with respect to the antagonism described above.

In fact, for the ICC, the contrast between effective prosecution and individual rights becomes even sharper than it is at the domestic level. As an international court, the ICC has jurisdiction only over crimes of a massive dimension, the so-called core crimes.[4] The idea that a perpetrator could go free may seem shocking where a single murder or rape goes unpunished. But how much more objectionable does it seem to risk that perpetrators of mass atrocities such as genocide or crimes against humanity are freed because investigators have disrespected legal rules? On the other hand, can the consequence truly be that an international criminal institution should regularly ignore the violation of individual rights and procedural safeguards in order to guarantee the effectiveness of its trials?

For other issues, commentators, as well as international judges, have argued in the past that the application of human and fair trial standards by international criminal courts and tribunals is subject to their applicability in the unique context in which these institutions operate.[5] International criminal proceedings are unique. This is not only so in view of the gravity of international crimes; investigations for these proceedings also give rise to challenges that go far beyond the difficulties investigators usually face at the domestic level. The collection of evidence for international criminal institutions is particularly challenging. None of the international criminal institutions has a fully competent enforcement machinery at its disposal. Instead, all of the existing international criminal courts and tribunals are

[3]Rome Statute of the International Criminal Court (ICC Statute), signed on 17 July 1998, entered into force on 1 July 2001; available at: http://www.icc-cpi.int/en_menus/icc/legal%20texts%20and%20tools/official%20journal/Pages/rome%20statute.asp (last visited: October 2013).

[4]See Article 5 of the ICC Statute.

[5]For an overview of this debate, see Fedorova and Sluiter 2009, p. 47 et seq.; Swoboda 2012, p. 87 et seq.

highly dependent on domestic authorities which may or may not be willing to cooperate. Further challenges arise from the large-scale dimension of international crimes both in geographical and temporal terms, as well as from the fact that evidence mostly has to be collected in conflict or post-conflict areas.[6]

At first sight, all of this seems to suggest that a different fair trial standard must apply to international criminal proceedings. Any discussion of the ICC's law of evidence will have to take into account these particularities. So will this research. It will nonetheless adopt the view that caution is advised before invoking these particularities to weaken the canon of procedural guarantees developed by modern criminal law systems. This research will show that while it may at times be hard to accept that evidence relating to grave crimes cannot be used in court, international criminal institutions in particular must stand by the basic principles of a fair trial and human rights protection. As we will see, institutions like the ICC are particularly vulnerable when it comes to their legitimacy. They cannot afford to compromise their integrity by using evidence that has been gained through breaches of basic procedural protections.

1.2 Setting the Context

Given the fundamental character of this issue, it does not come as a surprise that the admissibility of illicitly obtained evidence has generally been a very prominent topic in the domestic law of criminal procedure. This is at least so in systems governed by the rule of law. There is an abundance of legal literature on the topic. Academics, as well as legal practitioners, both in common law and civil law systems, have developed sophisticated theoretical approaches to the issue. In recent decades, the number of comparative approaches has increased as well. In a search for better solutions, academics have turned to the ideas developed by their colleagues abroad and to the case law of foreign courts. A number of scholarly writings have been published on the subject. These have contemplated both the approaches discussed in states whose procedural system belongs to their own legal family[7] and to those developed in systems that are part of a different legal family.[8] Recently, a whole volume of articles has approached the issue from a comparative law perspective.[9]

In comparison, at the level of international criminal proceedings, the subject has not yet been discussed in detail. Again, this does not come as a surprise as substantive criminal law has been the main focus of scholars in the field of

[6]See Combs 2011, p. 323.

[7]See for instance Choo and Nash 2007; Nasheri 1996; Osborn 2000.

[8]See for instance Ambos 2010; Bradley 1982; Harris 1991; Ma 1999; Pakter 1985; Slobogin 1999.

[9]Thaman 2013.

international criminal law for a long time. Of course, academic works have addressed the main problems that international criminal procedure had to face in its early years.[10] One important early volume dealt with the human rights implications of international criminal proceedings.[11] In addition, the many introductions and general books on international criminal law have always included discussions of the law of procedure and evidence, and the two main commentaries on the ICC Statute in particular provide a useful first insight into the law of international criminal procedure and evidence.[12] We can see, however, that it was mainly in recent years that the overall interest in the international law of criminal procedure and evidence has increased. Within the two years before the completion of this book, prominent scholars have published two comprehensive treatise on international criminal procedure.[13] In addition, different aspects of the law of evidence have been addressed in great detail in a number of volumes.[14] Very little, however, has been published on the specific issue dealt with in this research: Textbooks on international criminal law and procedure have devoted smaller sections to the issue[15]; a limited number of journal articles and contributions to anthologies have addressed the topic, mostly among other evidentiary issues[16]; and, to this author's knowledge, only one journal article on the procedural law of the ICC has so far has been devoted to the exclusion of illicitly obtained evidence.[17]

The scarce literature does not permit the inference that the issue has no relevance in international criminal proceedings. In practice, both United Nations *ad hoc* tribunals have had to decide on the admissibility of illicitly obtained evidence on several occasions.[18] Most importantly for this research, the judges of the ICC had to deal with requests for the exclusion of evidence in two different cases.

The first case ever completed by the ICC was the case against the former militia leader Thomas *Lubanga*. Among many other issues, the Court, in the course of these proceedings, was also confronted with a motion for the exclusion of evidence that the defence claimed had been gathered illegally. The evidence consisted of a number of documents that had been seized during a search at *Lubanga*'s home in the Democratic Republic of the Congo. The defence claimed that the collection of this evidence had violated the defendant's right to privacy. The issue was first

[10]For an early example with respect to the ICC, see Lattanzi and Schabas 1999.

[11]Zappalà 2003.

[12]Schabas 2010; Triffterer 2008.

[13]Safferling 2012; Gradoni et al. 2013.

[14]See in particular Combs 2010; Jackson and Summers 2012; Klamberg 2013.

[15]See for instance Zahar and Sluiter 2008, p. 379 et seq.; Schabas 2011, p. 317 et seq.

[16]See Alamuddin 2010; Berger 2012; Brady 1999; Caianiello 2011; Combs 2011; Edwards 2001; Fedorova and Sluiter 2009; Gallant 1999; Miraglia 2008.

[17]Vanderpuye 2005.

[18]For a number of examples, see in particular Sect. 3.1.3.

raised during the confirmation of charges proceedings. The ICC Pre-Trial Chamber decided to admit the evidence.[19] This decision was later confirmed by the Trial Chamber which took the opportunity to elaborate in more detail on the exclusion of evidence under the ICC Statute.[20]

The issue of the exclusion of tainted evidence arose again in the case against Germain Katanga, another former Congolese militia leader. This time, the defence based its motion for exclusion on the right to legal counsel. During a procès-verbal in Kinshasa, the defendant had not received legal assistance. The defence argued that, as a consequence, his statements could not be used as evidence by the ICC. When deciding on the confirmation of charges, the Pre-Trial Chamber once more admitted the evidence.[21] This time, however, the Trial Chamber disagreed with the decision and excluded the statements at the trial stage.[22]

In all likelihood, the ICC will have to deal with further such cases in the future. In fact, it seems clear that in criminal proceedings that are carried out in an international setting with the involvement of many, often very different, actors, the risk increases that individual rights will be violated, whether by mistake or intentionally. There seems therefore to be reason enough to try to fill the gap in the legal discussion described above.

1.3 Chapters Outline

This study is based on a decidedly comparative approach. The following chapters will look at the solutions found for the different problems relating to the exclusion of illicitly obtained evidence in domestic, human rights and international criminal law systems. These systems will be used as models to develop an approach that fits the peculiarities and needs of the International Criminal Court.

In light of the scarce literature at the international level, solutions developed by academics for domestic systems in particular will play a major role in breathing life into the ICC's legal framework on exclusion. Of course, this is not to say that the solutions of any of these systems can be transferred wholesale. The drafters of the Court's legal framework have established a system *sui generis* that does not favour any existing legal family, let alone one single domestic system.[23] But, at the

[19] *Prosecutor v. Lubanga* (Decision on the Confirmation of Charges), ICC (Pre-Trial Chamber), decision of 29 January 2007, paras 60 et seq.

[20] *Prosecutor v. Lubanga* (Decision on the Admission of Material from the 'Bar Table'), ICC (Trial Chamber), decision of 24 June 2009, para 41.

[21] *Prosecutor v. Katanga* (Decision on the Confirmation of Charges), ICC (Pre-Trial Chamber), decision of 30 September 2008, paras 79 et seq.

[22] *Prosecutor v. Katanga* (Decision on the Prosecutor's Bar Table Motions), ICC (Trial Chamber), decision of 17 December 2010, paras 55 et seq.

[23] See Calvo-Goller 2006, p. 147 et seq. For an introduction into the hybrid nature of the procedural law of the ICC, see Ambos 2007, p. 429 et seq.; Orie 2002, p. 1439.

same time, the Court's system is rooted in previously existing ideas of a modern law of criminal procedure. It was created by lawyers with their own legal backgrounds, influenced *inter alia* by their knowledge gained at the domestic level. This background can and must be taken into account when developing theoretical approaches to procedural issues under the ICC's legal framework.[24]

This latter finding was also important for the choice of domestic systems referred to in this book. All of these systems are part of either the civil or the common law legal family. Two prefatory remarks seem necessary in this respect. First of all, these are admittedly not the only legal families existing today. Limiting the choice in this way seems however reasonable in light of the predominant influence of these legal families on the content of the ICC's procedural law as it stands today. The second remark pertains to the categories of civil and common law as such. The categorization into these distinct legal families is not uncontroversial because, in reality, legal systems are not purely common law or purely civil law systems. They tend to be hybrid systems to a certain extent.[25] The debate around these comparative law categorizations, however, goes well beyond the scope of this study. For the sake of simplicity and comprehensibility, the following chapters will therefore refer to civil and common systems as readily intelligible categories.

With these preliminary deliberations in mind, this study is structured as follows. Chapter 2 will examine in more detail the sources and methods available to develop an ICC approach to the exclusion of evidence. This will include both an assessment of the kinds of legal sources that may be drawn from in terms of the ICC Statute and a short analysis of the applicable methods of interpretation. As part of the latter of these two assessments, special attention will be given to the purposes that have guided the establishment of the ICC. This analysis is necessary in order to subsequently develop the central rationale that guides exclusion under the ICC Statute. Chapter 3 will provide a general introduction to examples of approaches to the exclusion of illicitly obtained evidence at the international level, at the level of human rights law and at the domestic level. Chapter 4 will then constitute the central part of the research. Turning to the ICC, it will strive to develop the basic principles of a distinct approach to the exclusion of evidence that fits the Court. For this purpose, it will first depict the conditions ICC investigations operate under by describing the cooperation system between the ICC and domestic states. Taking into account the approaches of other systems, it will then set out and interpret the legal framework for exclusion under the ICC proper law. One of the main questions of this chapter will be the rationale that justifies the exclusion of evidence from ICC proceedings. This will be followed by a review of the kind of legal violations that may lead to the exclusion of evidence. Chapter 5 will deal with the factors that should guide the decision whether or not to exclude evidence in the specific case before the ICC and Chap. 6, in turn, will be dedicated to the relationship between the legal violation committed during an investigation and the

---

[24]Similar, Gradoni et al. 2013, p. 70.

[25]Mundis 2001, p. 367; Schuon 2010, p. 11.

evidence whose admissibility is at stake. This includes, in particular, an assessment of whether the ICC should apply its own version of the much discussed *'fruits of the poisonous tree doctrine'*, first developed in the United States. Finally, Chap. 6 will provide a brief consideration of a number of procedural aspects that determine the practical implementation of previous findings in ICC proceedings, such as who may file a motion for exclusion or who bears the burden of proof if the facts of a case remain contentious.

Naturally, not all questions related to the exclusion of illicitly obtained evidence can be discussed in such a comparatively short study. Neither will this research provide a definitive solution for how to treat tainted evidence in international proceedings. This would be presumptuous given the decades of discussion in domestic systems which remain ongoing today. By providing a possible approach to this issue in international criminal proceedings, it may, however, serve as one starting point for further discussion at this level. A further central contribution will hopefully be the fostering of mutual understanding in this debate. Both commentators on and actors in international criminal law are faced every day with the problem of how to develop solutions and compromises in a setting where a panoply of legal voices with diverse backgrounds come together. For the question of the exclusion of illicitly obtained evidence, this study is meant *inter alia* to contribute to a better understanding of the different views. In this way, it will hopefully help to trigger a sound discussion of this topic, taking into account the particularities of international criminal proceedings.

References

Alamuddin A (2010) Collection of evidence. In: Khan K, Buisman C, Gosnell C (eds) Principles of evidence in international criminal justice. Oxford University Press, Oxford, pp 231–305

Ambos K (2007) The structure of international criminal procedure: “Adversarial”, “Inquisitorial” or mixed? In: Bohlander M (ed) International criminal justice: a critical analysis of institutions and procedures. Cameron May, London, pp 429–503

Ambos K (2010) Beweisverwertungsverbote: Grundlagen und Kasuistik - internationale Bezüge Ausgewählte Probleme. Duncker & Humblot, Berlin

Berger M (2012) The right to silence in the Hague International Criminal Courts. Univ San Francisco Law Rev 47:1–54

Brady H (1999) The system of evidence in the Statute of the International Criminal Court. In: Lattanzi F, Schabas W (eds) Essays on the Rome Statute of the International Criminal Court, Vol. 1. Il Sirente, Ripa Fagnano Alto, pp 279–302

Bradley C (1982) The Exclusionary Rule in Germany. Harvard Law Rev 96:1032–1066

Caianiello M (2011) First decisions on the admission of evidence at ICC trials: a blending of accusatorial and inquisitorial models? J Int Crim Justice 9:385–410

Calvo-Goller N (2006) The trial proceedings of the International Criminal Court: ICTY And ICTR precedents. Martinus Nijhoff Publishers, Leiden

Choo A, Nash S (2007) Improperly obtained evidence in the commonwealth: lessons for England and Wales? Int J Evid Proof 11:75–105

Combs N (2011) Evidence. In: Schabas W, Bernaz, N (eds) Routledge handbook of International Criminal Law. Routledge, London, pp 323–334

Edwards G (2001) International Human Rights Law challenges to the New International Criminal Court: the search and seizure right to privacy. Yale J Int Law 26:323–412

Fedorova M, Sluiter G (2009) Human rights as minimum standards in international criminal proceedings. Hum Rights Int Legal Discourse 3:9–56

Gallant K (1999) Individual Human Rights in a New International Organization: The Rome Statute of the International Criminal Court. In: Bassiouni C (ed) International Criminal Law, Volume II: Procedural and Enforcement Mechanisms, 2nd edn. Transnational Publishers, New York, pp 693–723

Gradoni L, Lewis D, Mégret F, Nouwen S, Ohlin J (2013) General framework of international criminal justice. In: Sluiter G, Friman H, Linton S, Zappalà S, Vasiliev S (eds) International criminal procedure: principles and rules. Oxford University Press, Oxford, pp 39–130

Harris K (1991) Verwertungsverbot für mittelbar erlangte Beweismittel: Fernwirkungsdoktrin in der Rechtsprechung im deutschen und amerikanischen Recht. Strafverteidiger 7:313–322

Jackson J, Summers S (2012) The internationalisation of criminal evidence: beyond the Common Law and Civil Law traditions. Cambridge University Press, Cambridge

Klamberg M (2013) Evidence in international criminal trials: confronting legal gaps and the reconstruction of disputed events. Martinus Nijhoff Publishers, Leiden

Lattanzi F, Schabas W (eds) (1999) Essays on the Rome Statute of the International Criminal Court, Vol. 1 and 2. Il Sirente, Ripa Fagnano Alto

Ma Y (1999) Comparative analysis of exclusionary rules in the United States, England, France, Germany, and Italy. Polic Int J Police Strat Manage 22(280):303

Miraglia M (2008) Admissibility of evidence, standard of proof, and nature of the decision in the ICC confirmation of charges in Lubanga. J Int Crim Justice 6:489–503

Mundis D (2001) From towards: the evolution of the ICTY rules of procedure and evidence. Leiden J Int Law 14:367–382

Nasheri H (1996) The exclusionary rule: differing trends in Canada and the United States. Crim Justice Rev 21:161–180

Orie A (2002) Accusatorial versus inquisitorial approach in international criminal proceedings. In: Cassese A, Gaeta P, Jones J (eds) The Rome Statute of the International Criminal Court: a commentary, vol 2. Oxford University Press, Oxford, pp 1439–1495

Osborn D (2000) Supressing the truth: judicial exclusion of illegally obtained evidence in the United States, Canada, England and Australia', Murdoch University Electronic Journal of Law 7. http://www.austlii.edu.au/au/journals/MurUEJL/2000/44.html. Accessed 14 May 2015

Pakter W (1985) Exclusionary rules in France, Germany, and Italy. Hastings Int Comp Law Rev 1:1–57

Safferling C (2012) International criminal procedure. Oxford University Press, Oxford

Schabas W (2010) The International Criminal Court—a commentary on the Rome Statute. Oxford University Press, Oxford

Schabas W (2011) An introduction to the International Criminal Court, 4th edn. Cambridge University Press, Cambridge

Schuon C (2010) International criminal procedure: a clash of legal cultures. T.M.C. Asser Press, The Hague

Slobogin C (1999) Why liberals should chuck the exclusionary rule. University of Illinois Law Review, pp 363–446

Swoboda S (2012) Die Europäische Menschenrechtskonvention in Strafverfahren vor internationalen Gerichten. In: Höland A (ed) Wirkungen der Rechtsprechung des Europäischen Gerichtshofs für Menschenrechte im deutschen Recht. BMW Berliner Wissenschafts-Verlag, Berlin, pp 83–118

Thaman SC, ed. (2013) Exclusionary Rules in Comparative Law. Springer, Dordrecht et al.

Triffterer O (2008) (ed) Commentary on the Rome Statute of the International Criminal Court: observers' notes, article by article, 2nd edn. C.H. Beck et al., Baden-Baden

Vanderpuye K (2005) The International Criminal Court and discretionary evidential exclusion: toeing the mark? Tulane J Int Comp Law 14:127–177

Zahar A, Sluiter G (2008) International criminal law: a critical introduction. Oxford University Press, Oxford

Zappalà S (2003) Human rights in international criminal proceedings. Oxford University Press, Oxford

Chapter 2
Legal Sources and Legal Methodology Under the ICC Statute

Abstract Chapter 1 has provided a brief introduction into the topic of the present work. It was clarified that this work will not be yet another contribution to the debate on exclusionary rules within one or more domestic legal systems but that it will transfer the issue to the legal system of the first permanent international criminal court, the ICC. Before entering into the discussion on the exclusion of evidence itself however, Chap. 2 will examine in more detail the sources and methods available to develop an ICC approach to the exclusion of evidence. This includes, on the one hand, an assessment of the legal sources that may be drawn from under the ICC Statute and, on the other hand, a short analysis of the methods of interpretation applicable to these legal sources. As part of the latter of these two assessments, special attention will be given to the purposes that have guided the establishment of the International Criminal Court. This analysis is necessary to be able later on to develop the central rationale that guides the exclusion of illicitly obtained evidence under the ICC Statute.

Keywords Evidence · Exclusion · Legal resources · Interpretation · Purposes of the ICC · Rationale · Internationally recognized human rights · Hierarchy of norms · Article 21 of the ICC Statute

Contents

P. Viebig, *Illicitly Obtained Evidence at the International Criminal Court*,
International Criminal Justice Series 4, DOI 10.1007/978-94-6265-093-0_2

2.1 Introduction

Before entering into the discussion on the exclusion of evidence itself, some preliminary explanations are necessary. We will first have to determine the legal texts and authorities that this research can draw from and the methods that we can use to interpret the relevant provisions of the ICC Statute. Given the subject matter of this research, the focus of this assessment will be on the area of procedural law.

The starting point for the analysis must necessarily be Article 21 of the ICC Statute. This provision explicitly lists the legal sources applicable in ICC proceedings. Enumerating sources in this way is a novelty in the statute of an international criminal institution. None of the statutes of the previous international criminal tribunals contains a similar provision specifying the applicable law.[1] These tribunals have applied their own statutes first and then, as a secondary source, they have relied upon the proper sources of international law as stipulated by the authoritative codification contained in Article 38(1) of the International Court of Justice (ICJ) Statute.[2]

In order to be bound by international law, it would not have been necessary for the ICC to have such a provision as well. The Court is clearly an international organisation,[3] and the legal personality attributed to international organisations is considered the basis for their obligation to observe international law.[4] Nonetheless, the explicit enumeration in Article 21 of the ICC Statute was included in the Statute to promote the principle of legality.[5]

Article 21 of the ICC Statute modifies the approach taken by the ICJ Statute in order to adapt to the requirements of international criminal law. It does so in particular by defining a hierarchy between the different sources it sets out.[6] The ICC provision on sources contains three paragraphs: para (1) establishes a tripartite regime of applicable norms. Its subpara (a) refers to the proper law of the ICC, namely the Court's Statute, its Elements of Crimes[7] and its Rules of Procedure and

---

[1]Schabas 2010, p. 379.

[2]Triffterer 2008—Margaret McAuliffe de Guzman, Article 21, para 140.

[3]The term '*international organization*' has been defined as a "*collectivity of States established by a treaty, with a constitution and common organs, having a personality distinct from that of its member-States* [...]", see ILC, 'Report of the International Law Commission on the second part of its seventeenth session and on its eighteenth session', *Yearbook of the International Law Commission* (1963) II, p. 167, available at: http://untreaty.un.org/ilc/publications/yearbooks/1963.htm (last visited: October 2013).

[4]Fedorova and Sluiter 2009, p. 20. Legal personality is expressly attributed to the ICC by Article 4(1) of the ICC Statute.

[5]Triffterer 2008—McAuliffe de Guzman, Article 21, para 1 et seq. Critical with respect to the degree of detailedness, see Pellet 2002, p. 1083.

[6]Pellet 2002, p. 1076; Werle 2012, para 193.

[7]ICC Elements of Crimes, adopted on 9 September 2002, entered into force on 9 September 2002; available at: http://www.icc-cpi.int/en_menus/icc/legal%20texts%20and%20tools/official%20journal/Pages/elements%20of%20crimes.asp (last visited: October 2013).

Evidence.[8] Subparagraph (b) sets forth the applicability of a number of external sources, in particular "*applicable treaties and the principles and rules of international law*". Subparagraph (c) mentions as a further external source "*general principles of law derived by the Court from national laws of legal systems of the world*". The two remaining paragraphs are not conceived as legal sources in the strict sense but rather determine methodological parameters.[9] Article 21(2) of the ICC Statute allows for the consideration of the Court's previous decisions. At the same time, it clarifies that the Court is not bound by its own case law. It clearly rejects therefore the methodological notion of *stare decisis* used in common law systems.[10] Article 21(3) in turn provides for a general consistency rule with regard to "*internationally recognized human rights*". The content of this phrase and the implications of the provision will be dealt with below.[11]

The following section will elaborate in more detail on the different sources. It will in particular concentrate on the use of a number of legal texts and authorities that may be relevant for the research at hand. Firstly, the ICC proper law and the question of its interpretation shall be addressed. Secondly, the existing options of drawing from external legal texts and authorities will be considered.

2.2 The ICC Proper Law and Its Interpretation

2.2.1 General Considerations

As mentioned above, the main difference between Article 38(1) of the ICJ Statute and Article 21 of the ICC Statute is that the former lists the sources of international public law without ranking them, while Article 21 ICC Statute contains a hierarchy of its applicable sources.[12] According to this hierarchy, the primary source to be considered is the proper law of the ICC. This includes the ICC

[8]ICC Rule's of Procedure an Evidence, adopted on 9 September 2002, entered into force on 9 September 2002; available at: http://www.icc-cpi.int/en_menus/icc/legal%20texts%20and%20tools/official%20journal/Pages/rules%20of%20procedure%20and%20evidence.asp (last visited: October 2013).

[9]Safferling 2012, p. 114; Young 2011, p. 207. But see for a different view, Gradoni et al. 2013, p. 72, referring to Article 21(2) as a '*subsidiary source*'; see also Zahar and Sluiter 2008, p. 18, who characterize Article 21(3) as the most superior source of law in the hierarchy of norms set out by Article 21 of the ICC Statute.

[10]Safferling 2012, p. 119; Schabas 2010, p. 394. For a brief overview of the legal methodology in common law, including on the *stare decidis* rule, see Safferling 2012, p. 117 et seq.

[11]See Sect. 4.3.3.3.

[12]Fedorova and Sluiter 2009, p. 23; Pellet 2002, p. 1076; Schabas 2010, p. 385 et seq.; Werle 2012, para 193 et seq.

Statute, the Elements of Crimes and the Rules of Procedure and Evidence.[13] The first and the last of these documents both contain provisions on the procedure to be followed by the ICC. They are consequently most relevant for this research. In order to be able to properly apply these sources, we will first briefly consider some methodological aspects regarding their interpretation.

To date, no prevailing methodology of interpretation has emerged in the field of international criminal law. As far as the United Nations' *Ad hoc* tribunals are concerned, this lack of methodology can at least in part be attributed to the circumstances under which the statutes of these courts were created. Both tribunals were established within a short period of time under the pressure of the political events in the former Yugoslavia and Rwanda. As a consequence, their statutes remain vague in many respects. Neither statute contains interpretative guidance and their interpretation is complicated by the lack of a comprehensive and coherent legal system as would exist in a well-established area of law. Under these circumstances, a particularly broad discretion was granted to the judges to develop their own methods of interpretation. These methods, however, have been criticized for being inconsistent and strongly influenced by the legal training of the respective judges.[14]

For the interpretation of the ICC proper law, the situation is slightly different. This law has established a more sophisticated legal framework than that of its predecessors. Unlike the statutes of the *Ad hoc* tribunals, the ICC Statute was not created in short order as a result of a Security Council Resolution. It was rather created in a drafting process lasting over a decade and involving a wide range of states. As a result, the interpretation of the ICC Statute can resort to a more elaborate system, including with respect to its procedural law.[15] It has been presumed that there is consequently scope for greater reliance at the ICC on traditional methods of treaty interpretation.[16]

This progress notwithstanding, any interpretation of the ICC Statute will have to take into account persisting flaws in methodology: The Statute was negotiated among a great number of states with strongly diverging legal systems. 120 of these states finally adopted the result of the drafting process. At the end of the Rome Conference, they all had to come to an agreement within a relatively short period of time and in a situation of political pressure. It is the nature of such a negotiated instrument that it cannot create a fully comprehensive and coherent legal framework comparable to a domestic legal system. In fact, constructive ambiguity is often willingly used as a diplomatic tool under such circumstances.[17] Such ambiguity in certain provisions allows for a degree of consensus with regard to contentious

---

[13]Among the sources containing the proper law of the ICC, Article 21(1)(a) of the ICC Statute does not specify any hierarchy. The Statute however takes precedent over the Rules of Procedure and Elements according to Article 51(5) of the ICC Statute and over the Elements of Crimes according to Article 9(3) of the ICC Statute.

[14]Schabas 2003, p. 849 et seq.

[15]Currat 2007, p. 151; Orie 2002, p. 1493; Gradoni et al. 2013, p. 69.

[16]Staker 2010, p. 212.

[17]Safferling 2012, p. 113.

issues, while at the same time leaving it to the legal practitioner to find a solution for the respective problem. This diplomatic tool, however, is not necessarily beneficial for the creation of a coherent system of criminal procedure.[18] In fact, procedural law is one of the areas of international criminal law where the fragmentary nature of the system is particularly obvious. The ICC legal framework is still far from providing a comprehensive and fully developed procedural system as it would usually exist at the national level.[19] As a result, despite the higher degree of regulation when compared to the *Ad hoc* tribunals, a considerable amount of discretion remains with the ICC judges as well. So far, the exercise of this discretion has not led to a prevailing hermeneutic. In fact, the approach to interpretation chosen by the ICC judges has been criticized as sometimes arbitrary and unclear.[20]

2.2.2 The Vienna Convention on the Law of Treaties and Its Applicability to the ICC Statute and the Rules of Procedure and Evidence

Under general international law, the starting point for the interpretation of a convention is the Vienna Convention on the Law of Treaties.[21] The Vienna Convention, or VCLT, is a codification of customary international law and provides authoritative rules of treaty interpretation.[22] The general approach to treaty interpretation in international law is embodied in Article 31 of the VCLT. It sets forth that "[*a*] *treaty shall be interpreted in good faith in accordance with the ordinary meaning to be given to the terms of the treaty in their context and in the light of its object and purpose.*" This approach is primarily objective in nature. It focuses on the actual text of an agreement rather than on the intention of the parties that have adopted it.[23]

Article 31 of the VCLT alludes to three aspects of interpretation: literal interpretation, systematic or contextual interpretation and a teleological interpretation that concentrates on the object and purpose of a treaty.[24] None of these three aspects has primacy over the others. Instead, the three approaches are meant to be

[18]Gradoni et al. 2013, p. 50.

[19]Gray 2004, p. 290; Sluiter 2010, p. 589.

[20]Sluiter 2009, p. 477.

[21]Vienna Convention on the Law of Treaties, signed on 23 May 1969, entered into force on 27 January 1980, UN Doc A/CONF. 39/27; 1155 UNTS 331, available at http://untreaty.un.org/cod/avl/ha/vclt/vclt.html (last visited: October 2013).

[22]Ipsen et al. 2004, p. 141.

[23]Ipsen et al. 2004, p. 139.

[24]Cassese 2005, p. 179.

used by means of "*a single combined operation*".[25] Thus, any treaty interpretation will have to take into account all three aspects, the interaction of which will produce the legally relevant interpretative result.[26]

In addition, under Article 32 of the VCLT, legislative history can be used as an auxiliary for interpretation. This includes in particular references to the preparatory work of a treaty. The consideration of such supplementary means of interpretation is however only permissible where the ordinary meaning of a word remains unclear or where it would lead to a "*manifestly absurd or unreasonable result*". The fact that the legislative history of a treaty can only be considered subsidiarily is in line with the predominantly objective approach of the VCLT.[27]

In principle, the ICC Statute is subject to the Convention's rules of treaty interpretation. Unlike the Statutes of the *Ad hoc* tribunals, the ICC Statute is without question an international treaty.[28] At the same time, the specificities of the ICC Statute as the founding treaty of an international criminal court must be given due consideration. Ultimately, the interpretation of ICC provisions should function as follows:

Despite the equal rank of the different methods of interpretation, the general objective approach underlying the Vienna Convention implies that interpretation should start with a literal analysis. This demands an identification of the '*ordinary*' or plain meaning of the text of the respective treaty.[29] The starting point of any interpretation would therefore be the wording of the ICC Statute.

In order to establish the ordinary meaning of a particular formulation, guidance can be obtained from a systematic approach, by assessing the wording in its '*context*'. The Vienna Convention defines the context of a treaty narrowly. Article 31(2) of the Convention limits the context to intrinsic material such as the treaty text itself, its preamble and annexes, as well as to agreements and instruments concluded in connection with the treaty.[30] As a consequence, a systematic interpreta-

[25]See ILC, 'Report of the International Law Commission on the second part of its seventeenth session and on its eighteenth session', *Yearbook of the International Law Commission* (1966) II, p. 219 et seq., available at: http://untreaty.un.org/ilc/texts/instruments/english/commentaries/1_1_1966.pdf (last visited: October 2013).

[26]Ipsen et al. 2004, p. 141.

[27]Ipsen et al. 2004, p. 144.

[28]*Prosecutor v. Lubanga* (Judgment on the Prosecutor's Application for Extraordinary Review of the Pre-Trial Chambers I's 31 March Decision Denying Leave to Appeal), ICC (Appeals Chamber), decision of 13 July 2006, para 33; Volker Nerlich 2009, p. 295; Grover 2010, p. 546; Schabas 2010, p. 387. The applicability of the VCLT to the ICTY and ICTR Statutes is more in dispute but has mostly been recognized, see Lister 2005, p. 77 et seq.; it has also been confirmed by both tribunals, see *Prosecutor v. Delalić* et al., (Judgment) ICTY (Trial Chamber), decision of 16 November 1998, para 1161 et seq.; *Prosecutor v. Bagosara and 28 others* (Decision on the Admissibility of the Prosecutor's Appeal from the Decision of a Confirming Judge Dismissing an Indictment against Theoneste Bagosara and 28 Others), ICTR (Appeals Chamber), decision of 8 June 1998, para 28.

[29]Ipsen et al. 2004, p. 141 et seq.

[30]ILC, Summary records of the eighteenth session, *Yearbook of the International Law Commission* (1966) I/2, p. 188, available at: http://untreaty.un.org/ilc/publications/yearbooks/Ybkvolumes(e)/ILC_1966_v1_p2_e.pdf (last visited: October 2013); see also Nerlich 2009, p. 318.

tion in proceedings at the ICC would be restricted to the ICC Statute, the Final Act of the Rome Conference and to the instruments called for in the Statute, namely the ICC Elements of Crimes and the ICC Rules of Procedure and Evidence. It has been argued, however, that this limitation does not sufficiently take into account the evolution of the ICC and of its proper law. We will see that, accordingly, it can validly be argued that a contextual approach to the interpretation of ICC provisions may also rely on further instruments, in particular on the legal framework of the two *Ad hoc* tribunals.[31]

Further difficulties pertain to a teleological interpretation. This third aspect of interpretation requires the identification of the purpose of the ICC and of the impact of this purpose on the interpretation of its proper law. Teleological considerations will be of major significance for the present research and the following section will therefore contain a more thorough analysis of this subject. We will see that the main purpose of the ICC is a general preventive one, defined by the socio-pedagogical mandate of the Court. But the discussion of the overall purpose of the ICC can only be a starting point for this research. Building on this first assessment, the reasons that justify the exclusion of evidence in ICC proceedings will have to be clarified. This issue again calls for a closer examination. It will be dealt with in the section on the construction of Article 69(7) of the ICC Statute.[32]

Finally, it can be added that beyond these three central interpretative aspects, any interpretation of an ICC provision may have recourse, under Article 32 of the Vienna Convention, to the legislative history of the ICC Statute. This includes in particular the work of the Preparatory Committee,[33] as well as the documentation of the Rome Conference.[34]

2.2.3 The Purpose of the ICC

As a prominent scholar of comparative and international law has pointed out, the procedural features of any institution cannot be measured without some understanding of its goals.[35] This insight will guide this research and teleological considerations will be important for how we will interpret the ICC provisions on

[31]See Sect. 2.3.2 2.

[32]See Sect. 4.3.2.

[33]The *Preparatory Committee* was charged by the UN General Assembly in 1995 with the work on a draft statute for the future ICC. It held six sessions from 1996 to 1998. It is not to be confused with the *Preparatory Commission* that was appointed by the Final Act of the Rome Conference to work on further practical issues that where related to the establishment of the Court. See Werle 2012, paras 59 and 68.

[34]The preparatory materials for the ICC Statute are all available at http://untreaty.un.org/cod/icc/index.html (last visited: October 2013). For a critical view of the use of the preparatory materials of consensus-based international treaties see Young 2011, p. 197.

[35]Damaška 2009, p. 175.

exclusion. To this end, however, we must first consider the overall purpose of the Court and its proceedings.

As of today, there is no straightforward concept for the purpose of either the ICC or for the enforcement of international criminal law in general. In fact, such a panoply of different objectives has been advanced that it has been argued that the resulting agenda would overburden the young ICC.[36] A closer look at the possible objectives reveals indeed that not all of these goals are equally realistic or, where they are, equally significant. To some extent, the theoretical justification for the operation of international criminal justice can draw on the classical justifications supported in the respective domestic debates.[37] At the same time, the peculiarities of the international legal system must not be disregarded.

A look at the predecessors of the ICC reveals that both the Nuremberg Trial and the Tokyo War Crimes Trials focused primarily on the classical idea of retribution.[38] It is not surprising that these tribunals, which were marked by the victory of their creators, were guided by a concept that emphasizes expiation over more future-oriented goals. Admittedly, to some degree, retribution remains significant for modern international criminal trials as well.[39] It cannot, however, serve as the sole justification for the enforcement of international criminal law today. As a matter of principle, this rationale has been criticized for being anachronistic. Retribution as the only purpose of a criminal trial is in fact hardly compatible with a modern understanding of criminal law as a goal-oriented protection of legal values.[40] Moreover, at the international level, true retribution seems difficult to achieve. In light of the tremendous dimensions of international crimes, a fair compensation for the harm done is even more difficult to imagine than for domestic capital crimes.[41]

Accordingly, while the UN *Ad hoc* tribunals, in their early decisions, recognized retribution as a main purpose of their proceedings,[42] over the years, they have increasingly emphasized the significance of the more future-oriented concepts of prevention and deterrence.[43] This approach also seem to have been guiding for the adoption of the ICC Statute. In its preamble, the Statute stipulates that its State Parties are "[d]*etermined to put an end to impunity for the perpetrators of these crimes and thus to contribute to the prevention of such crimes.*"[44]

---

[36] Damaška 2009, p. 178.

[37] Werle 2012, para 97.

[38] Neubacher 2006, p. 967.

[39] Jäger 1995, p. 339; Werle 2012, para 98.

[40] On the latter notion, see Ambos 2002, p. 307 et seq.

[41] Neubacher 2006, p. 967 et seq.

[42] See *Prosecutor v. Kupreškić* et al. (Judgment) ICTY (Trial Chamber), decision of 14 January 2000, para 848 et seq., where the tribunal explicitly recognizes the different rationales for punishment known from domestic law.

[43] Nemitz 2002, p. 165; Neubacher 2006, p. 967.

[44] See Sect. 5 of the Preamble of the ICC Statute.

The preventive function of criminal proceedings can generally operate in a number of different ways and it includes special prevention, as well as general prevention, both in a positive and a negative form. For international criminal proceedings, the impact of these different aspects slightly deviates from the situation in domestic proceedings.

Special prevention relates to the asserted impact of criminal proceedings on the individual and is regularly considered particularly important at the domestic level. For international proceedings, however, this goal can at best be attributed a minor significance. One major aspect of special prevention is the positive idea of the rehabilitation and reintegration of a former criminal into society. Whether this is a workable mechanism at the level of international criminal law is doubtful. Perpetrators of macro-crimes generally do not display the usual kind of social shortcomings that characterize ordinary criminals. In fact, at the time of the commission of the crimes, they often rather act in conformity with societal expectations.[45] At most, the deterrent aspect of negative special prevention could be relevant for international criminal proceedings: A perpetrator who has been tried could be discouraged from committing further offences.[46] This goal may be advanced at least as one reason for the arrest of the respective person and for the conduct of proceedings. But it does not necessarily justify the punishment of a perpetrator of international crimes. Once the person has been deprived of power, repetition by the same offender will often become impossible in any case. Most of the time, not least because of this deprivation of power, the political circumstances will change and often the perpetrator will no longer be in a position to commit further international crimes.[47]

Preventive effects at the international level are in fact predominantly of a general character. Admittedly, the idea of negative general prevention, namely the deterrent effect on potential offenders, can be called into question as well. To support such an effect, it has been argued that persons in the position to commit international crimes tend to calculate rationally the costs and benefits of their actions. Accordingly, they should also be influenced by the risk of prosecution.[48] In fact, the opposite seems much more likely. The conflicts that lead to the commission of such crimes tend to evoke strong emotions attached, for instance, to nationalism or religion. In light of these motives, it is doubtful whether the risk of prosecution will often have much influence.[49]

The most compelling and most widely recognized rationale for international criminal proceedings pertains to the effects of positive general prevention. The underlying idea is that the notorious impunity of massive human rights violations has a negative influence on the general belief in the validity of international

---

[45] Neubacher 2006, p. 968.

[46] In favour of the significance of special prevention in general, Werle 2012, para 106.

[47] Ambos 2002, p. 319.

[48] Neubacher 2006, p. 969.

[49] Damaška 2009, p. 183.

humanitarian and criminal law. According to this view, international criminal proceedings have a socio-pedagogical effect. The proceedings provide information about the validity of said norms and strengthen the moral inhibition against massive crimes. This means that the best way in which these proceedings contribute to the prevention of future international crimes is through their exemplary function.[50] Such a purpose, however, necessarily implicates the public perception of the International Criminal Court: The ICC will only be able to promote the validity of international humanitarian and criminal law if it is perceived as a legitimate moral authority.[51]

In this context, difficulties arise, however, from the realities of the system of international criminal justice as it stands today. The power structures within the international community lead to shortcomings when it comes to the comprehensive execution of international criminal proceedings. This in turn threatens the socio-pedagogical effect of those proceedings that actually take place.

The problem can best be illustrated by reference to social contract theories. Under these theories, the obligation for an individual to abide by the law arises from an agreement between society and the individual. The individual sacrifices a certain amount of freedom. In return, he is promised protection from the freedom-restricting acts of other individuals but also from the arbitrary exercise of power of the sovereign that this agreement created in the first place.[52] The consideration of these theories reveals one of the biggest threats to the legitimacy of international criminal institutions. These institutions ultimately exercise a part of the power that was originally conferred upon the domestic sovereign. With the establishment of a system of international criminal justice, the pledge was made to both enhance the protection of the possible victims of international crimes and to do so by means of a system that would respect the rights of suspects and accused. But up to now, the international community, insofar as it is involved in this process, has not been able to deliver on this promise. The realities of global politics prevent the comprehensive prosecution of international crimes, as well as the implementation of a fair framework for their investigation. The prosecution of international crimes remains only fragmentary, which frustrates the hope for effective law enforcement. In addition, the international community fails to fulfil the duties that arise from the social contract vis-a-vis those that have broken the law. The selective implementation of international criminal law exposes the system to the criticism of arbitrariness.[53] Moreover, with respect to law enforcement, international criminal institutions, and the ICC in particular, are heavily dependent on states. This prevents the exercise of the supervision over investigating authorities that would be needed to guarantee the respect of the rights of potential perpetrators.[54]

---

[50]Ambos 2002, p. 320; Damaška 2009, p. 184; Neubacher 2006, p. 969; Werle 2012, para 99.

[51]Damaška 2009, p. 184.

[52]Jackson and Summers 2012, p. 17.

[53]Safferling 2012, p. 125.

[54]Jackson and Summers 2012, p. 114. For more details see on the cooperation between the ICC and states, see Sect. 4.2.

We can derive from this that it is both crucial and difficult for the ICC to be perceived as a legitimate moral authority. The question arises: What are the consequences for a teleological approach to the interpretation of the Court's evidentiary framework? The most important implication is one that will have a considerable impact on the present research: Since the Court can do only little to change the realities of global politics, it will have to take even greater care not to gamble away its moral authority. As a consequence, the ICC in its proceedings, including with respect to questions of evidence, will have to adhere to a particularly high standard where due process rights are concerned. Its socio-pedagogical mandate would be doomed to failure if its work could be assailed for disrespect of those guarantees that are regularly provided to the individual in modern criminal proceedings.

At the same time, we should not, in this research, forget about a different aspect of legitimacy. The previous findings notwithstanding, the perception of the Court as a legitimate and relevant actor in the international arena will not only depend on the fairness of its proceedings. It is also closely linked to its ability to effectively implement the substantive rules of international humanitarian and criminal law in those proceedings that it actually conducts. Closely related to this aspect of positive general prevention are two wider objectives which, beyond the classical justifications for criminal prosecution, have been advanced for international criminal proceedings. When it comes to the conception of the Court's evidentiary framework, these objectives in particular point in a different direction compared to what has been outlined above.

Firstly, international criminal proceedings are meant to demonstrate solidarity with the victims of gross human rights violations. It has been pointed out that recognizing the suffering of the victims is important in order to avoid a second victimisation through denial or even through a possible attribution of guilt to the victims themselves.[55] This brings us back to the assumptions of the social contract theories. We have seen that the system of international criminal justice, as it stands, is not able to truly protect the members of a supposed global society from international crimes. The proceedings, however, enable the international community at least to demonstrate its solidarity with the victims. This in turn has consequences for the teleological interpretation of rules of evidence. The demonstration of solidarity suggests that as much evidence as possible should be admitted at trial. Every exclusion of relevant evidence in order to protect the rights of an accused will be met with the understandable incomprehension of the victims.

Secondly, it is asserted that international criminal proceedings construct a historical record of the atrocities that took place during the respective conflicts. Proponents of this truth-telling function claim that remembrance of the past is necessary for reconciliation and in order to avoid future conflicts.[56] Doubt has been cast on whether courts are the proper forum for establishing a comprehensive

[55]Neubacher 2006, p. 969.

[56]Neubacher 2006, p. 969; Werle 1997, p. 822.

historical record.[57] A slightly more modest aspiration might be more realistic. Criminal proceedings contribute to national reconciliation by shedding at least some light on the history of events.[58] Such a documentary purpose in turn requires that an account of the facts is given that is as accurate as possible. An accurate documentation also calls for admitting as much evidence as possible.

For a teleological interpretation of evidentiary rules, both of the aforementioned objectives would then require focussing primarily on the reliability of evidence and not as much on the kind of external values that are affected by due process considerations.

As a consequence, these two latter functions add further aspects to the general preventive purpose of international criminal proceedings. The need for law enforcement and accurate truth finding will often stand in contrast to the rights and interests of the persons under the jurisdiction of the ICC.[59] Any procedural solution, including those pertaining to the admissibility of illicitly obtained evidence, will have to maintain a balance between these two poles. Only then will it comply with the legitimacy concerns of the ICC and ultimately foster its overall socio-pedagogical purpose.

2.3 The Use of External Sources and Models for Interpretation

The previous chapter has dealt with the interpretation of the proper law of the ICC. As mentioned above, this body of law covers procedural issues in greater detail when compared to the legal framework of the Court's predecessors. It nevertheless falls short of providing a comprehensive system of criminal procedure. Accordingly, we will see in this research that there is often no legal rule for evidentiary issues in the ICC proper law. This raises the question to what degree recourse may be had to other legal texts and authorities. This includes in particular the statutes and jurisprudence of the two *Ad hoc* tribunals, domestic law and, finally, the large body of human rights law, including human rights treaties and the jurisprudence of their monitoring bodies.

We have already determined that, while the ICC proper law is first and foremost applicable, the applicability of external legal texts and authorities is possible under Article 21(1) and (3) of the ICC Statute. The next section will first give some closer consideration to the relationship between the ICC proper law and external legal texts and authorities. This relates to the above-mentioned hierarchy set out in

---

[57] See Damaška 2009, p. 180, who doubts that historical documentation is a proper goal for an international criminal court given the constraints that legal relevancy and the need for expediency place on judicial fact-finding.

[58] Jackson and Summers 2012, p. 112. See also Douglas 2006, p. 513 et seq.

[59] Damaška 2012, p. 619.

Article 21. It will then deal in more detail with the application in practice of those external legal texts and authorities that are most important for this research, and with their applicability under Article 21(1) and (3) of the ICC Statute.

2.3.1 The Hierarchy of Norms in Article 21 of the ICC Statute

2.3.1.1 The Relation Between the Sources of Article 21(1) of the ICC Statute

If the ICC proper law is the primary legal source applicable in proceedings before the ICC, the question is: what are the conditions that should exist for the other legal sources enumerated in Article 21(1) of the ICC Statute to be considered? Looking at the plain wording of Article 21, those sources enumerated in subpara (b) are applicable "*in the second place, where appropriate*". The reference to domestic law as contained in subpara (c) in turn is only allowed "*failing*" the consideration of the previously mentioned sources. What the consequence of these formulations are, however, remains contentious.

Looking at the Court's jurisprudence, the ICC has understood Article 21 rather narrowly. Its judges have held that the sources both in Article 21(1)(b) and (c) of the ICC Statute were only applicable in the case of a *lacuna* in the written law that cannot be closed by dint of interpretation.[60] This jurisprudence favours an extremely positivist approach to the finding of justice. The primacy of the ICC Statute is strongly emphasized so as not to rely too much on legal rules that were not discussed and adopted in detail by the Assembly of States Parties as the Court's legislative authority.[61]

With respect to substantive criminal law, the preference for legal positivism can be explained with reference to the prohibition of retroactive criminality. While this notion is not as such transferable to procedural issues, the underlying legality principle also has its place in the law of criminal procedure. The implications are certainly less strict than with respect to substantive law.[62] However, the requirements of reliability and foreseeability, as well as of the equal treatment of affected persons, demand regulation of procedural matters that is as precise and definite as possible.[63] External legal sources such as customary law and general principles of

---

[60]See *Prosecutor v. Al Bashir* (Decision on the Prosecutor's Application for a Warrant of Arrest against Omar al Bashir), ICC (Pre-Trial Chamber), decision of 4 March 2009, para 126.

[61]Also see Safferling 2012, p. 111, who identifies a preference of both the ICC and the Ad hoc tribunals for a positivist approach.

[62]Gradoni et al. 2013, p. 71.

[63]On the principle of legality with respect to judicial decisions in general, see Cassese 2003, p. 21. With respect to the law of criminal procedure, see Safferling 2012, pp. 111 and 115; Gradoni et al. 2013, p. 70.

law are often vague and rest on uncertain foundations. Accordingly, they are less able to do justice to the requirements arising from the legality principle. On this basis alone, the jurisprudence of the Pre-Trial Chamber could be regarded as sensible even if one views it from the perspective of procedural law.

The approach of the ICC judges has nevertheless been criticised in general for overly restricting the use of external sources. On a level of principle, doubts have been raised about how often gaps in law that absolutely cannot be closed by interpretation will actually arise.[64] With respect to substantive issues, the—then very limited—possibility of considering external sources has been found to encourage a problematic fragmentation of international criminal law.[65] In fact, the wording used in Article 21(1) would also allow for a more open approach. This is most clear from the expression "*as appropriate*" used in Article 21(1)(b).[66] And while admittedly more restrictive, the formulation "*failing that*" used in para (c) is also open enough to allow for a broader understanding. Given the topic of this research, we shall assess this criticism from the perspective of procedural law. Our assessment will show that while, theoretically, a more open understanding of Article 21 would be advisable, the use of customary law and general principles of law as external legal sources in the strict sense is subject to practical limitations.

First of all, some remarks are necessary on the issue of fragmentation. The problem for procedural law is not the same as it is with respect to substantive law. In substantive law, fragmentation clearly has an adverse effect on the legitimacy of the ICC and of international criminal law in general. This is because international criminal law is based on the very idea of universal validity.[67] In procedural law, on the other hand, it is less problematic if each institution implements its own procedure, as long as it respects a common core of values. A possible fragmentation of procedural law does not automatically have an adverse impact on the rights of the accused or other persons affected by the proceedings. While these persons have a right to legal certainty with respect to the law of a certain institution, there is no right to be treated according to one specific legal procedure. In fact, there is often not one just solution for procedural problems but several.[68] The fairness of a solution depends not least on the overall procedural system applicable in a certain situation. To a large degree, procedural law is thus relative to the institution that applies it.[69] We will see in the next sections that this autonomy does not entirely bar recourse to external sources in the area of procedural law. It calls, however, for particular caution when assessing the transferability of solutions. And, most importantly at this point, it limits the danger that arises from fragmentation when compared to substantive law.

[64]Burghardt and Geneuss 2009, p. 132.

[65]Burghardt and Geneuss 2009, p. 133.

[66]Safferling 2012, p. 113.

[67]Burghardt and Geneuss 2009, p. 133; Safferling 2012, p. 111.

[68]With respect to general principles of law, see Gallant 1999, p. 709, fn. 86.

[69]Safferling 2012, p. 111.

More important than the danger of fragmentation is the methodological objection against the ICC case law mentioned above. This objection pertains to the difficulties in identifying gaps in the Court's procedural law as required by the ICC judges. In this context, we must once more take into account that the procedural system applicable at the ICC is not a coherent codification.[70] However, the very idea of identifying gaps in a legal system is based on the assumption of a theoretically coherent system of law. Where no such system exists, a generally more open approach to the consideration of external sources seems preferable.[71] Often, these sources will provide at least some legal guidance. In particular where a system remains fragmentary in many respects, the line between interpretation and a dangerously subjective creation of law is often thin. Admittedly, in light of the discretion vested in them, judges will always be law creators to a certain degree, especially in a system as new as the system of international criminal justice. But before developing entirely independent interpretations or creating completely new solutions, ICC judges should try to turn to pre-existing concepts and ideas. Such an approach is ultimately more fitting with the principle of legality. In general, the recourse to external texts and authorities seems less problematic than purely judge-made solutions.

Thus, under the hierarchy of Article 21 of the ICC Statute, external sources should theoretically be applicable to a larger extent than suggested in the ICC case law. But as we will see in more detail below, the consequences of this assessment are subject to considerable practical limitations. The reason is simply that external sources in the strict sense are often not very fruitful when it comes to questions of the law of criminal procedure. Accordingly, we will often not be able to rely on the sources set forth in Article 21(1)(b) and (c) of the ICC Statute in order to seek the external guidance that we have called for above. Instead, we will have to benefit from the guidance of external texts and authorities as a means of interpretation that will enhance our understanding of the proper law of the ICC.

2.3.1.2 The Status of Internationally Recognized Human Rights

The impact of human rights will be of paramount importance for determining the admissibility of illicitly obtained evidence. This is why the discussion on the hierarchy of sources needs to include some deliberations on the status of the explicit reference to "*internationally recognized human rights*" in Article 21(3) of the ICC Statute. This provision does not contain a legal source in the strict sense; it is rather to be considered a consistency rule. This does not however diminish the significance of human rights norms in the legal framework of the ICC. Quite the

[70]See Sect. 2.2.1.

[71]Safferling 2012, p. 113. In favour of a wider interpretation, see also Burghardt and Geneuss 2009, p. 133; Schabas 2010, p. 385; Triffterer 2008—McAuliffe de Guzman, Article 21, para 9; Werle 2012, para 189.

contrary: Article 21(3) represents a quasi-constitutional provision that enjoys a superior status when compared to the other paragraphs of Article 21.[72] Accordingly, all law applied by the Court has to be tested against the standard provided by this last paragraph.[73] In the case of an inconsistency, the provision authorizes the Court to find a legal norm inapplicable and to set it aside.[74]

Some have cast doubt on this understanding, stating that it would imply a considerable increase in the power of the Court, which might not have been intended by the drafters of the Statute.[75] However, the assumption of the superiority of human rights is not only indicated by a literal reading, the wording of the provision being unequivocal in this respect. Such a reading is also justified by a teleological interpretation. We have seen that the main rationale of international criminal proceedings is to be found in their socio-pedagogical effect.[76] This effect is dependent upon the perception of international criminal institutions as legitimate, which in turn necessitates their abidance by the fundamental protections of human rights law. Previous institutions have become aware of this necessity and have acknowledged the superior legal status of human rights. The International Criminal Tribunal for the former Yugoslavia for instance had been hesitant to apply human rights law at its beginnings.[77] Over time, however, it has successively recognized their fundamental role.[78] Likewise, other tribunals have shown readiness to set aside procedural provisions incompatible with human rights law.[79] The ICC itself has confirmed the fundamental role of Article 21(3), repeatedly citing it in its case law.[80]

According to the wide interpretation of Article 21(3) supported here, the provision not only requires a consistency test for other regulations but also broadens the power of the judges.[81] This understanding will have some impact in the context of this research.[82] It is derived from the word "*application*" which implicates some-

---

[72]Bitti 2009, p. 294; Fedorova and Sluiter 2009, p. 24; Sheppard 2010, p. 46; Werle 2012, para 206.

[73]Arsanjani 1999, p. 29; Pellet 2002, p. 1180.

[74]Pellet 2002, p. 1081; Gradoni et al. 2013, p. 83 et seq. and p. 93.

[75]Hafner and Binder 2004, p. 173 et seq. Declining a superiority of human rights over the Statute also Gallant 1999, p. 703.

[76]See Sect. 2.2.3.

[77]Safferling 2012, p. 119; Swoboda 2012, p. 86; Zahar and Sluiter 2008, p. 16. See also Sect. 2.3.2.4.

[78]See for instance *Prosecutor v. Tadić* (Decision on the Defence Motion for Interlocutory Appeal on Jurisdiction) ICTY (Appeals Chamber), decision of 2 October 1995, para 45: "*For a tribunal such as this one to be established according to the rule of law, it must be established in accordance with the proper international standards; it must provide all the guarantees of fairness, justice and even-handedness, in full conformity with internationally recognized human rights instruments.*" But see Swoboda 2012, p. 89 et seq. for a sceptical assessment of this decision.

[79]Gradoni et al. 2013, p. 93.

[80]See Schabas 2010, p. 398 with further references.

[81]Safferling 2012, p. 120; Gradoni et al. 2013, p. 93.

[82]See Sect. 4.3.3.5.3 with respect to the significance of Article 21(3) for the establishment of the requirement of a search warrant.

thing more than the mere interpretation of other legal sources.[83] The Court itself has in fact interpreted the provisions as performing a power-conferring function, thereby extending the role of its judges as law creators where this is necessary to make the ICC procedure compatible with human rights.[84] In this sense, while the provision is not conceived as a legal source in the strict sense, it clearly contains aspects quite similar to a legal source.

2.3.1.3 Interim Conclusion

It can be concluded that any interpretation of an ICC provision needs to proceed in the following way: The proper law of the ICC must first be considered; additionally the judges have the discretion to refer to a number of external sources of law, as well as to the Court's own jurisprudence. This jurisprudence, however, is not binding. Finally, any interpretation must take into account human rights law, which takes precedence in cases of incompatibility with human rights, and which allows for further development of the ICC legal system where this is required to achieve compatibility.

As this research is concerned with a procedural issue, external texts and authorities will have a distinct impact. We have seen that the necessity to refer to external texts and authorities arises from the fact that the drafters of the Statute could not regulate every conceivable matter and left the legal practitioner with an incomplete legal framework, including with regard to the details of criminal procedure. The following sections will attempt to classify those external legal sources that will be most important for the research at hand under the hierarchy laid out above. This assessment will show *inter alia* that these sources will mostly serve as a means of interpretation rather than as legal sources in the strict sense.

2.3.2 References Under Article 21 of the ICC Statute

2.3.2.1 General Considerations

The case law of the ICC contains numerous references to the jurisprudence of other courts and institutions such as the UN *Ad hoc* tribunals and human rights monitoring bodies. In their decision-making, ICC judges have also relied on legal

[83]Sheppard 2010, p. 62; Gradoni et al. 2013, p. 115.

[84]With respect to the power to stay the proceedings, see *Prosecutor v. Lubanga* (Judgment on the Appeal of Mr. Thomas *Lubanga* Dyilo against the Decision on the Defence Challenge to the Jurisdiction of the Court pursuant to Article 19(2)(a) of the Statute of 3 October 2006), ICC (Appeals Chamber), decision of 14 December 2006, para 37; *Prosecutor v. Lubanga* (Judgment on the appeal of the Prosecutor against the decision of Trial Chamber I entitled "Decision on the consequences of non-disclosure of exculpatory materials covered by Article 54(3)(e) agreements and the application to stay the prosecution of the accused, together with certain other issues raised at the Status Conference on 10 June 2008"), ICC (Appeals Chamber), decision of 21 October 2008, para 77.

texts outside the ICC Statute, in particular on the legal foundations of these courts and institutions. The practice of reference to the precedents and law of other institutions is generally widespread among international courts. It has been supported among scholars relying on the argument of its benefit for cross-fertilization among international judicial institutions and as a remedy against the fragmentation of international law.[85] While we have seen that fragmentation is not a central concern with respect to procedural matters,[86] this does not make the consideration of texts and authorities outside the ICC proper law futile *per se*. Useful cross-fertilization may still result from such examination.

It must, however, be noted that the ICC has been criticized because, like previous international courts and tribunals, it has refrained from developing clear methodological guidelines on the application of external law and jurisprudence. Such an absence of methodological accuracy bears the danger of lacking the predictability required under the principle of legality.[87] Closely linked, then, is the danger that a want of justification for the application of legal sources will have a negative impact on the legitimacy of a judicial institution like the ICC.[88]

Accordingly, referring to external texts and authorities in order to find solutions for the ICC requires some further assessment. We will therefore look more closely at those sources that will subsequently be referred to, which will include a classification of these sources in the hierarchy of Article 21 of the ICC Statute as depicted above. The sources examined below include the procedural systems and jurisprudence of the *Ad hoc* tribunals, domestic law and legislation and, finally, human rights treaties and the jurisprudence of their monitoring bodies.

As we will see, none of these sources as such is directly binding on the ICC. Article 21, however, provides for a number of options of including them in the legal assessment under the ICC system of procedure. Albeit to varying degrees, all of these texts and jurisprudence may be invoked when (1) determining the principles and rules of international law according to Article 21(1)(b) of the ICC Statute, which includes in particular customary law and[89] (2) when establishing the content of general principles of law according to Article 21(1)(c) of the ICC Statute,

---

[85]Miller 2002, p. 499; Nerlich 2009, p. 320.

[86]See Sect. 2.3.1.1.

[87]On the principle of legality with respect to the law of criminal procedure, see Sect. 2.3.1.1.

[88]Sheppard 2010, p. 44.

[89]The ICC would in any case be able to apply customary international law under Article 38 ICJ Statute since, as an international organisation, it is bound by general international law. Article 21 of the ICC Statute in turn does not explicitly refer to custom as a source of law. There is however consensus that customary law is encompassed by the "*principles and rules of international law*" as referred to in Article 21(1)(b) ICC Statute. While the exclusion of the word 'custom' is not entirely clear, the term might have been avoided for its vagueness in order to adhere to the principle of legality, see Pellet 2002, p. 1071. At the same time, the formulation "*principles and rules of international law*" can hardly be considered more precise. In particular, it is unclear which other notions besides customary international law are included in this term; see Schabas 2010, p. 390 et seq.

which allows for a comparative law perspective.[90] In addition, external texts and authorities play (3) a role in the interpretation of the rule of consistency with *internationally recognized human rights* contained in Article 21(3). The greatest impact that these sources will have, will not, however, be in the context of the previously named provisions but rather, as mentioned above, with respect to the interpretation of the ICC Statute and Rules of Procedure and Evidence under Article 21(1)(a).

2.3.2.2 References to the Procedural Systems and the Jurisprudence of the *Ad Hoc* Tribunals

The establishment of the *Ad hoc* tribunals in the last decade of the previous century brought about the resuscitation of international criminal law after a long period marked by a political climate unfavourable to any further practical implementation of the principles developed in Nuremberg and Tokyo.[91] The *Ad hoc* tribunals were the direct precursors of the first permanent international criminal court. It is therefore not surprising that the law and practice of these tribunals had a major impact both on the drafting of the ICC Statute and on its first jurisprudence.[92] For the drafters of the ICC Statute, the International Criminal Tribunal for the former Yugoslavia (ICTY) and the International Criminal Tribunal for Rwanda (ICTR) could be referred to for first-hand experience of the challenge of trying large scale mass crimes.[93] With respect to the present research, it may be added that the law of evidence was one of those areas where the influence of the *Ad hoc* tribunals was particularly strong. This is reflected by the high degree of similarity of the legal framework on evidence at the ICC when compared with the *Ad hoc* tribunals.[94]

Other international tribunals have of course emerged in the last two decades. This limited research will nevertheless be confined to the *Ad hoc* tribunals as examples of other international criminal institutions. The ICTY and ICTR are the only tribunals that are not hybrid or mixed with a procedure influenced by a specific domestic legal system. Furthermore, they are the most senior of the modern international courts and tribunals, which enhances the probability of deriving useful answers from their case law.

---

[90]There is some debate on whether Article 21(1)(c) of the ICC Statute parallels Article 38(1)(c) of the ICJ Statute or whether the "*general principles*" in the latter provision should better be subsumed under Article 21(1)(b) of the ICC Statute. Given the similarity in wording, a parallelism between Articles 21(1)(c) and 38(1)(c) will be assumed in this research; for this understanding see also Pellet 2002, p. 1073; Gradoni et al. 2013, p. 71. For a different view, see Safferling 2012, p. 114; Schabas 2010, p. 391.

[91]Werle 2012, para 45.

[92]Gray 2004, pp. 287 and 290.

[93]Currat 2007, p. 151; Nerlich 2009, p. 307.

[94]Gosnell 2010, p. 379 et seq.

Today, references to the jurisprudence of the *Ad hoc* tribunals remain popular among the actors involved in ICC proceedings. This practice has both sociological and practical reasons. There has been a great amount of movement of staff from the *Ad hoc* tribunals to the International Criminal Court, a phenomenon that is due *inter alia* to the approaching closure dates of the ICTY and the ICTR.[95] These staff members have obtained expert knowledge of the law and practice of the *Ad hoc* tribunals and are thus likely to be inclined to import solutions previously found by these tribunals.[96] Moreover, not only for former *Ad hoc* tribunal staff members, but for the actors involved in ICC proceedings in general, it has always been easier to refer to an already consolidated legal system than to create a completely new one.[97] Finally, the tendency observable in the submissions of participants in ICC proceedings to frequently refer to precedents of the *Ad hoc* tribunals might also be influenced by the fact that many of these participants have a common law background. It is only natural that these lawyers tend to refer to the case law of other courts as their legal training and work experience means they are familiar with the doctrine of judicial precedent.[98]

It goes without saying that while they served as models for the conception of the ICC Statute, the Statutes of the *Ad hoc* tribunals are not as such a legal source for the ICC. In particular, they are not "*applicable treaties*" according to Article 21(1)(b) of the ICC Statute. Likewise, the jurisprudence of the *Ad hoc* tribunals is in no way binding for the ICC.[99] Precedents in general are not binding on the Court. No rule of *stare decisis* exists for the Court's own case law,[100] let alone for the decisions of other institutions. The ICC judges themselves, while referring to the jurisprudence of the *Ad hoc* tribunals, have thus been cautious to repeatedly emphasize that this does not entail an automatic importation of this jurisprudence.[101] At the same time, Article 21(2) of the ICC Statute does not by a process

---

95 See for instance Møse 2005, p. 9.

96 Bitti 2009, p. 295; Nerlich 2009, p. 307.

97 Bitti 2009, p. 296.

98 On the use of ECtHR precedents by international criminal tribunals, see Cassese 2003, p. 20. For a critique of the use of precedents primarily by international lawyers with a common-law background, see Bantekas 2006, p. 132.

99 For a detailed rejection of the categorization of precedents of the *Ad hoc* tribunals as autonomous sources of law, see Nerlich 2009, p. 315 et seq.

100 See Sect. 2.1.

101 See for instance *Prosecutor v. Joseph Kony* et al., (Decision on the Prosecutor's Position on the Decision of Pre-Trial Chamber II to Redact Factual Descriptions of Crimes in the Warrants of Arrest, Motion for Reconsideration, and Motion for Clarification), ICC (Pre-Trial-Chamber), decision of 28 October 2005, para 19: "[T]*he rules and practice of other jurisdictions, whether national or international, are not as such 'applicable law' before the Court beyond the scope of Article 21 of the Statute.* [...]". See also *Situation in the Republic of Kenya* (Decision Pursuant to Article 15 of the Rome Statute on the Authorization of an Investigation into the Situation in the Republic of Kenya), ICC (Pre-Trial Chamber) decision of 31 March 2010, Dissenting Opinion Judge Kaul, para 29.

of *a contrario* reasoning preclude the ICC judges from taking into account the legislation of other courts and tribunals.[102]

One option would be to turn to the jurisprudence of the *Ad hoc* tribunals when determining customary law as part of the "*principles and rules of international law*" under Article 21(1)(b) of the ICC Statute.[103] However, the case law of neither tribunal is customary law in itself. In general, the case law of an international institution cannot itself contribute to the development of customary law. Under Article 38(1)(b) of the ICJ Statute, customary law arises out of a combination of the practice of states and their corresponding *opinio juris*.[104] Only states are therefore the decisive actors for the establishment of customary law. And while all members of the international community are bound by the statutes of the *Ad hoc* tribunals,[105] the routine function of these tribunals alone can hardly be considered evidence of customary law. With respect to state practice, the connection between judicial practice and states as law creators is rather remote. But even more importantly, it is doubtful whether an opinio juris could be determined among states that would involve the transferability of procedural solutions from the *Ad hoc* tribunals to other institutions by means of customary law. This finding alludes once more to the relativity of procedural law. We have seen that the correct procedural solutions depend to a great extent on the overall procedural system of the respective institutions. Correspondingly, even if states had an opinio juris with respect to a specific institution such as the ICTY or the ICTR, it might very well pertain only to this very institution. As a consequence, it cannot simply be transferred to another institution, operating with a different procedural system, such as the ICC.[106]

The significance of the jurisprudence of the *Ad hoc* tribunals for customary law is therefore not an obvious one. However, Article 38(1)(d) of the ICJ Statute can be used as a gateway to the consideration of the case law of the *Ad hoc* tribunals as indirect evidence of customary law. The provision mentions "*judicial decision* [...] *as subsidiary means for the determination of rules of law*". The general methodological approach that has been derived thereof is that judicial decisions are not sources of law as such but may be reflective of a rule of international law such as a

---

[102]Schabas 2010, p. 396. See also *Situation in the Republic of Kenya* (Decision Pursuant to Article 15 of the Rome Statute on the Authorization of an Investigation into the Situation in the Republic of Kenya), ICC (Pre-Trial-Chamber), decision of 31 March 2010, Dissenting Opinion Judge Kaul, para 30.

[103]For the subsumption of customary law under Article 21(1)(b) of the ICC Statute, see fn. 114.

[104]See *Germany v. Denmark/Germany v. The Netherlands* (North Sea Continental Shelf case), ICJ, decision of 20 February 1969, para 77. Also see Werle 2012, para 154, with references to the discussion of this term in public international law.

[105]The statutes of the *Ad hoc* tribunals were included in the Security Council resolutions that established these tribunals. These resolutions are binding upon all members of the United Nations, see Article 25 of the Charter of the United Nations, adopted on 26 June 1945, entered into force on 24 October 1945, available at: http://www.un.org/en/documents/charter/ (last visited: October 2013). See also Ipsen et al. 2004, p. 55.

[106]Safferling 2012, p. 115 et seq.

customary rule.[107] In other words, where one of the *Ad hoc* tribunals has established a rule of customary law, the ICC judges may use this as a resource for their own legal determination.

But even on this basis, the consideration of the case law of the *Ad hoc* tribunals for the determination of customary law is subject to considerable limits. First of all, the determination of international custom necessarily requires that the respective state practice manifests a relationship to international law.[108] This will only very rarely be the case with respect to the law of criminal procedure. It is, however, conceivable, especially where the determination of the human rights of persons affected by criminal proceedings is concerned.[109] But what is more, the determination of a custom is most likely to concern broad concepts rather than detailed procedural issues.[110] By and large determining customary law through ICTY and ICTR case law will often not be very fruitful for the development of procedural solutions for the ICC.

Secondly, ICTY and ICTR precedents can also be used indirectly when determining general principles of law according to Article 21(1)(c) of the ICC Statute. However, the recourse to such principles is constrained by similar limitations as that of international custom. These limitations will be discussed in more detail in the section on domestic law, where general principles are most significant.[111] For now, it suffices to say that the determination of general principles is often particularly assailable and that this determination will also usually establish only broad notions and thus fail to provide guidance for specific problems.

Two further remarks can be made on the indirect identification of general principles through ICTY and ICTR precedents. Article 21(1)(c) of the ICC Statute demands that these principles be "*derived by the Court*", thus explicitly entrusting this difficult legal assessment to the ICC judges. The judges should not circumvent this by simply referring to the determination of another judicial body. Instead, the persuasiveness of evaluations made by the judges of the *Ad hoc* tribunals has to be assessed carefully in every case. And what is more, Article 21(1)(c) emphasises the relevance of "*the national laws of States that would normally exercise jurisdiction over the crime*". Given the different states affected by the jurisdiction of the ICC when compared with the *Ad hoc* tribunals, this naturally requires a shift in perspective when compared to ICTY and ICTR case law.[112]

Thirdly, the *Ad hoc* tribunals also play a role when determining the content of "*internationally recognized human rights*" in Article 21(3). The significance of the tribunals' case law is plausible in this context since these tribunals are also

---

[107] Nerlich 2009, p. 313 et seq. See also Werle 2012, para 155.

[108] Werle 2012, para 156.

[109] See Sect. 4.3.3.5.1 on the customary law status of the prohibition of torture and Sect. 4.3.3.5.2 on the same assumption for the right to privacy.

[110] Swoboda 2012, p. 97.

[111] See Sect. 2.3.2.3.

[112] Altogether, see Nerlich 2009, p. 315.

regularly confronted with human rights related issues in international criminal proceedings.[113] The general consistency rule in Article 21(3) will be dealt with in more detail below when considering references to human rights law.[114]

Article 21(3) of the ICC Statute concerns *inter alia* the interpretation of the ICC proper law. This brings us to the last way in which the *Ad hoc* tribunals are relevant for this research. Beyond its limited influence on Article 21(3) of the ICC Statute, the law of the *Ad hoc* tribunals can be used for the interpretation of the ICC proper law. In fact, in light of the limited fruitfulness of comparative law and general principles in particular, the statutes and the jurisprudence of the *Ad hoc* tribunals will have their greatest impact not as sources in the strict sense but through the interpretation of the principal legal instruments of the Court. The next sections will show that this is the case for all of the external sources referred to in this research. Admittedly, the use of external sources for the interpretation of a specific legal instrument is not evident. With respect to the ICTY and the ICTR, the most convincing methodological foundation would be a consideration of their legal instruments and jurisprudence as part of a systematic interpretation of the proper law of the ICC. It can be argued that because the *Ad hoc* tribunals had such a major impact on the drafters of the ICC legal instruments, they may also be taken into consideration when analysing the significance of these instruments.[115]

However, irrespective of the methodology used, it is important to note that any consideration of the statutes and jurisprudence of the *Ad hoc* tribunals must take into account the aforementioned relativity of procedural law. We have seen that the law of procedure is generally dependent on the institution that applies it.[116] The ICC Statute establishes a legal system that differs, in some instances significantly, from the legal framework of the *Ad hoc* tribunals. This is especially true for procedural issues. Such differences result in particular from the different combination of adversarial and inquisitorial elements and from the different ways in which these institutions were created.[117] The different shape of the systems precludes any one-

[113]Gradoni et al. 2013, p. 90.

[114]See Sect. 2.3.2.4.

[115]Such an approach is not without problems. Article 31(2) of the Vienna Convention of the Law of Treaties defines the context of the terms of a treaty in a narrow way, as comprising only the text of the treaty, including its preamble, as well as agreements concluded in connection with the conclusion of the treaty. A broader definition for the founding documents of an international organisation seems however justified where this foundation was clearly influenced by the existence of a previous institution, see Nerlich 2009, p. 319. Another, albeit more assailable possibility would be to resort to Article 31(3)(c) of the VCLT. The Statutes and jurisprudence of the *Ad hoc* tribunals however can hardly be considered "*relevant rules of international law applicable between the parties*", see Young 2011, p. 195 et seq., fn. 37. But see Nerlich 2009, p. 320, who argues that the purpose of Article 31(3)(c) VCLT to avoid the fragmentation of international law might allow for a consideration on this basis anyhow.

[116]See Sect. 2.3.1.1.

[117]For more details, see Sects. 2.2.1 and 3.1.1.

to-one transfer of judicial solutions found by the judges of the *Ad hoc* tribunals.[118] The adoption of any solution will thus depend not only on its persuasiveness *per se* but also on its transferability to the ICC system of procedure.[119] This assessment will further limit the possibility of relying on the law and jurisprudence of the *Ad hoc* tribunals, including where they are simply used as interpretative aids.

In conclusion, the present research will, in principle, be able to refer to the jurisprudence of the *Ad hoc* tribunals. While this is possible in the course of the determination of customary law and general principles and "*internationally recognized human rights*", it will be of use mostly for the general interpretation of the ICC proper law. For all of these assessments, the systematic differences between the *Ad hoc* tribunals and the ICC will have to be given due consideration.

2.3.2.3 References to Domestic Law

The question whether domestic law may be considered is particularly relevant for the law of criminal procedure. Whereas substantive international criminal law can rely to a larger extent on international treaties and other international sources, procedural law is marked by a considerable lack of regulation, but also of models. Until recently, the law of criminal procedure was exclusively a matter of domestic law.[120] The only models available to the ICC at the international level are other international tribunals, which are also relatively young. This is particularly true for the so-called mixed or hybrid tribunals that have existed for a similar amount of time as the ICC.[121] But even the systems of procedure of the slightly more senior *Ad hoc* tribunals have not reached a level of development comparable to domestic systems, which have evolved over several decades and sometimes centuries.

From a methodological point of view, one option of using domestic law is, once again, to identify the content of the external sources of Article 21(1)(b) and (c) of

---

[118]For a much discussed procedural decision confirming this conclusion, see *Prosecutor v. Lubanga* (Decision Regarding the Practices Used to Prepare and Familiarise Witnesses for Giving Testimony at Trial), ICC (Trial Chamber), decision of 30 November 2007, where the Chamber prohibited witness proofing, thereby declining to adopt the respective jurisprudence of the ICTY; see in particular para 45, stating: "*The ICC Statute has, through important advances, created a procedural framework which differs markedly from the* ad hoc *tribunals,* [...]. *Therefore, the Statute moves away from the procedural regime of the* ad hoc *tribunals, introducing additional and novel elements to aid the process of establishing the truth.* [...] *Therefore, while acknowledging the importance of considering the practice and jurisprudence at the* ad hoc *tribunals, the Chamber is not persuaded that the application of* ad hoc *procedures, in the context of preparation of witnesses for trial, is appropriate.*"

[119]Nerlich 2009, p. 314.

[120]Kamardi 2009, p. 120 et seq.

[121]The first of the hybrid tribunals were the Special Panels for Serious Crimes (SPSC) in East Timor, which was created in 2000. For a summary on the establishment of the hybrid tribunals, see Werle 2012, para 326 et seq. For an introduction into their procedural systems, see Gradoni et al. 2013, p. 52 et seq.

the ICC Statute or of '*internationally recognized human rights*'. The latter of these options, the process of identifying '*internationally recognized human rights*', will be dealt with below.[122] For now, it suffices to say that while the term necessitates a degree of widespread approval, it does not require that a right be recognized in all societies worldwide. With respect to the determination of customary law in turn, domestic law can be evidence of a specific state practice or *opinio juris* and thus decisive for the determination of customary law.[123]

Domestic law may be considered primarily through the determination of general principles of law. The reference to such principles is an invitation to the judges to consult domestic law by way of a comparative law approach.[124] The ICC so far has been quite resistant to this invitation. Where this source is mentioned at all, the Court has ruled out the existence of a general principle of law.[125] While this seems to be in line with an overall reluctance of international courts and tribunals to use such principles, examples can nevertheless be found in the jurisprudence of other institutions. The jurisprudence of the ICTY offers examples of the use of general principles[126] and so does the jurisprudence of the ICJ.[127] Especially where new, partly unregulated areas of law have emerged, this legal source has been said to have a gap-filling function. In light of its incompleteness, the international law of criminal procedure is such a legal area.[128] The inclusion of this source in the ICC Statute was in fact based on this very consideration. Both in the Preparatory Commission and at the Rome Conference, scepticism was widespread about whether it was appropriate for the Court to assess the law of sovereign states. But the argument that the practical need to fill gaps had to be expected finally overruled such objections.[129]

On a practical level, it is, however, doubtful whether general principles are the most adequate way of considering domestic law and filling legislative gaps.

---

[122]See Sect. 4.3.3.

[123]Kamardi 2009, p. 120; Staker 2010, p. 201. Similar for general international law, Bothe 1976, p. 281.

[124]Cassese 2008, p. 22; Werle 2012, para 202.

[125]*Prosecutor v. Lubanga* (Decision Regarding the Practices Used to Prepare and Familiarise Witnesses for Giving Testimony at Trial), ICC (Trial Chamber), decision of 30 November 2007, para 41; *Situation in the Democratic Republic of the Congo* (Judgment on the Prosecutor's Application for Extraordinary Review of the Pre-Trial Chamber I, 31 March 2006 Decision Denying Leave to Appeal), ICC (Appeals Chamber), decision of 13 July 2006, para 32.

[126]See for instance *Prosecutor v. Erdemović* (Sentencing Judgment), ICTY (Trial Chamber), decision of 29 November 1996, para 31. *Prosecutor v. Furundžjia* (Sentencing Judgment), ICTY (Trial Chamber), decision of 10 December 1998, para 177 et seq. Also see *Prosecutor v. Furundžija* (Judgment), ICTY (Appeals Chamber), decision of 21 July 2000, Declaration of Judge Shahabuddeen, para 256.

[127]See for example *United Kingdom of Great Britain and Northern Ireland v. Albania* (Corfu Channel Case), ICJ, decision of 9 April 1949, p. 22; *Effects of awards of compensation made by the U.N. Administrative Tribunal* (Advisory Opinion), ICJ, decision of 13 July 1954, p. 10.

[128]Similar for international criminal law in general, Cassese 2005, p. 193.

[129]Edwards 2001, p. 406 et seq.

Similar to customary law, their generality often hampers their usefulness for practical purposes. General principles must not be confused with their specific manifestations within a legal system.[130] Whereas procedural systems in different states might share general principles, their solutions for a specific practical problem often greatly differ from each other.[131] Consequently, the finding of a general principle is usually limited to common denominators. This means that they are often unlikely to produce answers for questions of detail.[132] Moreover, the finding of such principles is difficult. It is often based on an uncertain epistemological basis.[133] The main difficulty consists in choosing among the legal systems to be compared. Theoretically, the identification of general principles would require a universal comparative analysis. Since this is not feasible in practice, it has been claimed that a representative number of legal orders belonging to all of the world's legal systems should be taken into consideration.[134] In the reality of international jurisprudence, this latter standard has not been met either. Comparative deliberations justifying the establishment of a general principle of law are often cursory.[135] Where such deliberations are made at all, the number of legal systems considered is regularly unrepresentative and the choice seems highly subjective.[136] Beyond this dogmatic criticism, the practice has also been opposed for being eurocentric because common law and civil law systems are usually the main, and often the only, systems consulted.[137] Such a reproach is naturally serious for a court that is as dependent on its perception as a legitimate institution as is the case for the ICC.

The question arises whether, as a consequence, the recourse to domestic law is flawed *per se*. For substantive law, the conclusion has been drawn that the true function of a comparative approach lies less in its benefits for the finding of justice and more in its ability to promote the understanding of international criminal law by translating the solutions found by the Court into the codes of domestic legal systems.[138] This assessment notwithstanding, for questions of international criminal procedure, the situation is slightly different. While fostering mutual understanding is an important goal, and hopefully also something that this research will contribute towards, a more direct impact of comparative analyses is easier to justify when it comes to procedural law.

---

[130]Staker 2010, p. 203.

[131]Bitti 2009, p. 300.

[132]Bothe 1976, p. 288.

[133]Gradoni et al. 2013, p. 71.

[134]This would include states belonging to the common law and the civil law system but also those of the Islamic world, as well as Asian and African states, see Cassese 2008, p. 22; Kamardi 2009, p. 130.

[135]Bothe 1976, p. 283.

[136]Burghardt 2011, p. 245. See also Nerlich 2009, p. 314.

[137]See Kamardi 2009, p. 131. On this choice of systems, see also Werle 2012, para 161, fn. 336, with further references.

[138]Burghardt 2011, p. 162 et seq.

We have seen that the international law of criminal procedure is both incomplete and in particular need of external sources and models to fill legislative gaps. At the same time, a comparative approach seems less problematic for procedural issues. The consequences of the principle of legality are less strict than for substantive law, where clear definitions of crimes are mandatory.[139] As mentioned above, in procedural law, there is often not only one single just way to proceed. It thus seems less problematic if judges draw from domestic solutions to find an adequate solution to procedural problems.[140]

This suggests the application of a pragmatic approach to the use of comparative assessments. Domestic systems can be used not as a discrete legal source under Article 21 of the ICC Statute, but as models from which to discover solutions that might work at the international level as well.[141] Numerous examples for references to domestic law on this basis can be found in international case law.[142] Such an approach seems also to have been applied at times in international criminal case law.[143]

This understanding of the comparative law exercise diminishes the importance of the choice of a representative sample of legal systems. The chance of finding the best possible approach to a legal problem admittedly increases if as many legal orders as possible are under scrutiny. But reasonable solutions can be found by looking at a few examples.[144] Moreover, it makes the critique of eurocentrism less appropriate. The procedural system of the ICC has been developed on the basis of

---

[139]Gradoni et al. 2013, p 68 and p 70.

[140]Gallant 1999, p 710. See also Sect. 2.3.1.1.

[141]Kamardi 2009, p. 124; Safferling 2012, p. 126; Staker 2010, p. 203. Similar for general international law, Bothe 1976, p. 291. Critical but eventually endorsing this approach for procedural law altogether, Gradoni et al. 2013, p. 71.

[142]For an enumeration of examples, see Staker 2010, p. 203.

[143]Most distinctively, see *Prosecutor v. Kupreškić* et al. (Judgment), ICTY (Trial Chamber), decision of 14 January 2000, para 738; *Prosecutor v. Mucić* et al. (Judgment), ICTY (Appeals Chamber), decision of 20 February 2001, para 412. On the approach adopted in these decisions, see also Staker 2010, p. 202. A similar approach seems to have guided the ICC judges when adopting the so-called '*control of the crime*' theory in the *Luganga* case. The ICC Pre-Trial Chamber, while referring to the acceptance of the theory in "*numerous legal systems*", did not explicitly mention whether its adoption of this theory was actually based on the establishment of a general principle. It rather seems to have adopted the approach that it considered most adequate among the approaches found at the national level, thus using domestic law rather as a source of inspiration than a legal source in the strict sense, see *Prosecutor v. Lubanga* (Decision on the Confirmation of Charges), ICC (Pre-Trial Chamber), decision of 29 January 2007, para 322 et seq. The ICC Trial Chamber in its very first judgment, has accepted this jurisprudence, see *Prosecutor v. Lubanga* (Judgment pursuant to Article 74 of the Statute), ICC (Trial Chamber I), decision of 14 March 2012, para 1018. For a critical assessment, see however the *Separate Opinion of Judge Adrian Fulford* annexed to this judgement, para 10 et seq. Judge Fulford rejects the '*control of the crime theory*', *inter alia* in view of the methodological approach applied by the Pre-Trial Chamber and by the Trial Chamber majority.

[144]Bothe 1976, p. 290 et seq.

the common law system and the civil law system. It is thus justifiable and often even indispensable to look at these systems to gain a better understanding of the ICC provisions that ultimately have arisen thereof.[145]

It should, however, be noted that many issues of procedural law have not been regulated from the outset even in domestic systems. A look at the domestic approaches on the admissibility of illegally gained evidence will reveal that the topic of this research is an illustrative example for a procedural issue which, in domestic orders, has mostly been solved through the development of legal doctrine and case law. In order to find solutions for the international level, it seems reasonable to look at these developments. With the case law of the ICC growing, a gradual autonomisation will become possible in the future.[146]

At the same time, it should be kept in mind that such a comparative approach cannot consist of a simple transposition. National solutions cannot simply be transferred to the international level because international criminal proceedings are different from national proceedings in many respects. The most important difference for the daily judicial practice is without doubt the lack of enforcement abilities of international courts and tribunals. In contrast to domestic courts, international criminal institutions cannot rely on a distinct branch of executive power at the international level that would enforce their decisions. They are completely dependent on the cooperation of states, which is often difficult to achieve.[147] One might also refer to the subject matter of trials before international criminal institutions. These institutions only have jurisdiction over crimes of a particular gravity,[148] whereas the procedural law of domestic states generally applies to crimes of any kind. Further differences pertain to the logistical challenges international prosecution is confronted with, to the broader participation of victims, as well as to the lapse of time since the commission of the crimes. The recourse to domestic law must therefore be subject to an adaptation of procedural solutions to the specific demands of international criminal justice.[149]

In conclusion, domestic law can be used to determine the content of the sources of international law such as customary law and general principles of law, as well as to construct the consistency rule of Article 21(3) of the ICC Statute. Since these sources of international law will often be of limited use, the most pragmatic approach is to draw from national solutions as models and sources of inspiration.

---

[145]See also Gradoni et al. 2013, p. 70, who consider it difficult to interpret the rules of international criminal procedure "*entirely independently from the legal-cultural setting and mental habits that shaped them*."

[146]See also Gradoni et al. 2013, p. 70, who, while acknowledging the necessity to turn to domestic law at this point of the development, already detect a beginning autonomization.

[147]For more details on the cooperation of these institutions with states, see Sect. 4.2.

[148]See Article 5 of the ICC Statute, Article 1 of the ICTY Statute and Article 1 of the ICTR Statute.

[149]Safferling 2012, p. 126; Gradoni et al. 2013, p. 70; Staker 2010, p. 203 et seq. See also *Prosecutor v. Furundžija* (Sentencing judgment), ICTY (Trial Chamber), decision of 10 December 1998, para 178.

This approach will be dominant in this research. Due consideration shall however be given to the contextual differences between domestic and international criminal proceedings.

2.3.2.4 References to Human Rights Treaties and the Jurisprudence of Human Rights Courts

Human rights are crucial for the protection of the rights of the persons involved in a criminal trial, in particular for the protection of the suspect or the accused. This is particularly true for international courts and tribunals that strive to serve as role models for the enforcement of international criminal justice. Quoting a comment made by the UN Secretary-General when the ICTY was established, respect for human rights standards by international criminal courts and tribunals is "*axiomatic*".[150]

In principle, international criminal courts and tribunals have long recognized this assessment. Their jurisprudence, including that of the ICC, regularly refers both to human rights treaties, such as the International Covenant on Civil and Political Rights (ICCPR),[151] the European Convention on Human Rights (ECHR),[152] the American Convention on Human Rights (ACHR)[153] and the African Convention on Human and Peoples Rights (ACHPR, also known as Banjul Charter),[154] and to the decisions and judgments of the respective monitoring bodies.[155] The way in which these conventions and this case law have been made use of has, however, been criticised for its lack of coherence. In fact, the

[150]See UNSC, Report of the Secretary-General pursuant to para 2 of the Security Council Resolution 808 (UN Doc. S/225704) (1993), para 106; available at http://www.icty.org/x/file/Legal%20Library/Statute/statute_re808_1993_en.pdf (last visited: October 2013): "*It is axiomatic that the International Tribunal must fully respect internationally recognized standards regarding the rights of the accused at all stages of its proceedings. In the view of the Secretary-General, such internationally recognized standards are, in particular, contained in article 14 of the International Covenant on Civil and Political Rights.*"

[151]International Covenant on Civil and Political Rights, signed on 16 December 1966, entered into force on 23 March 1976, available at http://www.ohchr.org/EN/ProfessionalInterest/Pages/CCPR.asp (last visited: October 2013).

[152]Convention for the Protection of Human Rights and Fundamental Freedoms, signed on 4 November 1950, entered into force on 3 September 1950, available at http://www.echr.coe.int/Pages/home.asp?p=basictexts&c=#n1359128122487_pointer (last visited: October 2013).

[153]American Convention on Human Rights, signed on 22 November 1969, entered into force on 18 July 1978, available at http://www.cidh.org/Basicos/English/Basic3.American%20Convention.htm (last visited: October 2013).

[154]African Charter on Human and Peoples' Rights, signed on 27 June 1981, entered into force on 21 October 1986, available at www.achpr.org/instruments/achpr/ (last visited: October 2013).

[155]Jackson and Summers 2012, p. 131; Miller 2002, p. 496; Sheppard 2010, p. 49 et seq.; Gradoni et al. 2013, p. 88; Swoboda 2012, p. 98.

judges have only rarely articulated in a clear way how these sources were used and to what extent they were applicable to the case before the respective international criminal tribunal.[156]

Of course, the various human rights conventions are not binding as conventional norms upon international criminal institutions,[157] which have not joined the respective conventions as parties and as international organizations, and they usually lack the legal ability to do so.[158] For the ICC, the immediate consequence is that human rights treaties are not "*applicable treaties*" according to Article 21(1)(b) of the ICC Statute.[159] As international institutions, the courts and tribunals are, however, bound where these norms have acquired the status of general international law. The fact that a certain treaty has been ratified by a number of states may play a role in determining a distinct state practice and thus a rule of customary law. And while the jurisprudence of monitoring bodies does not have any binding effect, it can be used through Article 38(1)(d) of the ICJ Statute as persuasive authority, reflecting the existence of such a customary rule. Similarly, human rights standards may be invoked when determining general principles of law.[160] In the case of the ICC, this binding effect is once more clarified by Article 21(1)(b) and (c) of the Statute.

Again, however, the findings filtered out through these two external sources will often not be of much help for the solution of procedural problems. Accordingly, human rights law, too, exercises its impact mostly through the interpretation of the ICC proper law. But in contrast to the law of the *Ad hoc* tribunals, this interpretative exercise is explicitly requested by the above-mentioned consistency rule of Article 21(3) of the ICC Statute. Moreover, the provision confers qualified power upon the Court, thus allowing it to create additional norms and remedies where this is necessary for the abidance by human rights law.[161]

The applicability of human rights law in the context of international criminal law and more specifically within the legal framework of the ICC can therefore easily be confirmed. The more complicated issues arise from the determination of the content of human rights standards. The phrase "*internationally recognized human rights*" is used not only in Article 21(3) of the ICC Statute but also in the main ICC rule on the exclusion of evidence, namely in Article 69(7) of the Statute. It will be further elucidated in Chap. 4 in the context of the latter provision.

At this point, we will address another contentious issue, the problem of transferability. Like domestic law and the law and jurisprudence of the *Ad hoc* tribunals, the validity of the use of human rights standards by the ICC is subject to their

---

[156]Cassese 2003, p. 20 et seq.; Sheppard 2010, p. 49.

[157]Gallant 1999, p. 695.

[158]Gradoni et al. 2013, p. 81.

[159]Fedorova and Sluiter 2009, p. 28; Pellet 2002, p. 1068.

[160]On the binding nature of human rights through this indirect mechanism, see Pellet 2002, p. 1068; Gradoni et al. 2013, p. 81; Villiger 1985, p. 197.

[161]See Sect. 2.3.2.

transferability to the Court's legal framework. Differences clearly exist between the conditions faced by international criminal tribunals and the context of the cases that human rights bodies are concerned with. While the former deal with individual criminal responsibility on an international level, the latter monitor the compliance of states with the requirements of conventions in their behaviour towards individuals.[162]

Closely related to this finding is a peculiarity of human rights regimes which pertains to the nature of human rights as minimum standards.[163] The addressees of these standards, traditionally states, are usually vested with a certain measure of flexibility in their implementation. The best example would be the *"margin of appreciation doctrine"* developed by the European Court of Human Rights (ECtHR), whereby the Strasbourg organs grant room to manoeuvre to domestic authorities in the fulfilment of their obligations under the ECHR.[164] The role of institutions such as the ECtHR, then, is only to review whether states have not exceeded the limits of their discretion. In comparison, the ICC is involved in criminal law issues as a direct consequence of the power conferred on it to adjudicate criminal matters. Unlike human rights monitoring bodies, it does not rule on the previous exercise of judicial power by a state but rather exercises such power itself. To this extent, the Court bears more similarities with a national criminal court than with a human rights court. Just like any national legal system, the ICC must find distinct solutions that fit into its own legal framework rather than leaving these solutions to other legal systems. Accordingly, the answers found by human rights monitoring bodies may at times not be specific enough to be adequate for the ICC.[165]

What is more, the cases before human rights monitoring bodies are generally settled in a national context. As a consequence, the previously mentioned differences between national and international proceedings, such as the different enforcement abilities or the different setting and character of the crimes, are also relevant for the use of human rights law.

These differences call into question an untransformed application of the existing standards and may warrant a reinterpretation of these standards for the purpose of international criminal trials. However, caution is required so as not to use the transferability question to overly restrict the application of human rights protections.[166]

This is more than a mere academic question. In its early days, the ICTY, for instance, relied on its uniqueness to justify a reinterpretation of human rights standards. Pointing to the horrific character of the crimes under its jurisdiction, the tribunal held that it was comparable to a military tribunal which often has limited rights of due

[162]Jackson and Summers 2012, p. 132.

[163]For a detailed discussion of the nature of human rights as minimum standards, see Fedorova and Sluiter 2009, p. 9 et seq.

[164]On the ECtHR's margin of appreciation doctrine, see Sect. 3.2.2.

[165]For a similar comparison between the ICTY and the ECtHR, see McIntyre 2003, p. 200. On the similarity between international tribunals and national courts as opposed to the monitoring bodies of human rights conventions, see Berger 2012, p. 4.

[166]For an overview of the different positions on the issue, see Damaška 2012, p. 612.

process.[167] This comparison with a military tribunal has naturally drawn intensive criticism since one of the basic arguments continuously raised against military jurisdiction has been its deplorable lack of compliance with human rights standards.[168]

In fact, an extensive detachment by international criminal tribunals from the established interpretation of human rights standards bears the risk of a relativisation of the rights of individuals in international criminal proceedings and puts at risk the legitimacy of international criminal justice institutions.[169] If international criminal tribunals do not fully abide by the basic requirements of human rights law, they will not be able to credibly advocate the sanctity of human rights within the international community.[170] It would be highly contradictory if, while arguing for human rights protection during their proceedings, at the same time, these tribunals themselves were not respecting human rights standards for defendants.[171] The gravity of the crimes in particular cannot be used as a generally applicable argument to outweigh such fundamental protections. Otherwise, given the horrific character of the crimes under the jurisdiction of international criminal tribunals, the rights of a suspect or an accused person would always be outbalanced.[172]

As a consequence, while a contextual interpretation of human rights standards is necessary in light of their specific setting, the basic boundaries set by human rights law must be guaranteed at all times. Today, all of the existing international courts and tribunals seem to accept these findings. The view prevails that the procedural rules of these institutions must be tested in view of their compliance with human rights law and not the other way around. Ultimately, this view was incorporated in the establishment of a superior standard of human rights law in Article 21(3) of the ICC Statute.[173]

Ultimately, a reinterpretation beyond the limits of human rights law will not be necessary to give consideration to the particularities of the ICC system. Human rights as minimum guarantees are not static concepts. As we have seen, they usually grant room to manoeuvre to those who implement them. They establish mandatory directives only very rarely.[174] In most instances, an interpretation for the purposes of international criminal proceedings will thus be possible without deferring from the flexible concepts provided for by the different human rights regimes.[175]

Finally, it should be noted that taking into consideration the structural differences of the ICC legal regime might not only warrant a restrictive interpretation of

---

[167] *Prosecutor v. Tadić* (Decision on the Prosecution's Motion Requesting Protective Measures for Victims and Witnesses), ICTY (Trial Chamber), decision of 10 August 1995, para 28.

[168] Swoboda 2012, p. 87 et seq.

[169] Swoboda 2012, p. 93.

[170] Similar, Edwards 2001, p. 334.

[171] Jackson and Summers 2012, p. 119; McIntyre 2003, p. 194.

[172] Torres Chedraui 2010, p. 228.

[173] Gradoni et al. 2013, p. 93. On the superior status of Article 21(3) of the ICC, see Sect. 2.3.1.2.

[174] Gradoni et al. 2013, p. 85.

[175] Altogether, Damaška 2012, p. 614 et seq.

human rights. These differences may at times even suggest a more generous interpretation. Examples would pertain to the specific difficulties for the defence arising from the lack of state cooperation or to the additional challenges that the defence faces due to the regime of increased victim participation.[176]

In conclusion, human rights standards are unequivocally applicable in proceedings before the International Criminal Court, as demonstrated in particular by Article 21(3) of the ICC Statute. The application of these standards, however, requires the consideration of the contextual differences between the legal frameworks. At the same time, the assessment of the transferability of solutions must be conducted cautiously so as not to exceed the limits set by human rights law.

2.4 Conclusion and Outlook

In order to fill the legislative gaps that arise at the ICC with respect to procedural issues, it is permissible to invoke, within limits, a number of texts and authorities outside of the proper law of the ICC. This includes the statutes and the jurisprudence of the *Ad hoc* tribunals, domestic law, and, finally, human rights treaties and the jurisprudence of their monitoring bodies. These may be taken into account either as legal sources or as sources of inspiration for the interpretation of the ICC legal framework.

It is without question that, from a methodological perspective, it is not obvious that the law and jurisprudence of other legal systems are used for the understanding of the legal instruments of an international court. It must however be recognized that at the present stage, strict reliance on positive law is not possible. Once a broader range of issues has been settled at the international level, and in particular by the ICC itself, comparative analyses will become less important and references to the Court's own precedents will more often be sufficient. At this point, however, the development of adequate solutions for procedural questions, such as in the present research, makes comparative analyses indispensable. Thus, in order to create a basis for the subsequent analysis of the admissibility of illicitly obtained evidence at the ICC, the basics of a number of external approaches to this issue will be elucidated in the next chapter.

References

Ambos K (2002) On the rationale of punishment at the domestic and international level. In: Marc Henzelin M, Roth R (eds) Le Droit Pénal à l'Épreuve de l'Internationalisation. Bruylant, Paris, pp 305–323

Arsanjani M (1999) The Rome Statute of the International Criminal Court. The American Journal of International Law 93:22-43

Bantekas I (2006) Reflections on some sources and methods of international criminal and humanitarian law. Int Crim Law Rev 6:121–136

[176]Fedorova and Sluiter 2009, p. 41.

Berger M (2012) The right to silence in The Hague international criminal courts. Univ San Franc Law Rev 47:1–54
Bitti G (2009) Article 21 of the Statute of the International Criminal Court and the treatment of the sources of law in the jurisprudence of the ICC. In: Carsten S, Goran S (eds) The emerging practice of the International Criminal Court. Martinus Nijhoff Publishers, Leiden, pp 285–304
Bothe M (1976) Die Bedeutung der Rechtsvergleichung in der Praxis internationaler Gerichte. Zeitschrift für ausländisches öffentliches Recht und Völkerrecht 36:280–299
Burghardt B (2011) Die Rechtsvergleichung in der völkerstrafrechtlichen Rechtsprechung – von der Rechtsvergleichung als Mittel der Rechtsfindung zur diskursiv-vermittelnden Rechtsvergleichung. In: Beck S, Burchard C, Fateh-Moghadam F (eds) Strafrechtsvergleichung als Problem und Lösung. Nomos, Baden-Baden, pp 235–254
Burghardt B, Geneuss J (2009) Der Präsident und sein Gericht. Zeitschrift für Internationale Strafrechtsdogmatik 4:126–142
Cassese A (2003) The influence of the European Court of Human Rights on international criminal tribunals—some methodological remarks. In: Bergsmo A, Eide A (eds) Human rights and criminal justice for the downtrodden: essays in honour of Asbjørn Eide. Martinus Nijhoff Publishers, Leiden, pp 19–52
Cassese A (2005) International law, 2nd edn. Oxford University Press, Oxford
Cassese A (2008) International criminal law, 2nd edn. Oxford University Press, Oxford
Currat P (2007) L'Interprétation du Statut de Rome. Revue québécoise de droit international 2:137–163
Damaška M (2009) Problematic features of international criminal procedure. In: Cassese A (ed) The Oxford companion to international criminal justice. Oxford University Press, Oxford, pp 175–186
Damaška M (2012) Reflections on fairness in international criminal justice. J Int Crim Justice 10:611–620
Douglas L (2006) The didactic trial: filtering history and memory into the courtroom. Eur Rev 14:513–522
Edwards G (2001) International human rights law challenges to the new International Criminal Court: the search and seizure right to privacy. Yale J Int Law 26:323–412
Fedorova M, Sluiter G (2009) Human rights as minimum standards in international criminal proceedings. Hum Rights Int Leg Discourse 3:9–56
Gallant K (1999) Individual human rights in a new international organization: the Rome Statute of the International Criminal Court. In: Bassiouni C (ed) International criminal law, Volume II: procedural and enforcement mechanisms, 2nd edn. Transnational Publishers, New York, pp 693–723
Gosnell C (2010) Admissibility of evidence. In: Khan A, Buisman C, Gosnell C (eds) Principles of evidence in international criminal justice. Oxford University Press, Oxford, pp 375–442
Gradoni L, Lewis D, Mégret F, Nouwen S, Ohlin J (2013) General framework of international criminal justice. In: Sluiter G, Friman H, Linton S, Zappalà S, Vasiliev S (eds) International criminal procedure: principles and rules. Oxford University Press, Oxford, pp 39–130
Gray R (2004) Evidence before the ICC. In: McGoldrick D, Rowe P, Donnelly E (eds) The permanent international criminal court: legal and policy issues. Hart Publishing, Oxford, pp 287–314
Grover L (2010) A Call to Arms: Fundamental Dilemmas Confronting the Interpretation of Crimes in the Rome Statute of the International Criminal Court. European Journal of International Law 21:543-583
Hafner G, Binder C (2004) The interpretation of Article 21(3) ICC statute opinion reviewed. Austrian Rev Int Eur Law 9:163–190
Ipsen K, Epping V, Heintschel von Heinegg W (2004) Völkerrecht, 5th edn. C.H.Beck, Munich
Jackson J, Summers S (2012) The internationalisation of criminal evidence: beyond the common law and civil law traditions. Cambridge University Press, Cambridge
Jäger H (1995) Markoverbrechen als Gegenstand des Völkerstrafrechts. In: Hankel G, Stuby G (eds) Strafgerichte gegen Menschheitsverbrechen: Zum Völkerstrafrecht 50 Jahre nach den Nürnberger Prozessen. Hamburger Edition, Hamburg, pp 325–354
Kamardi C (2009) Die Ausformung einer Prozessordnung sui generis durch das ICTY unter Berücksichtigung des Fair-Trial-Prinzips. Springer, Berlin

Lister C (2005) What's in a Name? Labels and the Statute of the International Criminal Tribunal for the Former Yugoslavia. Leiden Journal of International Law 18:77-92
McIntyre G (2003) Defining human rights in the arena of international humanitarian law: human rights in the jurisprudence of the ICTY. In: Boas W, Schabas W (eds) International criminal law: developments in the case law of the ICTY. Martinus Nijhoff Publishers, Leiden, pp 193–238
Miller N (2002) An international jurisprudence? The operation of across international tribunals. Leiden J Int Law 15:483–526
Møse E (2005) The ICTR: experiences and challenges. New Engl J Int Comp Law 12:1–16
Nemitz J (2002) Strafzumessung im, Völkerstrafrecht edn. Iuscrim, Freiburg
Nerlich V (2009) The status of ICTY and ICTR precedence in proceedings before the ICC. In: Stahn C, Sluiter G (eds) The emerging practice of the International Criminal Court. Martinus Nijhoff Publishers, Leiden, pp 305–326
Neubacher F (2006) Strafzwecke und Völkerstrafrecht. Neue Juristische Wochenschrift 14:966–970
Orie A (2002) Accusatorial versus inquisitorial approach in international criminal proceedings. In: Cassese A, Gaeta P, Jones J (eds) The Rome Statute of the International Criminal Court: a commentary, vol 2. Oxford University Press, Oxford, pp 1439–1495
Pellet A (2002) Applicable law. In: Cassese A, Gaeta P, Jones J (eds) The Rome Statute of the International Criminal Court: a commentary, vol 2. Oxford University Press, Oxford, pp 1084
Safferling C (2012) International criminal procedure. Oxford University Press, Oxford
Schabas W (2003) Interpreting the statutes of the *Ad hoc* tribunals. In: Vohrah LC et al. (eds) Man's inhumanity to man: essays on international law in honour of Antonio Cassese. Kluwer International Law, The Hague, pp 847–888
Schabas W (2010) The International Criminal Court—a commentary on the Rome Statute. Oxford University Press, Oxford
Sheppard D (2010) The International Criminal Court and "Internationally recognized human rights": understanding Article 21(3) of the Rome Statute. Int Crim Law Rev 10:43–71
Sluiter G (2009) Human rights protection in the ICC pre-trial phase. In: Stahn C, Sluiter G (eds) The emerging practice of the International Criminal Court. Martinus Nijhoff Publishers, Leiden, pp 459–476
Sluiter G (2010) Trends in the development of a unified law of international criminal procedure. In: Stahn C, Van den Herik L (eds) Future perspectives on international criminal justice. Asser Press, The Hague, pp 585–599
Staker C (2010) Interpretive methodologies and the use of precedent in cases before international criminal courts. In: Khan A, Buisman C, Gosnell C (eds) Principles of evidence in international criminal justice. Oxford University Press, Oxford, pp 185–213
Swoboda S (2012) Die Europäische Menschenrechtskonvention in Strafverfahren vor internationalen Gerichten. In: Höland A (ed) Wirkungen der Rechtsprechung des Europäischen Gerichtshofs für Menschenrechte im deutschen Recht. BMW Berliner Wissenschafts-Verlag, Berlin, pp 83–118
Torres Chedraui A (2010) An analysis of the exclusion of evidence obtained in violation of human rights in light of the jurisprudence of the European Court of Human Rights. Tilburg Law Rev 15:205–234
Triffterer O (2008) (ed) Commentary on the Rome Statute of the International Criminal Court: observers' notes, article by article, 2nd edn. C.H. Beck et al., Baden-Baden
Villiger M (1985) Customary international law and treaties: a study of their interactions and interrelations, with special consideration of the 1969 Vienna convention on the law of treaties. Martinus Nijhoff Publishers, Leiden
Werle G (1997) Menschenrechtsschutz durch Völkerstrafrecht'. Zeitschrift für die gesamte Strafrechtswissenschaft 109:808–829
Werle G (2012) Völkerstrafrecht, 3rd edn. Mohr Siebeck, Tübingen
Young R (2011) "Internationally recognized human rights" before the International Criminal Court. Int Comp Law Q 60:189–208
Zahar A, Sluiter G (2008) International criminal law: a critical introduction. Oxford University Press, Oxford

Chapter 3
Previous Approaches to the Exclusion of Illicitly Obtained Evidence

Abstract At the outset of this work, Chap. 1 has characterised the methodological approach to this research as being a decidedly comparative one. We have seen that given the scarce literature and jurisprudence at the level of international criminal law, solutions developed by academics for domestic systems of criminal procedure in particular will play a major role in developing an ICC approach to the exclusion of illicitly obtained evidence. In addition, there are first attempts to deal with the issue in the context of international criminal law and human rights law. In this chapter will provide a general introduction into examples of approaches at the international level, at the level of human rights law and at the domestic level. It will first outline the approaches of the predecessors of the ICC, the two UN *Ad hoc* tribunals, the International Criminal Tribunal for the former Yugoslavia (ICTY) and the International Criminal Tribunal for Rwanda (ICTR) and then add a human rights perspective by analysing the principles that the European Court of Human Rights (ECtHR) applies to cases concerning the exclusion of tainted evidence. Finally, in this chapter will look at the legal systems of Germany, the United States, England and Wales, as well as Canada. It will thereby explain and compare the different approaches taken in civil law systems as opposed to common law systems, as well as the approaches in systems more favourable to exclusion as opposed to systems with a more restrictive approach.

Keywords *Ad hoc* tribunals · Exclusionary rule · European court of human rights · Margin of appreciation · Bundesgerichtshof · Good faith · Independent source doctrine · Inevitable discovery doctrine · Attenuation doctrine · Police and investigation act 1984 · Conscriptive evidence · Bright-line rule

P. Viebig, *Illicitly Obtained Evidence at the International Criminal Court*,
International Criminal Justice Series 4, DOI 10.1007/978-94-6265-093-0_3

Contents

3.1 The Approach of the *Ad Hoc* Tribunals

3.1.1 Introduction

We have seen that the creation of a procedural law for the ICC was strongly influenced by the experience of the *Ad hoc* tribunals. For the drafters of the ICC legal framework, these tribunals were to some degree '*legal laboratories*' because they had already tested their procedural law in practice.[1] Establishing international tribunals for the situations in the former Yugoslavia and in Rwanda involved the task of developing a completely novel system of procedure for the adjudication of international crimes.[2] When the *Ad hoc* tribunals were established in the mid-nineties, hardly any precedent existed for how to organise and conduct international criminal proceedings.[3] The examples of the Nuremberg Trial and the Tokyo War Crimes Trials were not very instructive for procedural considerations. Admittedly, these tribunals had been comparatively progressive considering the time and

[1]Friman 1999, p. 376.

[2]Dixon 1997, p. 83 et seq.

[3]Gray 2004, p. 291.

historical circumstances of their formation. But they were still military tribunals in a period where the concept of due process rights was generally at an early stage of its development. Their procedure could not, as a consequence, serve as a model for modern, sophisticated international criminal tribunals.[4]

The creation of the *Ad hoc* tribunals differs from that of the ICC in two fundamental and closely linked aspects. Unlike the ICC, the *Ad hoc* tribunals were not established as a result of a treaty process. They were created by the UN Security Council pursuant to its powers under Chapter VII of the UN Charter. As a result, their procedural system was mainly judge-made. In contrast to the ICC, there was no Assembly of States Parties that could have served as a legislative power. The Security Council, by way of resolutions 827[5] and 955,[6] only created the statutes of the tribunals.[7] These statutes contain only very basic provisions on the law of procedure. The adoption of the majority of provisions was left to the judges who were given the power to create Rules of Procedure and Evidence.[8]

The procedural system that emerged at the *Ad hoc* tribunals has been labelled hybrid because it contains both common law and civil law elements. This system has, however, far more adversarial features than the procedural law of the ICC.[9] The proceedings have generally been conceived as a party process with a prosecution and a defence that bear the responsibility for the development of their cases themselves. This includes the collection and presentation of evidence.[10] The presentation of the evidence at trial also follows a typical common law order.[11] The strong influence of common law on the Rules of Procedure and Evidence of the *Ad hoc* tribunals was particularly apparent in their initial version. From the outset, however, this adversarial framework has been combined with a number of civil law features. And with the evolution of the procedural law of the tribunals, the influence of civil law has increased to some extent.[12]

---

[4]Berger 2012, p. 13; Jackson and Summers 2012, p. 117 et seq.

[5]UN Doc. S/RES/827 of 25 May 1993; available at: http://www.un.org/en/ga/search/view_doc.asp?symbol=S/RES/827%281993%29 (last visited: October 2013).

[6]UN Doc. S/RES/955 of 8 November 1994; available at: http://www.un.org/en/ga/search/view_doc.asp?symbol=S/RES/955%281994%29 (last visited: October 2013).

[7]Statute of the International Criminal Tribunal for the former Yugoslavia (ICTY Statute), last version of September 2009; available at: http://www.icty.org/sid/135 (last visited: October 2013); Statute of the International Criminal Tribunal for Rwanda (ICTR Statute), last version of 31 January 2010; available at: http://www.unictr.org/Legal/StatuteoftheTribunal/tabid/94/Default.asp (last visited: October 2013).

[8]See Article 15 of the ICTY Statute and Article 14 of the ICTR Statute.

[9]For a detailed description of the differences between these systems, see Orie 2002, p. 1439 et seq.

[10]Meron 2004, p. 522.

[11]See Rule 85 of the RPE. For more details, see Nemitz 2002, p. 54 et seq.

[12]Jackson and Summers 2012, p. 123.

3.1.2 The General Approach to the Law of Evidence

The influence of civil law on the *Ad hoc* tribunals' procedure is particularly strong when it comes to the admissibility of evidence.[13] While the presentation of evidence follows a common law order, the admissibility of evidence is characterized by a flexible approach more akin to inquisitorial concepts such as the French principle of '*la liberté de la preuve*' or the German notion of '*freie richterliche Beweiswürdigung*'.[14] Unlike in traditional adversarial systems, the procedural law of the *Ad hoc* tribunals is not governed by a large body of technical rules of evidence. The general standard for admissibility is set forth in Rules 89(C) of the Rules of Procedure and Evidence of the ICTY and ICTR respectively. In addition, only a dozen rules establish more detailed conditions for the introduction and admissibility of evidence.[15] Among these rules are *inter alia* Rule 89(D) of the RPE of the ICTY and Rule 95 of the Rules of both the ICTY and the ICTR, which pertain to the admissibility of illicitly obtained evidence.

The evidentiary framework that results from these provisions is characterized in particular by the broad discretion granted to the judges. As a general tendency, the exercise of this discretion was also guided by inquisitorial ideas. Under common law, tainted evidence would regularly be excluded at the outset of a trial. At the *Ad hoc* tribunals, the general tendency has instead been to admit evidence extensively and to assess its weight at a later stage together with the rest of the evidence.[16] This liberal approach to evidence was already applied by the historical tribunals at Nuremberg and Tokyo.[17] It may in fact be considered the general approach of international courts and tribunals.[18] There are different reasons for the overall reluctance of international criminal institutions to apply more technical rules of evidence. The prevalent rationale is a practical one. The parties in international criminal proceedings regularly face great difficulties when they strive to gather evidence, often during or in the aftermath of an armed conflict. Under these circumstances, it seems inappropriate to further complicate their efforts through a

---

[13]Jackson and Summers 2012, p. 123.

[14]Boas 2001, p. 48.

[15]For an overview of these rules, see Gosnell 2010, p. 376 et seq.

[16]See *Prosecutor v. Blaškić* (Judgment), ICTY (Trial Chamber), decision of 3 March 2000, para 34: "*The principle [...] is one of extensive admissibility of evidence—questions of credibility or authenticity being determined according to the weight given to each of the materials by the judges at the appropriate time*". See also Combs 2011, p. 326; Nemitz 2002, p. 57.

[17]See Article 19 of the IMT Charter: "*The Tribunals shall not be bound by technical rules of evidence. It shall adopt and apply to the greatest possible extent expeditious and non-technical procedure, and shall admit any evidence which it deems to have probative value.*" On the general approach of the historical tribunals, see Klamberg 2013, p. 337; May and Wierda 2003, p. 94 et seq.

[18]Gaynor et al. 2013, p. 1017; Zappalà 2002, p. 149.

complicated system of evidentiary rules.[19] Another key argument is that such rules are simply redundant in international criminal trials. In traditional adversarial systems, rules of evidence operate to guard a jury against unreliable or prejudicial information. International criminal trials in turn are conducted by professional judges. It is assumed that these judges, in contrast to jurors, are able to exclude from their minds any evidence they are not allowed to take into account when they take their final decision.[20]

3.1.3 The Ad Hoc Tribunals and the Exclusion of Illicitly Obtained Evidence

In the statutes of the *Ad hoc* tribunals, there are no provisions on the admissibility of evidence. Instead, the flexible approach to admissibility rests on Rule 89(C) of the Rules of Procedure and Evidence (RPE) of both tribunals. Under this provision, "[a] *Chamber may admit any relevant evidence which it deems to have probative value*". In pursuance of the policy depicted above, Rule 89(C) was drafted and has been interpreted in a way that enables the judges to admit evidence extensively in the first place. As an ICTY Chamber has held, "[t]*he approach adopted by the Rules is clearly one in favour of admissibility* [...]".[21] The basic requirements for admissibility are reliability and probative value.[22] The respective threshold is rather low. According to the case law, it suffices if evidence *prima facie* has "*some relevance and some probative value*".[23]

At the same time, both Statutes do allow for the exclusion of certain evidence even at an early stage of the proceedings. Rule 95 of the RPE of both tribunals requires the mandatory exclusion of evidence where such evidence was "[...] *obtained by methods which cast substantial doubt on its reliability or if its admission is antithetical to, and would seriously damage, the integrity of the proceedings*". According to this provision, exclusion is not a matter of means but one of result. The decisive factor for exclusion is not the way in which the evidence was collected but rather its impact on the trial. This was not the wording of Rule 95 in the initial version of both Rules of Procedure and Evidence. The original rule focused on the means used for collecting the evidence. A Chamber had to exclude evidence obtained by methods "*which constitute a serious violation of internationally*

---

[19]Friman 2003, p. 374; May and Wierda 2003, p. 94 et seq.

[20]Boas 2001; May and Wierda 2003, p. 99 et seq.; Nemitz 2002, p. 57; Safferling 2012, p. 495.

[21]*Prosecutor v. Delalić* et al. (Decision on the Motion of the Prosecution for the Admissibility of Evidence), ICTY (Trial Chamber), decision of 19 January 1998, para 16.

[22]On this general test for admissibility, see Gosnell 2010, p. 384 et seq. For the ICTY and ICTR in particular, see Gaynor et al. 2013, p. 1022 et seq.

[23]*Prosecutor v. Musema* (Judgment and Sentence), ICTY (Trial Chamber), decision of 27 January 2000, para 56. Also see Safferling 2012, p. 375.

recognized human rights".[24] The first version of the Rules was amended twice. The present text of the provision emanates from an amendment made in 1995 on the basis of proposals by the United Kingdom and the United States.[25] In addition, the title of the provision was changed in 1997. While the initial title was phrased "*evidence obtained by means contrary to internationally protected human rights*", it was then changed to "*exclusion of certain evidence*."[26]

These amendments were arguably meant to enhance the protection of the rights of the accused. Doubt has been cast, however, on whether this aim was achieved. Admittedly, under Rule 95 in its present form, the types of norms that may trigger exclusion are not explicitly enumerated.[27] Accordingly, exclusion is not limited to human rights violations but can also be the result of other violations, including violations of both the Statutes and the Rules of Procedure and Evidence.[28] According to the jurisprudence of the ICTY, this even includes the violation of the sovereignty rights of states, even though an accused is not directly affected by such a violation.[29] Theoretically, the present wording of Rule 95 would even allow for exclusion based on a violation of domestic law. This has, however, been rejected by case law.[30] By contrast, the initial version was generally limited to violations of '*internationally recognized human rights*'.

The focus of the initial version of the Rules on the means of evidence collection, however, had the benefit of unequivocally sanctioning violations from the very outset of the investigation. The wording as it presently stands adds another threshold by focusing on the effects at the trial stage.[31] The consequence is that, despite its mandatory wording, Rule 95 does not require automatic exclusion of all

[24]See ICTY Rules of Procedure and Evidence, *IT/32/Rev. 3,* from 30 January 1995 compared to ICTY Rules of Procedure and Evidence, *Original Version*, *IT/32*, from 11 February 1997. All versions available at: http://www.icty.org/sid/136 (last visited: October 2013).

[25]Calvo-Goller 2006, p. 97.

[26]See ICTY Rules of Procedure and Evidence, *IT/32/Rev. 12*, from 12 November 1997, compared to ICTY Rules of Procedure and Evidence, *Original Version*, *IT/32,* from 11 February 1997.

[27]Alamuddin 2010, p. 240.

[28]Zahar and Sluiter 2008, p. 382. Note that the RPE are covered by the wording of Rule 95. For the problem, which in turn arises for Article 69(7) of the ICC Statute in this respect, see Sect. 4.3.3.2.

[29]*Prosecutor v. Kordić and Čerkez* (Decision Stating Reasons for Trial Chamber's Ruling of June 1999 Rejecting Defence Motion to Suppress Evidence), ICTY (Trial Chamber), decision of 25 June 1999, para 10.

[30]*Prosecutor v. Haraqija and Morina* (Judgment), ICTY (Appeals Chamber), decision of 23 July 2009, paras 24 and 25; *Prosecutor v. Kordić and Čerkez*, ICTY (Trial Chamber), Transcript of 2 February 2000, p. 13694 and p. 13671, available at: http://www.icty.org/x/cases/kordic_cerkez/trans/en/000202it.htm (last visited: October 2013). See also Klamberg 2013, p. 400.

[31]Calvo-Goller 2006, p. 97; Safferling 2001, p. 249 et seq. For a critical assessment of the present version, see also Berger 2012, p. 37.

evidence gained improperly.[32] The key factor being the impact on the trial, the judges have the discretion to determine the conditions under which such an impact must be assumed. They are vested with a considerable margin of appreciation when defining the vague legal terms of Rule 95, such as '*substantial doubt*', '*anti-thetical*', '*seriously damage*' and '*integrity of the proceedings*'.[33]

When exercising this discretion, the Chambers of the *Ad hoc* tribunals have confirmed that the mere fact that evidence has been collected through illicit means does not necessarily require its exclusion. Other than some domestic exclusionary rules,[34] Rule 95 has never been applied as a matter of principle.[35] Quite the contrary, the Chambers have always interpreted its requirements rather restrictively.

This is particularly clear from the case law that applies the later version of Rule 95. Here, the judges have explicitly distinguished between the impropriety of certain means of collecting evidence and its subsequent admission at trial. They have emphasised that the admission of evidence must not be understood as an approval of a particular method of investigation.[36] All along, excluding evidence has only been considered appropriate as an exception. This ultimately requires a mechanism to determine which evidence must be excluded and which can be admitted. This decision has been reached through a balancing exercise in the course of which the tribunals consider a number of factors that we will discuss in more detail below.

In addition to rule 95, the ICTY Statute contains a provision that allows the consideration of the exclusion of evidence on a more manifestly discretionary basis. Under rule 89(D), the judges of the ICTY are authorized to exclude evidence "*if its probative value is substantially outweighed by the need to ensure a fair trial*". In comparison with Rule 95, the requirement of a weighing exercise results directly from the wording of the provision. This more explicit grant of

---

[32]Combs 2011, p. 328; Tochilovsky 2007, p. 407.

[33]Nemitz 2005, p. 70.

[34]An example is in particular the original version of the U.S. exclusionary rule, see Sect. 3.3.2.

[35]*Prosecutor v. Brđanin* (Decision on the Defence "Objection to Intercept Evidence"), ICTY (Trial Chamber), decision of 3 October 2003, para 55.

[36]See in particular a discussion on exclusion under rule 95 between the Trial Chamber and the Defence in *Prosecutor v. Kordić and Čerkez*, ICTY (Trial Chamber), Transcript of 2 February 2000, p. 13671, concerning the admissibility of a tape recorded in the course of an interception:
"*Judge Robinson: So the mere fact that it is inadmissible under domestic law doesn't make it inadmissible here.*
Mr. Stein: With respect, sir, the last words of 95 are "seriously damage the integrity of the proceedings.
Judge Robinson: The proceedings, yes.
Mr. Stein: If Your Honour agrees, assume it's relevant, assume it's accurate, assume it's material, but assume it's illegally obtained. Then Your Honours would be giving [...] *tacit approval to illegal conduct by admitting it into evidence as something we do.*
Judge May: Not necessarily. It doesn't mean that you are approving the conduct. The only question you have to decide in a case of this sort is whether it's admissible in these proceedings".

discretion is probably the reason why decisions on exclusion at the Yugoslavia Tribunal refer more frequently to Rule 89(D) than to Rule 95.[37]

This also explains why a chamber of the tribunal has called Rule 95 a "*residual exclusionary provision*".[38] Contrary to this jurisprudence, Rule 95 is actually the more restrictive of both norms. Rule 89(D), in contrast, is phrased in very general terms. As a result, the latter provision would also allow the exclusion of evidence on the basis, for example, of the method by which it is presented in court. In comparison, the expression "*obtained by methods*" in Rule 95 shows that this rule is confined to violations concerning the means of evidence collection.[39] Consequently, Rule 95 is in fact *lex specialis* where rights violations in the course of investigative measures constitute the bone of contention.[40]

The problem of the relationship between Rules 95 and 89(D) does not arise for the Rwanda Tribunal. The ICTR Rules of Procedure and Evidence do not contain an equivalent to Rule 89(D) of the RPE of the ICTY. Consequently, the Chambers of the Rwanda Tribunal have made greater use of Rule 95.[41] At the same time, since Rule 95 has also been interpreted to require a balancing exercise, this deviation does not lead to any divergence in substance. Moreover, the case law of the ICTR has ultimately referred to Rule 89(D) even though this rule does not appear in its RPE.[42] The Trial Chamber in the *Karemera* case applied the general admissibility test of Rule 89(C) of the ICTR Rules. Quoting the wording of Rule 89(D) of the ICTY Statute, the Chamber held that it had the "*inherent power to exclude evidence if its probative value is substantially outweighed by the need to ensure a fair trial.*"[43] In general, with respect to the exclusion of evidence, the Rwanda Tribunal seems to consider that it has to make the same considerations as the ICTY.

---

[37]Combs 2011, p. 328; Zahar and Sluiter 2008, p. 382.

[38]*Prosecutor v. Delalić* et al. (Decision on Zdravko Mucic's Motion for the Exclusion of Evidence), ICTY (Trial Chamber), decision of 2 September 1997, para 44.

[39]Zahar and Sluiter 2008, p. 382.

[40]Ambos 2007, p. 478, fn. 382.

[41]Combs 2011, p. 328.

[42]Note however the reference in Rule 70(F) of the ICTR Rules: "*Nothing in Sub-Rule (C) or (D) above shall affect a Trial Chamber's power under Rule 89(C) to exclude evidence if its probative value is substantially outweighed by the need to ensure a fair trial.*", which seems to interpret Rule 89(C) of the ICTR Rules in accordance with the wording of Rule 89(D) of the ICTY Statute.

[43]*Prosecutor v. Karemera* (Decision on the Prosecution Motion for Admission into Evidence of Post-Arrest Interviews with Joseph Nzirorera and Mathieu Ngirumpatse), ICTR (Trial Chamber), decision of 2 November 2007, para 3; *Prosecutor v. Karemera* (Decision on Defence Oral Motions for Exclusion of Witness XMB's Testimony, for Sanctions against the Prosecution and for Exclusion Outside the Scope of the Indictment), ICTR (Trial Chamber), decision of 19 October 2006, para 20.

3.1.4 Factors in the Balancing Exercise

We have seen that the *Ad hoc* tribunals base their decision on the exclusion of evidence on a balancing exercise. The question that follows pertains to the criteria that the tribunals consider relevant for this exercise. Not all of the case law of the *Ad hoc* tribunals is of much avail in this respect. Some decisions dealing with the exclusion of evidence do not specify the reasons for their findings.[44] Other decisions, however, are more instructive. In the *Brđanin* case in particular, the ICTY has explained its finding in more detail. The Trial Chamber in this case established a general test for the exclusion of illicitly obtained evidence. This test describes the antagonism between due process and effective law enforcement which, in essence, as we will see, guides the decision on exclusion in all modern systems of criminal procedure. The ICTY judges held that "[t]*he correct balance must be maintained between the fundamental rights of the accused and the essential interests of the international community in the prosecution of persons charged with serious violations of international humanitarian law.*"[45]

Furthermore, in order to find viable solutions, the judges in this and other decisions have referred to a number of factors that they have found to militate in favour of either one of the two opposing interests: 'due process' and 'effective law enforcement'.

A central factor has been the seriousness and nature of the contentious rights violation. In the *Brđanin* case, the Chamber found that exclusion of evidence as a remedy for a violation was only appropriate in case of a particularly serious violation. A "minor breach of procedural rules" in turn has not been considered sufficient to justify exclusion.[46] It seems, however, difficult to judge exactly what kind of mistakes the tribunals would qualify as serious enough.[47] The mere fact that human rights were concerned has not always been considered enough to make the violation sufficiently grave. While in some cases of human rights violations, the

[44]See for instance *Prosecutor v. Kordić and Čerkez* (Decision Stating Reasons for Trial Chamber's Ruling of June 1999 Rejecting Defence Motion to Suppress Evidence), ICTY (Trial Chamber), decision of 25 June 1999, paras 8 et seq.; *Prosecutor v. Karemera* (Decision on the Prosecutor's Motion for Admission of Certain Exhibits into Evidence), ICTR (Trial Chamber), decision of 25 January 2008, para 17.

[45]*Prosecutor v. Brđanin* (Decision on the Defence "Objection to Intercept Evidence"), ICTY (Trial Chamber), decision of 3 October 2003, para 62.

[46]*Prosecutor v. Brđanin* (Decision on the Defence "Objection to Intercept Evidence"), ICTY (Trial Chamber), decision of 3 October 2003, para 61. See also *Prosecutor v. Delalić* et al. (Decision on the Tendering of Prosecution Exhibits 104–108), ICTY (Trial Chamber), decision of 9 February 1998, para 20. *See Prosecutor v. Delalić* et al. (Decision on Zdravko Mucic's Motion for the Exclusion of Evidence), ICTY (Trial Chamber), decision of 2 September 1997, para 55.

[47]Alamuddin 2010, p. 302.

judges have excluded the evidence without further dwelling on any other factor,[48] they have declined exclusion in other instances.[49]

A further factor has been the seriousness of the crime the accused is charged with. The case law seems to establish that this is a factor that militates in favour of the admission of evidence. Again in the *Brđanin* case, the Trial Chamber referred to its mandate to try persons responsible for serious violations of international law and argued that "[...] *it would be utterly inappropriate to exclude relevant evidence due to procedural considerations, as long as the fairness of the trial is guaranteed*".[50] The Chamber, in this case, then set the seriousness of the crimes against the significance of the evidence, holding that it should not deprive itself of relevant and important evidence.[51] The specific impact of a piece of evidence thus seems to have been a further criterion for the tribunals's decision.

The ICTY has also taken into account the attitude of the investigators that were involved in the violation. According to the respective case law, the fact that the authorities have acted in good faith is a factor that militates in favour of the admission of the tainted evidence.[52]

A final criterion that has been discussed pertains to the actors involved in the collection of evidence. Three basic scenarios are possible in this respect. Either the national authorities have collected the evidence autonomously; or they have acted on behalf of the international prosecutor; or the latter has gathered the evidence himself. As a matter of principle, the standards against which the evidence is measured are the same in all of these scenarios. Even where national authorities have carried out acts of investigation, these acts must be measured not against national law but against the legal framework of the tribunals. We have already seen that, according to case law, a violation of domestic law as such is not sufficient to

[48]*Prosecutor v. Delalić* et al. (Decision on Zdravko Mucic's Motion for the Exclusion of Evidence), ICTY (Trial Chamber), decision of 2 September 1997, para 43; *Prosecutor v. Karemera* (Decision on the Prosecution Motion for Admission into Evidence of Post-Arrest Interviews with Joseph Nzirorera and Mathieu Ngirumpatse), ICTR (Trial Chamber), decision of 2 November 2007, paras 25 et seq.

[49]See *Prosecutor v. Kordic and Cerkez*, ICTY (Trial Chamber), Transcript of 2 February 2000, p. 13694; *Prosecutor v. Brđanin* (Decision on the Defence "Objection to Intercept Evidence"), ICTY (Trial Chamber), decision of 3 October 2003, para 61 et seq. Critical on this jurisprudence, Zahar and Sluiter 2008, p. 381.

[50]*Prosecutor v. Brđanin* (Decision on the Defence "Objection to Intercept Evidence"), ICTY (Trial Chamber), decision of 3 October 2003, para 63. See also *Prosecutor v. Karadžić* (Decision on the Accused's Motion to Exclude Intercepted Conversations), ICTY (Trial Chamber), decision of 30 September 2010, para 10.

[51]*Prosecutor v. Brđanin* (Decision on the Defence "Objection to Intercept Evidence"), ICTY (Trial Chamber), decision of 3 October 2003, para 63.

[52]*Prosecutor v. Haraqija and Morina* (Decision on Haraqija and Morina Second Request for a Declaration of Inadmissibility and Exclusion of Evidence), ICTY (Trial Chamber), decision of 24 November 2008, paras 20 and 26; *Prosecutor v. Haraqija and Morina* (Judgment), ICTY (Appeals Chamber), decision of 23 July 2009, para 28; *Prosecutor v. Brđanin* (Decision on the Defence "Objection to Intercept Evidence"), ICTY (Trial Chamber), decision of 3 October 2003, para 63. See also Alamuddin 2010, p. 304.

trigger the exclusion of evidence.[53] Conversely, where investigators have complied with national law, evidence can still be excluded if the national rules are not consistent with the tribunals' own standards, be it the standards set forth in the Statutes or RPEs, or applicable human rights standards.[54]

Turning to the influence on the balancing exercise, the issue is whether different weight should be attached to a violation of the aforementioned standards, depending on the identity of the participating actors. Commentators have argued that a violation becomes more serious if the international prosecutor was involved in the investigative measure.[55] This would apply where the staff of the Prosecutor's office has committed the violation or—albeit to a lesser extent—where it has at least triggered the investigative measure. This has also been suggested in the case law of the *Ad hoc* tribunals.[56]

3.1.5 Potential of the Approach of the Ad Hoc Tribunals for the Construction of the ICC Exclusionary Rule

The approach of the *Ad hoc* tribunals is the most immediate model to look to for guidance on how to deal with evidentiary issues in international criminal proceedings. The tribunals have conducted the first modern international criminal trials in which they had to reconcile the rights of the accused with the interests of the international community in the prosecution of international crimes. One issue among many has been when to exclude or admit illicitly obtained evidence. The ICC is faced with the same task. In many ways, as an international criminal institution, it is also confronted with the same problems as the tribunals. One example would be the above-mentioned difficulties involved in collecting evidence in an often unsteady environment. As we will see, this parallelism is reflected by the similarity of the norms on the exclusion of evidence.[57] As a consequence, the jurisprudence of the *Ad hoc* tribunals contains useful indications for the construction of an ICC exclusionary rule. This pertains in particular to the factors considered by the tribunals in their balancing exercise.

At the same time, a number of differences between the ICC and the tribunals have already become clear. Among these is the different process that led to the

---

[53] *Prosecutor v. Haraqija and Morina* (Judgment), ICTY (Appeals Chamber), decision of 23 July 2009, paras 24 and 25; *Prosecutor v. Kordić and Čerkez*, ICTY (Trial Chamber), Transcript of 2 February 2000, pp. 13694 and 13671.

[54] *Prosecutor v. Delalić* et al. (Decision on Zdravko Mucic's Motion for the Exclusion of Evidence), ICTY (Trial Chamber), decision of 2 September 1997, para 43.

[55] See Alamuddin 2010, p. 301; Sluiter 2002, p. 226.

[56] See for instance *Prosecutor v. Mrkšić* (Decision Concerning the Use of Statements Given by the Accused), ICTY (Trial Chamber), decision of 9 October 2006; *Prosecutor v. Barayagwiza* (Decision), ICTR (Appeals Chamber), decision of 3 November 1999, para 61.

[57] See Sect. 4.3.1.

creation of the *Ad hoc* tribunals and of their legal framework. Further differences would be the power conferred on the *Ad hoc* tribunals by the Security Council and the consequences for the cooperation system with states. These differences will have to be taken into account for the construction of the ICC exclusionary rule. In addition, we have seen that the impact of civil law and common law on the legal framework of the *Ad hoc* tribunals is not the same as for the ICC. The review of the different domestic systems will show, however, that the degree to which a system has a more adversarial or inquisitorial style of proceedings is less significant for the shape of the exclusionary rule as such. Its only true impact concerns the way the exclusionary rule is put into practice in the course of the proceedings.[58]

In addition to these systematic differences, the utility of the jurisprudence of the *Ad hoc* tribunals is not without limits. The case law on the exclusion of illicitly obtained evidence is far from providing a comprehensive framework. Consequently, the consideration of other sources will be necessary. This is particularly true for questions of detail. We will see that, here, the approaches developed by domestic legal systems will often be more useful.

3.2 The Approach of the European Court of Human Rights

3.2.1 Introduction

We have seen that human rights standards are applicable in proceedings before the ICC, as long as due consideration is given to the contextual differences between the legal frameworks. This includes the standards set by the ECHR, as well as its authoritative interpretation by the European Court of Human Rights. Another question is whether these standards are actually a fruitful legal source for the construction of the ICC exclusionary rule.

At the outset, we need to consider why this research concentrates on the European human rights framework. Admittedly, this choice only allows for a limited consideration of a human rights perspective. A consideration of all of the main human rights frameworks would, however, go beyond the scope of this research.

The ECtHR has been chosen because the case law of this court has been consulted more frequently by international criminal tribunals than the decisions of any other human rights body.[59] Linked to this is the consideration that, from the perspective of comparative law, the jurisprudence of the ECtHR is particularly interesting. Admittedly, the ECtHR itself only rarely carries out comparative law considerations in its judgments. However, all Member States of the Council of

[58]On the practical application of the exclusionary rule in ICC proceedings and on the significance of common and civil law elements in this context, see Sect. 6.1.

[59]Swoboda 2012, p. 98.

Europe are represented with a judge on its bench.[60] As a consequence, the Court takes into account the different legal systems that exist in the 44 Member States and, through its case law, contributes to their harmonization. These systems in turn are a very interesting sample for comparative law purposes. They are a mix of systems from both the civil law and the common law legal family. In this respect, the ECtHR case law is more interesting for international criminal law considerations than for example the Inter-American Court of Human Rights, whose Member States almost all have civil law based legal systems.

At the same time, the decisions of the ECtHR as a real court have greater authority than human rights institutions, such as the United Nations Human Rights Committee, which are not in fact judicial bodies in the strict sense.[61] What is more, the significance of the European human rights system also has a practical basis: its case law is the most developed among human rights institutions and it is continuously discussed by legal academics. Finally, the resulting material is usually available in the working languages of the ICC.[62]

3.2.2 The General Approach to the Law of Evidence

Turning to the law of evidence, the European Convention on Human Rights does not contain any explicit provision on either the gathering of evidence or on its use in criminal trials. Nor has the Court formulated any abstract rules on these issues. This absence can be explained in view of the nature of the Court as a human rights monitoring body. The European judges have repeatedly stressed that the ECtHR is not a court of fourth instance for the Member States. Its mandate does not cover the assessment of the correct application of domestic law. Neither is the ECtHR in a position to examine whether the domestic courts have ruled on the basis of accurately established facts.[63] Its exclusive task is to monitor the compliance of the Member States with the Convention. Accordingly, the Court is limited to determining the violation of a right contained in the Convention. In fact, even with respect to this intrinsic competence, the ECtHR assumes a subsidiary role. The main responsibility for the implementation of the Convention lies with the Member States.[64]

As a consequence, the Court has adopted a certain measure of self-restraint. It generally leaves a wide margin of appreciation to domestic authorities in order to

[60]Swoboda 2012, p. 96.

[61]Cassese 2003, p. 25.

[62]Young 2011, p. 204.

[63]*Jalloh v. Germany*, ECtHR, judgment of 11 July 2006 (Application no. 54810/00), para 94; *Khan v. United Kingdom*, ECtHR, decision of 12 May 2000 (Application no. 35394/97), para 34; *Schenk v. Switzerland*, ECtHR, decision of 12 July 1988 (Application no. 10862/84), para 45.

[64]For a manifestation of the primary responsibility of the domestic authorities, see Articles 13 and 53 of the ECHR.

respect the national institutions and their choices for the implementation of the obligations arising from the Convention.[65] With respect to evidentiary issues, the Court has concluded that it is not mandated to impose a specific approach to the admissibility and use of evidence because this is primarily a matter of national regulation.[66]

3.2.3 The ECtHR and the Exclusion of Illicitly Obtained Evidence

The discretion granted to the Member States does not mean of course that the use of illicitly obtained evidence by domestic criminal courts is not addressed by the ECtHR at all. The Court may find that this use constitutes a violation of the ECHR. Its case law deals with the issue under Article 6 of the Convention.

This provision, in its first section, guarantees the fundamental right to a fair trial. In addition, its third section enumerates a number of specific rights of the defence that are presented as minimum guarantees. This list of rights in Article 6(3) is not exhaustive. Where it omits basic procedural protections such as the privilege against self-incrimination or the principle of the equality of arms, such guarantees form part of the general right to a fair trial as set forth in Article 6(1).[67] In accordance with its previously described self-restraint, the Court is, however, very cautious when it assesses whether Article 6 has been violated. It assumes such a violation only where it considers, subsequent to an overall assessment, that a trial was unfair.

For this consideration, the Court proceeds in two steps. First, it determines whether any procedural guarantee covered by Article 6 has been violated. Such a violation however does not automatically lead to a violation of the fair trial principle. In a second step, a comprehensive evaluation of the respective proceedings is made in order to determine whether the trial "*as a whole*" was unfair.[68] In this context, the Court does not make a clear distinction between the general right to a fair trial in Article 6(1) and the specific rights of the defence in Article 6(3). It rather understands the latter rights as partial guarantees and components of an overall right to a fair trial. As a consequence, the assessment that the use of illicitly

[65] Satzger 2009, p. 761.

[66] See for instance *Jalloh v. Germany*, ECtHR, judgment of 11 July 2006 (Application no. 54810/00), paras 94 and 95; *Khan v. United Kingdom*, ECtHR, decision of 12 May 2000 (Application no. 35394/97), para 34; *Schenk v. Switzerland*, ECtHR, decision of 12 July 1988 (Application no. 10862/84), para 46. See also Gaede 2009, p. 494; Schroeder 2003, p. 295; Trechsel and Summers 2005, p. 83.

[67] Ambos 2011, para 7.

[68] For a comprehensive overview of this approach and its development in the case-law of the ECtHR, see Lubig and Sprenger 2008, p. 433 et seq.

obtained evidence amounts to a violation under the Convention is not based on the specific partial guarantees. Instead, the Court always justifies this finding by relying on the general right to a fair trial.[69]

3.2.4 Factors in the Balancing Exercise

In order to assess whether the trial "*as a whole*" was unfair, the ECtHR conducts a balancing exercise. To this end, it considers a number of criteria that it deems relevant for its evaluation. Firstly, the character and the seriousness of the violation alleged to have been committed by the authorities have been guiding factors for the Court. Violations of the prohibition of torture in Article 3 of the ECHR for example have been treated very differently from violations of Article 8 of the ECHR, which protects the right to privacy. The Court has assumed that the use of evidence gathered through an act of torture generally violates Article 6 of the ECHR.[70] It has not, however, drawn the same conclusion for violations of the right to privacy.[71] As a second factor, the European judges have considered that the seriousness of the alleged crime is relevant because it determines the public interest in its prosecution.[72] Moreover, the Court has taken into account the reliability of the evidence.[73] As a fourth relevant factor, the Court has assessed the impact of the evidence on the outcome of the trial. This factor pertains to whether this evidence would have been the decisive evidence for a conviction or whether it was only used for corroboration. Where the evidence was decisive for convicting the appellant, the determination of a violation of Article 6 has been more likely.[74] As a central factor, the Court has also considered whether the appellant had been able to fully exercise the procedural rights of the defence, especially whether he was able to contest the problematic evidence and whether he could introduce evidence of

---

[69] Trechsel and Summers 2005, p. 87.

[70] *Harutyunyan v. Armenia*, ECtHR, decision of 28 June 2007 (Application no. 36549/03), para 66. On the jurisdiction of the ECtHR on the prohibition of torture, see in particular Sect. 5.3.3.1.

[71] On Article 8 of the ECHR, see *Khan v. United Kingdom*, ECtHR, decision of 12 May 2000 (Application no. 35394/97), para 40. On the distinction between these rights, see Warnking 2009, p. 58 et seq.

[72] *Jalloh v. Germany*, ECtHR, judgment of 11 July 2006 (Application no. 54810/00), paras 119 and 122.

[73] *Jalloh v. Germany*, ECtHR, judgment of 11 July 2006 (Application no. 54810/00), para 96; *Khan v. United Kingdom*, ECtHR, decision of 12 May 2000 (Application no. 35394/97), para 37.

[74] *Jalloh v. Germany*, ECtHR, judgment of 11 July 2006 (Application no. 54810/00), paras 121 and 122; *Khan v. United Kingdom*, ECtHR, decision of 12 May 2000 (Application no. 35394/97), para 37; *Schenk v. Switzerland*, ECtHR, decision of 12 July 1988 (Application no. 10862/84), para 48.

his own.[75] According to this understanding, the notion of fairness is closely intertwined with the possibility of an accused actively taking part in the proceedings. This is based on the argument that an accused must be treated as an individual endowed with rights and not as a mere object of the proceedings.[76]

Finally, it needs to be added that the Court takes a very specific, retrospective view when it assesses the fairness of the proceedings. It does not only consider the proceedings and the trial itself. According to its case law, a verdict of unfairness is not justified if the respective Member State has subsequently compensated the appellant for the violation he has endured.[77]

3.2.5 Criticism of the ECtHR's Approach

The Court's jurisprudence on the exclusion of evidence has been subject to extensive criticism. These critics have held that the Court's approach is contrary to both the wording and purpose of Article 6 of the ECHR.[78] The main point of contention has been that the Court's approach does not sufficiently take into account the principle of legality. In this context, the holistic approach of the European judges in particular has been assailed for its unsound methodology. This is partly due to the fact that the decisions taken by the ECtHR have tended to simply refer to the holistic approach of trial fairness without going into more detail.[79] What is more, blurring the fair trial guarantee of Article 6(1) of the ECHR and the specific guarantees set forth in Article 6(3) has made it difficult to derive from the case law any clear guidance on the requirements relating to evidence under the Convention.[80] Similarly, the Court's retrospective perspective has been opposed because it makes it difficult to assess exactly what impact on trial fairness an original violation had.[81]

On a very basic level, it has been argued that the Court has exaggerated its restraint from interfering with national legal systems. The respective reasoning in its jurisprudence has been criticized for inviting Member States to find ways to

[75]*Khan v. United Kingdom*, ECtHR, decision of 12 May 2000 (Application no. 35394/97), para 35; *Schenk v. Switzerland*, ECtHR, decision of 12 July 1988 (Application no. 10862/84), para 47. For an enumeration of the different factors, see also Torres Chedraui 2010, p. 210; Satzger 2009, p. 767.

[76]Esser 2012, p. 134; Lubig and Sprenger 2008, p. 438.

[77]See *Gäfgen v. Germany*, ECtHR, decision of 30 June 2008 (Application no. 22978/05), para 76. In such a case, the appellant no longer holds the status of a victim that is required for a case to be admissible before the ECtHR. A previously filed complaint is considered *ex post* inadmissible, see Satzger 2009, p. 761. Also see Esser 2008, p. 661; Warnking 2009, p. 49.

[78]Rzepka 2000, p. 102 et seq.

[79]Schroeder 2003, p. 297.

[80]Trechsel and Summers 2005, p. 88. Critical also Gaede 2009, p. 495.

[81]Warnking 2009, p. 49.

circumvent the requirements of the ECHR.[82] Critics have pointed out that this self-restraint would not even be necessary because it would actually fall under the intrinsic competence of the Court to declare evidence inadmissible that had been collected in violation of the Convention. It has been added that while the Court has repeatedly stated that it was not mandated to judge the establishment of facts by national judges, its current jurisprudence does evaluate the factual basis of national decisions. This is based on the argument that the European judges have heavily relied on the significance of the evidence when conducting their balancing exercise.[83]

In addition, it has been argued that it was inconsistent to make a distinction between the violation of different Convention rights such as the right to torture and the right to privacy.[84] And finally, with respect to the factors considered, it has been found inappropriate to give primary consideration to the possibility of the accused fully exercising the procedural rights of the defence. It has been suggested that granting procedural rights to the defence only meant to refrain from committing even more rights violations.[85]

3.2.6 Potential of the ECtHR's Approach for the Construction of the ICC Exclusionary Rule

We have seen that the jurisprudence of the European Court of Human Rights in general is a very fruitful source for comparative law considerations. Since international criminal courts and tribunals have hybrid procedural systems with elements of both civil and common law, this jurisprudence should regularly have great potential for the interpretation of the normative framework of these institutions.[86] At the same time, the specific context in which the ECtHR operates calls for caution when utilizing its decisions, including for the present issue. Moreover, the criticism regarding the Court's case law on illicitly obtained evidence must be given due consideration.

When dealing with the exclusion of illicitly obtained evidence, both the ICC and the ECtHR are confronted with the same basic question: Which means are justified by the requirements of effective law enforcement? As a human rights monitoring body, however, the perspective of the ECtHR on this issue differs in many respects from that of the ICC as a criminal court. The role of human rights

[82]Schroeder 2003, p. 297.

[83]Gaede 2009, p. 495.

[84]See *Khan v. United Kingdom*, ECtHR, decision of 12 May 2000, Dissenting Opinion of Judge Loucaides (Application no. 35394/97); Gaede 2009, p. 494.

[85]Gaede 2009, p. 500.

[86]For a detailed description of the mergence of common law and civil law elements in the procedural law of the different international criminal courts and tribunals, see Orie 2002, p. 1439 et seq.

monitoring bodies is to review whether states have exceeded the limits of the discretion regularly accorded to them by human rights conventions. The consequence is that the Member States to the ECHR can choose between different approaches to the admissibility of illicitly obtained evidence. The approaches they adopt will regularly be closely related to the peculiarities of their respective procedural system.[87] The ECtHR in turn will only very rarely find that the use of illicitly obtained evidence amounts to a violation of the ECHR, namely only where a state has crossed even the broadly conceived limits of its discretion. This particular perspective explains in part the holistic and often imprecise approach of the ECtHR.

Irrespective of whether the critics are correct, and whether this lack of precision is inappropriate even for a human rights court, the ICC must, in any event, be more specific in its approach to illicitly obtained evidence. The ICC must deal with evidentiary issues in the context of its own criminal proceedings. As a criminal court it must give greater consideration to the principle of legality.[88] It cannot simply rely on trial fairness as a vague notion. Even more evidently, it cannot take a retrospective perspective or refer to the discretion of states because it is immediately confronted with the issue. Just like any national legal system, the Court must develop its own framework for evidentiary issues.

The decisions that the ECtHR reaches as a result of its specific balancing exercise cannot therefore be transposed as such to ICC cases. It is safe to say, however, that the jurisprudence of the ECtHR is useful in two respects. Firstly, the assessment of the ICC exclusionary rule will show that, as a basic requirement, the ICC will often have to determine the violation of an '*internationally recognized human right*'. When defining this notion, we will see that the recognition of a human right by the ECHR is significant for this assessment.[89] And secondly, while the results of its balancing exercise are not transposable, the factors the ECtHR considers relevant will be instructive for the construction of the ICC exclusionary rule. Here the criticism depicted above must, however, be kept in mind. One factor in particular will have to be treated differently. The ECtHR has considered as central whether an accused had the possibility to fully exercise the procedural rights of the defence. We have seen that this factor is problematic even with respect to the ECtHR. But beyond that it is heavily influenced by the specific perspective of a human rights monitoring body.[90] Asking whether an accused generally had the possibility to exercise his rights reflects the desire to leave as much discretion as possible to the Member States for adapting the concrete way in which they accord these rights to their own legal system. Such a broad consideration cannot guide the decision of a criminal court, such as the ICC, on a specific procedural problem. It

[87] Gaede 2009, p. 494.

[88] On the requirement of the principle of legality for the law of criminal procedure, see Sect. 2.3.1.1.

[89] See Sect. 4.3.3.3.

[90] On the relation between this factor and the overall approach of the ECtHR, see Gaede 2009, p. 495.

does not come as a surprise therefore that while the other factors addressed by the ECtHR appear in the discussions of the other systems reviewed in this research, this particular factor is only considered by the ECtHR.

3.3 Examples of Domestic Approaches

3.3.1 Germany

Turning to domestic systems, we will first look at Germany as an example of a system that is predominantly influenced by the civil law tradition. It seems reasonable to use this author's own system of origin as a starting point for the analysis of domestic legal systems. First of all, this author's understanding of the legal doctrine of the German system is inevitably more in-depth. At the same time, Germany also appears to be a useful example of a civil law system in light of the context of this research. The German delegation was closely involved in the process of negotiating the ICC proper law and shaped it considerably.[91]

Criminal proceedings in civil law systems are based on the assumption that it is possible to establish substantive truth by means of a trial. While adversarial proceedings confine themselves to the establishment of a distinct procedural truth, inquisitorial proceedings seek to establish a truth that largely corresponds to the historical facts behind a case.[92] In principle, rules excluding evidence run counter to this spirit of inquisitorial systems. The result of having such rules is that pieces of evidence possibly beneficial to the search for the truth are not at the disposal of the truth-finding authority.[93] At the same time, civil law systems generally recognize that the search for substantive truth cannot be unconditional. In the case of Germany, the German Federal Court of Appeals has noted in a regularly quoted dictum that it is not a principle of criminal procedure that the truth should be sought at any price.[94]

The reluctance against the use of rules of evidence is apparent in the German system of criminal procedure. A coherent set of rigid rules on the admissibility of evidence does not exist.[95] As is typical for a civil law system, the judge in German criminal proceedings is in control of the trial and is responsible for actively

---

[91]Werle 2012, para 367.

[92]Buisman et al. 2010, p. 10; Safferling 2012, p. 55. For a critical assessment of the truth-finding process of both systems, see Weigend 2003, p. 158 et seq.

[93]Weigend 2003, p. 168.

[94]German Federal Supreme Court (BGH), decision of 14 June 1960, *Neue Juristische Wochenschrift* 1960, p. 1580.

[95]See Amelung 1990, p. 3533.

seeking the truth.[96] He performs his task in view of the principle of the judge's freedom to evaluate the evidence.[97] According to this principle, judges in Germany are not bound by technical rules of evidence. This has sometimes led to the assumption by foreign commentators that the German system does not make use of any exclusionary rule at all.[98] But under the German principle of the judge's freedom to evaluate the evidence, the outcome of a trial is not simply subjected to the personal view of the responsible judge. And the German system is in fact not entirely without evidentiary rules. Those rules that do exist, however, are only rarely expressly laid down in statutory law.

The most well-known provision that does explicitly provide for an exclusionary rule is set forth in the German Code of Criminal Procedure, the *Strafprozessordnung* (StPO), in Section 136a, which concerns interrogations. It was incorporated into the Code of Criminal Procedure in 1950 as a reaction to the inhumane methods of persecution in Nazi Germany. Section 136a declares inadmissible all statements obtained by means of a number of methods of interrogation that are explicitly set forth by the provision. These include "*ill-treatment, induced fatigue, physical interference, administration of drugs, torment, deception or hypnosis*".[99] Exclusion is mandatory in these cases, even if the accused consents to the admission of such evidence.

In addition, the German legislator, in recent times, has created a number of new exclusionary rules. These rules were developed in light of a growing debate on exclusion in the legal literature and partly as a response to requirements established by the jurisprudence of the German Constitutional Court. Their scope of application, however, is limited to very specific cases concerning intensive investigative measures such as the intercepting of communication on private premises or the determination of mobile phone numbers.[100]

---

[96]See Section 244(2) of the German Code of Criminal Procedure, *Strafprozessordnung* (StPO), as amended and promulgated on 7 April 1987, last amended on 22 December 2010; an English version of the code is available at http://www.gesetze-im-internet.de/englisch_stpo/index.html (last visited: October 2013). See also Safferling 2012, p. 56.

[97]See Section 261 of the German Code of Criminal Procedure (StPO). On this principle, see Vogler and Huber 2008, p. 292.

[98]Bradley 1982, p. 1033.

[99]This prohibition is also applicable to the questioning of witnesses, see Section 69(3) of the StPO, as well as to that of experts, see Section 72 of the StPO.

[100]See Sections 100(c)(5)(3), (6)(2); 100(d)(5); 100(i)(2) of the StPO. For further specific exclusionary rules, see Sections 101(8)(3), 108(2),(3); 160(a)(1)(2), 161(2) and 477(2) of the StPO. Moreover, several such rules have been laid down in statutes other than the Code of Criminal Procedure itself, including Section 51 BZRG (dealing with findings on the accused originating from criminal investigations in previous cases); Sections 4(6), (7)(6) G 10 (dealing with wiretapping for intelligence and national security purposes), Section 101 VIII UHG (dealing with findings stemming from cases of copyright law violations) or Section 393(2) AO (dealing with the relationship between tax law and criminal proceedings). See also Mitsch 2008, p. 2297; Roxin and Schünemann 2012, p. 156.

The overwhelming majority of the rules on the admissibility of evidence in German law stems from procedural principles and case law. As a result of the incomplete statutory framework, the details of these rules are highly controversial and a much discussed topic among legal academics.

In Germany, the first academic approach to the problem of the admissibility of illegally gained evidence was developed at the beginning of the 20th century by the scholar Ernst von Beling.[101] Beling favoured a mandatory exclusionary rule. He started from the assumption that all means of collecting evidence are legal if they are not explicitly forbidden by law. Where in turn an explicit prohibition existed, the consequence of any violation had to be the exclusion of the tainted evidence.[102] This automatic inference needs to be viewed against the historical background: At the beginning of the last century, the legal constraints on police investigations were limited. Where a violation of law nevertheless occurred, the consequences had to be strict. Today, the situation is reversed: Under German constitutional law, investigative measures that affect individual rights are only allowed where this is explicitly permitted by statute.[103] This notion, which is generally alien to common law systems, naturally causes an increase in investigative violations.[104] As a consequence, there is a broad consensus among modern German scholars that not every investigatory mistake can result in the exclusion of the respective evidence.[105]

While, as we will see, the German judiciary applies a methodological approach to the exclusion of evidence which essentially differs from the approaches of German academics, this basic rejection of an automatic exclusionary rule is shared by German courts.[106] Based on this common premise, an abundance of different theoretical concepts have been developed in Germany in the last decades, all of

[101]Beling 1903. Prior to the academic debate, the German *Reichsgericht*, the old Supreme Court in the years 1879–1945, had developed a few basic principles but did not consider the issue in depth. While it mostly admitted evidence regardless of its provenance, in singular cases, it recognized the need for exclusion; see Effer-Uhe 2008, p. 335.

[102]Beling 1903, pp. 5 and 30. Also see Effer-Uhe 2008, p. 336; Rogall 1988, p. 386.

[103]This constitutional notion is called '*Gesetzesvorbehalt*', which may be translated by: '*reservation of legality*'.

[104]Muthorst 2009, p. 13. For a comparison of the notion of the '*Gesetzesvorbehalt*' with the U.S. legal system, see Lepsius 1997, p. 207 et seq.

[105]Gössel 1981, p. 650; Muthorst 2009, p. 14; Rogall 1988, p. 386. The dissenting opinion that still favours an automatic exclusionary rule is only rarely supported anymore. See however Kühne 2010, p. 547 et seq., p. 551.

[106]German Constitutional Court (BVerfG), decision of 27 April 2000, *Neue Juristische Wochenschrift* 2000, p. 3557; German Constitutional Court (BVerfG), decision of 30 June 2005, *Neue Zeitschrift für Strafrecht* 2006, p. 46; German Federal Supreme Court (BGH), decision of 17 March 1971, *Neue Juristische Wochenschrift* 1971, p. 1097; German Federal Supreme Court (BGH), decision of 14 March 1974, *Neue Juristische Wochenschrift* 1974, p. 1570.

which try to establish the conditions under which a violation committed during the investigation results in the exclusion of the tainted evidence.[107]

As mentioned above, two distinct methodological approaches can be distinguished within this debate. The academic approaches on the one hand differ in their detail but share the aspiration to establish a truly theoretical basis for exclusion. The judicial approach on the other hand is characterized by a more practical conception.

Academic approaches in Germany have regularly tried to identify a rationale for the exclusionary rule. Many scholars have held that this purpose must be defined from the perspective of society with a view to the aims that those procedural norms that have been violated in the course of an investigative measure are meant to serve. There has, however, been considerable disagreement on the determination of this purpose. The different opinions depend on the purpose that the respective scholars have attributed to the exclusion of evidence in general.[108] A number of justifications for exclusion have been identified. Among them are the establishment of the truth,[109] as well as the idea that exclusion is required by the aims of special prevention[110] or by the aims of general prevention.[111]

Another dominant view among German scholars favours a more subjectively shaped rationale. According to this approach, the basis for exclusion is the violation of individual rights. The exclusion of evidence is then considered a remedy for this violation. In Germany, this remedial approach has focussed in particular

---

[107]Systematically, German dogmatics distinguish between prohibitions of certain illegal means and methods by which evidence is obtained (termed '*Beweiserhebungsverbote*', which may be translated by: '*prohibitions regarding the collection of evidence*') and rules on the non-admissibility of this evidence in trial (termed '*Beweisverwertungsverbote*', which may be translated by: '*prohibitions regarding the use of evidence*'). The debate in Germany pertains to the circumstances under which a violation of the first of these groups of rules may result in a prohibition falling into the second category. Besides, it is uncontested that exclusion must not necessarily be based on previous police misconduct. It can also be grounded on independent considerations, namely where a violation of constitutional rights is not caused by the collection of the evidence but by its later admission into trial. An example would be German case law which prohibits that the defendant's legally seized diary is admitted into trial. Even where the seizure of the diary had been legal, German courts may consider that its admission as evidence violates the defendant's right to privacy; see German Federal Supreme Court (BGH), decision of 21 February 1964, *Neue Juristische Wochenschrift* 1964, p. 1139. Given the wording of Article 69(7) of the ICC Statute as the decisive provision, this last kind of exclusion falls outside of the ambit of this research, see Sect. 4.3.1.

[108]These approaches are called '*Schutzzwecklehren*', which may be translated by: '*theories of the protective purpose*'. Methodologically, they focus on the rule of evidence collection and argue that exclusion is only warranted if two requirements are met: (1) a prohibition on evidence gathering must serve a certain purpose and (2) this purpose can only be fulfilled where a violation results in exclusion. The determination of the purpose in turn depends on the overall rationale for exclusion favoured by the specific author. See Eisenberg 2011, p. 123; Muthorst 2009, p. 21 et seq.

[109]See Muthorst 2009, p. 44, with further references.

[110]Osmer 1966, p. 10 et seq. See also Muthorst 2009, p. 58 et seq.

[111]Dencker 1977, p. 59 et seq.

on the right of individuals to control certain information. Under this conception, a person is entitled to ask for the exclusion of evidence whenever the investigative authorities have gathered evidence in violation of the person's right to withhold certain information.[112]

The above mentioned approaches are highly controversial both in principal and in their detail. The German Federal Supreme Court (*Bundesgerichtshof* (BGH)) at first followed a different form of a subjectively shaped rationale. The Court stated that evidence only had to be excluded where the legal rule that had been violated by its collection was intended to protect the accused.[113] This approach has, however, been subject to intensive criticism by legal academics. Opponents have rightly claimed that the accused not only has the right to the observation of those rules aiming at his individual protection. Instead, he enjoys the right to a criminal trial that, in its entirety, is in line with the rule of law.[114] Subsequently, the BGH has referred to this concept more and more seldom.[115]

The German judiciary then applied the approach that it still abides by today. This approach is based on the idea that there is no overall explanation for the exclusion of evidence. It concentrates instead on a practically oriented methodology.[116] The solution for cases of tainted evidence is supposed to lie in an assessment on a case-by-case basis, involving a balancing exercise. In the course of this assessment, the judge has to balance the public interest in the prosecution of crimes against the defendant's interest in the protection of his rights.[117]

The postulation of a case-by-case approach has been criticized for being inconsistent with the principle of legality. Critics have argued that such such a large amount of freedom to evaluate the evidence on a case-by-case basis would be overly subjective and lead to the unpredictability of court decisions.[118] Others, however, have pointed to the fact that subjective decision-making is not a special

---

[112]This approach has been termed '*Informationsbeherrschungslehre*', which may be translated by: '*theory of the control of information*'. For more details, see Amelung 1991, p. 2533 et seq. See also Muthorst 2009, p. 62 et seq.

[113]German Federal Supreme Court (BGH), decision of 21 January 1958, *Neue Juristische Wochenschrift* 1958, p. 557. This approach is called '*Rechtskreistheorie*'. The term '*Rechtskreis*' can be translated by: '*circle of rights*'. It describes the number of all rules aiming at the protection of the accused. On this approach, see also Muthorst 2009, p. 33. Methodologically in turn, this approach is comparable to that of the '*Schutzzwecklehren*', see fn. 309, because it focusses on the purpose of the violated procedural rule, see Eisenberg 2011, p. 123.

[114]Eisenberg 2011, p. 123; Roxin and Schünemann 2012, p. 157.

[115]Effer-Uhe 2008, p. 336; Kühne 2010, p. 548; Rogall 1979, p. 26.

[116]Muthorst 2009, p. 69.

[117]This approach is called '*Abwägungslehre*', which can be translated by: '*theory of balancing*'. See German Federal Supreme Court (BGH), decision of 27 February 1992, *Neue Juristische Wochenschrift* 1992, p. 1463. This approach has been approved by the German Constitutional Court, see German Constitutional Court (BVerfG), decision of 28 July 2008, *Neue Juristische Wochenschrift* 2008, p. 3054. See also Meyer-Goßner 2013, para 55a.

[118]Amelung 1991, p. 2533 et seq.; Eisenberg 2011, p. 123; Trüg and Habetha 2008, p. 486.

feature of the admissibility of evidence but rather of judicial discretion in general.[119] Moreover, it has been argued that the allegation of unpredictability can be dispelled if the judicial evaluation is guided by sufficiently pre-defined criteria.[120] The higher courts in Germany have, in fact, striven to some extent to give guidance to the lower courts. But these attempts are still far from providing a comprehensive framework of generally applicable criteria. Instead, the jurisprudence of the higher courts has often focussed merely on the development of categories of cases. Such a categorization, however, at least allows one to derive a number of criteria that have been considered relevant.

Firstly, the seriousness of the violation alledgedly committed by the authorities is usually taken into account. Less serious and technical mistakes do not trigger exclusion under German case law. The violation, for example, of the right of an accused to be advised of his right to silence and to access legal advice under Section 136(1) of the StPO is considered so serious that it regularly triggers exclusion.[121] In comparison, the German Federal Supreme Court has held that this is not the case for violations of Article 36 of the Vienna Convention on Consular Regulations. The judges have argued that the seriousness of such violations is not comparable to violations of Section 136(1) of the StPO.[122] An example of a technicality in turn would pertain to the formal requirements of a search warrant.[123] A violation of these requirements does not lead to the exclusion of evidence found during the respective search.[124]

A second factor has been the significance that the evidence has for combating serious crimes.[125] This actually involves two factors. Firstly, it points to the significance of the evidence for the outcome of a trial, meaning whether this evidence is the only or at least the decisive proof in a trial. The second consideration is the seriousness of the crime that the accused is alleged to have committed. This latter point has also been considered a factor by itself.[126] Its consideration has been heavily criticized by legal scholars. It has been argued that the seriousness of the offence might militate in favour of exclusion but also against it. The critics admit

[119]Rogall 1979, p. 32.

[120]Muthorst 2009, p. 74 et seq.; Rogall 1979, p. 32.

[121]German Federal Supreme Court (BGH), decision of 27 February 1992, *Neue Juristische Wochenschrift* 1992, p. 1463.

[122]German Federal Supreme Court (BGH), decision of 20 December 2007, *Neue Juristische Wochenschrift* 2008, p. 1090.

[123]While under German law, a judicial search warrant may be issued orally under certain circumstances, the investigating authorities have a duty, in this case, to subsequently record its issuance in writing, see Meyer-Goßner 2013, Section 105, para 3.

[124]German Federal Supreme Court (BGH), decision of 13 January 2005, *Juristische Rundschau* 2005, p. 385 et seq.

[125]Trüg 2003, p. 230; Rogall 1979, p. 29 et seq.

[126]German Constitutional Court (BVerfG), decision of 31 January 1973, *Neue Juristische Wochenschrift* 1973, p. 891.

that society's interest in law enforcement increases with the seriousness of the crime. But at the same time, it has been held that the interest of the accused increases as well because of the higher sentence he risks in cases of more serious crimes.[127]

Beyond that, some factors have not been discussed generally but only with respect to specific case categories. One such factor is whether the authorities have acted in good faith. In Germany, this factor has been taken into account in particular in the context of searches and seizures. A classic example is the existence of exigent circumstances. In general, German law requires a judicial search warrant. In cases of exigent circumstances, however, the police and prosecution have the authority to decide on their own to enter private premises.[128] According to case law, misjudgements of the existence of exigent circumstances only lead to the exclusion of subsequently discovered evidence if the authorities have acted in bad faith.[129] Other such case-related factors have been whether the accused himself has suffered from the violation and whether the investigative authorities could have obtained the evidence through alternative means.[130]

In summary, it can be noted that the judicial approach and the above-mentioned academic approaches do not in principle run counter to each other. The case law in fact includes in its overall balancing exercise many of the considerations that also guide the academic solutions.[131] The concept of a balancing exercise in turn has also been supported and further developed by many legal scholars.[132] There continues, however, to be much debate over the factors that are relevant for the balancing exercise. In particular, the jurisprudence on these factors has been criticised by a2012cademics for being inconsistent and for overemphasising the public interest in law enforcement over individual rights.[133]

Finally, from a comparative law perspective, a comment is in order with respect to the justification for the exclusion of evidence. We have seen that German courts have generally refrained from adopting a particular rationale for exclusion and have concentrated, instead, on the methodology for exclusion. It is interesting to note, however, that the purpose of deterrence—which we will see is

---

[127]Muthorst 2009, p. 71.

[128]See Section 105(1) of the StPO.

[129]German Federal Supreme Court (BGH), decision of 25 February 1985, *Neue Zeitschrift für Strafrecht* 1985, p. 262.

[130]For an overview of the possibly relevant factors see Muthorst 2009, p. 71 et seq.; Meyer-Goßner 2013, *Einleitung*, para 55a; Volk 2010, p. 261 et seq.

[131]Muthorst 2009, p. 74.

[132]Effer-Uhe 2008, p. 338. The conception developed by Rogall in particular has strongly influenced this jurisprudence, see in particular Rogall 1979, p. 1 et seq.; Rogall 1996, p. 944 et seq. See also Meyer-Goßner 2013, *Einleitung*, para 55a; Roxin and Schünemann 2012, p. 159; Trüg and Habetha 2008, p. 486.

[133]Roxin and Schünemann, p. 159; Trüg and Habetha 2008, p. 490.

predominant in the United States[134]—has mostly been rejected in Germany. Among German scholars, the view is predominant that a disciplining function is alien to the concept of criminal proceedings. The pivotal argument is that there is no direct link between the wrong committed by the perpetrator and the injustice committed by the police. It has been held that the purpose of deterrence is better served by alternative remedies that have been created explicitly to this end. This would include actions under public law or criminal proceedings against the official involved.[135]

In conclusion, the approach of the German judiciary is interesting for the present research because it starts from the premise of a discretionary exclusionary rule. The decisions are based on a balancing exercise that is guided by a number of factors. We will see that this is ultimately true for the ICC exclusionary rule as well. The approach of the German judiciary, however, lacks a sufficient explanation of the reasons for the exclusion of evidence. In this context, it will be more interesting to assess the views discussed by German academics. Furthermore, we must take into account that the German jurisprudence on the admissibility of evidence tends to be inclusionary. It has been criticized for overemphasising law enforcement interests. We will see that a number of reasons indicate that the ICC Statue in turn should be interpreted in a manner that allows for a more generous application of its exclusionary rule.

3.3.2 United States

The motivation to include the U.S. legal system in a comparative analysis for the purpose of interpreting an ICC provision is not self-evident. The United States is not a State Party to the International Criminal Court. Article 21 of the ICC Statute, however, does not confine the judges to the consideration of legal systems of those states that have ratified the Statute. The ICC Statute instead grants the judges a great deal of discretion in determining which national laws to consider.[136] Against this methodological background, the U.S. legal system is a legally valid example of a domestic system that may be considered under Article 21.

---

[134]See Sect. 3.3.2.

[135]Amelung and Mittag 2005, p. 615; Amelung 1991, p. 2537; Eisenberg 2011, p. 125; Muthorst 2009, p. 55. But see Ransiek 2002, p. 567 et seq., who, while critical, approves of the deterrence rationale in the end. See also Nüse 1966, p. 284, who argues however that the deterrent effect is less relevant in Germany when compared to the United States because of the better education of police officials in Germany. See also Muthorst 2009, p. 53 et seq.

[136]Triffterer 2008—McAuliffe de Guzman, Article 21, para 17.

Beyond that, factual considerations justify taking the the U.S. system into account. Firstly, its influence on the legal framework of the ICC is indicated by the significant involvement of U.S. lawyers in the negotiation and drafting process of the ICC Statute.[137] Secondly, with regard to the research question at hand, a further consideration makes the legal situation in the United States worth examining: American jurisprudence and legal academics have extensively addressed the question of whether illegally gained evidence should be admitted in court. As a consequence, a consideration of the U.S. approach enables recourse to detailed research on the issue. Moreover, as a consequence of the extensive examination of this issue, the American exclusionary rule has inspired the development of exclusionary rules in other legal systems such as in England, France, Germany and Italy.[138] Its significance for a comprehensive discussion on evidentiary exclusion should thus not be disregarded.

The U.S. system is the first common law system examined in this research. The traditional common law approach did not attach much importance to the manner in which evidence was obtained. The only factors deemed relevant for the admissibility of evidence were accuracy and reliability. Today, however, it is widely recognized in systems influenced by the common law that reliance on rectitude alone is unsatisfactory and that not every means of obtaining evidence is acceptable.[139]

In the United States, exclusionary rules have been recognized since the end of the nineteenth century.[140] Today, modern U.S. law of criminal procedure is greatly influenced by constitutional law, in particular by the Bill of Rights in the first ten amendments to the U.S. Constitution, as well as by the due process clause set forth in the Fourteenth Amendment.[141] The interpretation of these provisions by the U.S. Supreme Court has shaped every aspect of criminal proceedings in the United States.[142] This includes the exclusionary rule for illicitly obtained evidence. Subsequent to a number of Supreme Court decisions, this rule is legally based on

---

[137]For details on the U.S. involvement in the negotiation process, see Scheffer 1999, p. 12 et seq. On the previous influence of the United States on the procedural law of the *Ad hoc* tribunals, see Jackson and Summers 2012, p. 122.

[138]Ma 1999, p. 286; Pakter 1985, p. 51; Slobogin 2013, p. 1; Thaman 2013, p. 338.

[139]Jackson and Summers 2012, p. 153.

[140]See *Hopt v. Utah*, United States Supreme Court, decision of 3 March 1884, 110 U.S. 574 (1884), which *inter alia* addresses the problem of the exclusion of involuntary confessions. See also Ambos 2010, p. 129.

[141]See United States Constitution, created on 17 September 1787, ratified on 21 June 1788; amended on 15 December 1791; available at: http://www.usconstitution.net/const.html last visited: October 2013).

[142]Hay 2011, p. 704.

the Constitution, in particular on the Fourth,[143] the Fifth,[144] the Sixth[145] and the Fourteenth Amendments.[146]

One of the most notable features of the exclusionary rule in the United States is its broad scope. Ever since its development, the U.S. exclusionary rule has been understood to cover a wide range of evidence. Already in its early jurisprudence, the U.S. Supreme Court established that the exclusionary rule not only includes evidence directly gained by means of a constitutional violation but also derivative evidence. From the outset, the Supreme Court has thus acknowledged what has been termed 'the fruit of the poisonous tree doctrine'.[147]

In addition to its constitutional foundation and its broad applicability, another noteworthy characteristic of the American exclusionary rule is its primary reliance on the so-called deterrence theory. In the U.S., the dominant argument for the exclusion of illicitly obtained evidence has traditionally been that it supposedly deters law enforcement authorities from committing similar violations.[148] This means that exclusion is ultimately based on a future-oriented rationale. American deterrence theorists recognize that there is no direct link between the specific official misconduct and the wrong committed by the perpetrator. They also acknowledge that, by definition, no deterrent effects can occur in the instant case. Instead,

[143]The 4th amendment provides protection against unreasonable searches and seizures; the Supreme Court has adopted the 4th Amendment exclusionary rule for federal trials for the first time in *Weeks v. United States,* United States Supreme Court, decision of 24 February 1914, 232 U.S. 383 (1914) and extended its applicability to state criminal trials in its decision in *Mapp v. Ohio,* United States Supreme Court, decision of June 19 1961, 367 U.S. 643 (1961).

[144]The 5th amendment pertains *inter alia* to the right against self-incrimination. On the related exclusionary rule, see in particular the landmark decision in *Miranda v. Arizona,* United States Supreme Court, decision of 13 June 1966, 384 U.S. 436 (1966), where the Supreme Court first relied on the 5th amendment to justify the exclusion of statements made in police custody unless the suspect had been advised of his constitutional rights and had waived them voluntarily.

[145]The 6th amendment *inter alia* sets forth defence rights, in particular the right to the assistance of counsel. On the related exclusionary rule, see in particular *Massiah v. the United States,* United States Supreme Court, decision of 8 May 1964, 377 U.S. 201 (1964), where the Supreme Court first recognized that exclusion was warranted where statements had been elicited from the accused in the absence of counsel.

[146]The 14th amendment contains a due process clause that protects life, liberty and property; this clause has been used to make most of the Bill of Rights applicable to the States. Altogether, for a concise summary of the development of the jurisprudence of the U.S. Supreme Court on the exclusionary rule, see Thaman 2013, p. 334.

[147]See *Silverthorne Lumber Co. v. U.S.,* United States Supreme Court, decision of 26 January 1920, 251 U.S. 385 (1920), in which the U.S. Supreme Court first recognized the indirect effect of the exclusionary rule: "*The essence of a provision forbidding the acquisition of evidence in a certain way is that not merely evidence so acquired shall not be used before the Court, but that it shall not be used at all.*"

[148]See for instance *Tehan v. United States, ex. Rel. Shott,* United States Supreme Court, decision of 19 January 1966, 382 U.S. 406 (1966): "[T]*he prime purpose of the rule* […] *was to deter the lawless action of the police and to effectively enforce the Fourth Amendment.*" See also Ambos 2010, p. 130; Harris 1991, p. 314; Safferling 2001, p. 299.

the exclusion of possibly reliable evidence is accepted as a negative side effect in order to diminish the incentive for law enforcement authorities to commit further violations in the future.[149]

Over the years, the Supreme Court has sometimes also recognized the maintenance of judicial integrity and the protection of individual rights as additional justifications for exclusion.[150] But while it had always prevailed, the significance attached to the deterrence rationale continued to grow and it was ultimately declared the sole rationale behind the exclusionary rule.[151]

This development is part of a general shift in the perspective on exclusion under the current conservative majority of the U.S. Supreme Court. Initially, the Supreme Court under liberal Chief Justice *Warren* interpreted the guarantees set forth by the Constitution in an extensive way. This shaped *inter alia* the initial concept of the constitutionally based exclusionary rule. The exclusionary rule was understood as a manifestation of the individual rights guaranteed by the respective amendments. Accordingly, exclusion was required as a constitutional mandate.[152] The result was an automatic exclusionary rule that was supposed to prevent any use of evidence gained through unconstitutional means.

It comes as no surprise that this extensive mandatory exclusionary rule faced severe criticism. It was argued in particular that such a doctrine unduly restricts effective law enforcement.[153] The successors of the *Warren* Court shared these concerns. They did not agree with the strong emphasis placed on the defendant's rights and were dissatisfied in particular with the mandatory aspect of the exclusionary rule.[154]

The consequence was an ideological shift: today the exclusionary rule is no longer conceived as a direct manifestation of constitutional guarantees, but rather as a mere remedy for the violation of constitutional rights.[155] It has, in other words, been decoupled from the guarantees provided for by the Constitution, which means that exclusion is no longer required as an automatic consequence of a rights violation. Rejecting the idea of exclusion as a part of individual constitutional rights allows in turn for a focus on deterrence as the only rationale for exclusion.[156]

---

[149]Roberts and Zuckerman 2010, p. 186.

[150]See *Mapp v. Ohio,* United States Supreme Court, decision of June 19, 1961, 367 U.S. 643 (1961); *Terry v. Ohio*, United States Supreme Court, decision of 10 June 1968, 392 U.S. 1 (1968). See Trüg 2003, p. 468. In this context, see also the '*shocks the conscience*' exception to the so-called '*international silver platter doctrine*', see Sect. 5.4.

[151]Jackson and Summers 2012, p. 154; Ma 1999, p. 296; Harris 1991, p. 314.

[152]Cammack 2010, p. 633. Also see Bradley 2010, p. 211 and p. 233, who points out that this concept partly derived from the assumption of the *Warren* Court that it had no power to make rules except if these rules were based directly on the Constitution.

[153]Harris 1991, p. 314.

[154]Bradley 2010, p. 212; Ma 1999, p. 297.

[155]Bradley 2010, p. 213; Cammack 2010, p. 633; Hessler 2000, p. 239.

[156]Cammack 2010, p. 646; Trüg 2003, p. 469.

With this premise as a starting point, the previously mandatory exclusionary rule has successively been demoted through a number of exceptions and its use has been restricted.[157] Ultimately, these exceptions are based on a weighting of interests which is geared towards the implementation of the deterrence rationale. The question that is asked is whether the deterrent effect of exclusion outweighs the costs of losing possibly cogent evidence.[158] The concept that remains is no longer that of a truly mandatory rule. Mandatory exclusion is rather a presumption that only constitutes the starting point for a number of further deliberations that a judge has to make when deciding whether or not to exclude tainted evidence. In many cases, this presumption will be refuted for reasons of proportionality by applying one of the exceptions mentioned below in this way, the Supreme Court has limited in particular the consequences of the fact that the U.S. exclusionary rule applies not only to direct but also to derivative evidence.[159]

A very obvious example of the Court's reasoning is the so-called '*good faith*' exception: According to the jurisprudence of the Supreme Court, the exclusionary rule does not apply where the authorities had reason to believe that their behaviour was legal. The Court has ruled, for instance, that the exclusionary rule is not applicable where the police, in good faith, have relied on a search warrant that was later declared invalid.[160] This conclusion is in line with the deterrence rationale: Where the authorities involved have engaged in neither wilful nor negligent conduct, no deterrent benefits can occur that would be able to outweigh the costs in terms of losing possibly cogent evidence.[161]

Similar considerations underlie further exceptions embraced by the Supreme Court in the last decades: Firstly, the '*independent source doctrine*' allows the admission of evidence that was initially discovered through illicit means but was then discovered again in a lawful way. Based on this doctrine, the Supreme Court has held for example that evidence that was discovered in the course of a warrantless search but then re-discovered during a second search after a warrant had been issued is admissible.[162] Once more, the Court reached its conclusion by applying a balancing exercise and by presuming that the deterrent benefits could not outweigh the loss of evidence. It reasoned that while the exclusionary rule is meant to prevent the authorities from benefiting from constitutional violations, it does not justify putting them in a worse position than without such a violation.[163]

---

[157]Cammack 2010, p. 633; Slobogin 2013, p. 7.

[158]Harris 1991, p. 314; LaFave et al. 2004, p. 510; Thaman 2013, p. 379.

[159]Ambos 2010, p. 146.

[160]*Arizona v. Evans*, United States Supreme Court, decision of 1 March 1995, 514 U.S. 1 (1995); more recently *Herring v. United States,* United States Supreme Court, decision of 14 January 2009, 07–513 (2009).

[161]Cammack 2010, p. 645 et seq.; Harris 1991, p. 314.

[162]See *United States v. Murray,* United States Supreme Court, decision of 27 June 1988, 487 U.S. 533 (1988).

[163]For more details on the '*independent source doctrine*', see Ambos 2010, p. 131 et seq.; Cammack 2010, p. 642 et seq.; Harris 1991, p. 316 et seq.; LaFave et al. 2004, p. 511 et seq.

By the same logic, the Court has developed the so-called '*inevitable discovery doctrine*'. Under this doctrine, illicitly obtained evidence is admissible if the prosecution proves by a preponderance of evidence that this evidence would inevitably have been discovered in a legal manner. As a consequence, the Supreme Court has, for instance, admitted into evidence the body of a victim that had been found on the basis of statements elicited from the defendant in violation of his right to counsel. The Court argued that the body would inevitably have been found in the course of a search that had already been under way.[164] This assumption goes a step further than the '*independent source doctrine*'. Instead of relying on the fact that an actual investigative measure has ultimately procured the evidence, this doctrine relies on purely hypothetical considerations.[165] In the end, however, it is based on the same justification, namely that deterrence cannot result in a situation that is worse for the authorities than the one that would have arisen without the violation.[166]

Finally, the logic of balancing deterrence against the interests of effective law enforcement is also apparent in a further exception to the exclusionary rule labelled the '*attenuation doctrine*'. According to the jurisprudence of the Supreme Court, evidence is admissible where the connection between a constitutional violation and the gathered evidence is diminished. This would be the case where intervening factors have the effect of making this connection "*so attenuated as to dissipate the taint*".[167] According to this doctrine, a confession made by a defendant arrested subsequent to an illegal search would be inadmissible, but if, on the basis of this statement, another person is arrested, the confession that this person later makes of her own will could be admitted.[168] The weak connection is used to argue that the gathered evidence can no longer reasonably be attributed to the violation. As a result, the detrimental consequences of the violation would no longer justify exclusion.[169] Again, the underlying intention of this exception is to restrict the application of the exclusionary rule by weighing the interests involved.[170]

This approach of the Supreme Court has also drawn severe criticism. Most fundamentally, the reliance on deterrence as a rationale has been criticised. On a

---

[164] *Nix v. Williams*, United States Supreme Court, decision of 11 June 1984, 467 U.S. 431 (1984).

[165] Ambos 2010, p. 135.

[166] Cammack 2010, p. 643. On the '*inevitable discovery doctrine*', see also Harris 1991, p. 317 et seq.; LaFave et al. 2004, p. 513 et seq.

[167] See *Nardone v. The United States*, United States Supreme Court, decision of 11 December 1939, 308 U.S. 338 (1939).

[168] Ambos 2010, p. 139.

[169] See *Brown v. Illinois*, United States Supreme Court, decision of 26 June 1975, Concurring Opinion Justice Powell, 422 U.S. 590 (1975), who first formulated this justification of the '*attenuation doctrine*'. See also Cammack 2010, p. 644 et seq. For a more recent decision, see *Hudson v. Michigan*, United States Supreme Court, decision of 15 June 2006, 547 U.S. 586 (2006); on this decision, see also Bradley 2010, p. 213.

[170] Ambos 2010, p. 141. On the '*attenuation doctrine*', see also Harris 1991, p. 315 et seq.; LaFave et al. 2004, p. 510 et seq.

factual basis, it has been doubted that the exclusionary rule is actually able to achieve its purported deterrent effect.[171] On a theoretical level, the same argument has been raised as in Germany. It has been argued that the goal of deterring the authorities from future misbehaviour is better served by means outside of the trial forum. This argument is based on the fact, admitted by deterrence theorists themselves, that there is no direct connection between the violation and the crime that the defendant has allegedly committed. In view of this lack of connection, opponents argue that where there is a strong epistemic case against the defendant, deterrence is not a sufficiently significant consideration to outweigh the public interest in prosecution.[172]

What is more, this jurisprudence has been criticised for the lack of clarity that results from the development of the many exceptions embraced by the Supreme Court.[173] Commentators have pointed to the ideological tension between the *Warren* Court and its successors to explain this lack of clarity. It has been held that the latter disapproved of the initially mandatory nature of the exclusionary rule but, at the same time, were reluctant to simply overrule the respective decisions. Instead, the judges adopted numerous exceptions to the rule, which has lead to contradictions and obscurities.[174] The consequences derived thereof depend on the general position of the respective commentator. Some have assumed that the Supreme Court should limit exclusion more openly.[175] Conversely, others have deplored the fact that the exclusionary rule has been restricted to this extent.[176]

In summary, the U.S. legal system recognizes the necessity of excluding illegally gained evidence. At the same time, the exclusionary rule in its current shape is far from creating an automatism. On the contrary, the expansion of exceptions has lead to a gradual contraction of the previously mandatory exclusionary rule in the U.S. This means that the difference between the current U.S. approach and the approaches of those systems which more openly conduct a balancing exercise, instead of applying rules of exception, is less significant than it might first seem.[177] The difference is less whether exclusion is mandatory or whether judges must take their decisions on a discretionary basis. Ultimately, all these systems weigh up the different interests affected by admissibility decisions. The difference rather lies in the factors guiding these decisions. This in turn is highly dependent upon the justification for the exclusion of illicitly obtained evidence.[178] Here, the U.S. system differs from other domestic systems in that its exclusionary rule today is entirely based on the deterrence theory.

[171] Jackson and Summers 2012, p. 154; Ma 1999, p. 297; Slobogin 2013, p. 15 et seq.

[172] Jackson and Summers 2012, p. 155.

[173] Hessler 2000, p. 240 et seq.

[174] Ma 1999, p. 297.

[175] For an example of an alternative, more restrictive approach, see Bradley 2010, p. 231 et seq.

[176] Cammack 2010, p. 633.

[177] Similar, Ambos 2010, p. 151.

[178] Jackson and Summers 2012, p. 153 et seq.

For this research, the consequence is that the application of the U.S. exclusionary is guided by criteria that could in principle also be relevant for the construction of the discretionary ICC exclusionary rule. We will see, however, that the ICC exclusionary rule is not based on deterrence. As a result, the factors considered relevant for exclusion in the U.S. will have to be assessed in view of their plausibility in terms of the justification that underlies Article 69(7) of the ICC Statute.

3.3.3 England and Wales

Even though English and American law both originate from the same legal background, these systems have for a long time adopted entirely contrary approaches to the exclusion of illicitly obtained evidence. While the American position was initially characterized by a mandatory exclusionary rule, English law followed the traditional common law approach for much longer.

We have already seen that the common law position was unsympathetic to exclusion. Investigative mistakes as such were considered meaningless for the admissibility of evidence. In general, any evidence was deemed admissible as long as it was relevant and reliable. Admittedly, judges under common law had the discretion to exclude evidence if they considered it to be more prejudicial than probative. There was however considerable reluctance among the judiciary to exercise this discretion.[179] The only instance where official impropriety had to result in exclusion were cases of involuntary confessions. But what might seem like an exception was in fact consistent with the general approach to evidentiary exclusion. The reason for excluding involuntary confessions on a mandatory basis was that induced or coerced confessions were considered unreliable. Other values were not taken into consideration.[180]

This general reluctance towards evidentiary exclusion meant that for most abuses, citizens could only resort to civil remedies against the police. The British common law theoretically provides grounds for citizens to seek civil remedies against the police. In addition, it was possible under common law to file complaints against investigators in order to institute internal disciplinary proceedings within the police force. In practice, however, there was repeated criticism that civil remedies were difficult to access, in particular for the economically disadvantaged group of citizens that are most often confronted with police investigations. Disciplinary proceedings, on the other hand, were often criticized for their alleged lack of impartiality.[181]

---

[179]Osborn 2000, para 30; Roberts and Zuckerman 2010, p. 177. On the whole, see also Ma 1999, p. 284; Stone 1995, p. 1 et seq.

[180]Ma 1999, p. 284. For an overview of the common law position, see Mellifont 2007, p. 62 et seq.

[181]Roberts and Zuckerman 2010, p. 184; Ma 1999, p. 286.

The general inclusionary approach to admissibility prevailed until the last quarter of the twentieth century. Since the mid-1980s, the English law of criminal procedure has undergone a major transformation. This change was triggered to a great extent by the need to comply with human rights standards. These standards require that law enforcement be conducted in accordance with the law and, to this end, demand a written statutory basis for investigatory measures which the traditional case law based common law did not provide.[182]

The consequence was a systematic procedural reform. The first in a series of legislative acts that implemented modern rules on criminal procedure was the Police and Investigation Act 1984 (PACE).[183] Together with a number of related Codes of Practice, PACE, for the first time, provided a statutory framework for the conduct of investigations in England and Wales. Section 78 of PACE allows for the exclusion of evidence "[…] *if it appears to the court that, having regard to all the circumstances, including the circumstances in which the evidence was obtained, the admission of the evidence would have such an adverse effect on the fairness of the proceedings that the court ought not to admit it.* […]".

Section 78 seems only to repeat the discretionary rule of exclusion that already existed under common law. Consequently, commentators were sceptical from the outset about its practical impact. They doubted whether judges would actually make much use of their discretion.[184] This scepticism seems to have been well-founded. To start with, there were indications that the English judiciary would avail itself of the new rule to widen the application of the exclusionary rule.[185] But, as commentators have pointed out, this initial willingness of judges to fully use their discretionary power slowly dried up.[186]

The development that PACE has triggered with respect to the exclusion of evidence should not therefore be overestimated. In fact, the common law reluctance to exclude evidence other than for reasons of unreliability still exercises a strong influence on today's jurisprudence. So far, the judiciary uses its power under Section 78 mostly in egregious cases. In general, the English approach continues to be characterised by scepticism towards the exclusion of evidence whose quality is not at stake.[187]

Similar to the situation under common law, the discretionary rule in Section 78 of PACE is supplemented by a mandatory exclusionary rule for illegally gained confessions. Section 76 of PACE requires the exclusion of involuntary confessions. Again, it can be assumed that it was the lack of reliability of induced or

[182]See for instance Article 5(1) and Article 8(2) of the ECHR.

[183]See Police and Criminal Evidence Act 1984 (PACE), in force since 31 October 1984, available at: http://www.legislation.gov.uk/ukpga/1984/60/contents (last visited: October 2013). See also Roberts and Zuckerman 2010, p. 197.

[184]Roberts and Zuckerman 2010, p. 176.

[185]Ma 1999, p. 285; Stone 1995, p. 2.

[186]Mellifont 2007, p. 83.

[187]Mellifont 2007, p. 85. Similar, Safferling 2001, p. 298 et seq.

coerced confessions that justified the addition of an explicit exclusionary rule to this extent.[188] The consideration of aspects other than the determination of truth in turn is primarily guaranteed by Section 78 of PACE.[189] An early decision on PACE confirms this understanding of both rules as complementary to each other. In 1987, the Court of Appeal had to decide on the admissibility of a confession obtained through deception. It did not consider Section 76 to be *lex specialis* for confessions. Instead, the judges made clear that even where a confession triggered the applicability of Section 76, this would not affect the ability of a court to exclude confessions based on Section 78.[190] Section 78 is therefore understood as the decisive test of fairness with regard to all categories of evidence.[191]

Section 78 of PACE is an open-ended provision that grants a large amount of discretion to the judges. Its content and boundaries remain controversial to this day. In face of the overall general reluctance to use Section 78, it is not surprising that there has been little authoritative guidance by the highest English courts. Where they have applied the rule at all, the Supreme Court (formerly the House of Lords) and the Court of Appeal have focused on the facts of the immediate case rather than providing a general authoritative position.[192]

In particular, there has been hardly any judicial statement regarding the justification of exclusion. This issue is debated intensively by English academics. Rationales such as the compensation of the defendant for the violation, the deterrence of authorities or the maintenance of judicial legitimacy have been supported in this debate.[193] English judges in turn have mostly refrained from unequivocal teleological considerations.[194] The only specific statement in this respect, relates to the rejection of the deterrence theory. Unlike in the United States, English judges have frequently repeated that the exclusionary rule contained in Section 78 does not serve the purpose of disciplining the police.[195]

Some further indication on the judges' understanding of Section 78 can be extracted from case law. English courts have usually approached the application of Section 78 to cases of illegally obtained evidence in two phases. The preliminary step is an examination of "*the circumstances in which the evidence was obtained*". This regularly implies the determination of the violation of a right of the defendant or of a breach of another procedural requirement. Modern English law of

[188]Mellifont 2007, p. 77; Stone 1995, p. 10.

[189]But see Mellifont 2007, p. 83, who claims that reliability is also the prevalent rationale for exclusion under Section 78 of PACE.

[190]*Regina v. Mason*, Court of Appeal of England and Wales, decision of 21 May 1987, [1988] 1 W.L.R. 139.

[191]Roberts and Zuckerman 2010, p. 191; Stone 1995, p. 6.

[192]Ashworth and Redmayne 2010, p. 348.

[193]For an overview of the debate, see Roberts and Zuckerman 2010, p. 179.

[194]Roberts and Zuckerman 2010, p. 193.

[195]Osborn 2000, para 46; Ma 1999, p. 284. See also Mellifont 2007, p. 87, who states that the rejection of the deterrence rationale was even guiding the governmental drafting of Section 78 PACE.

criminal procedure contains a large body of rules on the gathering of evidence, whose breach can trigger exclusion under Section 78 of PACE. The procedural reforms described above have led to a detailed framework for the conduct of criminal investigations, which includes PACE, as well as other primary legislation on different aspects of criminal procedure. These primary sources are usually accompanied by Codes of Practice that also set forth relevant rules in this respect. In addition, the European system of human rights protection has strongly influenced the English law of criminal procedure. This has been particularly true since the Human Rights Act of 1998 came into force, which gave direct effect to the ECHR in English courts. A further important source for a rights violation is therefore the European Convention on Human Rights.

It should be noted, however, that Section 78 of PACE requires neither the violation of a specific individual right nor the breach of a specific procedural norm. It simply refers to fairness. Certain methods of investigation, such as deceit, even though not legally prohibited, might also have a negative impact on the fairness of the proceedings. English courts have excluded evidence on this basis. They have, however, been more reluctant to do so than in case of distinct infringements.[196]

But even where an infringement has been determined, Section 78 has not been understood as requiring exclusion for every kind of violation.[197] In a second step, judges have to consider whether admitting the tainted evidence would have an adverse effect on the fairness of the proceedings. It is recognized in English law as well that determining those rights that impact on the fairness of the proceedings requires a balancing of the interests of the accused against those of the public.[198] While English courts have not linked this balancing exercise to any particular justification for exclusion, they have considered a number of factors that can also be found in the case law of other systems.

A preliminary question has usually been the nature of the breach. In this context, the courts have asked whether the breach was "*significant and substantial*".[199] This formula is meant to exclude technical breaches. This pertains to trivial violations of the very detailed requirements set forth in modern English law of criminal procedure. Examples that have been advanced for such technical breaches are the requirement that police station detainees must be offered two light meals and a main meal in any period of 24 h[200] or that detainees must be vis-

---

[196]Ashworth and Redmayne 2010, p. 349.

[197]Roberts and Zuckerman 2010, p. 193.

[198]Ma 1999, p. 286; Mellifont 2007, p. 82.

[199]*Regina v. Keenan*, Court of Appeal of England and Wales, decision of 26 April 1989, [1990] 2 Q.B. 54; *Regina v. Absolam*, Court of Appeal of England and Wales, decision of 1 July 1988, [1988] Cr. App R. 332. See also Mellifont 2007, p. 85 and p. 86.

[200]See para 8.6 of Code C of the PACE Codes of Practice on "Detention, Treatment and Questioning of Persons by Police Officers"; available at: https://www.gov.uk/government/publications/pace-code-c-2012 (last visited: October 2013).

ited at least every hour.[201] Such requirements without doubt serve a valid purpose. Depending on the circumstances of the specific case, however, it is argued that insisting on strict adherence can amount to holding on to a technicality. This would be the case, for example, where the detainee is given three light meals without adverse effect on his well-being or where he is visited only every 90 min without there being any relevant incidents.

Taken by itself however, the fact that a breach was "*significant and substantial*" is not decisive for an exclusion of the tainted evidence under English case law. In fact, torture has so far been the only instance where the seriousness of the violation has been understood as requiring exclusion on a mandatory basis.[202] For all other breaches, further deliberations are required.

An important consideration has been whether the police have acted in bad faith.[203] Thus it has been stated that the fact that the investigative authorities have deliberately violated legal requirements is likely to tip the scales in favour of exclusion. The same is not true the other way around. Good faith errors do not necessarily prevent exclusion under English case law.[204] This assertion is in line with the previously mentioned position of the judges that the discretion granted by Section 78 of PACE should not be exercised in order to discipline the police.[205]

In addition, the seriousness of the crime also seems to have been a relevant factor in the exercise of discretion. However, while this point is mentioned in the case law, it remains unclear to what extent it is deemed to have significance. The respective comments are rather of a general nature.[206]

A more significant factor for English courts seems to have been whether the outcome of the trial would be different if the evidence were admitted. This depends on the importance of the evidence. It has been held that excluding tainted evidence would be useless in those cases where there is sufficient other evidence. The argument is that in such cases, admitting the evidence would, in any event,

---

[201] See para 9.3 of Code C of the PACE Codes of Practice on "Detention, Treatment and Questioning of Persons by Police Officers". On these examples, see Roberts and Zuckerman 2010, p. 194.

[202] Roberts and Zuckerman 2010, p. 219.

[203] *Regina v. Walsh*, Court of Appeal of England and Wales, decision of 13 July 1989, [1990] 91 Cr. App R. 161; *Regina v. Alladice*, Court of Appeal of England and Wales, decision of 8 May 1988, [1988] WL 624104. See also Mellifont 2007, p. 86.

[204] See for example *Regina v. Alladice*, Court of Appeal of England and Wales, decision of 8 May 1988, [1988] WL 624104: "*If the police, albeit in good faith, have nevertheless fallen foul of Section 58, it is still necessary for the Court to decide whether to admit the evidence would adversely affect the fairness of the proceedings* [...]."

[205] Deterrence mainly targets the consciously acting investigator; where the investigator has acted in good faith, there is little need for exclusion under a deterrence rationale, see Sect. 4.4.5.

[206] See for instance *Regina v. Khan*, Court of Appeal of England and Wales, decision of 15 June 1992, [1993] Crim. L.R. 54: "[I]*t would be a strange reflection on our law if a man who has admitted his participation in the illegal importation of a large quantity of heroin should have his conviction set aside on the grounds that his privacy has been invaded*".

have no impact on the outcome of the trial. Conversely, where this evidence is decisive for the final judgment, because it is the only or the strongest evidence, exclusion has been deemed necessary because "*the temptation to do what the provisions are aimed to prevent is greatest, and the protection of the rules is most needed.*"[207]

Finally, the same hypothetical considerations have been made with respect to the course of investigations as in other domestic systems. It has been asked whether the violation was instrumental in obtaining the evidence or whether this evidence would have emerged either way. The argument is that where the violation was not instrumental, it did not disadvantage the defendant. Consequently, the fairness of the proceeding would not be affected. The most well-known examples in English case law involve the right to have access to legal advice. In cases where the defendant was denied access to a solicitor, English courts have made their decision on exclusion subject to whether the accused was aware of his right to remain silent. Where he was and still testified, it has been held that there was no reason to suppose that this confession would not have occurred in the presence of a solicitor. Consequently, the evidence has been admitted.[208] The evidence has in turn been excluded where it was likely that a confession would not have been made had the access to legal advice been granted.[209]

In conclusion, the English system also weighs the different interests involved in order to decide whether to exclude tainted evidence. English courts, in contrast to the U.S. system, openly conduct a balancing exercise instead of applying rules of exceptions. We will see that in terms of methodology, the English approach is therefore closer to the ICC exclusionary rule than the U.S. approach. What is more, unlike U.S. courts, the English judiciary has not chosen to rely on deterrence as a rationale for their exclusionary rule, which, as we will see, cannot guide the application of the ICC exclusionary rule either.

At the same time, a similar conclusion can be drawn as with respect to the German system. We will see that the approach to the ICC exclusionary rule that will be adopted in this research will be more open to exclusion than English case law. English judges, in theory, have a broad discretion under Section 78 of PACE. In practice, however, the inclusionary approach at common law still influences today how this discretion is used by the judiciary. As a result, the modern English approach is characterized by a general reluctance to exclude. The consequence for this research is that, while the factors considered by English courts will be relevant for this research, there will be a certain shift when it comes to the evaluation of the different interests affected by decisions on exclusion. We will see that the

---

[207] *Regina v. Keenan*, Court of Appeal of England and Wales, decision of 26 April 1989, [1990] 2 Q.B. 54.

[208] *Regina v. Alladice*, Court of Appeal of England and Wales, decision of 8 May 1988, [1988] WL 624104.

[209] *Regina v. Samuel*, Court of Appeal of England and Wales, decision of 17 December 1987, [1988] Q.B. 615.

relationship between the interests of law enforcement and the respect for due process is different under the ICC exclusionary rule as conceived in this research than the one reflected by the inclusionary approach under English case law.

3.3.4 Canada

Finally, a third domestic system with a common law background shall be given some consideration. We will see that similarities exist between the Canadian and the ICC exclusionary rule which make the Canadian approach to illicitly obtained evidence particularly interesting for this research. This is perhaps not surprising. Canada in fact played a significant role in the work on Article 69 within the Preparatory Committee that prepared a draft text for the negotiation of the ICC Statute.[210]

For a long time, Canadian law followed the inclusionary approach typical to common law.[211] The Canadian Supreme Court, in its leading case, rejected the idea of a general judicial discretion with respect to the admission of illicitly obtained evidence. It held instead that exclusion was limited to cases of substantial unfairness.[212] Under this jurisprudence, the circumstances under which exclusion was possible were so restricted that evidence was almost always admitted. One exception to this jurisprudence resulted from the so-called '*confessions rule*'. Under this common law doctrine, statements made to state authorities were inadmissible unless the prosecution established beyond a reasonable doubt that they had been made voluntarily.[213]

The generally restrictive approach of the Canadian courts was fundamentally overthrown after the adoption of the Canadian Charter of Rights and Freedoms in 1982.[214] The Charter sets forth an explicit exclusionary rule in its Section 24(2),

[210] Triffterer 2008—Piragoff, Article 69, para 17.

[211] Osborn 2000, para 16.

[212] See *Regina v. Wray*, Supreme Court of Canada, decision of 26 June 1970, [1971] S.C.R. 272, 273: "*The trial judge has no general discretion to exclude admissible evidence because, in his opinion, its admission would be unjust or unfair to the accused. The exercise of a discretion by him arises only if the admission of the evidence, would operate unfairly.* [...] *It is only the allowance of evidence gravely prejudicial to the accused, and whose probative force in relation to the main issue before the Court is trifling, which can be said to operate unfairly.*"

[213] Vanderpuye 2005, p. 131. Technically, the 'confessions rule' remains applicable today, despite the existence of Section 24(2) of the Charter; see *Regina v. Grant*, Supreme Court of Canada, decision of 17 July 2009, [2009] 2 S.C.R. 353, para 90. We will nevertheless concentrate on the modern framework under Section 24(2) of the Canadian Charter of Rights and Freedoms. Treating all common law aspects to exclusion under Canadian law would go far beyond the scope of this research.

[214] The Canadian Charter of Rights and Freedoms is part of the Canadian Constitution adopted on 17 April 1982, into force on 17 April 1982; available at http://laws-lois.justice.gc.ca/eng/Const/page-15.html (last visited: October 2013).

which stipulates that "[w]*here* [...] *a court concludes that evidence was obtained in a manner that infringed or denied any rights or freedoms guaranteed by this Charter, the evidence shall be excluded if it is established that, having regard to all the circumstances, the admission of it in the proceedings would bring the administration of justice into disrepute.*"

This provision was conceived against the backdrop of the U.S. exclusionary rule. Like the U.S. rule, the Canadian exclusionary rule is part of constitutional law; its explicit mention in the text of the constitution even goes a step further than the judicially conceived U.S. rule. At the same time, the Canadian version of the exclusionary rule reflects a desire to dissociate itself from the American rule. By the time the Canadian Charter was adopted, the U.S. Supreme Court had already started to gradually soften the U.S. exclusionary rule. In Canada, however, the U.S. rule was still understood by many as requiring exclusion in any case of tainted evidence. Section 24(2) was conceived in order to avoid such a consequence. It necessarily involves a balancing of different factors[215] and is therefore a compromise between a mandatory rule and its general inclusionary counterpart under the traditional common law approach.[216]

The way the judicial discretion granted by Section 24(2) is exercised, however, demonstrates a position of the Canadian judiciary that is on the whole in favour of a stronger exclusionary rule than, for instance, under the German or the English approach depicted above. If the Canadian exclusionary rule is compared with the modern U.S. exclusionary rule in turn, a differing trend can be detected. While the U.S. exclusionary rule has been gradually restricted, the trend in Canada is rather in favour of its expansion.[217]

Another marked difference between the U.S. and the Canadian approach to exclusion has been identified with reference to the wording of Section 24(2) of the Canadian Charter of Rights and Freedoms. The provision allows for exclusion only where the admission of the evidence risks "*[bringing] the administration of justice into disrepute*". The Canadian Supreme Court has drawn conclusions from this formulation for the rationale of the exclusionary rule. Unlike their American colleagues, Canadian judges have rejected the idea that deterring the police from further violations of individual rights is the primary rationale for evidentiary exclusion. The judges have considered deterrence, where it actually occurs, to be but a fortunate side effect.[218] Moreover, they have also explicitly rejected another justification that is often discussed in domestic debates, namely the idea that exclusion is a remedy for the defendant in order to compensate him for the

---

[215]Hessler 2000, p. 339.

[216]Penney 2003, p. 107.

[217]See already Nasheri 1996, p. 161 et seq. Similar, see Stuart 2010b, p. 320 et seq.

[218]See for instance, *Regina v. Grant,* Supreme Court of Canada, decision of 17 July 2009, [2009] 2 S.C.R. 353, para 70; *Regina v. Genest*, Supreme Court of Canada, decision of 26 January 1989, [1989] 1 S.R.C. 59.

violation he has suffered.[219] Instead, the Canadian Supreme Court judges have held explicitly that the purpose of the exclusionary rule is to preserve the integrity of the justice system. Under the Canadian exclusionary rule, excluding evidence is meant to maintain public respect for and confidence in the administration of justice.[220]

Such a purpose obviously risks overemphasising public opinion, which might not always be in line with the requirements of the rule of law. The Canadian Supreme Court has admitted that the concept of disrepute involves some element of the views of the general community. But at the same time, it has indicated that it is aware of the risks. The Court has emphasized that integrity should not concentrate on immediate public reaction to individual cases. It should rather be understood as focussing on the long-term reputation of the justice system.[221] We can already note at this point that this justification is very similar to the one that this research will endorse in view of the ICC exclusionary rule.

Despite the determination of this overall perspective, the notion of the repute of the justice system remains vague. Taking a middle course between automatic exclusion and general admission necessarily grants discretion to the judges. While this implies a balancing of different values and interests, Section 24(2) does not provide much insight into the exact test that needs to be applied.[222] As a consequence, the criteria to be considered in such a test have been intensively discussed both by the Canadian judiciary and academia. The Canadian Supreme Court in particular has thoroughly dealt with this issue in order to develop principles to guide trial judges.[223]

The Supreme Court jurisprudence can be divided in two distinct phases. Initially, the Court developed its interpretation of Section 24(2) in two leading cases, *Collins* and *Stillman*.[224] The framework that emerged from this jurisprudence demanded that the trial judge apply a rather difficult test, which de facto only allowed him to exercise his discretion to a limited degree. This framework was mainly based on the distinction between two categories of evidence, so-called

---

[219]*Regina v. Grant*, Supreme Court of Canada, decision of 17 July 2009, [2009] 2 S.C.R. 353, para 70. On the remedial theory, see Sect. 4.3.2.2.4.

[220]See for instance, *Regina v. Therens*, Supreme Court of Canada, decision of 23 May 1985, [1985] 1 S.C.R. 613, para 75: "*The central concern of s. 24(2) would appear to be the maintenance of respect for and confidence in the administration of justice, as that may be affected by the violation of constitutional rights and freedoms.*"

[221]*Regina v. Grant*, Supreme Court of Canada, decision of 17 July 2009, [2009] 2 S.C.R. 353, para 68; *Regina v. Collins*, Supreme Court of Canada, decision of 9 April 1987, [1987] 1 S.C.R. 265. On the integrity rationale underlying the Canadian exclusionary rule, see Ashworth and Redmayne 2010, p. 346; Choo and Nash 2007, p. 94 et seq.; Vanderpuye 2005, p. 139 et seq. Further Sect. 4.3.2.2.5.

[222]Eberdt 2001, p. 67.

[223]Penney 2003, p. 108.

[224]*Regina v. Collins*, Supreme Court of Canada, decision of 9 April 1987, [1987] 1 S.C.R. 265; *Regina v. Stillman*, Supreme Court of Canada, decision of 10 March 1997, [1997] 1 S.C.R. 607.

'*conscriptive*' evidence and '*non-conscriptive*' evidence. The exact scope of what was to be considered conscriptive evidence remained controversial. In its essence, however, the term describes evidence that exists only as the result of an involuntary contribution by the defendant. The latter is thereby compelled to incriminate himself in violation of his rights under the Canadian Charter. This could include the production of a statement, as well as the use of the body or the production of bodily samples.[225]

The judgment in *Stillman* introduced a bright-line rule to this effect. In case of conscriptive evidence, exclusion was supposed to be virtually automatic.[226] The only way the prosecution could secure that the evidence would be admitted was to demonstrate that it could have been discovered through legal, non-conscriptive means, which was often impossible.[227] In the case of evidence that was considered non-conscriptive in turn, the trial judge was entrusted with a greater amount of discretion. He had to apply a balancing exercise that included as main factors the seriousness of the violation and the effect that exclusion would have on the outcome of the trial.[228]

This distinction was supposed to emphasize the special concern for unconstitutional self-incrimination. The Supreme Court's jurisprudence was, however, constantly subjected to criticism by the Canadian legal academia, which ultimately seems justified.

The main point of criticism was the rigid bright-line rule. In fact, the underlying assumption that a violation of the right against self-incrimination is more intrusive than other violations is open to challenge. There seems to be no apparent reason why, for instance, producing a statement under duress should in principle be considered a more serious violation than a warrantless search of private premises.[229] Beyond that, the distinction made by the Canadian Supreme Court has been criticized in particular for the flaws in its analytical method. Section 24(2) of the Charter clearly provides for a contextual analysis. The trial judge is supposed to exercise his discretion by taking into account "*all the circumstances*". Critics have pointed out that this opposes rigid and inflexible categorizations. While the bright-line rule, at first sight, might be applauded for its benefits for legal certainty, it in fact restricts the judicial discretion granted by Section 24(2). What is more, the bright-line rule has been less beneficial to legal certainty than it might at first seem. In view of the lack of an exact definition of the category of conscriptive evidence, the emerging case law has been criticised for being both too complex and too opaque. The combination of a bright-line rule with an unsettled definition of

---

[225]*Regina v. Stillman*, Supreme Court of Canada, decision of 10 March 1997, [1997] 1 S.C.R. 607.

[226]Choo and Nash 2007, p. 96; Stuart 2010b, p. 324.

[227]Eberdt 2001, p. 68; Penney 2003, p. 129; Vanderpuye 2005, p. 133.

[228]Choo and Nash 2007, p. 96; Penney 2003, p. 133.

[229]Penney 2003, p. 132; Stuart 2010b, p. 324.

the respective categories has resulted in disputable findings. In order to avoid undesired results, trial judges have sometimes arrived at questionable results when categorizing evidence as conscriptive or non-conscriptive.[230]

As a consequence, in 2009, the Supreme Court in two bellwether rulings, formulated a revised approach to exclusion. The primary feature of this new jurisprudence was that it abandoned the conscription bright-line rule. Instead of placing the focus on the conscriptive or non-conscriptive dichotomy, the Court opted for a general discretionary standard, no matter the nature of the evidence. The criteria that had previously been considered in cases of non-conscriptive evidence were revised. The ensuing balancing exercise is now applicable to all kinds of evidence. The new jurisprudence takes into account three factors: the seriousness of the Charter violation, the impact of the violation on the rights of the accused and the interest of society in the adjudication of the case on its merits.

Under the first heading, the seriousness of the Charter violation, the trial judge is supposed to consider in particular whether the investigating authorities have acted in bad faith. Where this is the case, there is a presumption for exclusion. Under the new framework, the attitude of the authorities towards the infringement is deemed crucial.[231] This is particularly interesting when compared with the '*good faith*' exception adopted by the U.S. Supreme Court. In the U.S., this exception is based on the argument that exclusion is of little use where no deterrent effect can be achieved because the authorities have acted in good faith.[232] The new Canadian Supreme Court jurisprudence in turn continues to consider deterrence to be a side effect.[233] At the same time, the Court has asserted that the attitude of investigators impacts on the consequences that the admission of evidence has on judicial integrity. The judges have held that "'[g]*ood faith' on the part of the police will also reduce the need for the court to dissociate itself from the police conduct*."[234] Their jurisprudence shows that the significance of bad or good faith can be based on a different argument, namely the maintenance of the reputation of the justice system.

In addition, the second factor takes into account the interests of the accused at the time of the infringement. This involves the seriousness and character of the violation committed by the authorities. The question to be asked here is whether the breach was only of a technical nature or whether it was in fact intrusive.[235]

[230]Eberdt 2001, p. 68 et seq.; Stuart 2010a, p. 596 et seq.; Stuart 2010b, p. 324 et seq.

[231]For a critical assessment of this focus, see Eberdt 2001, p. 73 and p. 82.

[232]On this consideration, see in particular Sect. 4.4.5.

[233]*Regina v. Grant,* Supreme Court of Canada, decision of 17 July 2009, [2009] 2 S.C.R. 353, para 70.

[234]*Regina v. Grant,* Supreme Court of Canada, decision of 17 July 2009, [2009] 2 S.C.R. 353, para 75. See also Stuart 2010b, p. 318.

[235]*Regina v. Grant,* Supreme Court of Canada, decision of 17 July 2009, [2009] 2 S.C.R. 353, para 76. See also Stuart 2010b, p. 318.

The last factor asks "*whether the truth-seeking function of the criminal process would be better served by admission of the evidence or by its exclusion*".[236] This includes in fact two different criteria. Firstly, the Canadian judges, at this point, consider the reliability of the evidence. Moreover, they take into account the importance of the evidence for the outcome of the trial. This means that they have to evaluate whether the evidence is the only or decisive evidence for the crime or whether other reliable evidence exists.[237] Interestingly, quite in contrast to their English colleagues, who also consider this factor, the Canadian Supreme Court judges have deemed the significance of the evidence for the prosecution's case to be a factor militating against and not in favour of exclusion.[238]

In the context of the effect of exclusion on the outcome of the trial, a further aspect of the Supreme Court's jurisprudence needs to be noted. There was disagreement among the judges who conceived the new approach on the impact of the seriousness of the crime the defendant is charged with. One of the judges strongly favoured the consideration of this aspect.[239] The rationale behind her view is that society has a greater interest in admission in trials concerning serious crimes than it has in cases of less serious crimes. The majority disagreed. The original Supreme Court jurisprudence on exclusion had been ambiguous with regard to the seriousness of the crime. In its new decision, the Canadian Supreme Court emphasized, however, what the former case law had already indicated: that, theoretically, the seriousness of the crime might be able to tip the scales both in favour of exclusion and in favour of admission.[240]

In general, Canadian legal academics have reacted positively to the revision of the jurisprudence of their Supreme Court. This was not surprising since such a change had long been demanded. A number of aspects of this case law is of interest to this research.[241] On a general level, the change of jurisprudence confirms a conclusion already made in view of the development of the case law of the U.S. Supreme Court. The question of the admissibility of illicitly obtained evidence is too complex for automatic rules. While the introduction of a bright-line rule in Canada was intended to promote legal certainty, its practical implementation had the opposite effect because judges often chose to circumvent the predetermined results. In the end, the judges returned to what Section 24(2) of the Charter had initially intended to provide for, namely a decision-making on the basis of broad judicial discretion.

---

[236]*Regina v. Grant,* Supreme Court of Canada, decision of 17 July 2009, [2009] 2 S.C.R. 353, para 79.

[237]Stuart 2010b, p. 318 and p. 319, with further references.

[238]See Sect. 3.3.3.

[239]See *Regina v. Grant,* Supreme Court of Canada, decision of 17 July 2009, Dissenting Opinion Justice Deschamps [2009] 2 S.C.R. 353, paras 216 et seq.

[240]*Regina v. Grant,* Supreme Court of Canada, decision of 17 July 2009, [2009] 2 S.C.R. 353, para 84.

[241]Eberdt 2001, p. 66; Stuart 2010b, p. 314, both with further references.

Most importantly, however, Section 24(2) of the Canadian Charter of Rights and Freedoms bears significant similarities with the ICC exclusionary rule in terms of the underlying justification for the exclusion of evidence. As we will see in more detail when treating the purpose of the ICC exclusionary rule, both rules refer to the importance of the public perception of the legitimacy of the judicial system. In light of this parallelism, the jurisprudence of the Canadian Supreme Court will serve as a useful example when determining the consequences of the importance of judicial integrity for the interpretation of Article 69(7) of the ICC Statute. The focus of the Canadian Supreme Court on a particular rationale, as well as its thorough discussion of the factors to be considered in a balancing exercise, will be particularly helpful. Naturally, this cannot lead to any one-to-one adoption of the Canadian approach by the ICC. The jurisprudence of the Canadian Supreme Court will still have to be assessed in more detail, in particular in view of the transferability of the solutions from the domestic to the international level.

3.4 Conclusion and Outlook

We have seen that, from a methodological point of view, it is generally possible to draw from both domestic and international law to find solutions for procedural issues at the ICC. The adoption of the solutions of other systems, however, is subject to the consideration of the particularities of the respective system and its differences when compared to the ICC system.

On a substantive level, the assessment of a number of systems has demonstrated that there is a common baseline with respect to the exclusion of illicitly obtained evidence. All of the systems reviewed recognize the need to exclude illicitly obtained evidence under certain circumstances. Moreover, in essence, all of these systems weigh the different interests involved in order to decide which evidence should be excluded. This is ultimately a reflection of the tension that has already been addressed at the very outset of this research. All of these systems must find a balance between the interests of due process and the interest in effective law enforcement. The way in which this balance is achieved differs, however, depending on the emphasis the respective system places at either of these two poles, as well as on its justification for exclusion and on the factors it deems relevant for weighing the different interests.

For many questions of international criminal procedure, a line has been drawn between civil and common law concepts. Discussions often turn around whether the ICC proper law has opted for a civil law or a common law concept for a certain question or whether it has opted for its own solution. For the research at hand, this issue does not arise. Even though this is only a small sample, one insight that can be gained from the above assessment of domestic legal systems is that there is no direct link between the legal family a system belongs to and its solutions regarding the exclusion of evidence. The civil law and common law distinction does not, for instance, decide where this system positions itself between the two poles of due process and effective law enforcement. Systems belonging to different legal families, such as the English and the German system, may follow a similar line by choosing to adopt a more inclusionary approach that favours the interests of effective law enforcement. Systems that are part of the same legal family may in turn follow different approaches. This is demonstrated by the common law systems assessed above. While the English system adopts an inclusionary approach, the Canadian system in particular has opted for a much stronger exclusionary rule. The same is true for the question of justification. This is again indicated by a comparison of the three common law systems, with the U.S. system being the only one to rely on the deterrence theory.

For the research question at hand, this means that the civil law and common law dichotomy is not of much help. Instead of looking at the mixture of these elements in the ICC proper law, we will have to find answers to the questions related to exclusion that best suit the ICC as an international criminal court. In order to find proper solutions for the ICC, the systems reviewed above will serve as a guideline, as well as a point of demarcation.

References

Alamuddin A (2010) Collection of evidence. In: Khan K, Buisman C, Gosnell C (eds) Principles of evidence in international criminal justice. Oxford University Press, Oxford, pp 231–305

Ambos K (2007) The structure of international criminal procedure: "adversarial", "inquisitorial" or mixed? In: Bohlander M (ed) International criminal justice: a critical analysis of institutions and procedures. Cameron May, London, pp 429–503

Ambos K (2010) Beweisverwertungsverbote: Grundlagen und Kasuistik—internationale Bezüge Ausgewählte Probleme. Duncker & Humblot, Berlin

Ambos K (2011) Art. 6 EMRK. In: Radtke H, Hohmann O (eds) Strafprozessordnung: StPO. VerlagFranz Vahlen, Munich, pp 2518–2535

Amelung K (1990) Informationsbeherrschungsrechte im Strafprozeß. Dogmatische Grundlagen individualrechtlicher Beweisverbote. Duncker & Humblot, Berlin 1990

Amelung K (1991) Grundfragen der Verwertungsverbote bei beweissichernden Hausdurchsuchungen im Strafverfahren. Neue Juristische Wochenschr 40:2533–2540

Amelung K, Mittag M (2005) Beweislastumkehr bei Haussuchungen ohne richterliche Anordnung gemäß § 105 StPO. Neue Z Strafrecht 11:614–617

Ashworth A, Redmayne M (2010) The criminal process, 4th edn. Oxford University Press, Oxford, 2010

Beling E (1903) Die Beweisverbote als Grenzen der Wahrheitserforschung im Strafprozess. Wissenschaftliche Buchgesellschaft, Breslau

Berger M (2012) The right to silence in The Hague international criminal courts. Univ San Francisco Law Rev 47:1–54

Boas G (2001) Creating laws of evidence for international criminal law: the ICTY and the principle of flexibility. Crim Law Forum 12:41–90

Bradley C (1982) The exclusionary rule in Germany. Harvard Law Rev 96:1032–1066

Bradley C (2010) Reconceiving the fourth amendment and the exclusionary rule. Law Contemp Probl 73:211–238

Buisman C, Bouazdi M, Costi M (2010) Principles of civil law. In: Khan K, Buisman C, Gosnell C (eds) Principles of evidence in international criminal justice. Oxford University Press, Oxford, pp 7–95

Calvo-Goller N (2006) The trial proceedings of the International Criminal Court: ICTY And ICTR PRECEDENTS. Martinus Nijhoff Publishers, Leiden, 2006

Cammack M (2010) The rise and fall of the constitutional exclusionary rule in the United States. Am J Comp Law 58:631–658

Cassese A (2003) The influence of the European Court of Human Rights on international criminal tribunals—some methodological remarks. In: Bergsmo A, Eide A (eds) Human rights and criminal justice for the downtrodden: essays in honour of Asbjørn Eide. Martinus Nijhoff Publishers, Leiden, pp 19–52

Choo A, Nash S (2007) Improperly obtained evidence in the Commonwealth: lessons for England and Wales? Int J Evid Proof 11:75–105

Combs N (2011) Evidence. In: Schabas W, Bernaz, N (eds) Routledge Handbook of International Criminal Law. London, pp 323–334

Dencker F (1977) Verwertungsverbote im Strafprozess: ein Beitrag zur Lehre von den Beweisverboten. Carl Heymanns Verlag, Cologne

Dixon R (1997) Developing international rules of evidence for the Yugoslav and Rwanda Tribunals. Transnatl Law Contemp Probl 7:81–102

Eberdt B (2001) Impaired exclusion: exploring the possibility of a new bright line rule of good faith in impaired driving offences. Rev Curr Law Law Reform 16:65–83

Effer-Uhe D (2008) Die Entwicklung der Lehre von den Beweisverboten. Jura – juristische Ausbildung 5:335–340

Eisenberg U (2011) Beweisrecht der StPO: Spezialkommentar, 7th edn. C.H. Beck, Munich

Esser R (2008) EGMR in Sachen Gäfgen v. Deutschland (22978/05), Urt. v. 30.06.2008. Neue Z Strafrecht 12:657–662

Esser R (2012) Article 7 IPBPR and article 6 EMRK. In: Rosenberg L (ed) Die Strafprozessordnung und das Gerichtsverfassungsgesetz: StPO Band 11: EMRK/IPBPR, 26th edn. De Gruyter, Berlin

Friman H (1999) Rights of persons suspected or accused of a crime. In: Lee R (ed) The International Criminal Court: the making of the Rome Statute: issues, negotiations, results. Kluwer Law International, The Hague, pp 247–262

Friman H (2003) Inspiration from the international criminal tribunals when developing law on evidence for the International Criminal Court. Law Pract Int Courts Tribunals 2:373–400

Gaede K (2009) Beweisverbote zur Wahrung des fairen Strafverfahrens in der Rechtsprechung des EGMR insbesondere bei verdeckten Ermittlungen. Juristische Rundsch 12:493–502

Gaynor F, Jackson J, Klamberg M, Tochilovsky V (2013) Appeals, reviews and reconsideration. In: Sluiter G, Friman H, Linton S, Zappalà S, Vasiliev S (eds) International criminal procedure: principles and rules. Oxford University Press, Oxford, pp 1051–1150

Gosnell C (2010) Admissibility of evidence. In: Khan A, Buisman C, Gosnell C (eds) Principles of evidence in international criminal justice. Oxford University Press, Oxford, pp 375–442

Gössel K (1981) Kritische Bemerkungen zum gegenwärtigen Stand der Lehre von den Beweisverboten im Strafverfahren. Neue Juristische Wochenschr 13:649–656

Gray R (2004) Evidence before the ICC. In: McGoldrick D, Rowe P, Donnelly E (eds) The permanent International Criminal Court: legal and policy issues. Hart Publishing, Oxford, pp 287–314

Harris K (1991) Verwertungsverbot für mittelbar erlangte Beweismittel: Fernwirkungsdoktrin in der Rechtsprechung im deutschen und amerikanischen Recht. Strafverteidiger 7:313–322

Hay P (2011) US-Amerikanisches Recht, 5th edn. C.H. Beck, Munich

Hessler S (2000) Establishing inevitability without active pursuit: defining the inevitable discovery exception to the fourth amendment exclusionary rule. Mich Law Rev 99:238–278

Jackson J, Summers S (2012) The internationalisation of criminal evidence: beyond the common law and civil law traditions. Cambridge University Press, Cambridge

Klamberg M (2013) Evidence in international criminal trials: confronting legal gaps and the reconstruction of disputed events. Martinus Nijhoff Publishers, Leiden

Kühne H (2010) Strafprozessrecht: eine systematische Darstellung des deutschen und europäischen Strafverfahrensrecht, 8th edn. C.F. Müller, Heidelberg

LaFave W, Israel J, King N (2004) Criminal procedure, 4th edn. West Academic Publishing, St Paul
Lepsius O (1997) Verwaltungsrecht unter dem Common Law: Amerikanische Entwicklungen bis zum New Deal. Mohr Siebeck, Thübigen
Lubig S, Sprenger J (2008) Beweisverwertungsverbote aus dem Fairnessgebot des Art. 6 EMRK in der Rechtsprechung des EGMR. Zeitschrift für Internationale Strafrechtsdogmatik 9:433–440
Ma Y (1999) Comparative analysis of exclusionary rules in the United States, England, France, Germany, and Italy. Polic: Int J Police Strat Manag 22:280–303
May R, Wierda M (2003) International criminal evidence. Transnational Publishers, New York
Mellifont K (2007) The derivative imperative: how should Australian criminal trial courts treat evidence deriving from illegally or improperly gained evidence? Professional Doctorate thesis, Queensland University of Technology. http://eprints.qut.edu.au/16388/1/Kerri_Mellifont_Thesis.pdf. Accessed 14 May 2015
Meron T (2004) Evolution in the ICTY. J Int Crim Justice 2:520–525
Meyer-Goßner L (2013) Strafprozessordnung, 56th edn. C.H. Beck, Munich
Mitsch W (2008) Strafprozessuale Beweisverbote im Spannungsfeld zwischen Jurisprudenz und realer Gefahr. Neue Juristische Wochenschr 32:2295–2301
Muthorst O (2009) Das Beweisverbot: Grundlegung und Konkretisierung rechtlicher Grenzen der Beweiserhebung und der Beweisverwertung im Zivil-, Straf- und Verwaltungsverfahren. Mohr Siebeck, Tübingen
Nasheri H (1996) The exclusionary rule: differing trends in Canada and the United States. Crim Justice Rev 21:161–180
Nemitz J (2002) Strafzumessung im Völkerstrafrecht. Edition Iuscrim, Freiburg
Nemitz J (2005) Die Hauptverhandlung unter besonderer Berücksichtigung des Beweisrechts. In: Kirsch S (ed) Internationale Strafgerichtshöfe. Nomos, Baden-Baden, pp 53–74
Nüse K (1966) Zu den Beweisverboten im Strafprozeß. Juristische Rundsch 8:281–288
Orie A (2002) Accusatorial versus inquisitorial approach in international criminal proceedings. In: Cassese A, Gaeta P, Jones J (eds) The Rome statute of the international criminal court: a commentary, vol 2. Oxford University Press, Oxford, pp 1439–1495
Osborn D (2000) Supressing the truth: judicial exclusion of illegally obtained evidence in the United States, Canada, England and Australia'. Murdoch Univ Electron J Law 7. http://www.austlii.edu.au/au/journals/MurUEJL/2000/44.html. Accessed 14 May 2015
Osmer J (1966) Der Umfang des Beweisverwertungsverbotes nach § 136a StPO. Doctoral thesis, University of Hamburg, Hamburg
Pakter W (1985) Exclusionary rules in France, Germany, and Italy. Hastings Int Comp Law Rev 1:1–57
Penney S (2003) Taking deterrence seriously: excluding unconstitutionally obtained evidence under section 24(2) of the Charter. McGill Law J 49:105–144
Ransiek A (2002) Durchsuchung, Beschlagnahme und Verwertungsverbot. Strafverteidiger 10:565–571
Roberts P, Zuckerman A (2010) Criminal evidence, 2nd edn. Oxford University Press, Oxford
Rogall K (1979) Gegenwärtiger Stand und Entwicklungstendenzen der Lehre von den strafprozessualen Beweisverboten. Z Gesamte Strafrechtswissenschaft 191:1–44
Rogall K (1988) Hypothetische Ermittlungsverläufe im Strafrecht—ein Beitrag zur Lehre der Beweiserhebungs—und Beweisverwertungsverbote. Neue Z Strafr 9:385–393
Rogall K (1996) Über die Folgen der rechtswidrigen Beschaffung des Zeugenbeweises im Strafprozeß. Juristenzeitung 51:944–955
Roxin C, Schünemann B (2012) Strafverfahrensrecht: ein Studienbuch, 27th edn. C.H. Beck, Munich
Rzepka D (2000) Zur Fairness im deutschen Strafverfahren. Vittorio Klostermann, Frankfurt am Main
Safferling C (2001) Towards an international criminal procedure. Oxford University Press, Oxford
Safferling C (2012) International criminal procedure. Oxford University Press, Oxford

Satzger H (2009) Der Einfluss der EMRK auf das deutsche Straf- und Strafprozessrecht—Grundlagen und wichtige Einzelprobleme. Jura - Juristische Ausbild 31:759–768
Schroeder F (2003) Die Gesamtprüfung der Verfahrensfairness durch den EGMR. Goltdammer's Arch Strafr 5:293–298
Slobogin C (2013) A comparative perspective on the exclusionary rule in search and seizure cases. Vanderbilt Public Law Research Paper No. 13-21. http://papers.ssrn.com/sol3/papers.cfm?abstract_id=2247746. Accessed 14 May 2015
Sluiter G (2002) International criminal adjudication and the collection of evidence: obligations of states: obligations of states. Intersentia, Antwerpen
Stone R (1995) Exclusion of evidence under section 78 of the Police and Criminal Evidence Act: practice and principles. www.worldlawbook.com/attachments/312.pdf. Accessed 14 May 2015
Stuart D (2010a) Charter justice in Canadian criminal law, 5th edn. Carswell, Toronto
Stuart D (2010b) Welcome flexibility and better criteria from the Supreme Court of Canada for exclusion of evidence obtained in violation of the Canadian Charter of Rights and Freedoms. Southwest J Int Law 16:313–332
Swoboda S (2012) Die Europäische Menschenrechtskonvention in Strafverfahren vor internationalen Gerichten. In: Höland A (ed) Wirkungen der Rechtsprechung des Europäischen Gerichtshofs für Menschenrechte im deutschen Recht. BMW Berliner Wissenschafts-Verlag, Berlin, pp 83–118
Thaman S (2013) Fruits of the poisonous tree in comparative law. Southwest J Int Law 16:333–384
Tochilovsky V (2007) Jurisprudence of the International Criminal Courts and the European Court of Human Rights: Procedure and Evidence. Martinus Nijhoff Publishers, Leiden
Torres Chedraui A (2010) An analysis of the exclusion of evidence obtained in violation of human rights in light of the jurisprudence of the European Court of Human Rights. Tilburg Law Review 15:205–234
Trechsel S, Summers S (2005) Human rights in criminal proceedings. Oxford University Press, Oxford
Triffterer O (2008) (ed) Commentary on the Rome Statute of the International Criminal Court: observers' notes, article by article, 2nd edn. C.H. Beck, Baden-Baden
Trüg G (2003) Lösungskonvergenzen trotz Systemdivergenzen im deutschen und US-amerikanischen Strafverfahren. Mohr Siebeck, Tübingen
Trüg G, Habetha J (2008) Beweisverwertung trotz rechtswidriger Beweisgewinnung—insbesondere mit Blick auf die "Liechtensteiner Steueraffäre". Neue Z Strafr 9:481–492
Vanderpuye K (2005) The International Criminal Court and discretionary evidential exclusion: toeing the mark? Tulane J Int Comp Law 14:127–177
Vogler R, Huber B (2008) Criminal procedure in Europe. Duncker & Humblot, Berlin
Warnking V (2009) Strafprozessuale Beweisverbote in der Rechtsprechung des europäischen Gerichtshofs für Menschenrechte und ihre Auswirkungen auf das deutsche Recht. Peter Lang, Frankfurt am Main
Weigend T (2003) Is the criminal process about truth: a German perspective. Harvard J Law Public Policy 26:157–173
Werle (2012) Völkerstrafrecht, 3rd edn. Mohr Siebeck, Tübingen
Young R (2011) "Internationally recognized human rights" before the International Criminal Court. Int Comp Law Q 60:189–208
Zahar A, Sluiter G (2008) International criminal law: a critical introduction. Oxford University Press, Oxford
Zappalà S (2002) The rights of the accused. In: Cassese A, Gaeta P, Jones J (eds) The Rome Statute of the International Criminal Court: a commentary, vol 2. Oxford University Press, Oxford, pp 1319–1354

Chapter 4
Development of an Approach to the Exclusion of Evidence by the International Criminal Court

Abstract Chapters 2 and 3 have provided a base of knowledge concerning, on the one hand, the legal framework the ICC operates in and, on the other hand, the approaches that other systems have taken to the exclusion of illicitly gained evidence. The present chapter will constitute the central part of the research. Turning to the ICC, it will develop the basic principles of an own approach to the exclusion of evidence that fits the International Criminal Court. To this end, it will first depict the conditions ICC investigators operate in by describing the cooperation system between the ICC and domestic states. Based on the findings of the previous chapters, it will then set out and interpret the legal framework for exclusion under the law applicable to the ICC. In this context, one of the main questions of this chapter pertains to the rationale that should guide the exclusion of evidence from ICC proceedings. In domestic legal systems, excluding tainted evidence is usually justified on the basis of four different rationales: a lack of reliability of the respective evidence, deterrence, the vindication of individual rights and the maintenance of procedural integrity. The chapter will demonstrate that in case of the ICC, the last of these justification models, the integrity rationale, is not only the rationale that is most consistent with the wording of Article 69(7) of the ICC Statute but that it must also be given preference over other approaches in light of teleological considerations. Finally, this chapter will give an outline of the kind of legal violations that may at all lead to the exclusion of evidence in ICC proceedings.

Keywords Cooperation regime · Admissibility · Vindication of rights · Deterrence · Theory of integrity · Unreliable evidence · Internationally recognized human rights · Article 69(7) of the ICC statute · Torture · Right to silence · Right to privacy

P. Viebig, *Illicitly Obtained Evidence at the International Criminal Court*,
International Criminal Justice Series 4, DOI 10.1007/978-94-6265-093-0_4

Contents

4.1 Introduction

The procedural part of the ICC Statute is the manifestation of a highly ambitious compromise. It constitutes an attempt to reconcile for the international level the sometimes widely diverging views among legal cultures on the appropriate procedure for criminal trials. As commentators have emphasized, finding a common system of procedure for the ICC revealed a deep chasm between the ideas of lawyers with a common law background and those with a civil law background in particular.[1] The law of evidence was among those procedural areas that triggered a lot of controversy.[2]

For the specific issue of the admissibility of illicitly obtained evidence, the underlying controversy is somewhat different than for most questions of criminal procedure. As we have seen in the review of domestic systems, the dividing lines here are not so much between common law and civil law. They are rather between more liberal and more restrictive approaches. This controversy will also impact on the development of solutions for the ICC. At the same time, the dichotomy between civil law and common law ideas cannot be entirely disregarded. It sometimes provides useful insights and helps one to understand the emergence of the different approaches to the admissibility of illicitly obtained evidence that we will now try to transfer to the ICC.

The legal regulations that govern the law of evidence in the ICC proper law are rather scarce. During the Preparatory Committee's session in 1996, an agreement was reached that only fundamental and substantive principles of evidence should appear in the Statute itself. The rationale behind this decision was to guarantee that the Court's evidentiary law would later be able to adapt to new procedural issues. It was therefore decided that less important matters would appear in the more easily amendable Rules or would be left to the jurisprudence of the Court. When drafting the Rules, adaptability was again the prevailing guideline. Instead of providing detailed evidentiary rules, the Preparatory Commission opted for the inclusion into the Rules only of a selected number of previously controversial areas. The decision on most evidentiary issues was left to the jurisprudence of the

[1]Brady 2001, p. 286.

[2]Behrens 1999, p. 243.

future judges.[3] As a result, only one article of the ICC Statute, Article 69, deals with matters of evidence. The Rules relating to this provision remain fragmentary as well.

This fragmentary nature of the law of evidence was not, however, only the result of diplomatic ambiguity. We have seen that a liberal approach to evidence is a common feature of international criminal institutions.[4] The normative framework adopted by the States Parties to the ICC Statute follows therefore the lines of the approach adopted by previous international criminal tribunals. At the ICC, the flexibility in the law of evidence goes even a step further than it does at the *Ad hoc* tribunals. The applicable law at the tribunals is shaped by the combination of an adversarial order in which evidence is presented with a liberal admissibility regime akin to the civil law principle of the judge's freedom to evaluate the evidence.[5] The ICC proper law in turn grants discretion to the judges in both respects.[6]

With respect to admissibility, Article 69(4) of the ICC Statute and Rule 63(2) of the Rules of Procedure and Evidence contain a delicate compromise between the diverging approaches of the different domestic systems. This compromise consists of eschewing a number of technical rules of evidence while, at the same time, generally allowing the judges to make a decision on the admissibility of evidence. It follows from these provisions that the bench is free in terms of the analytical method it chooses to apply. It can either rule on the admissibility of evidence at the outset or it can initially admit all evidence and consider the question of its admissibility at a later stage together with its weight.[7] So far, the judges have mainly followed the line of the *Ad hoc* tribunals: They have opted for an adversarial style for the presentation of evidence, while they have admitted evidence rather generously.[8]

4.2 The Collection of Evidence in Light of the ICC Cooperation Regime

The question whether evidence collected through improper means is admissible in ICC trials cannot be answered without first looking at the way evidence generally reaches the Court. To this end, we have to consider a number of peculiarities that shape international investigations. The most important of these peculiarities

---

[3]Behrens 1999, p. 242; Fernández de Gurmedi 2001, p. 240.

[4]See Sect. 3.1.1.

[5]See Sect. 3.1.1.

[6]The mode of submission of evidence is left entirely to the judges, see Article 64(8)(b) of the ICC Statute. Also see Damaška 2009, p. 176; Schuon 2010, p. 292.

[7]Piragoff 2001, p. 351.

[8]Combs 2011, p. 326; Schuon 2010, p. 292.

pertains to the absence of international enforcement agencies. Criminal prosecution has a major significance for the sovereignty of states. Accordingly, it was out of the question to create an international body that would bear the primary responsibility for ICC investigations.[9] As a consequence, the Court, like its predecessors, is dependent to a large extent on the cooperation of national authorities.

The importance of effective state cooperation for the successful operation of the Court has been pointed out repeatedly.[10] This concerns *inter alia* the collection of evidence. The modalities of this evidence gathering naturally also influence the later judicial assessment of evidentiary issues. The legal regime for cooperation is a decisive factor, for example, for the actors that will usually play an active part in investigations. We will see that this has consequences for the attribution of responsibility for investigative mistakes committed by national authorities.[11] Another example would pertain to the burden of proof for violations, which we will see is also influenced by the shape of a cooperation system.[12]

The cooperation regime established by the ICC proper law is different from the traditional concepts of mutual legal assistance between states. It also differs from the cooperation regimes that govern the relationship between states and the *Ad hoc* tribunals. The ICTY Appeals Chamber in the *Blaškić* case introduced a widely accepted terminology that was meant to describe the distinction. The ICTY judges termed the consensual and reciprocal cooperation regime between sovereign states a *horizontal* cooperation system while the cooperation regime between the *Ad hoc* tribunals and states has been called a *vertical* cooperation system.[13] This latter term results from the stricter obligations of national authorities vis-à-vis the international tribunals, which have the power to unilaterally impose duties on states under the powers conferred to them by the UN Security Council.[14]

The regime adopted by the States Parties to the ICC Statute in turn is a mixture of both of these cooperation models. It imposes obligations on the States Parties and requires explicitly that these states "*cooperate fully with the Court*".[15] At the same time, sovereignty concerns have prevented the adoption of a truly vertical scheme of cooperation. As a result, the treaty-based system of the ICC falls short of allocating the same kind of power to the Court that the *Ad hoc* tribunals have enjoyed, at least from a legal perspective, by virtue of their relationship with the UN Security Council.[16]

---

[9]Cryer 2009, p. 201.

[10]Cryer et al. 2010, p. 509.

[11]See Sect. 5.4.

[12]See Sect. 7.6.

[13]*Prosecutor v. Blaškić* (Judgment on the Request of the Republic of Croatia for the Review of the Decision of Trial Chamber II of July 1997), ICTY (Appeals Chamber), decision of 29 October 1997, paras 47 and 50.

[14]See Sect. 3.1.1.

[15]See Article 86 of the ICC Statute.

[16]Sluiter 2002, p. 344.

The details of the ICC cooperation regime are set forth in Part 9 of the ICC Statute. This cooperation regime is based on the primary responsibility of the States Parties to conduct investigative measures. The most significant provision for the present research is Article 93 on '*other forms of legal assistance*'. The norm makes it possible for the ICC to make '*requests*' regarding *inter alia* the collection of evidence. This includes, for instance, the questioning of both suspects and witnesses, the examination of places and sites or the execution of searches and seizures. The term '*request*' instead of '*obligation*' underlines the difference to the vertical cooperation scheme of the *Ad hoc* tribunals.[17]

Admittedly, when compared to ordinary horizontal systems of inter-state cooperation, the ICC Statute reduces significantly the grounds for a refusal to execute an ICC request.[18] But while this appears to constitute an advantage compared to the traditional cooperation between sovereign states, a number of features in the ICC cooperation regime reflect the will of the States Parties to put in place safeguards for the protection of their sovereignty. Cooperation duties can, for instance, be diminished or the compliance with them can at least be slowed down.[19] What is more, when compared to horizontal cooperation systems, these constraints are further compounded by the fact that the ICC lacks the means traditionally at the disposal of states to enforce their requests for cooperation on a bilateral level. In contrast to horizontal cooperation systems, the ICC, as an international organisation, is unable to implement economic or diplomatic sanctions against an uncooperative state, at least not without the support of its further States Parties or of the UN Security Council.

Sovereignty concerns have also shaped the modalities of the involvement of the ICC Office of the Prosecutor in the collection of evidence. Under the ICC Statute, independent on-site investigations by ICC staff are only allowed to a very limited degree. According to Article 99(4) of the ICC Statute, the power of the Prosecutor to act on his own is generally confined to non-compulsory measures. This explicitly includes the taking of voluntary witness statements and the examination

[17]Cryer et al. 2010, p. 510. The term '*obligation*' is used in *Prosecutor v. Blaškić* (Judgment on the Request of the Republic of Croatia for the Review of the Decision of Trial Chamber II of July 1997), ICTY (Appeals Chamber), decision of 29 October 1997, para 53.

[18]For the '*other forms of legal assistance*', only two grounds for refusal remain possible. States can deny cooperation firstly on national security grounds, see Articles 72, 73 and 93(4) of the ICC Statute; and secondly where the measure requested by the Court "*is prohibited in the requested State on the basis of an existing fundamental legal principle of general application*", see Article 93(3) of the ICC Statute. None of the more extensive traditional grounds for refusal, such as for example the requirement of double criminality, is permissible; see Cryer et al. 2010, p. 523.

[19]States have the possibility for instance to seek consultation, see Article 97 of the ICC Statute; or to demand for a postponement of the compliance with a request, see Articles 94 and 95 of the ICC Statute. In addition, they may also ask for a modification of the content of a request, see Article 93(3) of the ICC Statute.

without modification of a public site or other public place.[20] But even here, consultations may be required and, under certain conditions, the affected state can determine conditions that the international investigators must respect.

In addition, the Pre-Trial Chamber has the power to authorize investigative measures by the Office of the Prosecutor, including coercive measures under Article 57(3)(d) of the ICC Statute. This possibility, however, is limited to the scenario of so-called '*failed states*', meaning the case where no domestic authorities that could authorize the measure exist. No such possibility exists where the authorities are simply unwilling to conduct or permit the respective measures. In this case, as well as in any other case of non-compliance with cooperation duties, the Court is confined to refer the matter to either the Assembly of States Parties or the UN Security Council.[21]

The reluctance to allow independent investigations by the ICC Prosecutor has been criticised in view of the resulting lack of efficiency of ICC investigations.[22] In fact, a stronger involvement of OTP staff members in investigative activities would promote the efficiency of the respective measures. This concerns in particular the collection of evidence. International investigators will regularly have a better awareness of the requirements that evidence must meet in order to contribute to the success of an ICC indictment. It can *inter alia* be assumed that their presence would be likely to promote compliance with the requirements of the ICC proper law and with international human rights standards. With a view to the present research, this could avoid a later motion for the exclusion of evidence. Moreover, there are instances where witnesses will be less reluctant to speak if international investigators question them without the presence of national authorities.[23]

However, it must be conceded that despite the above, the results achieved by the negotiators of the ICC Statute with respect to OTP investigations should not be underestimated. The fact that international investigators can even conduct measures on the territory of a State Party without its consent constitutes an advantage in comparison to the options investigators in a horizontal cooperation system have.[24] Even though greater investigative powers would have been desirable, a political consensus on such a strong OTP mandate was not to be expected.[25]

[20]In practice, even the exercise of these limited powers might be hampered. The legislation of a number states on the implementation of the ICC Statute into national law expressly excludes the operation of Article 99(4) of the ICC Statute. This amounts to a violation of their obligations under Article 88 of the ICC Statute to "*ensure that there are procedures available under their national law*" for all kinds of cooperation envisaged by the ICC Statute; see Rastan 2008, p. 437.

[21]See Article 87(7) of the ICC Statute. The latter possibility is limited to situations that were referred to the Court by the UN Security Council under Article 13(b) of the ICC Statute.

[22]Sluiter 2002, p. 347.

[23]Cryer et al. 2010, p. 525.

[24]Rastan 2008, p. 437.

[25]On the difficulties to reach a consensus even for non-compulsory measures, see Kaul and Kreß 1999, p. 169.

What is more, on a practical level, the question has been raised whether, in the course of past investigations, ICC investigators have even exhausted those options for independent investigations that are legally available to them.[26] In this context, the OTP has been criticised for the large extent to which it has outsourced investigative tasks to so-called intermediaries. Intermediaries are individuals on the ground that are regularly used by the OTP to facilitate contact with victims and witnesses in view of the often precarious security situations in areas affected by ICC proceedings. The assessment of their involvement in investigations was a major issue in the *Lubanga* case. In this context, the ICC Trial Chamber has criticized the lack of proper oversight of intermediaries by the OTP.[27] In the context of the present research, the use of such intermediaries raises the question whether and to what extent misconduct by the latter is relevant for the exclusion of evidence.[28]

Turning to the comparison with the vertical cooperation system of the *Ad hoc* tribunals, it has been argued that the differences between the ICC and the *Ad hoc* tribunals in terms of cooperation are less significant in practice than in theory. In fact, the legal powers allocated to the *Ad hoc* tribunals by the Security Council have not prevented problems of non-compliance.[29] Ultimately, both the ICC and the *Ad hoc* tribunals are predominantly governed by indirect enforcement systems.[30] Such systems depend in any case on the willingness of states to cooperate. Moreover, courts and tribunals should not expect much action from those bodies which, unlike the courts and tribunals themselves, could theoretically impose sanctions on recalcitrant states. Such measures are highly contentious from a political point of view. Accordingly, the *Ad hoc* tribunals have in practice often followed a procedure that was not that different from the one under the ICC Statute. In an attempt for diplomacy, the ICTY and ICTR judges have urged their prosecutors to first call upon the domestic authorities. The judges decided that the use of direct enforcement powers was constrained to situations where these authorities were not available.[31]

---

[26]See Buisman 2013, p. 30 et seq. for a critical discussion from the perspective of a defence lawyer involved *inter alia* in the ICC proceedings in the cases *Katanga* as well as *Ruto*.

[27]*Prosecutor v. Lubanga* (Judgment pursuant to Article 74 of the Statute), ICC (Trial Chamber), decision of 14 March 2012, paras 178 et seq. and 482.

[28]See Sect. 5.4.

[29]Cryer 2009, p. 187 and p. 198; Cryer et al. 2010, p. 528 et seq.; Jackson and Summers 2012, p. 114.

[30]Rastan 2008, p. 455.

[31]*Prosecutor v. Blaškić* (Judgment on the Request of the Republic of Croatia for the Review of the Decision of Trial Chamber II of July 1997), ICTY (Appeals Chamber), decision of 29 October 1997, para 55. A similar conclusion has been drawn by the ICTR, see for instance *Prosecutor v. Bagosora et al.* (Decision on the Defence for Bagosora's Request to Obtain the Cooperation of the Republic of Ghana), ICTR (Trial Chamber), decision of 25 May 2004, para 6. See also De Meester et al. 2013, p. 283 et seq. Note however that the cooperation of the ICTR with the Rwandan government has been particularly complicated and has at times been characterized by considerable power struggles; see Peskin 2009, p. 170 et seq.

Despite these reservations, when compared to the ICC, a considerable difference, at least with the ICTY, lies in the fact that the ICTY judges have made an exception to the approach outlined above for the states and entities of the former Yugoslavia. In these areas, which are particularly important for the investigations of the ICTY, the prosecution has been granted a right of direct enforcement without first involving domestic authorities.[32] In comparison, the ICC faces problems of enforcement in particular in those areas that are crucial for its investigations. Under the principle of complementarity, the Court can only exercise its jurisdiction where the state that would normally have jurisdiction is either unwilling or unable to prosecute the allegedly committed crimes.[33] Accordingly, for measures that do not fall under Articles 99(4) and 57(3)(d) of the ICC Statute, the prosecution regularly needs the cooperation of states that have been labelled either unwilling or unable to take action. It is obviously no easy task to ensure that such a state will help effectively with investigative measures, including the taking of evidence.[34] It can be added that the ICC is also in a more difficult situation than the *Ad hoc* tribunals for factual reasons: unlike the latter, the former partly operates in conflicts that are still ongoing, which makes the taking of evidence an even greater challenge.[35]

In summary, a consideration of the process of evidence gathering requires taking a number of differences between investigations for the ICC and domestic investigations, as well as between the ICC and investigations for the *Ad hoc* tribunals, into account.

Any comparison with the *Ad hoc* tribunals must take into account the different legal frameworks governing these judicial bodies, in particular the—albeit restricted—greater powers of the *Ad hoc* tribunals under their vertical cooperation regime. And it must also consider the factual differences between the situations these bodies operate in.

Any comparison with national investigations, on the other hand, must make allowance for the indirect enforcement model that the States Parties to the ICC have agreed upon. This model sets ICC investigations apart from national proceedings, which regularly operate in a system of direct enforcement. The ICC, in

---

[32]The tribunal has justified this exception by referring to the possible implication of authorities in the crimes in these areas, see *Prosecutor v. Blaškić* (Judgment on the Request of the Republic of Croatia for the Review of the Decision of Trial Chamber II of July 1997), ICTY (Appeals Chamber), decision of 29 October 1997, paras 53 and 55.

[33]Rastan 2008, p. 455. The *Ad hoc* tribunals on the other hand have jurisdiction over the states on the territory of the former Yugoslavia since 1991 and on the territory of Rwanda and—where Rwandan citizens are alleged to be responsible—for such violations committed in the territory of neighbouring States between 1 January 1994 and 31 December 1994 respectively, independently of any own jurisdictional competence of the affected states, see Article 1 of the ICTY Statute and Article 1 of the ICTR Statute.

[34]Even in case of a self-referral, where full compliance should be expected, a state may fail to live up to these expectations due to practical circumstances, see Cryer et al. 2010, p. 529.

[35]Cryer et al. 2010, p. 529.

comparison, is often confronted with a lack of overview and control over investigations. Compared in turn to domestic cases concerning cross-border crime, the ICC may, theoretically, enjoy larger powers than states in cases of inter-state cooperation. In practice, however, these advantages are unlikely to compensate for the lack of political pressure available to the Court.

4.3 The Legal Framework for the Exclusion of Evidence

4.3.1 The Admissibility of Evidence in General

The general approach of the ICC to the admissibility of evidence, as set forth in Article 69(4) of the ICC Statute, parallels what is demanded at the ICTY and at the ICTR. By stipulating that the ICC judges "*may rule on the relevance or admissibility of any evidence, taking into account,* inter alia, *the probative value of the evidence and any prejudice that such evidence may cause to a fair trial*", the provision refers to the same basic requirements as the *Ad hoc* tribunals.[36]

While, according to this provision, relevance and admissibility are distinct from each other, the case law applies a comprehensive approach covering both notions.[37] To this effect, the Trial Chamber in the *Lubanga* case established a threefold test. This test consists of a *prima facie* evaluation firstly of whether the evidence is relevant and, secondly, of whether it has probative value. In a third step, the Chamber must then "*weigh the probative value of the evidence against its prejudicial effect*".[38]

Once again, the threshold for the first two requirements is not very high. Relevance is merely a precondition for admissibility.[39] For evidence to be relevant, it must only relate to the matters that the Chamber has to consider in view of the charges.[40] The second requirement, probative value, is an established concept of common law. It has been defined as "*evidence that tends to prove or disprove a point in issue*".[41] According to the jurisprudence of international courts and tribunals, to have probative value, the evidence must, in particular, have some

---

[36]On the similarities between the requirements for admissibility, see Gosnell 2010, p. 376 et seq.

[37]Safferling 2012, p. 492.

[38]*Prosecutor v. Lubanga* (Corrigendum to Redacted Decision on the Defence Request for the Admission of 422 documents), ICC (Trial Chamber), decision of 8 March 2011, para 39. On this test, see also Safferling 2012, p. 490; Gaynor et al. 2013, p. 1023.

[39]*Prosecutor v. Katanga and Chui* (Decision on the Prosecutor's Bar Table Motions), ICC (Trial Chamber), decision of 17 December 2010, para 16. See also on the jurisprudence of the *Ad hoc* tribunals, Sect. 3.1.3.

[40]*Prosecutor v. Lubanga* (Corrigendum to Redacted Decision on the Defence Request for the Admission of 422 documents), ICC (Trial Chamber), decision of 8 March 2011, para 39.

[41]Gaynor et al. 2013, p. 1022.

component of reliability.[42] In addition, the ICC Trial Chamber has held that probative value entails that the evidence has some significance.[43] The third prong of the test is the most interesting for the admissibility of illicitly obtained evidence. The balancing required between the probative value of the evidence and its prejudicial effect on trial fairness may theoretically be used as a legal basis for the exclusion of tainted evidence. This part of Article 69(4) is reminiscent of Rule 89(D) of the ICTY Statute. But unlike in the latter provision, the balancing exercise is not conceived as a distinct exclusionary rule. Instead, fair trial considerations are inserted in the legal basis for the general decision on the admissibility of evidence.[44]

There is, however, in the ICC Statute a provision that does contain a distinct exclusionary rule, namely Article 69(7). Before turning to the relationship between Articles 69(4) and 69(7), the latter norm shall be presented in more detail.

In general, Article 69(7) implements a similar approach to the one laid down in Rule 95 of the ICTY and ICTR Rules of Procedure and Evidence. The provision, which will subsequently be referred to as the ICC exclusionary rule, reads as follows:

> Evidence obtained by means of a violation of this Statute or internationally recognized human rights shall not be admissible if:
>
> a. The violation casts substantial doubt on the reliability of the evidence; or
> b. The admission of the evidence would be antithetical to and would seriously damage the integrity of the proceedings.

There was, at first, no agreement within the Preparatory Committee on the general basis for exclusion. The central issue was whether the emphasis should be placed on the manner in which the evidence was collected or whether the focus should be on the effects that such a violation might have on the proceedings. The first of these proposals would have corresponded to the original wording of Rule 95 of the RPE of both of the *Ad hoc* tribunals, while the latter would have been similar to the tribunal's rule in its amended version.[45]

The consensus that finally emerged combines both prerequisites: The starting point of any exclusion is that evidence was collected in violation of a person's

---

[42]See Gosnell 2010, p. 384 et seq.; Gaynor et al. 2013, p. 1022.

[43]*Prosecutor v. Katanga and Chui* (Decision on the Prosecutor's Bar Table Motions), ICC (Trial Chamber), decision of 17 December 2010, paras 20 and 34. See also Safferling 2012, p. 493. Significance refers to "[…] *the measure by which an item of evidence is likely to influence the determination of a particular issue in the case.*", see *Prosecutor v. Katanga and Chui* (Decision on the Prosecutor's Bar Table Motions), ICC (Trial Chamber), decision of 17 December 2010, para 35. But where the test of admissibility is made at the end of the trial, this second criterion can hardly be distinguished as an own requirement from the overall weight of the evidence, see *Prosecutor v. Bemba* (Decision on the admission into evidence of materials contained in the prosecution's list of evidence), ICC (Trial Chamber), decision of 19 November 2010, para 9, where probative value is defined as pertaining "[…] *inter alia, to the reliability and weight to be attached to the evidence concerned.*"

[44]Combs 2011, p. 328.

[45]For more details on Rule 95 of the RPE of the *Ad hoc* tribunals, see Sect. 3.1.3.

rights. At the same time, exclusion as a remedy for such a violation is only available in case of a specific negative impact on the proceedings, namely that the evidence either lacks reliability or that its admission "*would be antithetical to and would seriously damage the integrity of the proceedings*".[46]

This combination has important consequences. At first sight, the provision is formulated as a mandatory rule. The inclusion of additional requirements, however, changes its character into a discretionary rule.[47]

This formulation of the provision has met a lot of criticism, both among delegates during the consultations and among commentators. This criticism is directed against Article 69(7)(b) in particular. The argument is that it seems difficult to imagine any instance where the admission of evidence gained in violation of human rights would not damage the integrity of the proceedings.[48] As a consequence, commentators have argued, even after the adoption of the final wording, that the provision should be interpreted based on the assumption that every human rights violation *ipso facto* fulfils the requirements of the second prong.[49]

The formulation of the provision however does not seem to allow for such an equation. It would lead, at least with regard to human rights violations, to an automatic exclusion of the tainted evidence. The drafters of the ICC Statute, however, have clearly opted for a different policy. To this extent, a similar assessment can be made as for Rule 95 of the RPE of the ICTY and ICTR.[50] Despite the fact that Article 69(7) of the ICC Statute is formulated as a mandatory rule, its wording contains a number of vague legal terms whose interpretation requires the exercise of evaluation and thus grants discretion to the judges.[51] This is done in particular through the interpretation of its two subparagraphs, providing for tests of reliability and prejudice.[52] This assessment corresponds to the existing case law on the provision. The Pre-Trial Chamber in *Lubanga* explained the general principle governing the exclusion of evidence at the ICC claiming that "[…] *article 69(7) of the ICC Statute rejects the notion that evidence procured in violation of internationally recognised human rights should be automatically excluded. Consequently, the judges have the discretion to seek an appropriate balance between the Statute's fundamental values in each concrete case.*"[53] The Trial Chamber confirmed this

---

[46]Triffterer 2008—Piragoff, Article 69, para 16 et seq.

[47]Miraglia 2008, p. 492; Safferling 2012, p. 499.

[48]Sluiter 2002, p. 226; Triffterer 2008—Piragoff, Article 69, para 70; Zahar and Sluiter 2008, p. 382; Zappalà 2002, p. 152.

[49]Zahar and Sluiter 2008, p. 382; Zappalà 2003, p. 152.

[50]See Sect. 3.1.3.

[51]Triffterer 2008—Piragoff, Article 69, para 66.

[52]Schabas 2010, p. 848.

[53]*Prosecutor v. Lubanga* (Decision on the confirmation of charges), ICC (Pre-Trial Chamber), decision of 29 January 2007, para 84. For a review of this decision, see Miraglia 2008, p. 492 et seq. In addition, also see *Prosecutor v. Mbarushimana* (Decision on the confirmation of charges), ICC (Pre-Trial Chamber), decision of 16 December 2011, para 61.

understanding in the same case, explicitly rejecting the view that automatic inferences follow from human rights violations.[54]

In other words, the provision follows the approach outlined above accepted in many legal systems, both at the international and at the domestic level, to predicate the decision on the exclusion of evidence on a discretionary decision of the judges. The execution of this judicial discretion is an integral part of the interpretation of the constituent elements of Article 69(7) of the ICC Statute. Discretion guides in particular the decision in the more contentious situation where reliable evidence is challenged on the basis of a violation. In this situation, Article 69(7)(b) calls for a balancing exercise.

It is not possible therefore to claim that human rights violations generally lead to the exclusion of tainted evidence. However, it may very well be argued that exclusion is generally warranted in cases of a certain category of violations. This is not as such contrary to the discretionary nature of the provision. Where a certain violation is generally severe enough, the discretion of the bench may be constricted to a point where the balancing exercise can lead to no other decision than exclusion. This has been held to be the case, for instance, where evidence has been obtained as a result of torture.[55]

Article 69(7) ostensibly requires a higher threshold than its equivalent in the Rules of the *Ad hoc* tribunals. Unlike the latter, it provides for a two-part exclusionary rule, namely a violation in the obtaining of evidence *and* a detrimental effect with regard to its admission to the trial.[56] Rule 95 of the RPE of the ICTY and ICTR in contrast only contains the second part of this test. This does not mean, however, that the different formulations necessarily lead to diverging results. In essence, both provisions require a balancing exercise. We will see that in Article 69(7) of the ICC Statute, just as in the ICTY and ICTR Rule, the crucial element is the second part, namely the detrimental effect on the proceedings. This is the part that gives rise to problems of interpretation.[57] Moreover, Rule 95 implicitly requires a prior violation leading to the subsequent detrimental effect. Admittedly, in contrast to the ICC provision, the types of norm whose violation may trigger exclusion are not expressly delimited in Rule 95.[58]

The explanations above have demonstrated that, theoretically, two provisions allow for the exclusion of illicitly obtained evidence: the general admissibility rule of Article 69(4) and the exclusionary rule of Article 69(7). Similar to the Rules of the ICTY, the parallel existence of two norms raises the question of their relationship.[59] In particular, the difference between "*fair trial*" and the "*integrity of the*

[54] *Prosecutor v. Lubanga* (Decision on the admission of material from the "bar table"), ICC (Trial Chamber), decision of 24 June 2009, para 41.

[55] Triffterer 2008—Piragoff, Article 69, para 71. For more details, see Sect. 5.4.3.

[56] Combs 2011, p. 328; Sluiter 2002, p. 224.

[57] Sluiter 2002, p. 224.

[58] Alamuddin 2010, p. 240.

[59] On the parallel question with regard to Rules 89 (D) and 95 of the RPE of the ICTY, see Sect. 3.1.3.

proceedings" does not seem evident.[60] The Trial Chamber in *Lubanga* clarified the relationship between these two paragraphs, stating that Article 69(7) of the ICC Statute was *lex specialis* to other rules on admissibility, including Article 69(4).[61]

Despite the different formulation of the provision, Article 69(4) of the ICC Statute bears similarity to Rule 89(D) of the ICTY RPE. Like the latter, the former is not confined to fair trial infringements resulting from the methods of collection of evidence. In accordance with their assumption that Article 69(7) is to be considered *lex specialis*, the ICC judges, unlike their colleagues at the ICTY, have refrained from using the general rule on admissibility for their decision when confronted with illicitly obtained evidence.[62] Instead, they have dealt with this issue under the more specific exclusionary rule of Article 69(7). The fact that Article 69(4) was not conceived as a further exclusionary rule has probably benefited this jurisprudence.

As a consequence, the following research will focus on Article 69(7) of the ICC Statute as the decisive ICC exclusionary rule. The scheme followed by Article 69(7) can be summarized in the following way: The main ICC exclusionary rule requires a test that consists of two steps. The first step is described in the first part or *chapeau* of the provision. It consists of a determination of all of those violations in the gathering of evidence that may trigger the exclusionary rule. These may be either violations of the Statute or of "*internationally recognized human rights*". The discretionary nature of the exclusionary rule is most evident from the fact that the inquiry does not stop here. Instead, Article 69(7) of the ICC Statute provides for a second step that allows to the judges to filter out, from the abundance of violations possible during the gathering of evidence, those violations that result in exclusion.

This inquiry demands justification. More precisely: why do certain violations lead to exclusion, while others do not? In order to guide the discretion of the judges, Article 69(7) contains two options that describe the justification for this selection. In other words, subparas (b) and (c) pertain to the purposes of exclusion. Only where at least one of these purposes is fulfilled is the exclusion of evidence gathered for ICC trials warranted. Naturally, the purposes that are prominently described in these two subparagraphs must also be taken into account when interpreting the rest of the provision. As a consequence, the deliberations below will not follow the composition of Article 69(7) of the ICC Statute. Instead, they will first concentrate on the justification of the ICC exclusionary rule reflected in subparas (a) and (b). This will include reflections on the reason for the choice of these very purposes for the ICC exclusionary rule, when compared to other possible justifications that guide exclusion in domestic legal systems. Only then will this research turn to the interpretation of the *chapeau* and to the details of the balancing exercise under Article 69(7) of the ICC Statute.

---

[60] Alamuddin 2010, p. 241 and p. 242.

[61] *Prosecutor v. Lubanga* (Decision on the admission of material from the "bar table"), ICC (Trial Chamber), decision of 24 June 2009, paras 34 and 43.

[62] On the respective jurisprudence of the *Ad hoc* tribunals, see Sect. 3.1.3.

4.3.2 *The Purpose of the ICC Exclusionary Rule*

4.3.2.1 Introduction

Some of the uncertainties regarding the exclusion of evidence in international proceedings result from a lack of theoretical foundations. At the domestic level, exclusion is usually justified on the basis of four different rationales: a lack of reliability of the respective evidence, deterrence, the vindication of individual rights and the maintenance of procedural integrity. All of these concepts have already been mentioned when explaining the different domestic approaches to exclusion. At the international level, none of the bodies of international criminal adjudication have clearly explained their approach to the exclusion of evidence. Neither has the problem been discussed in detail in the legal literature.

In the case of the ICC, the Statute provides insight into the purposes that must guide ICC judges when exercising their discretion under Article 69(7). Subparagraphs (a) and (b) reflect the purposes that the drafters of the Statute thought most appropriate in ICC proceedings, namely guaranteeing the reliability of evidence and preserving the integrity of the Court. Despite this legislative decision, references to other rationales have sometimes emerged in the literature and in international case law, including that of the ICC. The following deliberations will therefore consider all of the previously mentioned rationales. This will enable an understanding of the choice that was made for Article 69(7) and a determination whether other justifications play a role in addition to those reflected in the wording of the provision. The exclusion of reliable evidence is comparatively uncontroversial. As a consequence, the discussion will concentrate on the more contentious cases under Article 69(7)((b). These cases will be the starting point of the following analysis. It will then give some consideration to the exclusion of reliable evidence under subpara (a).

4.3.2.2 The Purpose of Excluding Reliable Evidence

The exclusion of reliable but tainted evidence is one of the most controversial topics in the law of criminal procedure of many countries. The different and sometimes overlapping approaches that can be identified in domestic debates vary both with respect to the degree to which they endorse the idea of an exclusionary rule and, if they do so at all, to the way they justify this rule.

The first line of argument opposes exclusion altogether; on the other end of the scale, the proponents of a mandatory exclusionary rule argue that the exclusion of evidence should be the automatic consequence of every violation. While the arguments of the remaining views are sometimes drawn upon to justify a mandatory exclusionary rule, most of their advocates today adopt a middle course between the general admissibility and the automatic exclusion of illicitly obtained evidence. These views offer rival rationales underpinning the exclusion of illicitly obtained evidence under certain conditions. In this latter category, the analysis of the domestic approaches has identified as one rationale the so-called theory of deterrence, namely the idea that exclusion serves as a tool to discipline investigating authorities. The exclusion of cogent but tainted evidence has also been justified by resorting to what is usually labelled the remedial or protective approach, according to which exclusion is principally concerned with the vindication of the individual rights of the accused. Finally, it has been held that exclusion can best be explained by resorting to a theory of integrity or legitimacy. The overall idea of this last conception is that by admitting improperly obtained evidence, a court endangers its moral authority.

The wording of Article 69(7)(b) of the ICC Statute suggests that it is essentially the integrity rationale that may serve as a basis for the ICC exclusionary rule.[63] Where the reliability of evidence is not at issue, the provision demands that the admission of tainted evidence "*would be antithetical to and would seriously damage the integrity of the proceedings*".

As we will see, this choice was a sensible one. Not only is the integrity theory probably the best justification for the exclusion of reliable evidence in general, including in trials at the domestic level, it is also the only justification that sufficiently takes into account the particular context of international criminal proceedings. Before turning to the integrity theory, however, the competing approaches shall be assessed.

4.3.2.2.1 Opposing Arguments

In domestic proceedings, the exclusion of evidence solely on grounds of a rights violation has sometimes been rejected altogether. The starting point of such views is that the focus of admissibility should be on reliability and accuracy only. The traditional common law approach in particular did not consider as relevant the manner in which evidence was obtained except for cases where its reliability was thereby affected.[64]

Such an argument is clearly incompatible with the wording of the ICC Statute. The initially cumulative effect requirements of Article 69(7) of the Statute were ultimately made disjunctive.[65] By introducing in this way an alternative for exclusion independent from reliability, the drafters of the ICC Statute made clear that importance is to be attached to values other than the mere trustworthiness of the evidence.

But beyond this evident policy choice of the ICC Statute, the arguments put forward to oppose a value based exclusionary rule can also be dismissed in principle. In domestic systems, the position that rejects the exclusion of reliable evidence altogether has usually been labelled the 'separation thesis'.[66] The separation

[63] Zahar and Sluiter 2008, p. 380.

[64] See Sect. 3.3.1.

[65] Triffterer 2008—Piragoff, Article 69, para 18.

[66] Jackson and Summers 2012, p. 155.

thesis includes the argument that there is no real connection between a rights violation in the investigative phase and the admissibility of evidence in trial. Moreover, it is claimed that investigating authorities on the one hand and the judiciary on the other are entirely separate institutions.[67]

The first of these claims has been countered at the national level by an argument that equally applies in the international context. The pre-trial and trial phases are not in fact distinct sequences within criminal proceedings. They are rather intimately linked. The former is only a means of laying the foundations for the latter. This may include arresting the suspect or, more relevantly, gathering the evidence required for a conviction.[68] As a consequence, courts, be it at the national or at the international level, cannot simply deny any connection with those acts that have produced the very evidence on which their verdicts are based.

The assertion, however, that the police and the judiciary are entirely separate institutions seems easier to refute at the national than at the international level. In the domestic context, opponents to the separation thesis have pointed to the fact that both the police and the courts are parts of the same state and its criminal justice system. In light of this common institutional embedding, they are in fact two closely linked components of law enforcement.[69]

At the international level, there is no uniting under the auspices of a state. There is a clear institutional separation between the ICC and the national authorities, which are mostly active at the investigative phase. At first sight, this seems to be a strong argument for not holding the former responsible for the failures of the latter. But such an allegation would ignore that this separation is the result of a deliberate choice of the ICC States Parties. Instead of creating a proper enforcement mechanism for the ICC, the States Parties have decided to assign the main part of the investigative tasks to national authorities.

This decision is based on the understandable desire of states to safeguard their sovereignty. It cannot however be intended to entirely circumvent those responsibilities that arise from the enforcement of international criminal justice. The Court and the investigating authorities are part of the same international criminal justice system. They have a shared responsibility for the guarantee of fundamental rights in the international context.[70] We will see later that the loose institutional connection between the ICC and domestic authorities does in fact influence to a certain degree the attribution of violations to the Court.[71] As a matter of principle, however, this type of connection cannot be relied upon to create the illusion of a general separability.

---

[67]For an example of a prominent proponent of this thesis, see Wigmore 1922, p. 479 et seq.

[68]Ashworth 2003, p. 114; Roberts and Zuckerman 2010, p. 189.

[69]Ashworth 2003, p. 115.

[70]Similar, Zahar and Sluiter 2008, p. 380.

[71]See Sect. 5.4. In this context, see also the parallel question of the accountability of the ICC in case of investigative mistakes committed by intermediaries.

4.3.2.2.2 Exclusion as an Automatic Rule

The separation thesis examined above is one of the two extreme positions with respect to the exclusion of illicitly obtained evidence. At the opposite end of the scale, proponents of a mandatory exclusionary rule in different legal systems have supported the idea that tainted evidence should never be admitted as evidence in a court of law. As we have seen above, despite first appearances, Article 69(7) of the ICC Statute is not conceived as an automatic exclusionary rule. Its discretionary nature results in particular from the inclusion of the two subparas (a) and (b).[72] This discretionary nature was confirmed by the ICC in its first decisions.[73] Given that the present research is meant as an analysis of the status quo of an existing provision of the ICC Statute, the inquiry could simply stop here, by pointing to the obvious policy choice of the drafters of the ICC Statute, embodied in Article 69(7) of the ICC Statute. For the sake of completeness, however, we will briefly address the question of whether this was a sensible policy choice policy.

As mentioned above, the existing version of the ICC exclusionary rule with its restricting additional subparagraphs was heavily criticized both by participants at the Rome Conference and by commentators.[74] Some commentators have even argued that, despite its wording, Article 69(7) should be interpreted, at least with respect to all human rights violations, as a mandatory exclusionary rule.[75] It has been argued above that this view cannot be sustained given the clear wording of the provision. The criticism, however, reflects the need to answer a very basic question. How can it be that a court such as the ICC is put in a more favourable position through the possibility of using evidence that has evidently been obtained by means contrary to its own law and even contrary to human rights? In other words, would the drafters of the ICC Statute have been better advised to adopt a mandatory exclusionary rule after all?

This research is based on the assumption that applying a mandatory exclusionary rule to the Court's proceedings would not be appropriate for reasons beyond the positivistic argument of the policy choice made by the drafters of the ICC Statute. We will see below that all of the classical rationales for the exclusion of evidence could, in principle, be construed in a way that would call for a mandatory exclusionary rule. Theoretically, the deterrence theory, as well as the remedial theory and the theory of integrity, can be understood either in a more restrictive and inclusionary or in a more liberal way. At first sight, an automatic exclusionary rule may even seem more appropriate for an international court with a firm commitment to due process rights. Proportionality concerns, however, suggest refraining from such an all-purpose rule.

---

[72]See Sect. 4.3.1.

[73]See *Prosecutor v. Lubanga* (Decision on the Admission of Material from the "Bar Table'), ICC (Trial Chamber), decision of 24 June 2009, para 41; *Prosecutor v. Lubanga* (Decision on the Confirmation of Charges), ICC (Pre-Trial Chamber), decision of 29 January 2007, paras 84 and 90.

[74]See Sect. 4.3.1.

[75]Zahar and Sluiter 2008, p. 382; Zappalà 2003, p. 152.

The review of domestic systems has revealed, as a very basic principle, that bright line rules are doomed to failure when it comes to the question whether or not to exclude tainted evidence.[76] Such rules fail to sufficiently do justice to the moral and legal complexity of the issue.[77] This conclusion also applies to the imposition of a mandatory exclusionary rule. The respect for the different rights affected in the course of an investigation is without any doubt paramount. At the same time, these rights are not the only values that must be upheld in criminal proceedings. The interests of both society in general and of the victims of a crime are valid concerns that must equally be taken into account.

This brings us back to the tension between the protection, in particular,[78] of individual rights on the one hand and the need for the effective prosecution of crimes on the other, which was mentioned at the very outset of this research.[79] In view of these competing values, automatic exclusionary rules are in danger of yielding disproportionate results because they focus exclusively and too narrowly on the rights protected in the course of evidence gathering.[80] The idea of a mandatory exclusionary rule has been challenged because such rules force courts to categorically ignore the discovery of cogent evidence without ever considering other interests and values. Critics have invoked the crime control responsibilities of states. Once evidence has been discovered, the official knowledge of the facts puts the state and its authorities in a problematic position. Having a responsibility towards its citizens to control crime, the state cannot categorically pretend not to know of a crime and of the danger that the suspect possibly poses to society.[81]

It is because of their one-sided focus that mandatory exclusionary rules have not prevailed in domestic systems. This is most explicitly illustrated by the mandatory exclusionary rule initially conceived by the U.S. Supreme Court.[82] Despite the development by the Supreme Court of a mandatory exclusionary rule, its critics ultimately prevailed. Up until today, this mandatory exclusionary rule has been eroded through a number of important exceptions. Leaving aside the question of whether the U.S. exclusionary rule in its current form strikes the appropriate balance, the erosion of the automatic exclusionary rule shows that one-sided solutions are not viable and socially acceptable in the long-term.

In the case of the ICC, the focus of crime control is less on averting the danger posed by a specific perpetrator than in domestic criminal proceedings. It is rather on the enhancement of the general belief in the validity of international criminal

---

[76]See in particular Sects. 3.3.2 and 3.3.4.

[77]Cryer et al. 2010, p. 190. Similar, Muthorst 2009, p. 75. For the opposite view with respect to the ICC, Vanderpuye 2005, p. 129 et seq.

[78]On the protection of the rights of states during the collection of evidence, see in particular Sect. 4.3.2.2.4.

[79]See Sect. 1.1.

[80]Penney 2003, p. 112. Critical with respect to this argument, Potter 1983, p. 1396.

[81]Dennis 2010, p. 106; Roberts and Zuckerman 2010, p. 183.

[82]Roberts and Zuckerman 2010, p. 182.

law.[83] This belief, however, would also be threatened by a strong mandatory rule of exclusion. We have already mentioned that the legitimacy of the Court does not only depend on its respect for due process rights. It is also closely linked to its capacity to enforce international criminal law.[84] It would be disproportionate to categorically ignore credible evidence related to gross human rights atrocities. These arguments were central to the creation of the ICC exclusionary rule in its present form. Accordingly, the drafters of the ICC Statute were well advised to implement an exclusionary rule that leaves sufficient room to the Court's judges to take into account the interests of effective law enforcement.

4.3.2.2.3 The Deterrence Rationale

In domestic law, one of the strongest justifications for the exclusion of evidence has traditionally been the alleged disciplining effect on the police. We have seen that the so-called deterrence rationale has been discussed in a number of domestic legal orders and has had a particularly strong impact on the U.S. exclusionary rule. But even in the domestic debates, this approach has drawn severe criticism both for practical and for theoretical reasons. At the international level in turn, the ICTY has held that exclusion in international proceedings cannot be directed at disciplining domestic authorities.[85] The ICC in *Lubanga* adopted this jurisprudence. It has not, however, conclusively assessed the question of deterrence for investigative measures carried out by OTP staff itself.[86] The following section will show that, not least because of the particularities of the system of international criminal justice, the deterrence theory is generally not the appropriate justification for exclusion in ICC proceedings.

In the domestic context, doubt exists as to whether, from a practical point of view, the exclusionary rule is actually able to achieve the purported deterrent effect.[87] It has been pointed out that, often, there will be no such effect because officials believe that their misconduct will not come to light. In addition, it has also been held that the behaviour of the police is usually not motivated by the conviction of an individual suspect. It is rather encouraged by other considerations such as maintenance of order or intelligence gathering.[88]

In general, it is safe to say that the practical effect of deterrence is in any event difficult to prove. Proponents of the theory have repeatedly sought to demonstrate

---

[83]On the purposes of special and general prevention at the international level, see Sect. 2.2.3.

[84]See Sect. 2.2.3.

[85]*Prosecutor v. Brđanin* (Decision on the Defence "Objection to Intercept Evidence"), ICTY (Trial Chamber), decision of 3 October 2003, para 63.

[86]*Prosecutor v. Lubanga* (Decision on the Admission of Material from the 'Bar Table'), ICC (Trial Chamber), decision of 24 June 2009, para 44.

[87]Jackson and Summers 2012, p. 154; Ma 1999, p. 297.

[88]Ashworth and Redmayne 2010, p. 344; Roberts and Zuckerman 2010, p. 187; Slobogin 2013, p. 16.

that there is a visible deterrent effect even if it is not perfect.[89] A considerable amount of research has been conducted on the subject. The results of the respective empirical studies, however, remain ambiguous.[90]

On a theoretical level, domestic scholars have argued that the objective of deterrence is better served by means outside of the trial forum. This may involve criminal investigations or the imposition of disciplinary measures against the officials involved. These arguments are based on the view that a disciplining function is alien to the concept and aim of criminal proceedings and thus better left to alternative mechanisms. This point has had a major impact on the debate in a number of domestic systems. In Germany, for instance, it is this very argument that has led the majority of legal academia to oppose the deterrence rationale.[91] Similar deliberations can be found in the English,[92] Canadian[93] and U.S. literature.[94] Where the decision on exclusion has been predicated on a balancing exercise, deterrence has often been considered a weak factor at best, unable to outweigh the public interest in prosecution[95]

In the specific context of ICC proceedings, the previous arguments apply all the more, particularly in cases of violations committed by domestic officials. The success of deterrence with respect to domestic authorities must be doubted for a number of practical reasons. It is first of all questionable whether the ICC as a court situated in a foreign country that has no legal power in the states themselves is sufficiently recognized as an authority by domestic police forces. These police forces will actually often have little knowledge about ICC proceedings at all. Furthermore, only a small number of domestic cases actually fall under the jurisdiction of the Court. Deterrence, however, can only be successful if the exclusion of evidence is a regular repercussion of official misconduct. The exclusion of evidence in single cases before the ICC is unlikely to make much of an impression on investigators when compared to the many cases they are confronted with that fall under national jurisdiction.[96]

The ICTY, when rejecting deterrence as an objective of Rule 95 in the *Brđanin* case, seems to have relied *inter alia* on such practical considerations. We have seen above that the system of cooperation between the *Ad hoc* tribunal and states is a vertical one. This means that the ICTY is an international criminal institution that is endowed with stronger authority over states than the ICC. Regardless of this relationship, the judges stated that they were not convinced that they had the power to discourage domestic authorities from using such measures in the

[89]Penney 2003, p. 114.

[90]See Bilz 2012, p. 150, with further references.

[91]Amelung and Mittag 2005, p. 615; Eisenberg 2011, p. 125; Muthorst 2009, p. 55.

[92]Roberts and Zuckerman 2010, p. 188.

[93]See Penney 2003, p. 120 et seq. with further references.

[94]Slobogin 1999, p. 363 et seq.

[95]Jackson and Summers 2012, p. 155.

[96]Similar, Berger 2012, p. 38.

future.[97] This must be true all the more for a court like the ICC whose cooperation system is characterized by a weaker position vis-à-vis states.

In addition, theoretical arguments can be advanced against the validity of the deterrence theory with respect to ICC proceedings. To this effect, two further differences between national proceedings and ICC proceedings need to be taken into account.

The first is closely connected to the practical arguments advanced above. It concerns the weak institutional connection between domestic investigating authorities and the Court. The discussion of the separation thesis has demonstrated that these actors of international criminal justice cannot be regarded as entirely disconnected.[98] At the same time, the link between them is clearly weaker than it is between investigators and courts at the domestic level. As a result of this weak institutional connection, ICC trials are an even more inappropriate forum to address investigative misconduct than domestic trials. To obtain evidence, the Court depends to a large extent on domestic authorities, which carry out many investigative measures independently. The ICC, in this setting, has only very little influence on the actual way investigative measures are implemented. As a result of the non-vertical nature of the ICC cooperation regime, this is even the case where evidence gathering is carried out at the behest of the international prosecutor. It seems however misplaced in a trial conducted by an international court to deal with acts carried out by officials of a sovereign state that this court cannot control. Attempts by the Court to not only serve as a moral role model but to openly discipline national investigation forces would in fact be regarded as infringing upon state sovereignty.[99] It should be noted that these arguments are not to be confused with the claims made by proponents of the separation thesis. There is no general disconnection between the acts of the Court and the investigating authorities. But the existing connection does not justify the conferral of responsibility on the ICC to exercise influence over the future conduct of domestic investigations through its procedure. Where exclusion nevertheless has an educational impact on national authorities, this is rather to be considered merely a positive side effect.

The second difference between national proceedings and ICC proceedings relevant in this context pertains to the subject matter of the ICC. The Court is dealing with crimes that are considerably more serious than the average crime at the domestic level. As a consequence, applying the deterrence rationale would cause an imbalance. The seriousness of the crimes is certainly not a reason to generally restrict the validity of human rights.[100] But the purpose to exercise, with very uncertain outcomes, a deterrent influence on national investigators is certainly too weak a factor to outweigh the public interest in the prosecution of such crimes.[101]

---

[97] *Prosecutor v. Brđanin* (Decision on the Defence “Objection to Intercept Evidence”), ICTY (Trial Chamber), decision of 3 October 2003, para 63.

[98] On the separation thesis, see Sect. 4.3.2.2.1.

[99] Safferling 2001, p. 313; Gaynor et al. 2013, p. 1034.

[100] See in particular Sect. 5.2.

[101] Safferling 2012, p. 502.

In conclusion, where national authorities have gathered evidence through illicit means, deterrence must be rejected as a purpose of an ICC exclusionary rule. This is irrespective of whether the measures were carried out independently or on behalf of the international prosecutor.

But what about deterrence where OTP staff itself carries out the respective investigative measure? There certainly is a strong institutional connection between the Chambers of the ICC and its Office of the Prosecutor. This may call for a disciplining role of the former vis-à-vis the latter.

The ICC in the *Lubanga* case seems to have considered at least the possibility that exclusion may have a disciplining effect on OTP staff. It has, however, doubted its significance in light of the limited power of the international prosecutor to carry out investigative measures himself.[102] Indeed, deterrence cannot play a considerable role for ICC proceedings as long as the structure of the ICC cooperation regime limits the direct intervention of OTP to exceptional cases. But even beyond this limited impact under the cooperation regime as it stands today, the validity of deterrence for OTP violations is doubtful. Firstly, the practical benefit of deterrence will once more be difficult to assess. Admittedly, one may argue that the Prosecutor will usually have a strong interest in every individual conviction and not be driven by considerations such as the maintenance of order. But at the same time, ICC investigations often take place in unstable regions far away from The Hague. Prosecution staff may therefore believe that violations will not come to light. Beyond that, and even more importantly, the question of adequacy arises once more. In particular with respect to the seriousness of the crimes under the Court's jurisdiction, it seems more appropriate to punish prosecutorial rights violations by means other than the exclusion of evidence.[103]

4.3.2.2.4 The Vindication of Individual Rights

A second explanation for the exclusion of reliable evidence advanced in domestic debates concentrates on the protection of the individual rights of the accused. According to this approach, the state itself has set legal limits on its access to evidence. Where these limits are not respected by the investigating authorities, the accused has a right to a remedy. It is argued that the best way to vindicate the rights of the accused is to exclude illicitly gathered evidence. As a consequence of such an exclusion, both the accused and the state are supposed to be put back in

---

[102] *Prosecutor v. Lubanga* (Decision on the Admission of Material from the 'Bar Table'), ICC (Trial Chamber), decision of 24 June 2009, para 44.

[103] For existing possibilities to sanction ICC staff, see Rules 23 et seq. of the Rules of Procedure and Evidence. See also Rules 110.1 et seq. of the Staff Rules of the International Criminal Court, available at http://www.icc-cpi.int/en_menus/icc/legal%20texts%20and%20tools/official%20journal/Pages/staff%20rules%20of%20the%20international%20criminal%20court%20%20annex%20to%20icc%20ai%202005%20003.asp (last visited: October 2013).

the same position they would have been in had the violation not occurred. This approach has also been endorsed for the ICC exclusionary rule.[104]

The idea that exclusion is closely connected to the protection of individual rights is the basis of a number of domestic approaches. It constitutes, for instance, the gist of the originally strong mandatory exclusionary rule in the United States.[105] In its initial form, the U.S. exclusionary rule was conceived as a direct manifestation of the individual rights guaranteed by the U.S. Constitution.[106] This view has also been endorsed in the discussions in England.[107] In Germany, individual rights concepts have been supported at times by the judiciary. The so-called '*Rechtskreistheorie*' that was first followed by the German Federal Supreme Court was based on the assumption that evidentiary exclusion is only triggered in the case of a violation of individual rights.[108] Other approaches referring to the exclusionary rule as a remedy for the violation of individual rights have been developed by German scholars.[109]

Like the deterrence rationale, these propositions have been subject to much criticism in domestic debates. Depending on the specific embodiment of the remedial concept, it has either been considered too wide or too narrow.[110] We will see that the criticism raised at the domestic level is also valid for international criminal proceedings.

First of all, a strict understanding of the remedial theory has been criticized as too wide. Where the remedy of exclusion is seen as a direct consequence of the violation of individual rights, there is a danger of yielding disproportionate results.[111] In principle, it could be held that exclusion is triggered automatically whenever a violation occurs in the course of the collection of evidence. The mandatory exclusionary rule initially conceived by the U.S. Supreme Court is, once again, an illustrative example of such an approach.[112] As we have seen before, however, such a mandatory conception of the exclusionary rule is problematic because it forces courts to simply ignore cogent evidence, which is problematic with respect the official responsibility to enforce criminal law.[113]

The remedial theory however does not necessarily have to be conceived in such a categorical way. At the national level, even strong proponents of the theory have

---

[104]Safferling 2001, p. 313.

[105]Roberts and Zuckerman 2010, p. 182.

[106]On the initial concept of the U.S. mandatory exclusionary rule, see Sect. 3.3.2.

[107]See for instance Ashworth 1977, p. 723 et seq.

[108]On the '*Rechtskreistheorie*', see Sect. 3.3.1.

[109]A prominent example is the so-called '*Informationsbeherrschungslehre*', an approach that conceives most of the rules on the exclusion of evidence as resulting from subjective rights to control information, see Amelung 1990. Also see Sect. 3.3.1.

[110]Roberts and Zuckerman 2010, p. 189.

[111]Penney 2003, p. 112. Critical with respect to this argument, Potter, 1983, p. 1396.

[112]Roberts and Zuckerman 2010, p. 182.

[113]See Sect. 4.3.2.2.2.

conceded that, for reasons of proportionality, the obligation to provide a remedy may not be applicable to every kind of violation.[114] Theoretically, Article 69(7) of the ICC Statute could therefore be understood as limiting the right to a remedy to cases where the additional requirements of subparas (a) and (b) are fulfilled.

But even if the right to a remedy is restricted in this way, other points of criticism have been raised against the remedial theory. First of all, the remedial theory has naturally been rejected by the proponents of the separation thesis.[115] This criticism can be refuted right away. It maintains that there is no connection between the violation and the trial. Accordingly, there would be no reason that a court would have to provide a remedy. This argument, however, disregards the fact that investigators and courts have a shared responsibility for the fair administration of justice.

At the same time, the criticism raised by the separation thesis points to an aspect which, in a similar form, has already been discussed in relation to deterrence. While there is a connection between the official misconduct and the trial, the question emerges whether the trial is the appropriate forum to remedy the violation. Admittedly, the Latin principle '*ubi remedium, ibi jus*' is recognized in both common and civil law. It postulates that any violation of a right requires a remedy. And certainly, this principle is all the more applicable where a human rights violation is concerned. Such a remedy, however, could also be provided by resorting to the law of tort. Accordingly, as for deterrence, there is an alternative way to reach the objectives pursued by the remedial theory.

One could object that tort law remedies would only provide for material compensation whereas the exclusion of evidence is meant to entirely redress the violation suffered by the accused. But in many cases, it is doubtful whether the remedy of excluding tainted evidence actually fully eliminates the adverse effects of the violation. In most domestic proceedings, as well as in ICC proceedings, the decision on exclusion is taken by the same judicial authority that also passes the final judgment. Once introduced into trial, the judicial awareness of the existence of the evidence can never be entirely reversed.[116] As a consequence, there will often be a risk that the evidence has nevertheless influenced the decision, at least to some degree. Accordingly, the choice is between two imperfect remedies, material compensation, which only provides for a substitute, and the exclusion of the evidence from trial, which cannot guarantee that its objective will actually be achieved.

In cases, on the other hand, where the bench actually ignores the evidence, the question of proportionality arises once again. In such cases, the remedy provided to the accused may affect the enforcement of criminal law to a considerable degree and possibly even lead to the acquittal of the accused. This is why the remedial theory has been criticised for benefiting the accused in a manner disproportionate

---

[114]Ashworth 2003, p. 112.

[115]On the separation theory, see Sect. 4.3.2.2.1.

[116]Dennis 2010, p. 106; Roberts and Zuckerman 2010, p. 183.

to the violation of his rights.[117] Admittedly, as we have previously found, in order to avoid entirely disproportionate results, the remedial theory can be limited to serious cases of rights violations. If however, the remedy of exclusion is restricted in this way, the question arises how those violations which, for reasons of proportionality, cannot be compensated through the exclusion of evidence will be remedied. Such violations would have to be remedied by means of the law of tort after all, thus creating disparities between the different violations. Ultimately, it would seem more appropriate to have one common mechanism for the remedy of violations committed during the collection of evidence. The allocation of damages through the law of tort is equally available in all cases and provides a remedy as a matter of right and not of judicial discretion.[118]

The possibility of providing material compensation instead of excluding the evidence has been used as a strong argument against the remedial theory at the national level. At the international level, one may raise the objection that it could be difficult to obtain damages from the responsible authorities.

First of all, there is no comprehensive scheme on rights compensation in the ICC proper law that could be invoked where OTP staff commits a violation. Article 85 of the Statute creates an enforceable right to compensation. This right is limited, however, to instances of unlawful arrest or detention or to cases where a person has been punished as the result of a miscarriage of justice. On a discretionary basis, the Court may also award compensation to a detained person who has not been convicted because of a grave and manifest miscarriage of justice. Neither of the instances of compensation for miscarriages of justice applies, however, to cases where a person has suffered a violation and was still justly convicted and sentenced. As a result, there seems to be no right to compensation where the violation does not reach the extent that would warrant a release. Neither does Article 71 of the Statute establish such a claim. The provision is limited to misconduct before the Court and not at the investigative phase.[119]

Where domestic authorities have gathered the tainted evidence independently, the matter is often not less difficult. The access to a remedy then depends both on the domestic legal framework for government liability and on the actual enforceability of such claims. But it must be taken into account that evidence relevant to ICC proceedings often stems from states in conflict or post-conflict situations. Under such conditions, it will be difficult for an individual to assert his claim under domestic law.

In addition, persons affected by violations committed by domestic authorities could be eligible for damages under human rights conventions. In practice, however, the claims for compensation will often be difficult to enforce. While Article (2)(3)(a) of the ICCPR, Article 41 of the ECHR, as well as Article 63 of

---

[117]Potter 1983, p. 1396.

[118]Dennis 2010, p. 106.

[119]Altogether, see Acquaviva et al. 2013, p. 800.

the IACHR and Article 27 of the Additional Protocol to the ACHPR,[120] stipulate the right to an effective remedy, compensation for abuses is not always accessible to the individual. This is particularly true for those individuals who, under the present circumstances, are actually affected by the jurisdiction of the International Criminal Court. All of them originate from states on the African continent. Despite the comprehensive ratification of the African Charter of Human Rights by African States, access to a remedy is not likely to be readily available, be it at the domestic level or through the human rights monitoring body. As of today, the jurisprudence of the African Court of Human Rights is still fragmentary and the young institution is at this point far from being a reliable guarantor for the allocation of remedies for human rights abuses.[121]

But despite this unsatisfactory situation, it is not evident that its consequence should be to integrate the vindication of rights into the ICC law of evidence. The appropriate way to address such deficiencies would rather be the same as with any other deficiencies in the access to legal recourse: improve existing remedial mechanisms.[122] With respect to violations by OTP staff, this is a matter to be dealt with by the ICC's Assembly of States Parties and not by its judges. Regarding the lack of compensation at the domestic level, it is beyond the scope of tasks of the ICC to provide for improvement. Reforms are the responsibility of domestic states and human rights systems.

Another important objection against the remedial theory then again is that its scope of protection is too narrow. If exclusion is based on a remedial effect, the exclusionary rule can only apply to violations of those rights that explicitly protect the accused. It could not therefore be triggered by violations of the rights of third parties. At the domestic level, this has rightly been criticized. It has been argued that the accused not only has the right to the observation of rules that aim at his individual protection; instead, he is entitled to a criminal trial that, in its entirety, is in line with the rule of law.[123]

This argument is all the more convincing in view of an international criminal court that has an enhanced need to preserve and improve its perception as a legitimate institution. The legitimacy of the ICC would be affected if the rights of third parties would not sufficiently be taken into account in its trials. This includes the rights of victims, in particular where they participate as witnesses in the proceedings. We have seen that safeguarding the interests of victims is one of the major

---

[120]Article 27 of the Additional Protocol to the ACHPR is technically only a provision on competence which confers the jurisdiction for such a claim to the AfCHPR. Given its similarity to Article 41 of the ECHR and Article 63 of the IACHR, it can however be regarded as a substantive legal basis for a tort remedy; see Seegers 2005, p. 148.

[121]For an introduction into the development and current situation of the African Court of Human and Peoples Rights, see Viljoen 2012, p. 410 et seq.

[122]Roberts and Zuckerman 2010, p. 184.

[123]For the respective critics of the German '*Rechtskreistheorie*', see Eisenberg 2011, p. 123. See also Sect. 3.3.1.

purposes of international criminal trials.[124] This has also left its marks on the ICC proper law. It is an often emphasized characteristic of the procedural regime of the ICC that it accords special importance to the rights of victims and witnesses.[125] It would be contrary to this key value if these rights were completely disregarded when it comes to the exclusion of evidence.

Moreover, a failure to guarantee the respect for the rights of third parties would provide a convenient argument for states to refuse cooperation. This argument does not only pertain to the rights of the citizens of a state; it is also important that the rights of states themselves are guaranteed, in particular their sovereignty rights. International courts have a distinct responsibility to ensure that their decisions are consistent with international law and that they respect state sovereignty.[126] Accordingly, the ICTY, for instance, has not precluded the accused from raising the violation of state sovereignty, including with respect to the exclusion of evidence.[127] The same conclusion has been suggested with respect to Article 69(7)(b) of the ICC Statute.[128]

In conclusion, the exclusion of illicitly obtained evidence by the ICC cannot be explained as a tool to vindicate individual rights. The exclusion of evidence is not the appropriate mechanism to compensate for abuses. Moreover, such a justification would not sufficiently take into account the rights of third parties which play a paramount role in the legal system of the Court.

4.3.2.2.5 The Theory of Integrity

Having sketched the main rival theories, we will now turn to the last rationale, the theory of integrity. At the core of this concept is the idea that the moral authority of a court is brought into disrepute where this court does not dissociate itself from illicit investigative methods. We will see that in spite of justified criticism, there is no real alternative to the integrity theory.

This is particularly true for ICC proceedings. Among the theoretical approaches presented here, the integrity rationale is not only the one that is most consistent with the wording of Article 69(7)(b) of the ICC Statute. The assumption that the

---

[124] See Sect. 2.2.3.

[125] For an introduction into the status of victims under the ICC legal framework, see Greco 2007, p. 531 et seq.

[126] Sluiter 2002, p. 226.

[127] With respect to the exclusion of evidence, see *Prosecutor v. Kordić and Čerkez* (Decision stating Reasons for Trial Chamber's Ruling of 1 June 1999 Rejecting Defence Motion to Suppress Evidence), ICTY (Trial Chamber), decision of 25 June 1999, para 10. Generally, see *Prosecutor v. Tadić* (Decision on the Defence Motion for Interlocutory Appeal on Jurisdiction), ICTY (Appeals Chamber), decision of 2 October 1995, para 55.

[128] See Alamuddin 2010, p. 261. This seems also to be implied by *Prosecutor v. Lubanga* (Decision on the admission of material from the 'Bar Table'), ICC (Trial Chamber), decision of 24 June 2009, para 42.

integrity theory must be given preference over other approaches follows in particular from teleological considerations. As we have seen, the main purpose of ICC proceedings is positive general prevention, meaning the socio-pedagogical effects of the prosecution and punishment of international crimes.[129] As a consequence, it is particularly important that the Court is perceived as a legitimate institution possessing moral authority and acting with integrity, including with respect to the evidence that it relies upon in its proceedings.[130]

Among the domestic legal orders considered above, the strongest example for the appreciation of this rationale can be found in Canadian law. The Canadian Charter of Rights and Freedoms predicates decisions on exclusion on whether the admission of evidence obtained in breach of a Charter right "*would bring the administration of justice into disrepute*".[131]

But the maintenance of judicial integrity is also part of the debate on exclusion in other states. References to this idea can be found in decisions of the United States Supreme Court dating from its liberal era,[132] as well as in the case law of the English Supreme Court (formerly the House of Lords).[133] Integrity based approaches have been discussed in English,[134] American[135] and German[136] legal discourse. In general, the theory has become increasingly popular in recent times among legal scholars throughout different domestic systems.[137]

Within any system governed by the rule of law, the courts are tasked with promoting legal and societal values. The discharge of this task necessarily requires a certain level of public acceptance. Such acceptance in turn depends heavily on the moral authority of the courts. Authority, however, cannot be sustained where the courts themselves do not adhere to the values they are entrusted to protect. These assumptions have implications not only for the actual behaviour of the judges themselves, but also for the attitude they need to adopt towards official impropriety.

---

[129]See Sect. 2.2.3.

[130]Safferling 2001, p. 302.

[131]See Article 24(2) of the Canadian Charter of Rights and Freedoms. See in particular Sect. 3.3.4.

[132]See *Mapp v. Ohio,* United States Supreme Court, decision of June 19, 1961, 367 U.S. 643 (1961); *Terry v. Ohio*, United States Supreme Court, decision of 10 June 1968, 392 U.S. 1 (1968). In contrast, for a decision opposing integrity as a benchmark, see *Stone 1995 v. Powell*, United States Supreme Court, decision of 6 July 1976, 428 U.S. 465 (1976).

[133]For a clear example, see *A. and others v. Secretary for Home Department (No. 2)*, House of Lords (Appellate Committee), decision of 8 December 2005, [2005] UKHL 71, para 87: "[…] *that the courts will not shut their eyes to the way the accused was brought before the court or the evidence of his guilt was obtained. Those methods may be such that it would compromise the integrity of the judicial process, dishonour the administration of justice, if the proceedings were to be entertained or the evidence admitted.*"

[134]Roberts and Zuckerman 2010, p. 188 et seq.

[135]See Slobogin 2013, p. 17 et seq.

[136]See Muthorst 2009, p. 56, with further references.

[137]Jackson and Summers 2012, p. 156.

If judges were to overlook such impropriety on a regular basis, they would quickly be perceived as applying a double standard. Their attitude would create the impression that regular citizens are required to comply with legal values while the same behaviour is not expected from state officials.[138] Even worse, where courts not only fail to identify a violation but even make use of its outcome, they risk being perceived as its accomplices.[139] A court that does not proceed against violations of due process rights eventually loses its authority to teach citizens moral lessons through its judgments.[140] Proponents of the integrity theory argue that, consequently, courts must place an emphasis on due process and distance themselves from illegally gained evidence. A possible reaction to official violations of due process rights would be excluding the evidence gathered by such means.

The judicial attitude towards official impropriety, however, is not the only criterion that impacts on the moral authority of a criminal court. As we have seen, the authority and credibility of a court are also closely linked to its ability to enforce substantive criminal law.[141] Public confidence is undermined where excluding evidence results in a failure to convict a guilty person.[142] Thus, the aim of effective law enforcement would be served best by admitting as much cogent evidence as possible.

As a result, a tension arises between due process guarantees and the public interest in the enforcement of substantive criminal law. Proponents of the integrity theory recognize this tension. The theory tries to dissolve it through a balancing exercise between the two poles 'due process' and 'effective law enforcement'.[143] This process of balancing ultimately reflects the common methodological approach deduced from the review of national and international systems. All of the systems reviewed above have, to some degree, balanced against each other the different interests affected in cases of tainted evidence. This is not surprising from the teleological point of view of the integrity theory. It simply results from the fact that every system needs to dissolve the tension between due process rights and effective prosecution in order to maintain the legitimacy of its judicial system.

But while, in recent times, the approach has become increasingly popular within domestic debates, it has not been without its opponents. A first line of attack against the integrity rationale is based on the separation thesis rejected above. Commentators have argued that the integrity rationale is unable to refute the argument that pre-trial breaches do not affect the trial itself.[144] Interestingly, a similar argument seems to have been raised by the ICTY. In *Kordić and Čerkez*,

---

[138]Roberts and Zuckerman 2010, p. 188.

[139]Ashworth 2003, p. 108.

[140]Roberts and Zuckerman 2010, p. 188.

[141]See Sect. 2.2.3.

[142]See Muthorst 2009, p. 59 et seq., who claims that excluding evidence may have a worse effect on public confidence than admitting it. See also Rogall 1979, p. 14; Penney 2003, p. 111.

[143]Ashworth 1977, p. 346; Roberts and Zuckerman 2010, p. 190.

[144]Ashworth 2003, p. 121; Muthorst 2009, p. 57.

the issue was the admissibility of a tape that had been recorded by means of an interception, allegedly in violation of domestic law. During the discussion, the bench refuted the argument that admitting the evidence would be tantamount to tacitly approving illegal measures. Judge May held that the only decision to be made related to the admissibility of the tape. And, in his words, admitting this evidence "*doesn't mean that you are approving the conduct*".[145] He was not convinced therefore that admitting illegally gained evidence would reveal anything about the tribunal's attitude towards the violation, let alone affect the tribunal's integrity. The argument rather presents the violation and the trial as completely unrelated.

In fact, a loose institutional connection between the actors at the pre-trial and those at the trial phase has consequences for how deeply a violation affects a court's integrity. But be it at the national or at the international level, presuming a complete disconnection neglects the bonds that actually exist between the different procedural stages, as well as between the actors involved in them. What is more, the tenets of the integrity theory necessitate going even one step further than with respect to the rationales discussed above. Despite the connection between the different phases and actors of criminal proceedings, both the deterrence and the remedial theory were rejected above *inter alia* because there are alternatives to reach the objectives pursued by them. The trial is neither the appropriate forum for deterrence nor for the vindication of individual rights. This argument is not transferable to the integrity theory. Deterrent and remedial goals may be achieved outside of a criminal trial. The purpose of sustaining the integrity of a court, however, is inseparably connected to the trial forum.

Another counter-argument commonly raised against the integrity theory seems to be more relevant, namely that the integrity theory risks putting too much emphasis on public reaction. Where crimes are serious enough to attract revulsion, public opinion is likely to reject considerations of due process altogether. At the national level, cases involving the sexual abuse of children or terrorism have been advanced as examples.[146] The same risk certainly exists with respect to the grave crimes under international jurisdiction.

Most advocates of the integrity theory, however, are aware of this risk. As a reaction, commentators have drawn a distinction between two versions of the integrity principle. The first of these versions is based on '*public attitude integrity*', while the second is based on '*court-centred integrity*'. In the latter, preferable version, the integrity rationale is understood as focussing on the consistency of judicial decisions. This means that courts must first of all guarantee respect for a certain set of values irrespective of whose behaviour they assess.[147] Accordingly,

---

[145]See *Prosecutor v. Kordić and Čerkez*, ICTY (Trial Chamber), Transcript of 2 February 2000, p. 13671. See also *Prosecutor v. Brđanin* (Decision on the Defence "Objection to Intercept Evidence"), ICTY (Trial Chamber), decision of 3 October 2003, para 63.

[146]Ashworth 2003, p. 111; Ashworth and Redmayne 2010, p. 346.

[147]Ashworth 1977, p. 110. Also see Bilz 2012, p. 166, who points out that according to psychological research, inconsistency has a negative impact on the perception of a judicial system.

the moral authority of a court is not sustained through the widespread consensus with a particular decision. It rather builds on growing public respect for the consistent affirmation by this court of its own values. The case law of the Canadian Supreme Court is exemplary for this line of thought. With the risk of opportunism in mind, Canadian judges have concentrated on the long-term effects of exclusion to the reputation of the justice system rather than on immediate public reaction when interpreting Section 24(2) of the Canadian Charter.[148]

Such an understanding must also govern the conception of the integrity rationale in the case of the ICC. The aim of sustaining the Court's integrity should not indiscriminately make it subject to public opinion. This is not least confirmed by the teleological considerations advanced above.[149] If the purpose of ICC proceedings is a socio-pedagogical one, the Court cannot promote its perception as legitimate by simply complying with the status quo of prevailing societal values. The socio-pedagogical purpose rather suggests that the Court must impart knowledge about the validity of legal standards through a consistent application of its own values.

Moreover, a '*public attitude*' version of the integrity rationale would also be particularly problematic for international proceedings for reasons of definition. At the domestic level, the theory as such has been criticized for the relativity of the notion of integrity. This is true in particular if the definition of integrity depends on public opinion. The public perception of what integrity means varies considerably across space and time.[150] At the international level in turn, the range of public opinions naturally differs to a much greater degree than within one domestic society. Any attempt at defining the already vague term 'integrity' on this basis would be a hopeless endeavour.

Admittedly, the problem of vagueness remains important. Albeit to a somewhat lesser extent, a 'court-centred' conception must also face the notorious vagueness of the integrity rationale. Here, the main point of criticism has been the danger of an inherent subjectivity of decisions on exclusion. Domestic opponents to the integrity rationale have argued that the performance of the required balancing exercise is highly dependent on the views of the judge responsible for taking the decision.[151] The fear is that judicial decisions on the exclusion of evidence would become unpredictable.[152] This danger may come with a risk that decisions would differ greatly depending on the composition of the bench. This would entail an inequality of treatment of defendants. It has been argued in general that the

[148]On this approach by the Supreme Court of Canada, see Sect. 2.3.4.

[149]See Sect. 2.2.3.

[150]Bilz 2012, p. 168.

[151]Ashworth and Redmayne 2010, p. 347. See also, Ashworth 2003, p. 118 et seq.

[152]The vagueness of the integrity theory has been criticized in particular by the U.S. Supreme Court in the more conservative post-*Warren* area, see for instance *Stone 1995 v. Powell*, United States Supreme Court, decision of 6 July 1976, 428 U.S. 465 (1976).

discretion allocated to the judges would be disproportionate because they would be given the authority to make policy decisions that should be left to the legislator.[153]

Beyond the domestic debates, this is a contentious point, most particularly for the application of an integrity based rationale by an international court. Generally speaking, granting a very broad discretion to judges is considered even more problematic at the international level than it is in domestic proceedings. This reluctance to give too much leeway to international judges results in particular from the fragmentary nature of international law. Given the lack of legal framework, it seems particularly difficult to predict the standards international judges will abide by.[154] What is more, this lack of regulation comes in addition to a panoply of legal backgrounds among international judges. The resulting divergence of opinion is no less problematic for creating confidence in their exercise of discretion.

Thus, in principle, the aforementioned criticism is not unjustified. At the same time, it must be acknowledged that there is no real alternative to granting judicial discretion for cases of reliable but illicitly obtained evidence. It is no coincidence that all of the systems analysed above have, to some extent, balanced the different interests affected in such cases. Mandatory requirements do not generate workable solutions for evidentiary exclusion. This is best illustrated by the development of the formerly automatic exclusionary rule in the U.S. The matter is simply too complex to allow for predetermined moral certitude embodied by a simple all-purpose rule.[155] Ultimately this is also acknowledged by the deterrence and the remedial theories. In their modern shapes, both of these approaches recognize that the objectives they consider relevant are not absolute. As a consequence, they both limit the consequences of their presumptions: Where the deterrence rationale is used as an explanation, this has led to resorting to rules of exception. Here, the U.S. rule is once again an illustrative example.[156] The remedial theory in turn is confronted with the same problem of deciding which rights violation are serious enough to require exclusion. By openly resorting to a balancing exercise, the integrity theory concedes to the moral and practical complexities of the issue. To openly allocate discretion to the judges simply means to recognize that no legislator would ever be able to regulate all possible cases.[157]

In the end, predicating decisions on an exercise of discretion is also less problematic than the critics suggest. Granting leeway to judges is not a tool alien to law. The ICC Statute makes no exception and recognizes such judicial power not

[153]For a critique with respect to international criminal proceedings, see Gallant 1999, p. 719; Vanderpuye 2005, p. 130; Zappalà 2003, p. 51 et seq.

[154]Kamardi 2009, p. 108.

[155]Cryer et al. 2010, p. 190. Similar, Muthorst 2009, p. 75. For the opposite view with respect to the ICC, Vanderpuye 2005, p. 129 et seq.

[156]See Sect. 3.3.2.

[157]Similar, with respect to the jurisprudence, see Rogall 1979, p. 32.

only in Article 69(7) but in a number of provisions.[158] If one were to reject the integrity rationale on that basis, the same would have to apply to all instances where evaluation and the weighing of interests are demanded from a judge.[159] What is more, discretionary rules are even less assailable in matters of criminal procedure. The requirements of the principle of legal certainty are not as strict here as they are for substantive law.[160]

Finally, exercising discretion does not necessarily need to be equated with a complete lack of predictability. Admittedly, discretion inevitably implies a core amount of freedom to decide on the part of the responsible judge.[161] But this decision-making process can be guided. In the case of evidentiary exclusion, it is at least to some extent possible to structure the balancing process with a framework of principles that applies beyond the single case. Such an approach, however, is conditional on a sound methodology. It requires the identification of factors that are relevant for the balancing exercise.[162]

The development of such a methodology is not left up in the air. As stated at the outset of this chapter, the theoretical foundations of an exclusionary rule are of considerable importance for its implementation. The integrity theory has now been determined as the best explanation for exclusion in international criminal proceeding. This rationale represents the point of reference for the development of abstract factors. We have seen that the judiciary in a number of systems has striven to identify relevant factors for a balancing exercise. This case law may serve as a starting point to determine adequate criteria for the ICC. The validity of every possible factor will however have to be examined in light of the peculiarities of the ICC legal system and, in particular, in light of its significance for the promotion of judicial integrity.

4.3.2.3 The Exclusion of Unreliable Evidence

Some consideration shall finally be given to the first of the two alternatives in Article 69(7). This instance of evidentiary exclusion is rather straightforward. The need to guarantee the reliability of evidence is deeply rooted as one rationale for exclusion in domestic legal systems. In common law systems, unreliability was initially even regarded as the sole reason for the exclusion of evidence.[163] In civil law systems in turn, the importance of not relying on inaccurate evidence necessarily results from the strong emphasis on the truth-ascertaining function accorded

[158]For just some of the many examples, see Article 19(1), Article 57(3)(a), Article 64(6) or Article 77 of the ICC Statute.

[159]Similar with respect to the German jurisprudence, see Rogall 1979, p. 32.

[160]See Sect. 2.3.1.1.

[161]Roberts and Zuckerman 2010, p. 219.

[162]Rogall 1979, p. 33; Roberts and Zuckerman 2010, p. 191.

[163]Jackson and Summers 2012, p. 153.

to criminal trials.[164] Moreover, basing convictions on evidence whose reliability is doubtful is naturally also problematic from a human rights point of view. Accordingly, the ECtHR has included the reliability of disputed evidence in its overall assessment of the fairness of a trial under Article 6 of the ECHR.[165] Finally, this alternative of the ICC exclusionary rule can be found verbatim in Rule 95 of both of the *Ad hoc* tribunals.

Today, it is widely agreed that reliability is not the only rationale for exclusion. This view also prevailed among the drafters of the ICC Statute and drove them to include a separate subpara (b) that would allow for the exclusion of possibly reliable evidence.[166] At the same time, guarding fact finders against risks of error evidently remains one major purpose of exclusion. This applies without doubt to ICC trials as well. Convictions resting on a wrong factual basis would endanger the fulfilment of the mandate of the ICC to prosecute those persons who are in fact liable for international crimes. Moreover, wrongful convictions are also problematic in view of the previously emphasized need of the Court to be perceived as a legitimate institution. This last assessment has an impact on the relation between subpara (a) and (b) of the ICC exclusionary rule. Even though the two requirements of unreliability and threat to integrity were finally made disjunctive, there continues to be a degree of overlap between the two alternatives of Article 69(7). While Article 69(7)(b) more immediately aims at the protection of the Court's integrity, this is indirectly also a concern of Article 69(7)(a). It is hard to imagine that the requirements of the first alternative of the ICC exclusionary rule would be met without there being also an adverse effect on the integrity of the proceedings in terms of Article 69(7)(b). At the same time, the relation between the two alternatives of the provision is not one of lex specialis and lex generalis. In aiming directly not at integrity but at the discovery of material truth, Article 69(7)(a) to some extent has a protective function that differs from Article 69(7)(b). Ultimately, this alternative was probably maintained as a separate option because of the paramount importance of the reliability issue for the exclusion of evidence in many domestic legal systems.

So far, no evidence has been excluded by the ICC on the basis of Article 69(7)(a) of the Statute. It has even been suggested that this alternative of the ICC exclusionary rule is redundant, not because of the above-mentioned overlap with subpara (b), but because unreliable evidence would in any case not be admissible in

---

[164] Weigend 2003, p. 168.

[165] See *Gäfgen v. Germany*, ECtHR, decision of 1 June 2010 (Application no. 22978/05), para 164: "*In addition, the quality of the evidence must be taken into consideration, as must the circumstances in which it was obtained and whether these circumstances cast doubts on its reliability or accuracy.*" On the *Gäfgen* case, see in particular Sect. 6.2.2.

[166] Initially, the draft language of the ICC exclusionary rule predicated exclusion cumulatively on doubts about reliability and an adverse effect on the integrity on the proceedings. At the Rome Conference, it was agreed that it would be sufficient that either of these requirements be met. See Triffterer 2008—Piragoff, Article 69, para 18.

ICC proceedings.[167] In fact, reliability is also a criterion for the general decision on admissibility. The drafters of the ICC Statute did not include it as a distinct factor in either Article 69(4) or Rule 63.[168] The question of reliability is, however, of major significance for the probative value of a piece of evidence.[169] But while the exclusion of unreliable evidence is possible on this basis, the *lex specialis* nature of Article 69(7) vis-à-vis Article 69(4) needs to be taken into account. Accordingly, where the unreliability results from the use of illicit methods of evidence gathering, exclusion under Article 69(7) takes precedence.[170]

What kind of cases are covered by this first alternative of the ICC exclusionary rule? The most obvious example are confessions obtained as a result of torture. In cases of torture, the violation raises doubts about whether the confession was truthful or merely the result of the coercion resulting from the manner of questioning.[171] In fact, together with humanitarian concerns, the unreliability of evidence was one of the main reasons for abolishing torture in enlightened 18th century European states.[172] The same conclusion can be drawn for other instances of undue pressure during interrogation that do not amount to torture.[173] Accordingly, the ICTY has held *inter alia* with respect to their lack of reliability that "*statements, which are not voluntary but are obtained by oppressive conduct, cannot pass the test under Rule 95*".[174]

In addition, the reliability of evidence may be impaired where rules relating to its preservation are violated. Article 56(2) of the ICC Statute for instance sets forth a number of measures aimed at the preservation of evidence in the case of unique investigative opportunities.[175] Moreover, Rule 112(1) of the RPE demands that interrogations of suspects and arrested person shall be recorded.

When compared to subpara (b), the alternative set forth in subpara (a) of the ICC exclusionary rule allows less leeway to the judges. We have seen that generally, the margin of appreciation in Article 69(7) does not result from the formulation of a discretionary rule *per se*. Rather it is an inherent part of the interpretation of the vague terms included in particular in the two subparagraphs of the provision.[176]

---

[167]Schabas 2011, p. 317.

[168]There was some discussion to include reliability in Rule 63 of the RPE as a distinct criterion for the general admissibility of evidence. No agreement could however be reached, see Combs 2011, p. 326; Gaynor et al., p. 1027.

[169]See Gosnell 2010, p. 384 et seq.; Gaynor et al. 2013, p. 1022. See also Sect. 4.3.1.

[170]On the relation between Articles 69(4) and 67(9) of the ICC Statute, see Sect. 4.3.1.

[171]Triffterer 2008—Piragoff, Article 69, para 67.

[172]Ambos 2010, p. 369.

[173]Triffterer 2008—Piragoff, Article 69, para 67.

[174]*Prosecutor v. Stakić* (Provisional Order on the Standards Governing the Admission of Evidence and Identification), ICTY (Trial Chamber), decision of 25 February 2002, para 8.

[175]Triffterer 2008—Piragoff, Article 69, para 67.

[176]See Miraglia 2008, p. 492; Safferling 2012, p. 499. Also see Sect. 4.3.1.

Article 69(7)(b) covers cases where evidence that is reliable is excluded nevertheless due to its adverse effect on the integrity of the proceedings. Where evidence is excluded despite its reliability, a tension arises between due process guarantees and the interest of the international community in the enforcement of international criminal law. This tension results in a balancing of these two interests. No such balancing exercise is necessary in turn where the methods of evidence gathering impair the reliability of the evidence. Instead, in cases covered by Article 69(7)(a), the admission of evidence does not further any of the previously mentioned interests. In particular, there can be no public interest in convicting an accused on the basis of possibly erroneous facts. Likewise, such a conviction would not serve the related goal of international trials to recognize the suffering of victims of gross human rights violations.[177] But while a balancing exercise is not necessary in this case, the judges still enjoy a certain margin of appreciation when interpreting the terms "*reliability*" and "*substantial doubt*".

The ICC itself has interpreted the term "*reliability*" only in the context of Article 69(4). In the Katanga case, the Trial Chamber provided a non-exhaustive list of criteria that it deemed appropriate to determine whether evidence was reliable, including its source, its nature and characteristics, its contemporaneousness and purpose and, finally, the way in which the evidence was gathered.[178] This list was intended, however, to deal with the admissibility of documentary evidence and seems only partly transferable to Article 69(7)(a). It may be useful for instance in cases of violations of Article 56 of the Statute.

The ICTY has held in the context of hearsay evidence that in order to be reliable, evidence must be "*voluntary, truthful and trustworthy*" and that the judges, in order to make that determination, may look in particular at the content of the evidence, as well as at the circumstances under which it arose.[179] This jurisprudence has in turn been adopted by the ICC.[180] In the end, however, reliability seems too broad a concept to be defined conclusively. The ICC Trial Chamber in *Katanga* thus seems correct in holding that any determination of reliability is dependent on a case-by-case assessment.[181]

The more problematic question with respect to Article 69(7)(a) is whether the effect of a violation is severe enough to "*cast substantial doubt*" on the reliability of the evidence. It has been held that evidence produced by the Prosecutor would

---

[177]See Sect. 2.2.3.

[178]*Prosecutor v. Katanga and Chui* (Decision on the Prosecutor's Bar Table Motions), ICC (Trial Chamber), decision of 17 December 2010, para 27.

[179]*Prosecutor v. Aleksoviski* (Decision on Prosecutor's Appeal on Admissibility of Evidence), ICTY (Trial Chamber), decision of 16 February 1999, para 15.

[180]*Prosecutor v. Lubanga* (Decision on the admissibility of four documents), ICC (Trial Chamber), decision of 13 June 2008, para 28.

[181]*Prosecutor v. Katanga and Chui* (Decision on the Prosecutor's Bar Table Motions), ICC (Trial Chamber), decision of 17 December 2010, para 28. Altogether on the interpretation of the term '*reliability*' in international case law, see Safferling 2012, p. 495 et seq.

likely be held to a high standard of reliability.[182] This might suggest that the degree of probability of unreliability would be rather low, at least where Article 69(7)(a) is used to contest the admissibility of prosecution evidence.

The wording of the provision and the ratio of admissibility decisions, however, call for a certain restraint in this regard. The inclusion of the qualifier "*substantial*" implies that not every allegation of unreliability is sufficient to trigger exclusion on the basis of Article 69(7)(a). The French version of the provision uses the word "*sérieusement*" which unequivocally demands that a certain degree of doubt be reached before excluding the evidence.

What is more, the preliminary nature of admissibility decisions needs to be taken into account. It is important to distinguish between the admissibility of a particular item of evidence and the weight attached to it in the overall assessment in the final decision. The generally liberal, more civil law oriented, approach to admissibility in international criminal law suggests that ICC judges will tend to admit evidence rather generously except for cases where there are strong indicia of unreliability. Accordingly, the threshold for admissibility would have to be lower for the admissibility of evidence than for the final determination of its weight.[183]

The jurisprudence of the *Ad hoc* tribunals confirms this approach. According to case law, the tribunals cannot base their decisions on evidence whose reliability is not confirmed beyond a reasonable doubt.[184] However, including with respect to the application of Rule 95, both tribunals have considered a *prima facie* assessment of reliability to be sufficient at the admissibility stage.[185] The ICTR has pointed out that mere speculation cannot lead to exclusion on the basis of that rule.[186]

At the same time, Article 69(7)(a) of the ICC Statute does not require that it be virtually certain that the evidence is unreliable. This does not only result from the use of the word "*doubt*": Any other interpretation would make the provision a dead letter. If nothing else, a higher threshold would be inconsistent with the previously mentioned influence of legitimacy concerns on Article 69(7)(a). Thus, the Court is well advised not to make the hurdles for unreliability too high. Otherwise, its legitimacy would be threatened where evidence was admitted despite there being clear indications that its trustworthiness is questionable. Again, this corresponds to the line followed by the *Ad hoc* tribunals. The ICTY, despite its reluctance, described above, to exclude unreliable evidence early in the proceedings, has most clearly held in the *Brđanin* case that it "[…] *finds that it is necessary,*

[182] Triffterer 2008—Piragoff, Article 69, para 67.

[183] See with respect to the *Ad hoc* tribunals, Gaynor et al. 2013, p. 1026.

[184] *Prosecutor v. Brđanin* (Decision on the Defence "Objection to Intercept Evidence"), ICTY (Trial Chamber), decision of 3 October 2003, para 66. *Prosecutor v. Milosević* (Preliminary Decision on the Admissibility of Intercepted Communications), ICTY (Trial Chamber), decision of 16 December 2003.

[185] *Prosecutor v. Brđanin* (Decision on the Defence "Objection to Intercept Evidence"), ICTY (Trial Chamber), decision of 3 October 2003, para 68. *Prosecutor v. Karemera* et al. (Decision on the Prosecutor's Motion for Amission of Certain Exibits into Evidence), ICTR (Trial Chamber), decision of 25 January 2008, para 17.

[186] *Prosecutor v. Bagosora* (Decision on Exclusion of Evidence under Rule 95), ICTR (Trial Chamber), decision of 27 January 2004, para 5.

even at this stage, to be satisfied that there is a prima facie indication of reliability failing which it would be incumbent on it to exclude them [the intercepted communications] *straightaway*".[187] Depending on the particular case, a decision on reliability may require further inquiry into the factual situation. In the *Milosević* case, the admission of intercepted communications was also contested by the defence *inter alia* under Rule 95. The tribunal admitted the evidence only after court-appointed experts had dispelled alleged doubts about their reliability.[188]

In general, Article 69(7)(a) of the ICC Statute does not require a balancing exercise. The judges of the ICC are, however, given a certain margin of appreciation when interpreting the norm. When exercising their discretion, they should find a reasonable middle ground for the interpretation of the vague legal terms of this subparagraph. While taking into account the preliminary nature of the admissibility decision, they should be careful not to make this first alternative of Article 69(7) a dead letter. In particular, they should take into account the legitimacy concerns of the ICC.

In the following sections, subpara (b) will not be analysed in further detail. Instead, the focus will be on the more contentious case of when the admissibility of reliable evidence is contested for conflicting reasons of fairness. However, where the following sections pertain to the general requirements of Article 69(7), the discussion implicitly includes exclusion on the basis of unreliability. This concerns the discussion of the requirements of the chapeau of Article 69(7), including the causality requirements that will be discussed in Chapter 6. Given the overlap between both alternatives of Article 69(7) mentioned at the outset of this section, a separate discussion is not required. This is in particular because, as we have seen, legitimacy concerns underlie both of the rationales of the ICC exclusionary rule. We will see that, ultimately, this common concern must also guide the interpretation of the general requirements of the ICC exclusionary rule.

4.3.3 The Relevant Violations

The next basic question we have to address pertains to the norms that must have been violated in order to trigger the ICC exclusionary rule. In its *chapeau,* Article 69(7) of the ICC Statute expressly enumerates these norms. Exclusion may rely either on a violation of the Statute itself or of "*internationally recognized human rights*".[189] The notoriously vague wording of the latter category in particular constitutes a major challenge for the interpretation of the ICC exclusionary rule.

---

[187] *Prosecutor v. Brđanin* (Decision on the Defence "Objection to Intercept Evidence"), ICTY (Trial Chamber), decision of 3 October 2003, para 68.

[188] *Prosecutor v. Milosević* (Final Decision on the Admissibility of Intercepted Communications), ICTY (Trial Chamber), decision of 14 June 2004.

[189] Brady 2001, p. 293.

Questions also arise from the fact that neither violations of the Rules of Procedure and Evidence, nor violations of domestic law are mentioned in the wording of the provision. We will see, however, that it can be argued that the Rules are implicitly included in the scope of Article 69(7). A violation of domestic law as such is in turn never a sufficient reason for the exclusion of evidence by the ICC.

4.3.3.1 Violations of the ICC Statute

The first alternative, a violation of the Statute, is a rather straightforward notion among the many ambiguous terms of Article 69(7). On the basis of this alternative, the exclusionary rule can be triggered by, for instance, a violation at the investigation stage of the rights of the accused or of the rights of witnesses. The ICC Statute contains a rather broad set of human rights guarantees. Wherever such a violation occurs, it is not necessary to rely on the notoriously vague category of "*internationally recognized human rights*". The applicability of Article 69(7) is not limited to individual rights.[190] Such violations are likely, however, to be the most frequent way in which the ICC exclusionary rule will be triggered. A brief overview of the main rights explicitly stipulated in the ICC Statute will demonstrate what kind of human rights guarantees exclusion under this first alternative may rely on.

During the debates on the ICC Statute, there was a general consensus on the need to apply a high standard of protection for both suspects and accused persons.[191] In part, this attitude was based on similar considerations to those underlying this research. The drafters of the ICC Statute were aware of the fact that the legitimacy of the Court would depend *inter alia* on its respect for the persons affected by its jurisprudence.[192] In addition, this position was certainly also prompted by less idealistic motives. The negotiations having been conducted by states, the participants probably also had in mind that these rights might be accorded to their own citizens in future proceedings.[193]

A panoply of proposals on the concrete design of the respective ICC provisions, mostly based on domestic law, were introduced in the consultations. The general consensus, however, was that the minimum threshold would be the major international human rights instruments.[194] The framework finally adopted would, however, go further than that. Most of these international instruments were designed to

---

[190]Alamuddin 2010, p. 261. See also Sect. 4.3.2.2.4.

[191]Friman 1999, p. 248.

[192]Edwards 2001, p. 344.

[193]Zappalà 2003, p. 48.

[194]Friman 1999, p. 248 et seq. This meant above all the International Covenant on Civil and Political Rights (ICCPR), whose significance has already been pointed out with respect to the *Ad hoc* tribunals, see Sect. 2.3.2.4, in particular, fn. 175. On the broader protection of the ICC Statute when compared to the law of the *Ad hoc* tribunals, see Gallant 1999, p. 701; Alamuddin 2010, p. 235.

protect persons at the trial stage of criminal proceedings. So far, both international human rights bodies and international criminal institutions had given but little attention to the protection of suspects or other persons at the investigation stage. The ICC Statute broke new ground by inserting provisions that focus exclusively on individual protections at this early stage of the proceedings.[195]

The provision that incorporates the core human rights protections at the investigation stage is Article 55 of the ICC Statute. This provision is central to the legality of evidence gathering under the ICC proper law. It contains a rather broad set of minimum guarantees. The protection applies to the accused but also to other persons affected by investigations, such as victims and witnesses. The extension of pre-trial rights to this latter category of persons is another aspect that makes this provision particularly innovative. Given its ample scope, Article 55 has been labelled a "*mini human rights convention for the period before trial*".[196]

Article 55 distinguishes two steps in the process of investigation, which depend on the status of the person affected by an investigative measure. Its first paragraph grants a number of core rights to any such person. This pertains in particular to victims, witnesses and to those persons who may be indicted later on but for whom there is not yet enough indication that they have committed a crime. The provision involves protections that are important for the law of evidence, such as the right against self-incrimination, a protection against torture and other ill-treatment, as well as the right to an interpreter. The rights stipulated by paragraph 1 remain applicable from the outset to the end of the investigation phase. Accordingly, their applicability is not affected when a suspicion becomes more concrete.

Article 55(2) in turn is only applicable where the suspicion is sufficiently high, namely where "*there are grounds to believe that a person has committed a crime within the jurisdiction of the Court and that person is about to be questioned*". It adds a number of additional rights equally important for evidentiary issues, namely the right to be informed that the said suspicion exists, the right to silence and the right to counsel. It would have been expected that the drafters of the Statute would employ the word '*suspect*' in this context. The use of this term was, however, deliberately avoided. One reason was to prevent any premature criminalization of the respective person. Another consideration was that it would be exceedingly difficult to find an agreement for a notion for which such widely diverging concepts exist under domestic law.[197] It has nevertheless been presumed that the term would still be used in practice.[198] This has been confirmed by the

[195]Gradoni et al. 2013, p. 76; Triffterer 2008, Article 21, para 1 (McAuliffe de Guzman).

[196]Alamuddin 2010, p. 235; Triffterer 2008, Article 55, para 1 (McAuliffe de Guzman).

[197]Friman 1999, p. 254; Triffterer 2008, Article 55, para 10 (McAuliffe de Guzman).

[198]Critical, Zappalà 2003, p. 48, who holds that the lack of definition is likely to bring about more interpretative difficult than were avoided by using the term 'suspect'. Commentators have employed the term as well, see Triffterer 2008, Article 55, para 10 (McAuliffe de Guzman).

case law that exists thus far on Article 55(2).[199] Consequently, the term suspect will also be used in this research to refer to persons falling under Article 55(2) of the ICC Statute.

In light of the cooperation regime of the ICC, acts of national authorities play a distinct role in the context of investigations, including for the collection of evidence. One question that arises in this respect is the applicability of the protections that the ICC Statute provides in its Article 55 to acts of domestic law enforcement.

There are two scenarios where national authorities conduct investigative measures. Either they act on a request of the ICC Prosecutor in accordance with Chap. 9, or the measures are carried out independently and exclusively under national law. The ICC Trial Chamber has clarified that where national authorities conduct their own investigations, states are not bound by the ICC proper law. As a consequence, the Chamber concluded that in the absence of an ICC request, evidence gathered by domestic authorities "*cannot be said to have been obtained by means of a violation' of the Statute*".[200]

This jurisprudence is based *inter alia* on the wording of Article 55(2) of the ICC Statute. The provision only explicitly extends the applicability of its protections to questioning by national authorities where national acts are based on an OTP request.[201] Beyond the wording, the Trial Chamber has held that there was no indication that the States Parties had agreed, simply by adopting Article 55(2), to comply with the standards set by the Statute in their own, independent investigations.[202]

Article 55(1) of the ICC Statute in turn does not contain any reference to the acts of national authorities. At the same time, the wording of the first paragraph does not necessarily preclude its applicability to national investigative acts. In light of the above-mentioned jurisprudence, this is at least worth consideration where domestic authorities act on behalf of the ICC Prosecutor. To this effect, it has been argued that because the investigative process is clearly designed to involve national authorities, Article 55(1) must apply to their acts as well.[203] Rule 111(2) of the RPE has been referred to in support of this argument. This rule

---

[199] *Prosecutor v. Katanga and Chui* (Decision on the Prosecutor's Bar Table Motions), ICC (Pre-Trial Chamber), decision of 17 December 2010, para 59; *Prosecutor v. Katanga and Chui* (Decision on the Defences' Applications for Leave to Appeal the "Decision on the admissibility for the confirmation hearing of the transcripts of interview of deceased witness 12"), ICC (Pre-Trial Chamber), decision of 22 May 2008, p. 6 and p. 19; *Prosecutor v. Lubanga* (Decision on the Defence Request for Order to Disclose Exculpatory Materials), ICC (Pre-Trial Chamber), decision of November 2006, p. 5.

[200] *Prosecutor v. Katanga and Chui* (Decision on the Prosecutor's Bar Table Motions), ICC (Pre-Trial Chamber), decision of 17 December 2010, para 59.

[201] See Article 55(2) of the ICC Statute: "*Where there are grounds to believe that a person has committed a crime within the jurisdiction of the Court and that person is about to be questioned* [...] *by national authorities pursuant to a request made under Part 9* [...]."

[202] *Prosecutor v. Katanga and Chui* (Decision on the Prosecutor's Bar Table Motions), ICC (Pre-Trial Chamber), decision of 17 December 2010, para 59.

[203] Gallant 1999, p. 712.

stipulates that in all cases where a person is questioned, be it by the Prosecutor or by national authorities, "*due regard shall be given to Article 55*". It does not restrict this requirement to para 1 of the provision.[204] The argument, however, does not seem entirely convincing. The reference to Article 55 only includes the order to respect those rights that are in fact stipulated by the provision. Given that Article 55(1) does not expressly provide for an extension to national authorities, such reasoning appears to lead to a circular argument.

Conversely, a systematic consideration could in turn be advanced to argue to the contrary. It could be argued that a comparison between Article 55(1) and (2) indicates the will of the States Parties not to submit their authorities to obligations at the very early stage of investigations covered by Article 55(1). This would explain why national authorities are only mentioned in Article 55(2).

There are, however, strong teleological arguments pointing to the opposite conclusion. An extension to national authorities seems to be required by the very purpose of the provision, which is to provide for comprehensive human rights guarantees at all stages of the proceedings. In a cooperation system where national authorities are so prominently involved in investigations, states cannot be free from the duty to respect these fundamental guarantees. The consequence would be their regular inapplicability. In view of the high human rights standard required from the ICC, the rights under Article 55(1) should also therefore be regarded as applicable where national authorities act on behalf of the ICC Prosecutor.

In addition to a violation of the human rights protections under Article 55, any other disregard of a provision of the ICC Statute may trigger the application of Article 69(7). This pertains in particular to a number of additional provisions in the ICC Statute that also protect the rights of persons during investigations.[205] It can be added that the idea that has just been developed for Article 55(1) should be applicable to all of the protections contained in the ICC proper law. Regardless of whether this is mentioned in a provision, the rights of individuals must generally be respected where states act on behalf of an ICC request.

Beyond individual protections, the ICC exclusionary rule can also be triggered by other infringements. We have already seen that the rule is not limited to the violation of individual rights. More precisely, unlike it has been held in some domestic legal systems, there is no requirement contained in Article 69(7) for the provision that is violated to be aimed at the protection of the rights of the accused himself. As a result, the accused is entitled to file a motion for exclusion even where legal requirements that do not affect him directly have been violated. This includes violations of the rights of states such as those contained in the provisions

---

[204] Alamuddin 2010, p. 234; Triffterer 2008, Article 55, para 4 (McAuliffe de Guzman).

[205] See for example Article 54(1)(c), requiring that the Prosecutor shall "[f]*ully respect the rights of persons arising under this Statute.*", Article 59(2)(c), demanding for the respect of the rights of a person upon arrest by national authorities and Article 66, which pertains to the presumption of innocence.

on the cooperation regime set out in Part 9 of the Statute.[206] There is no reason why the ICC, in this respect, should not follow the parallel assessment by the ICTY.[207]

4.3.3.2 Violations of the Rules of Procedure and Evidence

Violations of the Rules of Procedure and Evidence are not explicitly mentioned in Article 69(7) of the ICC Statute. This raises the question whether violations of the Rules may trigger the ICC exclusionary rule.

To begin with, it can be noted that a comparison with the jurisprudence of the *Ad hoc* tribunals is not helpful in this respect. The ICTY has indeed considered that violations of the Rules of Procedure and Evidence are sufficient to trigger the exclusion of evidence.[208] We have seen, however, that the wording of Rule 95, in its amended version, does not list the types of norms that may trigger exclusion.[209] What is more, many of the key provisions that are part of the ICTY Rules, have, in the case of the ICC, been inserted into the Statute rather than into the Rules. Accordingly, this is one of those instance where the different shape of the ICC procedural system leads to a lack of comparability with the *Ad hoc* tribunals.[210]

Looking at the drafting process of the ICC Statute, it is unclear whether omitting the Rules from Article 69(7) was a deliberate choice or not. This omission might in fact stem from a clerical error. The inclusion of a violation of the Rules was discussed during the debates in the Preparatory Committee. At that time, however, the central draft provision on the Rules, which was then Article 52, involved different wording than the finally adopted Article 51. It contained the option to include a reference stating that the "*Rules of Procedure and Evidence* [...] *shall be an integral part of this Statute*" and would be annexed to it.[211] Consequently, in the early days of the Rome Conference, many of the debates in the different working groups might have been based on the premise that the Rules were an integral part of the Statute. At the Rome Conference, the said option was deleted. Instead, Article 51 in its final version contains another option which determines that the Rules "*shall enter into force upon adoption by a two-thirds majority of the members of the Assembly of States Parties*". The working group responsible for the provision on the Rules was different from the one working on Article 69(7).

[206]Triffterer 2008—Piragoff, Article 69, para 60, fn. 126. See also Sect. 4.3.2.2.4.

[207]See *Prosecutor v. Kordić and Čerkez* (Decision Stating Reasons for Trial Chamber's Ruling of June 1999 Rejecting Defence Motion to Suppress Evidence), ICTY (Trial Chamber), decision of 25 June 1999, para 10. On this ICTY jurisdiction, see also Sect. 3.1.3.

[208]See *Prosecutor v. Delalić* (Decision on Zdravko Mucić's Motion for the Exclusion of Evidence), ICTY (Trial Chamber), decision of 2 September 1997, para 55.

[209]Alamuddin 2010, p. 240. See also Sect. 3.1.3.

[210]Alamuddin 2010, p. 241.

[211]See Rome Statute, Official Records, Volume III, 41; available at http://untreaty.un.org/cod/icc/rome/proceedings/E/Rome%20Proceedings_v3_e.pdf (last visited: October 2013).

The consequence of this development might have been that out of a lack of cooperation, the latter simply did not take this deletion into account.[212]

Even if one considers Articles 69(7) and 51 as they were finally adopted, one may argue that the Rules are still an integral part of the ICC Statute, even without an express reference. As a consequence, it has been held that violations of the Rules are covered by the wording of the exclusionary rule.[213] This view however has not gone unchallenged. It has been opposed on the basis that restricting the exclusionary rule to the Statute was intentional and a result of the lesser significance of the Rules when compared to the Statute.[214] This opinion is certainly more in accordance with the strict wording of Article 69(7). There is, however, some argument in support of a wider interpretation that includes the Rules. Admittedly, the Rules are legally subordinate to the Statute.[215] One might nevertheless argue that they are still significant enough to trigger the application of the exclusionary rule.

The modes of drafting and adoption chosen for the Rules reveals the importance that the States Parties attached to many of the issues addressed in them. Unlike the Rules of the *Ad hoc* tribunals, the drafting and adoption of the ICC Rules was not entrusted to the judges. Many delegations were concerned about ratifying the Rome Statute without being able to exercise a certain amount of control over the many significant issues that were to be covered by the Rules. As a consequence, it was agreed that these Rules would have to be adopted by the Assembly of States Parties itself.[216] This not only highlights the significance attached to the Rules by the delegations; the mode of adoption also enhances the consistency of the Rules with the principle of legality and ultimately invests them with a higher degree of legitimacy.

The deletion of former Article 52 in turn seems not to have been due to the Rules' legal status. It was rather related to practical considerations that concerned the adoption of the Rules. The States Parties strove to prevent the Rome Conference from being overburdened with questions of procedural details. Accordingly, they chose not adopt the Rules as an annex to the Statute but instead to adopt them at a later time. The option described above was then deleted because states did not want to subject themselves in advance to a legal text that they did not know at the time.[217]

Ultimately, the overall scheme of Article 69(7) ICC Statute militates in favour of an inclusion of the Rules at this stage of the inquiry. Article 69(7) provides a

---

[212]Triffterer 2008—Piragoff, Article 69, para 62.

[213]Triffterer 2008—Piragoff, Article 69, para 62.

[214]Rwelamira 1999, p. 172. For a critical view, see Safferling 2012, p. 500.

[215]See Article 51(4) of the ICC Statute.

[216]Rwelamira 1999, p. 172.

[217]Rwelamira 1999, p. 172 et seq. See also Rome Statute, Official Records, Volume II, 238 et seq.; available at http://untreaty.un.org/cod/icc/rome/proceedings/E/Rome%20Proceedings_v2_e.pdf (last visited: October 2013).

twofold test consisting of, first, the establishment of a violation and second, the determination of its consequences. In this structure, the seriousness of a violation is not a consideration in the context of the first step, but rather in the context of the second step.[218] The Pre-Trial Chamber has held with respect to the determination of the violation under Article 69(7) that "*the Statute does not 'quantify'*" this violation.[219] Minor breaches must rather be sorted out when considering their detrimental effect in the single case. In light of this distinction, the argument seems unconvincing that the Rules should generally be disregarded because of their alleged minor significance. Whether a Rule is significant enough to call for exclusion must rather be decided in a second step on the basis of a comprehensive balancing exercise.

4.3.3.3 Violations of Internationally Recognized Human Rights

In addition to statutory violations, the ICC exclusionary rule can be triggered by a violation of '*internationally recognized human rights*'. In view of the Court's legitimacy concerns, it is evidently crucial that judgments do not rely on human rights violations. The more difficult question is how to determine those protections that are covered by the human rights reference in Article 69(7) of the ICC Statute. The notoriously vague formulation '*internationally recognized human rights*' precludes any conclusive definition. The choice of such a broad reference, however, bears advantages in light of the dynamic nature of human rights law. Human rights standards are constantly subjected to the development of societal values. Any comprehensive coverage of contemporary human rights protections requires therefore that judges be given enough discretion to be able to adapt to developments. Of course, here again, the margin of appreciation is not entirely without limits. We will see that it is possible at least to delineate the term to a certain degree.

The ICC Statute uses the formulation '*internationally recognized human rights*' both in Article 69(7) and in Article 21(3). Neither of these provisions provides any further guidance on its content. The elusive wording of the formulation makes it difficult in turn to simply determine any ordinary or plain meaning in terms of Article 31 of the Vienna Convention on the Law of Treaties.[220]

Neither has international jurisprudence established a common definition that would suggest an ordinary meaning. A look at the case law reveals that while both the ICC and the *Ad hoc* tribunals have repeatedly used the expression, their jurisprudence has not provided any substantial, let alone common, definition. Instead, the case law usually refers cumulatively to a number of human rights conventions

---

[218] See also Sect. 5.4.

[219] *Prosecutor v. Lubanga* (Decision on the admission of material from the 'bar table'), ICC (Trial Chamber), decision of 24 June 2009, para 35.

[220] On the applicability of the Vienna Convention on the Law of Treaties, see Sect. 2.2.2.

to demonstrate that a right is an '*internationally recognized human right*'.[221] Reference is regularly made to international conventions such as the International Covenant on Civil and Political Rights (ICCPR), but also to regional conventions, including the European and the American Convention on Human Rights, and sometimes the African Charter of Human and Peoples Rights and the Arab Charter of Human Rights.[222] It can been noted that the ICC, in its first decisions dealing with Article 69(7) has most heavily relied on the case law of the ECtHR.[223]

Furthermore, no ordinary meaning can be derived from the use of the expression in international legal sources.[224] The phrase appears regularly in international instruments such as in resolutions of the UN Security Council or the UN General Assembly, as well as in declarations and guidelines of different UN organs, in documents issued by regional organisations and in international treaties. It has also been employed by NGOs such as Amnesty International and Human Rights Watch.[225] But, in general, these instruments do not elaborate any further on the meaning of the phrase. Where further specification is included, reference is usually made to major human rights treaties such as the Universal Declaration of Human Rights (UDHR)[226] or the ICCPR.[227] Some texts also enumerate specific rights solely for the understanding of the term in the respective treaty.[228] There is not, however, any common understanding of the phrase as of today.

An approach to the expression seems nevertheless possible. Some basic assumptions can be drawn from teleological and methodological arguments permissible under Article 31 of the Vienna Convention on the Law of Treaties.

First of all, a teleological approach indicates that the ICC is always bound by the highest human rights standards. We have established earlier that the main purpose of ICC proceedings lies in positive general prevention and that the main

---

[221]Critical, Sheppard 2010, p. 48.

[222]Bitti 2009, p. 301; Gradoni et al. 2013, p. 88.

[223]See *Prosecutor v. Katanga and Chui* (Decision on the Prosecutor's Bar Table Motions), ICC (Trial Chamber), decision of 17 December 2010, para 60 et seq.; *Prosecutor v. Lubanga* (Decision on the confirmation of charges), ICC (Pre-Trial Chamber), decision of 29 January 2007, para 73 et seq.; confirmed in *Prosecutor v. Lubanga* (Decision on the admission of material from the "bar table"), ICC (Trial Chamber), decision of 24 June 2009, para 19; *Prosecutor v. Katanga and Chui* (Decision on the confirmation of charges), ICC (Pre-Trial Chamber), decision of 30 September 2008, para 93 et seq.

[224]Hafner and Binder 2004, p. 183.

[225]For an enumeration of instruments referring to the phrase, see Hafner and Binder 2004, p. 178 et seq.

[226]Universal Declaration of Human Rights, signed on 16 December 1966, adopted on 10 December 1948, available at http://www.un.org/en/documents/udhr/index.shtml (last visited: October 2013).

[227]See for instance *The United Nations Millenium Declaration*, UN Doc. A/55/49 (2000), paras 24, 25, available at: http://www1.umn.edu/humanrts/instree/millennium.html (last visited: October 2013).

[228]See for instance Dayton Peace Accords, Annex 6: *Agreement on Human Rights*, entered into force on 14 December 1995. See also Young 2011, p. 204.

reason to exclude evidence beyond reliability is to maintain the Court's integrity. In view of its need for legitimacy, the Court has a decisive interest in applying a high human rights standard. Ultimately, this high standard is also implied in the simple fact that the reference includes '*internationally recognized human rights*' without any distinctions. It is only possible to guarantee that no human rights are violated by always adhering to the highest standard among the relevant rights.[229] It has in fact been held that, beyond the ICC Statute, it is a general principle of human rights law that the highest possible standard of protection is authoritative.[230]

Secondly, a wide interpretation should also be applied to the geographical dimension of Article 69(7). The term '*internationally*' presupposes a certain degree of widespread approval. The question that arises is how broad the recognition must be in order to become '*international*'. A systematic comparison with Article 7(1)(h) of the ICC Statute is helpful in this respect. It suggests that this qualifier should not be used to overly restrict the applicability of the ICC exclusionary rule. In the context of crimes against humanity, Article 7(1)(h) refers to "*grounds that are universally recognized as impermissible under international law*". The use of the expression '*universally*' in the ICC Statute indicates that a higher level of recognition exists when compared to an '*international*' recognition and that the latter encompasses a broader category of human rights. Universal recognition would demand a right to be recognized in all world societies. For recognition to be international in turn, a less comprehensive endorsement would suffice.[231] This assessment is confirmed by a look at the legislative history of the provision. The use of the qualifier '*universal*' was discussed during the consultations on the ICC Statute. In the end, however, it was rejected because it was considered too limiting.[232]

This means, first of all, that for the most basic human rights protections, establishing that a certain right is '*internationally recognized*' does not pose much difficulty. With respect to these rights, there is a considerable amount of overlap between the different human rights conventions.[233] Rights such as the right to silence or the right to legal assistance, for instance, are so comprehensively covered by human rights treaties that at least their core content definitely meets the degree of recognition required by the qualifier '*international*'. It is irrelevant in turn whether the protection of such rights is acknowledged in all world societies.

In addition, beyond the core rights covered by treaty law, the reference without doubt also covers any right that has acquired the status of customary law.

---

229 Gradoni et al. 2013, p. 86.

230 See *Prosecutor v. Mrkšić* et al. (Judgment), ICTY (Trial Chamber), decision of 5 May 2009, Dissenting Opinion Judge Pocar, para 7: "*One of the key principles in the international protection of human rights is that when there are diverging international standards, the highest should prevail.*" See also Gradoni et al. 2013, p. 86.

231 Bitti 2009, p. 301; Edwards 2001, p. 377 et seq.

232 Triffterer 2008—Piragoff, Article 69, para 64.

233 Gradoni et al. 2013, p. 88.

The determination of customary law requires broad recognition among states.[234] Where these relatively strict conditions are met, the necessary degree of recognition will automatically be satisfied.[235]

The previous deliberations are reflected in the general practice of the ICC and the *Ad hoc* tribunals of mentioning conventions cumulatively and interchangeably which was considered at the outset.[236] The citations include regional instruments, such as the ECHR, the ACHR and the AChHPR. In the ICC jurisprudence, regional instruments alone have been cited as an indication for the existence of an *internationally recognized human rights* standard.[237] With respect to the exclusion of evidence, we have seen that the ICC has heavily relied on the case law of the ECtHR. International criminal institutions have more generally never considered regional instruments irrelevant only because of their geographically limited scope.[238] The question arises, however, whether quoting single regional human rights instruments or the jurisprudence of their monitoring bodies truly suffices to establish an '*internationally*' recognized right.

In accordance with the above, the practice to refer interchangeably to regional conventions and case law is rather unproblematic where main human rights instruments set forth identical protections.[239] As we will see in more detail below, mentioning more than just one regional convention will always improve the transparency of judicial reasoning. But where a right is sufficiently widespread, shortcomings to this effect do not affect the establishment of the right as such. The geographical dimension of the human rights reference raises questions, however, where a right is not as broadly recognized.

There is no indication that the wording of the human rights reference precludes the reliance on single regional human rights instruments. A literal interpretation of the word '*international*' does not *per se* indicate that any minimum level of recognition must be reached.[240] A systematic reading of the human rights reference even suggests that it is characterized by a high amount of flexibility. This in turn indicates that there is a broad discretion as to the legal instruments that may be relied upon.

[234]On the determination of customary law, see Werle 2012, para 154. See also Sect. 2.3.2.2.

[235]Similar, Sheppard 2010, p. 48.

[236]Gradoni et al. 2013, p. 88.

[237]See e.g. *Prosecutor v. Lubanga* (Judgment on the appeal of the Prosecutor against the decision of Trial Chamber I entitled "Decision on the consequences of non-disclosure of exculpatory materials covered by Article 54(3)(e) agreements and the application to stay the prosecution of the accused, together with certain other issues raised at the Status Conference on 10 June 2008"), ICC (Appeals Chamber), decision of 21 December 2008, para 46; *Prosecutor v. Harun and Kushayb* (Decision on the Prosecution Application under Article 58(7) of the Statute), ICC (Pre-Trial Chamber I), decision of 27 April 2007, para 28.

[238]Alamuddin 2010, p. 236; Gradoni et al. 2013, p. 87; Sluiter 2009, p. 466.

[239]Sheppard 2010, p. 50.

[240]Sheppard 2010, p. 64.

The words '*internationally recognized*' can be contrasted with other formulations in the ICC Statute. The reference to external sources in Article 21(1)(c) for instance includes '*international law and internationally recognized norms and standards*'. The wording indicates that there is a difference between '*international*' and '*internationally recognized*'. The conjunction with '*law*' on the one hand and '*norms and standards*' on the other seems to imply that '*internationally recognized*' refers to a more flexible concept than the term '*international*'. This is also supported by the formulation in Article 36(3)(b)(ii) of the ICC Statute that alludes to the '*law of human rights*, which again seems to refer to a more rigid body of law than '*internationally recognized human rights*'.[241]

The broad and flexible interpretation of the reference is also supported by a look at the genesis of the provision. In the early debates, a reference to '*rules of international law*' was considered.[242] Subsequently, this reference was, however, deleted in favour of a formulation that was explicitly meant to be broader, namely the formulation '*internationally protected human rights*'.[243] Later, the word '*protected*' was changed because it was considered misleading. Critics argued that it was unclear which human rights were not protected.[244]

As a matter of principle, these considerations suggest that the ICC judges have the discretion to consider that a right that is set forth in a regional convention is '*internationally recognized*'.

This kind of flexibility cannot, however, result in arbitrariness. Where different human rights instruments provide different standards, judges cannot simply choose among these instruments without further explanation. In most cases, the question of diverging standards can easily be solved by relying on the teleological arguments raised above. We have seen that in light of the legitimacy concerns of the ICC, the Court should generally adopt the highest among different standards.

The determination of the correct standard of a right would then only be problematic where, in the circumstances of the case, different rights are affected and these rights come into conflict.[245] This is the situation where the adequate protection of one right rules out another right being protected to a similar degree. In such a situation, the different human rights regimes have often found different solutions for the balancing of the various interests involved. Where this is the case, applying

---

[241]Young 2011, p. 193.

[242]The wording was supposed to include in particular the International Covenant on Civil and Political Rights, without however being limited to it; see Preparatory Committee, *Decisions Taken By The Preparatory Committee At Its Session Held From 1 To 12 December 1997* of 18 December 1997, endnote 60; available at: http://www.iccnow.org/?mod=prepcommittee5 (last visited: October 2013).

[243]See Preparatory Committee, *Decisions Taken By The Preparatory Committee At Its Session Held From 1 To 12 December 1997* of 18 December 1997, endnote 60.

[244]Altogether, see Triffterer 2008—Piragoff, Article 69, para 64.

[245]Gradoni et al. 2013, p. 86; Sheppard 2010, p. 64 et seq.

the highest standard naturally becomes relative. While one human rights system may emphasize a certain right, another may focus on the conflicting protection.[246]

In the context of Article 69(7) of the ICC Statute, however, such cases are likely to be a rare exception. It presupposes a conflict of rights that arises already at the stage of evidence collection. Only then would such a conflict influence the existence of an '*internationally recognized human right*' under the chapeau of Article 69(7). Such rare cases may include the use of force during the investigative measure in order to protect the investigators against an attack. This would result in a conflict between the right to physical integrity of the defendant and of the same right of the investigators. Another example could be that the evidence results from a journalist whose work has impinged upon the defendant's right to privacy, which would result in a conflict of the latter right with the freedom of the press. Where human rights instruments have found different solutions for such conflicts, the ICC can obviously not simply rely on one instrument. It will have to disclose the different standards in its judgments. It will then have to find its own solution by weighing the different human rights affected in light of its own values and in view of the peculiarities of its legal framework. Reference to single regional human rights instruments and related case law is not precluded under the ICC exclusionary rule. Such a reference falls short, however, where instruments provide different standards of protection. Here, the ICC must disclose its line of reasoning in more detail.

While the focus on single instruments is not prohibited, we have already alluded to the fact that it would generally be advisable to rely on a broader legal basis. Such a practice would enhance the transparency of the Court's legal reasoning. This would contribute to the fulfilment of its legitimacy aspirations. In particular, the Court would be well advised to include more often in its assessments the legal norms and standards considered legitimate in those communities that are directly affected by its jurisdiction.[247] The focus of the ICC judges on the ECtHR is understandable to some extent. The significance of the European human rights regime has been depicted above.[248] At the same time, all of the ICC's prosecutions today affect African communities. Critics have claimed that the ICC is a Western court that targets African states in an inappropriate way.[249] This is why the socio-pedagogical purpose of the ICC requires, to the extent that is possible, the inclusion of affected societies in a dialogue about shared human rights beliefs. Thus, the African human rights system in particular should not be overlooked in the

[246]Sheppard 2010, p. 64.

[247]The same idea is also supported by Article 21(1)(c) of the ICC Statute which allocates particular significance to the consideration of "[…] *the national laws of States that would normally exercise jurisdiction over the crime* […]".

[248]See in particular Sect. 3.2.1.

[249]See for instance Ssenyonjo 2013, p. 385 et seq. For a summary of the discussion, see also Kimani 2009, p. 12 et seq.; available at: http://www.un.org/africarenewal/fr/magazine/october-2009 (last visited: October 2013).

Court's decision-making.[250] Open-ended clauses such as the human rights reference in Article 69(7) are a particularly important tool in this respect. We have seen that the procedural law of the ICC was developed on the basis of Western legal systems. As a consequence, theses systems are usually also considered for the purpose of interpretation, including in this research.[251] Open-ended clauses such as the notion of '*internationally recognized human rights*' in turn are gateways for the consideration of different values in the international arena and in particular of those prevailing in the affected communities. Naturally, this cannot mean following norms and standards that reflect the very attitude that the effects of positive general prevention are supposed to overcome. But local legal regimes must not be ignored where they are consistent with the Court's own values.[252]

In conclusion, it comes as no surprise that it is not possible to positively define the exact content of a phrase as vague as '*internationally recognized human rights*'. Ultimately, this ambiguity was a deliberate choice by the Statute's drafters, giving the ICC judges a wide margin of discretion. The only practical approach to gain some understanding of the term is by considering some reference points. This includes the assumption of a high human rights standard, as well as of a generally flexible approach, in particular with regard to the geographical dimension of the phrase. At the same time, the Court should be careful to make use of the possibility of addressing local standards and values through the open-ended human rights references set forth in its Statute.

4.3.3.4 The Insignificance of Violations of Domestic Law

The final question that arises relates to the treatment of violations of domestic law under Article 69(7) of the ICC Statute. The issue whether such violations should be able to trigger the ICC exclusionary rule was raised in the debates in the Preparatory Committee. Some states argued in favour of the creation of a mechanism that would allow the Court to decide whether evidence had been collected in conformity with domestic law. The majority, however, was concerned that the Court would have to adjudicate on national law, thereby interfering with the sovereignty of the respective state.[253] This latter view, according to which "*the Court*

[250]Young 2011, p. 205 and p. 207. For an introduction into the African human rights system, see Viljoen 2012, p. 151 et seq., see in particular p. 213 et seq. (on substantive human rights law in Africa, including in particular the Bajul Charter), p. 289 et seq. (on the work of the African Commission on Human Rights) and p. 410 et seq. (on the work of the African Court of Human and Peoples' Rights).

[251]See Sect. 2.3.2.3. See also Gradoni et al. 2013, p. 70.

[252]Damaška 2009, p. 184.

[253]Edwards 2001, p. 361.

should not get involved in intricate inquiries about domestic law and procedure", finally prevailed.[254]

Accordingly, Article 69(8) of the ICC Statute precludes the Court from ruling on the application of domestic law. It has been criticised that to generally exclude the possibility of challenging domestic illegalities does not do justice to the fundamental significance of the exclusionary rule for trial fairness. In addition, it has been considered inconsistent with the requirement placed on States Parties by Article 88 of the ICC Statute to ensure that their domestic law provides for sufficient procedures for all forms of cooperation. And the same has been said about Article 93, which requires that States Parties, under their national procedures, comply with ICC requests.[255]

As justified as this criticism may be, the basic legislative decision in favour of state sovereignty that is contained in Article 69(8) seems quite clear. Accordingly, the ICC Trial Chamber, in the *Lubanga* case, adopted the same approach to violations of domestic law as the ICTY.[256] It has emphasised that domestic rules, even if they implement national standards protecting human rights, do not automatically trigger the ICC exclusionary rule.[257] Naturally, this is as long as they do not likewise constitute a violation of internationally recognised human rights. But a violation of domestic law will never be able as such to trigger the exclusion of evidence.

This is not, however, to say that such violations will never have any impact on admissibility. It has been doubted whether the categorical stipulation to refrain from any consideration of national law can always entirely be complied with. In fact, compliance with formal requirements under domestic law will have to be taken into account when determining whether an '*internationally recognized human rights*' has been violated.[258] This is because formal correctness as such is a procedural guarantee for persons affected by investigative measures. To this extent, Article 69(8) will have to be interpreted narrowly, prohibiting an overall reliance on domestic violations and a comprehensive assessment of national law, but not its consideration altogether.

Early ICC case law also seems to have followed this line. The Trial Chamber, when deciding on an alleged violation of *internationally recognized human rights* in the context of a house search in *Lubanga*, alluded to the fact that the order to conduct this investigative measure was "*given by the competent authority in order*

---

[254] ICC Preparatory Committee, *Report of the Preparatory Committee on the Establishment of an International Criminal Court* Volume I, *Proceedings of the Preparatory Committee during March-April and August 1996*, U.N. Doc. A/51/22 of 13 September 1996, p. 60 et seq.

[255] Edwards 2001, p. 362.

[256] For the ICTY, see *Prosecutor v. Kordić and Čerkez* (Decision Stating Reasons for Trial Chamber's Ruling of June 1999 Rejecting Defence Motion to Suppress Evidence), ICTY (Trial Chamber), decision of 25 June 1999, para 10. See also Sect. 3.1.3.

[257] *Prosecutor v. Lubanga* (Decision on the admission of material from the "Bar Table"), ICC (Trial Chamber), decision of 24 June 2009, para 36.

[258] See Orie 2002, p. 1486; De Meester et al. 2013, p. 294.

to gather evidence for the purpose of lawful criminal proceedings".[259] The compliance with domestic formalities is thus one consideration in the overall establishment of a violation under Article 69(7).[260]

This approach can be welcomed in light of the comprehensive respect for procedural rights that it reflects. Not least, it seems to bear out to some degree the fundamental criticism of Article 69(8) summed up at the outset. At the same time, it can be noted that the Trial Chamber did not go into a detailed analysis of domestic law, but confined itself to a *prima facie* assessment. This reflects the challenge posed by the consideration of domestic legal aspects when determining a violation under Article 69(7). ICC judges cannot disregard entirely blatant illegalities under national law. But the express restrictions contained in Article 69(8) of the ICC Statute make it difficult for the judges in individual cases to find the right margin for such considerations and to not trespass on legislative orders.

4.3.3.5 Examples of Violations of Under Article 69(7) of the ICC Statute

The spectrum of rights covered by the chapeau of Article 69(7) of the ICC Statute cannot be determined exhaustively. To get a better idea of the kind of protections that fall into the scope of the ICC exclusionary rule, we will nevertheless look at a few examples. These examples will also serve as a background for later considerations. The following chapters will refer to specific rights violations. The most significant ones will be treated in the following sections. Where these rights are expressly mentioned in the ICC Statute, the applicability of the ICC exclusionary rule would not require a determination of whether they also exist as an 'internationally recognized human right'. For reasons of completeness, and in order to fully understand the significance and the scope of these rights for later considerations, we will, however, address their status under international law as well.

4.3.3.5.1 The Prohibition of Torture

The first example of a right covered by the chapeau of Article 69(7) is also the most obvious, namely the right not to be tortured. This right is explicitly protected by Article 55(1)(b) of the ICC Statute. In light of the previous discussion on the applicability of Article 55(1) of the ICC Statute to acts of domestic authorities,[261] it is interesting to note that commentators have argued that the primary aim of Article 55(1)(b) seems to be the protection of persons against violations

---

[259] *Prosecutor v. Lubanga* (Decision on the confirmation of charges), ICC (Pre-Trial Chamber), decision of 29 January 2007, para 76.

[260] Similar Triffterer 2008—Piragoff, Article 69, para 75.

[261] See Sect. 4.3.3.1.

committed by state authorities that assist OTP investigations.[262] Furthermore, where the admissibility of statements is concerned, acts of torture regularly also result in a violation of the right to silence under Article 55(1)(b) and (2)(b).[263]

The right not to be tortured is without doubt also an 'internationally recognized human right'. The rather moderate level of recognition required by the human rights reference is certainly met.[264] Torture is prohibited under international treaties, namely under Article 7 of the ICCPR and under Article 5 of the UDHR, as well as under regional human rights norms such as Article 5(2) of the ACHR, Article 3 of the ECHR and Article 5 of the Banjul Charter. Most importantly, it is banned by the UN Convention against Torture, which by May 2012 had acquired 153 States Parties.[265] The Convention, in Article 2, contains an absolute ban on torture. States Parties to the Convention are explicitly forbidden to derogate from this prohibition whatever the circumstances.[266]

Beyond treaty law, torture is also banned by customary law. What is more, this ban is not only a simple rule of customary international law but one of *jus cogens*. As a result, derogations are also forbidden by custom.[267] The consequence of this broad recognition is that evidence obtained through torture must always be inadmissible under Article 69(7) of the ICC Statute. As we will see, despite the discretionary nature of the ICC exclusionary rule, this consequence is mandatory.[268] This includes not only primary but also secondary evidence.[269]

4.3.3.5.2 The Right to Silence

Some preliminary remarks are also in order with respect to the right to silence, also referred to as the privilege against self-incrimination or the right not to confess guilt. Irrespective of the idiom, the core substance of this right appears to be identical.[270] It guarantuees the right of a suspect not to be compelled to particpate

---

[262] Calvo-Goller 2006, p. 167; Triffterer 2008, Article 55, para 6 (McAuliffe de Guzman).

[263] Zappalà 2003, p. 55.

[264] On the necessary level of recognition, see Sect. 4.3.3.3.

[265] See The United Nations Treaty Collection, available under: http://treaties.un.org/Pages/ViewDetails. asp?src=TREATY&mtdsg_no=IV-9&chapter=4&lang=en (last visited: October 2013).

[266] It should be noted that except for the Central African Republic, all of the states currently concerned by the ICC's jurisdiction have ratified UNCAT. Furthermore, all of them, including the Central African Republic have ratified the Banjul Charter. The suggestion, made in Sect. 4.3.3.3, to take into account human rights protections explicitly recognized in the affected communities would therefore be complied with if such a case were currently to be decided.

[267] For a comprehensive deduction of both the customary status and the *jus cogens* nature of the prohibition against torture, see Stein 2007, p. 240 et seq.

[268] See Sect. 5.4.3.

[269] See Sect. 6.2.3.4.

[270] Zappalà 2003, p. 77.

in his or her own conviction and the ensuing right to make a self-determined choice about whether and to what extent to speak to the authorities. This right is one of the most basic guarantees of the law of criminal procedure.[271] It is explicitly included in human rights instruments such as the ICCPR[272] and the ACHR.[273] The European Convention on Human Rights in turn does not expressly refer to the right to silence. The guarantee has however been recognized by the ECtHR in its case law as part of Article 6(1) of the ECHR. Finally, the Statutes of the *Ad hoc* tribunals also contain respective safeguards.[274]

At the domestic level, not all modern systems of criminal procedure recognize this right and where they do, the scope of protection varies considerably.[275] Critics have in fact deplored a weakening of the right to silence in recent years.[276] At the same time, the comprehensive protection by supranational and international legal instruments is still mirrored in a widespread recognition and enforcement by domestic legal orders. Despite these reservations, it appears safe to claim that the right to remain silent is an '*internationally recognized human right*' in the sense of Article 69(7) of the ICC Statute. This is all the more plausible in light of the assumption made above that this formula does not require universal recognition.[277]

While this interpretative exercise underlines the significance of the right to silence, as for the right not to be tortured, the recourse to '*internationally recognized human rights*' is not necessary for the applicability of the ICC exclusionary rule. In its Articles 55 and 64, the ICC Statute contains the most modern phrasing of the right to silence. Article 55 establishes a twofold protection at the investigation stage. Any person in general is protected by a right "*to not be compelled to incriminate himself or herself or to confess guilt*", as set forth in Article 55(1)(a) of the ICC Statute. Once a person becomes a suspect, this protection is reinforced by the right "[t]*o remain silent, without such silence being a consideration in the determination of guilt or innocence*" under Article 55(2)(b) of the ICC Statute. The scope of these provisions clearly overlaps. Yet Article 55(1)(a) is primarily meant to protect persons from providing the prosecution with evidence against themselves and especially from being pressured into doing so. Article 55(2) in turn adds a distinct notion to the protection of the right to silence. It focusses on the right to be free of procedural sanctions for refusing to answer questions.[278]

---

[271] Safferling 2009, p. 784.

[272] See Article 14(3)(g) of the ICCPR.

[273] See Article 8(2)(g) of the ACHR.

[274] See Article 21(4)(g) of the ICTY Statute and Article 20(4)(g) of the ICTR Statute.

[275] Pradel 2008, p. 444.

[276] Safferling 2009, p. 784.

[277] See Sect. 4.3.3.3.

[278] Zappalà 2003, p. 78 et seq.

According to the arguments made above, both subparagraphs apply not only to interrogations conducted by the international prosecutor but also where domestic investigators operate on his behalf.[279]

4.3.3.6 The Right to Privacy and the Requirement of a Search Warrant

The last right that we will consider is the right to privacy. Generally speaking, the right to privacy is widely recognized, not only for criminal proceedings. Its exact content is not easy to determine. It has been described as pertaining to the extent to which a person must be 'left alone', to his or her choice to interact and exist with or without others and to the degree to which his or her identity, integrity, autonomy, intimacy, sexuality or emotions may not be interfered with against his or her will.[280] In the context of criminal investigations, the right to privacy contains in particular the right to be free from unreasonable, arbitrary or unlawful searches and seizures. One important aspect of this right is the question whether this entails the right to have one's premises searched only subsequent to the issuance of a search warrant.

Unlike the rights described above, the right to privacy is not expressly mentioned in the ICC Statute. Its inclusion was discussed in the course of the negotiation process.[281] But, in the end, proposals to this effect were not accepted.[282] We will see, however, that, in general, the right to privacy can be considered an 'internationally recognized human right' in terms of Article 69(7) of the ICC Statute. At the same time, we will have to give some consideration to the extent to which the human rights reference covers this right and in particular to the question whether it includes the necessity of a search warrant. This latter question is of paramount importance for the practice of evidence gathering. It will also be relevant at a later stage in this research in the context of the significance of hypothetical courses of investigations for the exclusion of evidence.[283]

In principle, the right to privacy can easily be classified as an 'internationally recognized human right'. The required threshold of recognition is evidently satisfied. Provisions on the right to privacy exist in both international and regional human rights instruments. At the international level, these include in particular Article 12 of the UDHR, as well as Article 17 of the ICCPR. At the regional level, both Articles 8 of the ECHR and Article 11 of the ACHR protect the right to

---

[279]See Sect. 4.3.3.1.

[280]Edwards 2001, p. 331.

[281]See for instance the proposal contained in the Draft Report of the Intersessional Meeting from 19 to 30 January 1998 in Zutphen, The Netherlands, 30 January 1998, as reprinted in De Meester et al. 2013, p. 294.

[282]For a detailed description of the negotiation process with respect to the right to silence, see Edwards 2001, p. 349 et seq.

[283]See Sect. 6.4.3.

privacy.[284] In addition, the right is also widely recognized at the domestic level. A large number of those states with written constitutions have privacy safeguards incorporated in their fundamental legal texts. This includes the constitutions of states affected by the jurisdiction of the ICC.[285] This latter point indicates that privacy is not only a Western concept.[286] As a consequence of its broad recognition and application, the right to privacy has even been claimed to have acquired the status of customary law.[287] It does not therefore come as a surprise that the ICC, in its early jurisprudence, has confirmed that the right to privacy is an 'internationally recognized human right' under the ICC Statute.[288]

A question that has not yet been discussed in the case law of the Court is whether, under this right, searches in the context of international prosecutions require a search warrant. Given the practical significance of the requirement and its implications for the applicability of the ICC exclusionary rule to warrantless searches, we will address this issue in more detail.

In many domestic systems, the conduct of a search requires a judicial authorization by way of a search warrant granted before the search. But a look just at the domestic systems reviewed so far reveals that the requirement is dealt with in a variety of ways. This includes differences in terms of its legal basis, as well as with respect to its scope.

Both in the United States and in Germany, the warrant requirement is codified as a matter of constitutional law.[289] In Canada in turn, while the constitution contains a provision prohibiting unreasonable searches, this provision does not explicitly mention the need for a search warrant.[290] The warrant requirement has however been established through case law. According to the jurisprudence of the Canadian Supreme Court, there is an assumption that a search is unreasonable where no warrant was previously issued. This assumption is based on the

[284]The African Charter on Human Rights and Freedoms in turn has been criticized as incomplete *inter alia* because it does explicitly mention the right to silence, see Heyns 2003, p. 687. In light of the otherwise comprehensive coverage by human rights onstruments, this does not affect the status of the right as '*internationally recognized*'.

[285]See Article 27 of the Constitution of Uganda; Article 31 of the Constitution of the Democratic Republic of Congo; Article 14 of the Constitution of the Central African Republic; Article 4 of the Constitution of Côte d' Ivoire; Article 29 of the Constitution of the Republic of Sudan; as well as Article 31 of the Constitution of Kenya.

[286]Also see Edwards 2001, p. 401.

[287]See Edwards 2001, p. 388 et seq.

[288]See *Prosecutor v. Lubanga* (Decision on the confirmation of charges), ICC (Pre-Trial Chamber), decision of 29 January 2007, paras 74 and 75, confirmed by *Prosecutor v. Lubanga* (Decision on the admission of material from the "bar table"), ICC (Trial Chamber), decision of 24 June 2009, para 19.

[289]See the 4th amendment of the United Stated Bill of Rights, as well as Article 13(2) of the German Grundgesetz.

[290]See Section 8 of the Canadian Charter of Rights and Freedoms.

argument that a prior judicial authorization, when compared to a subsequent validation, is the most effective instrument to prevent unjustified searches.[291]

In the English legal system, warrantless searches are handled less strictly than in the other three systems. Under English law, a warrant is required by statutory law.[292] At the same time, in a large number of cases, a broad variety of exceptions enable investigators to enter private premises without a warrant. These exceptions include, for instance, the far-reaching power to generally conduct warrantless searches subsequent to a suspect's arrest.[293] Exceptions to the general warrant requirement admittedly also exist in other systems of criminal procedure, including, in particular, in cases of urgency. But at least among the other domestic systems reviewed here, this exceptional power of police and prosecutors is not as broad as in the English system.[294]

Turning to the international level, none of the statutes of the ICC's predecessors has explicitly required judicial authorization for searches and seizures or other coercive measures. At both the International Military Tribunal at Nuremberg (IMT) and the International Military Tribunal for the Far East (IMFTE), searches and other coercive measures were simply carried out without any formal legal basis justifying the measure, let alone setting conditions.[295] The extensive powers of the prosecution at the *Ad hoc* tribunals in turn include in principle the authority to conduct searches and seizures.[296] The prosecutor theoretically has the power to conduct such measures on the territory of domestic states without involving the domestic authorities. However, as we have seen before, the policy of the tribunals has often been to leave it to the domestic authorities to carry out investigative measures.[297]

Irrespective of who conducts a search, there is no express warrant requirement in either the statutes or the RPE of the tribunals. In those cases where domestic

---

[291]*Hunter et al. v. Southam Inc.*, Supreme Court of Canada, decision of 17 September 1984, [1984] 2 S.C.R. 145.

[292]See Section 8 et seq. of PACE.

[293]See Section 18 of PACE. This power already existed under common law. Altogether, see Safferling 2001, p. 157.

[294]In the United States, the Supreme Court has developed a comprehensive doctrine on search and seizure. According to this jurisprudence, there is a number of instances, where searches may be conducted without warrant. Incident to a lawful arrest for example, the police has the right to search a person, as well as those areas in the arrestee's immediate physical surroundings. Other examples for lawful warrantless searches include exigent circumstances, such as a search in the context of a so-called '*hot pursuit*', or where there is the danger that evidence will be destroyed. Altogether, see LaFave et al. 2004, p. 194 et seq. A very similar jurisprudence exists under Canadian law, see Stuart 2010, p. 247 et seq. In Germany, in case of exigent circumstances, Section 105 of the StPO allows for a search to be conducted without judicial warrant, on the order of either the public prosecutor or the police officers that investigates the crime. For a general definition of exigent circumstances under German law, see Meyer-Goßner 2013, Section 98, paras 6 et seq.

[295]De Meester et al. 2013, p. 283.

[296]For the legal basis, see Articles 18(2) of the ICTY Statute and 17(2) of the ICTR Statute.

[297]See Sect. 4.2.

authorities carry out the measure, the warrant requirement depends of course first of all on domestic law.[298] Moreover, commentators have suggested that where the domestic procedural rules do not contain a respective demand or where the international prosecutor acts himself, the need for a warrant should be derived from Rules 39(iv) and 54 of the ICTY and ICTR RPE respectively. Such a warrant would have to be issued by the judges of the tribunals.[299]

The jurisprudence of the tribunals on this matter has been rather ambiguous. On the one hand, the ICTY Trial Chamber II has expressly stated that "*there seems to be no identifiable rule of public international law according to which it is mandatory to request a judge's warrant before conducting a search and seizure*".[300] At the same time, in those cases where the international prosecutor exceptionally acts independently of domestic authorities, it has been the common practice of the international investigators to seek a warrant.[301] Given that the ICTY judges have complied with these requests, they seem to approve of this practice.[302] A mandatory demand for a judicial authorization, however, that would include those cases where the measure is carried out by domestic authorities but without previous domestic authorization, cannot be identified in the case law.[303]

With respect to the ICC, we have seen that the ICC Prosecutor is compelled to rely on domestic cooperation to an even greater extent than his colleagues at the *Ad hoc* tribunals. In the vast majority of cases, searches will be carried out by domestic authorities upon a request of the international prosecutor under Articles 54(3)(a) and 93(1)(h) of the ICC Statute. The ICC Prosecutor himself only has the very limited possibility to carry out searches himself under Article 54(3)(d) of the ICC Statute in so-called failed state scenarios.[304]

It has been argued that lawful searches for ICC investigations also require a previous judicial authorization. Others have held that a prior judicial authorization of coercive measures is dispensable in light of the different nature of international criminal proceedings as opposed to domestic law.[305]

---

[298]De Meester et al. 2013, p. 283. A violation would of course not as such trigger the exclusionary rules of the tribunals, see Sect. 3.1.3.

[299]De Meester et al. 2013, p. 284; Safferling 2001, p. 159; De Meester 2008, p. 281.

[300]*Prosecutor v. Stakić* (Decision on the Defence request to exclude evidence as inadmissible), ICTY (Trial Chamber), decision of 31 July 2002.

[301]De Meester et al. 2013, p. 284; Cryer et al. 2010, p. 527.

[302]See for instance the search warrants issued in the *Karadžić* case: *Prosecutor v. Karadžić and Mladić* ("Mandat de perquisition"), ICTY (Duty judge), two warrants issued under seal on 24 February 1998; *Prosecutor v. Karadžić* (Search warrant for the Public Security Center (CJB) Srpsko Sarajevo), ICTY (Duty judge), decision issued under seal and *ex parte* on 11 September 2003. All of these decisions were unsealed by *Prosecutor v. Karadžić* (Decision on the accused's requests for copies of search warrants), ICTY (Trial Chamber), decision of 29 August 2008.

[303]De Meester et al. 2013, p. 285.

[304]For more details, see the general explanations on the ICC cooperation regime in Sect. 4.2.

[305]Klamberg 2013, p. 252. See also Cryer et al. 2010, p. 526, fn. 138, who advance doubts in particular on the practicability of judicial authorizations.

The argument that a warrant issued by the ICC judges is necessary has been based on Article 57(3)(a) of the ICC Statute. Under this provision, the ICC Pre-Trial Chamber has the power to "*issue such orders and warrants as may be required for the purposes of an investigation*".[306] Admittedly, Article 57(3)(a) of the ICC Statute does not give any information about the nature of the orders and warrants that it requires. Instead, it leaves this determination to the discretion of the judges.[307]

Beyond this specific grant of discretion, the establishment of a warrant requirement could also be based on the general human rights clause in Article 21(3) of the ICC Statute. As we have seen, this provision does not only set forth a consistency test with respect to '*internationally recognized human rights*'; it also has a power-conferring function that allows to the judges of the ICC to act as law creators where this is necessary to make the ICC procedure compatible with human rights.[308]

A number of arguments support the view that the discretion in Article 57(3)(a) and the power of the judges under Article 21(3) should be exercised in favour of the establishment of a general warrant requirement. It can be argued that the warrant requirement is part of the right to privacy as an 'internationally recognized human right' under Article 69(7) and, more generally, under Article 21(3) of the ICC Statute.

In this respect, a look at the guidance of human rights institutions is revealing. Generally speaking, the right to privacy is not absolute under either the human rights instruments or the case law of their monitoring bodies. It can to some extent be limited, *inter alia*, for the purpose of criminal prosecution.[309] An interference with privacy rights can, however, only be justified under certain restrictive conditions. This includes the existence of a precise legal basis and that the measure is proportionate to its aim.[310] Proportionality in turn presupposes the limitation of

---

[306]De Meester et al. 2013, p. 285 et seq.; Zahar and Sluiter 2008, p. 367.

[307]De Meester et al. 2013, p. 293.

[308]See Sect. 2.3.1.2.

[309]Article 8(2) of the ECHR provides for the lawful interference for overriding reasons. This includes the public prosecution of crimes, see Ambos 2011, para 20; Safferling 2012, p. 277. Article 11 of the ACHR, while not this explicit, has been interpreted in a similar way by the Inter-American Commission on Human Rights, see *Garcia v. Peru*, Inter-American Commission on Human Rights, Report No. 1/95 of 11 February 1995: "[T]*he right to privacy is not absolute; quite the contrary, exercise of this right is routinely restricted by the domestic laws of States.*" At the international level, Article 17 of the ICCPR, which echoes Article 12 of the UDHR, has been understood in the same way by the Human Rights Committee, see Human Rights Committee, General Comment no. 16 of 8 April 1988, para 7: "*As all persons live in society, the protection of privacy is necessarily relative.*"; available at: http://www.unhchr.ch/tbs/doc.nsf/%28Symbol%29/23378a8724595410c12563ed004aeecd?Opendocument (last visited: October 2013).

[310]On Article 8 of the ECHR, see Ambos 2011, paras 18 and 22; Safferling 2012, p. 277. On Article 17 of the ICCPR, see Human Rights Committee, General Comment no. 16 of 8 April 1988, para 3: "*The term 'unlawful' means that no interference can take place except in cases envisaged by the law.*", and para 4: "[T]*hat even interference provided for by law should be* […] *reasonable in the particular circumstances.*"

the discretion of the authorities. This is most clear from the prohibition of '*arbitrariness*' which explicitly appears in the privacy guarantees of the UDHR and the ICCPR, as well as the ACHR. Admittedly, in the jurisprudence of human rights monitoring bodies, a search warrant has not always been regarded as mandatory to meet the requirements of proportionality. The warrant requirement has, however, been considered the central safeguard for the rights of affected persons. Where this safeguard does not exist, this omission must be adequately compensated through other legal protections.[311] This could be the formulation of strict and concise rules that would limit prosecutorial discretion.[312]

At the ICC, the judges have recognized proportionality as a requirement for the lawful interference with the right to privacy.[313] The warrant requirement was not at issue in this case. Were this issue to arise, it would, however, seem difficult for the Court, in light of the above-mentioned human rights case law, to guarantee respect for the principle of proportionality and to generally reject the warrant requirement at the same time.

The ICC should take into account the view, supported in the human rights case law, that a warrant issued prior to the measure has the character of a general guarantee for the proportionality of searches. This is in particular supported by the high human rights standard required with view to the Court's legitimacy concerns. Interestingly, this view has also been supported in domestic law.[314]

Moreover, in the absence of a warrant, it would be difficult for the ICC to determine that a search was proportionate based on alternative conditions being met which, under human rights law, may compensate for a missing warrant requirement. At the international level, there are no strict and concise rules that would limit the power of investigators to conduct searches and seizures and that would thereby be able to compensate for the lack of a search warrant. With respect to the complete absence of such rules in international criminal procedure, a warrant is in

[311] See for instance *Miailhe v. France*, ECtHR, decision of 25 February 1993 (Application no. 12661/87), para 38, where the ECtHR identified a violation of Article 8 of the ECHR because it considered that the fact that there was no warrant requirement was not sufficiently compensated under domestic law: "[I]*n the absence of any requirement of a judicial warrant the restrictions and conditions provided for in law* [...] *appear too lax and full of loopholes for the interferences with the applicants' rights to have been strictly proportionate to the legitimate aim pursued.*". On the case law of the ECtHR on searches, also see Edwards 2001, p. 396 et seq. Similarly, the IACtHR has found a violation of Article 11 of the ACHR in case of a warrantless search in *Garcia v. Peru,* Inter-American Commission on Human Rights, Report No. 1/95 of 11 February 1995, where it emphasized the significance of a search warrant for the justification of privacy interferences. On the case law of the IACtHR, see also Edwards 2001, p. 398 et seq.

[312] Altogether, see Zahar and Sluiter 2008, p. 367 et seq.

[313] See *Prosecutor v. Lubanga* (Decision on the confirmation of charges), ICC (Pre-Trial Chamber), decision of 29 January 2007, para 79; interestingly, this decision quotes exactly the ECtHR's case *Miailhe v. France*, ECtHR, decision of 25 February 1993 (Application no. 12661/87), confirming the approach of the ECtHR to the warrant requirement laid out before.

[314] See the jurisprudence of the Canadian Supreme Court depicted before, in particular *Hunter et al. v. Southam Inc.*, Supreme Court of Canada, decision of 17 September 1984, [1984] 2 S.C.R. 145.

fact the only possibility to limit the discretion of the authorities and to put in place safeguards against arbitrary decisions.[315]

This affects in particular those cases where the international prosecutor carries out the measure. But where a domestic system lacks a warrant requirement, it will also be difficult for the Court to assess the proportionality of the measure ex post facto. In order to establish whether a coercive measure meets the demands of '*internationally recognized human rights*', the judges would have to thoroughly assess the domestic rules allegedly compensating for the lack of a warrant. A comprehensive review of domestic legal rules, however, is not envisaged by the ICC Statute. This was a deliberate choice, which, as we have seen, was meant to avoid politically sensitive assessments of domestic investigation procedures. While it has been argued above that, despite Article 69(8), domestic rules cannot be disregarded altogether, a thorough legal analysis is exactly what this provision strives to avoid.[316] Under these conditions, advocating for a general warrant requirement seems to be the most simple and adequate means to respect both the rights of the accused and the decision of the drafters of the ICC Statute.

In contrast to this view, the particularities of the international system have been advanced to argue against a warrant requirement. It has been argued that the issuance of a warrant can be extremely difficult and time-consuming in international criminal cases.[317] This may be correct. The increased complexity of cases, however, cannot be a general argument against the guarantee of fundamental rights. In an individual case, the issuance of a warrant can also be difficult at the domestic level without the need arising to challenge the warrant requirement as such. Moreover, time-related difficulties could be handled based on the concept of exigent circumstances. It would be possible to establish conditions in the case law under which investigators in international proceedings have the exceptional power to carry out coercive measures independently.

The question remains in which cases a warrant is required. This depends on the actors that are responsible for the respective search. For the more frequent case that the domestic authorities carry out the measure, a warrant issued by the ICC would be necessary where no equivalent procedural demands exist under domestic law. The requirement of an international warrant in such cases would guarantee the proportionality of the measure by ensuring at least one level of judicial supervision.[318]

Beyond these cases, it has been suggested that an international warrant should also be issued by the ICC even where the domestic law does provide for a similar mechanism. It has been argued to this effect that domestic judges lack a sufficient overview with respect to international investigations.[319] While such a practice

---

[315] Zahar and Sluiter 2008, p. 368.

[316] On the policy behind Article 69(8) of the ICC Statute, see Sect. 4.3.3.4.

[317] See Cryer et al. 2010, p. 526, fn. 138.

[318] See De Meester et al. 2013, p. 293.

[319] Zahar and Sluiter 2008, p. 367.

would be beneficial to a uniform treatment of affected persons, it seems less compelling from a proportionality point of view to demand two levels of judicial supervision. What is more, the specific ICC cooperation system should be given due consideration. A parallel assessment of the same matter on the domestic as well as on the international level would bear the risk of diverging decisions and related conflicts of competence.

In contrast, a warrant should be necessary where the prosecutor exceptionally carries out a coercive measure himself. In such a case, there would be no other level of judicial assessment.[320] It may be argued that the authorization requested by Article 57(3)(d) of the ICC Statute already provides for such an assessment. This authorization alone cannot, however, be sufficient to justify the interference with the right to privacy.[321] The permission under Article 57(3)(d) is meant to confer upon the Prosecutor the power to act without turning to the domestic authorities. A decision under this provision is thus meant to address the sovereignty concerns that arise in the relationship between the ICC and states. A search warrant, in comparison, pertains to the relationship between the investigating authorities and the individual affected by a search. The legal test for such a warrant is different and necessarily independently of the former authorization.

References

Acquaviva G, Combs N, Heikkilä M, Linton S, McDermott Y (2013) Trial Process. In: Sluiter G, Friman H, Linton S, Zappalà S, Vasiliev S (eds) International criminal procedure: principles and rules. Oxford University Press, Oxford, pp 489–938

Alamuddin A (2010) Collection of Evidence. In: Khan K, Buisman C, Gosnell C (eds) Principles of Evidence in International Criminal Justice. Oxford University Press, Oxford, pp 231–305

Ambos K (2010) The transnational use of torture evidence. Israel Law Rev 42:362–397

Amelung K (1990) Informationsbeherrschungsrechte im Strafprozeß. Dogmatische Grundlagen individualrechtlicher Beweisverbote. Duncker & Humblot, Berlin 1990

Amelung K, Mittag M (2005) Beweislastumkehr bei Haussuchungen ohne richterliche Anordnung gemäß § 105 StPO. Neue Z Strafrecht 11:614–617

Ashworth A (1977) Excluding evidence as protecting rights. Crim Law Rev 3:723–735

Ashworth A (2003) Exploring the integrity principle in evidence and procedure. In: Mirfield P, Smith R (eds) Essays for Colin Tapper, London, pp 107–125

Ashworth A, Redmayne M (2010) The criminal process, 4th edn. Oxford

Berger M (2012) The right to silence in the Hague International Criminal Courts. Univ San Francisco Law Rev 47:1–54

Bilz K (2012) Dirty hands or deterrence? An experimental examination of the exclusionary rule. J Empirical Legal Stud 9:149–171

Bitti G (2009) Article 21 of the Statute of the International Criminal Court and the treatment of the sources of law in the jurisprudence of the ICC. In: Carsten S, Goran S (eds) The emerging practice of the International Criminal Court. Martinus Nijhoff Publishers, Leiden, pp 285–304

[320] For this argument, albeit with respect to the larger powers of the prosecutor of the *Ad hoc* tribunals, see Klamberg 2013, p. 252 et seq.

[321] But see De Meester et al. 2013, p. 292, who seem to suggest otherwise.

Brady H (2001) The system of evidence in the Statute of the International Criminal Court. In: Lattanzi F, Schabas W (eds) Essays on the Rome Statute of the International Criminal Court, vol 1. Il Sirente, Ripa Fagnano Alto 2001, pp 279–302

Buisman C (2013) Delegating investigations: lessons to be learned from the Lubanga Judgment. Northwestern J Int Hum Rights 11:30–82

Calvo-Goller N (2006) The trial proceedings of the International Criminal Court: ICTY and ICTR precedents. Martinus Nijhoff Publishers, Leiden

Combs N (2011) Evidence. In: Schabas W, Bernaz, N (eds) Routledge Handbook of International Criminal Law. London, pp 323–334

Cryer R (2009) Means of gathering evidence and arresting suspects in situation of state's failure to cooperate'. In: Cassese A (ed) The Oxford companion to international criminal justice. Oxford University Press, Oxford, pp 201–207

Cryer R, Friman A, Robinson D, Wilmshurst W (2010) An introduction to international criminal law and procedure, 2nd edn. Cambridge University Press, Cambridge

Damaška M (2009) Problematic features of international criminal procedure. In: Cassese A (ed) The Oxford companion to international criminal justice. Oxford University Press, Oxford, pp 175–186

De Meester K (2008) Coercive Measures, Privacy Rights and Judicial Supervision in International Criminal Investigations: In Need of Further Regulation?. In: Sluiter K, Vasiliev S (eds) International Criminal Procedure: Towards a Coherent Body of Law. Cameron May, London, pp 273-309

De Meester K, Pitcher K, Rastan R, Sluiter G (2013) Investigation, coercive measures, arrest and surrender. In: Sluiter G, Friman H, Linton S, Zappalà S, Vasiliev S (eds) International criminal procedure: principles and rules. Oxford University Press, Oxford, pp 171–380

Dennis I (2010) The law of evidence, 4th edn. Sweet and Maxwell, London

Edwards G (2001) International human rights law challenges to the New International Criminal Court: the search and seizure right to privacy. Yale J Int Law 26:323–412

Eisenberg U (2011) Beweisrecht der StPO: Spezialkommentar, 7th edn. C.H. Beck, Munich

Fernández de Gurmedi S (2001) In: Lee R (ed) The International Criminal Court: elements of crimes and rules of procedure and evidence. Transnational Publishers, New York, pp 235–258

Friman H (1999) Rights of persons suspected or accused of a crime. In: Lee R (ed) The International Criminal Court: the making of the Rome Statute: issues, negotiations, results. Kluwer Law International, The Hague, pp 247–262

Gallant K (1999) Individual human rights in a new international organization: The Rome Statute of the International Criminal Court. In: Bassiouni C (ed), International criminal law, Volume II: Procedural and enforcement mechanisms, 2nd edn. Transnational Publishers, New York, pp 693–723

Gaynor F, Jackson J, Klamberg M, Tochilovsky V (2013) Appeals, reviews and reconsideration. In: Sluiter G, Friman H, Linton S, Zappalà S, Vasiliev S (eds) International criminal procedure: principles and rules. Oxford University Press, Oxford, pp 1051–1150

Gosnell C (2010) Admissibility of evidence. In: Khan A, Buisman C, Gosnell C (eds) Principles of evidence in international criminal justice. Oxford University Press, Oxford, pp 375–442

Gradoni L, Lewis D, Mégret F, Nouwen S, Ohlin J (2013) General framework of international criminal justice. In: Sluiter G, Friman H, Linton S, Zappalà S, Vasiliev S (eds) International criminal procedure: principles and rules. Oxford University Press, Oxford, pp 39–130

Greco G (2007) Victims' rights overview under the ICC legal framework: a jurisprudential analysis. Int Crim Law Rev 7:531–547

Hafner G, Binder C (2004) The interpretation of article 21(3) ICC Statute opinion reviewed. Aust Rev Int Eur Law 9:163–190

Heyns C (2003) The African Regional Human Rights System: The African Charter. Penn State Law Review 108:670-702

Jackson J, Summers S (2012) The internationalisation of criminal evidence: beyond the common law and civil law traditions. Cambridge University Press, Cambridge

Kamardi C (2009) Die Ausformung einer Prozessordnung sui generis durch das ICTY unter Berücksichtigung des Fair-Trial-Prinzips. Springer, Berlin et al

Kaul H, Kreß C (1999) Jurisdiction and cooperation in the Statute of the International Criminal Court: principles and compromises. Yearb Int Humanit Law 2:143–175

Kimani M (2009) Pursuit of justice or western plot? International indictments stir angry debate in Africa. Afr Renew 23(3):12–15

Klamberg M (2013) Evidence in International Criminal Trials: Confronting Legal Gaps and the Reconstruction of Disputed Events. Martinus Nijhoff Publishers, Leiden

LaFave W, Israel J, King N (2004) Criminal Procedure, 4th edn. West Academic Publishing, St Paul

Meyer-Goßner L (2013) Strafprozessordnung, 56th edn. C.H.Beck, Munich

Muthorst O (2009) Das Beweisverbot: Grundlegung und Konkretisierung rechtlicher Grenzen der Beweiserhebung und der Beweisverwertung im Zivil-. Straf- und Verwaltungsverfahren, Mohr Siebeck, Tübingen

Orie A (2002) Accusatorial versus inquisitorial approach in international criminal proceedings. In: Cassese A, Gaeta P, Jones J (eds) The Rome Statute of the International Criminal Court: a commentary, vol 2. Oxford University Press, Oxford, pp 1439–1495

Penney S (2003) Taking deterrence seriously: excluding unconstitutionally obtained evidence under section 24(2) of the Charter. McGill Law Journal 49:105–144

Peskin V (2009) International justice in Rwanda and the Balkans. Cambridge University Press, Cambridge

Piragoff D (2001) Evidence. In: Lee R (ed) The International Criminal Court: elements of crimes and rules of procedure and evidence. Transnational Publishers, New York, pp 349–401

Potter S (1983) The road to Mapp v. Ohio and beyond: the origins, development and future of the exclusionary rule in search-and-seizure cases. Columbia Law Rev 6:1365–1404

Pradel J (2008) Droit pénal comparé, 3rd edn. Dalloz-Sirey, Paris

Rastan R (2008) Testing co-operation: the International Criminal Court and national authorities. Leiden J Int Law 21:431–456

Roberts P, Zuckerman A (2010) Criminal evidence, 2nd edn. Oxford University Press, Oxford

Rogall K (1979) Gegenwärtiger Stand und Entwicklungstendenzen der Lehre von den strafprozessualen Beweisverboten. Zeitschrift für die gesamte Strafrechtswissenschaft 191:1–44

Rwelamira M (1999) Composition and administration of the Court. In: Lee R (ed) The International Criminal Court: the making of the Rome Statute: issues, negotiations, results. Kluwer Law International, The Hague, pp 153–174

Safferling C (2001) Towards an international criminal procedure. Oxford University Press, Oxford

Safferling C (2009) Das Recht zu Schweigen und seine Konsequenzen. Zeitschrift für Internationale Strafrechtsdogmatik 13:784–794

Safferling C (2012) International criminal procedure. Oxford University Press, Oxford

Schuon C (2010) International criminal procedure: a clash of legal cultures. T.M.C. Asser Press, The Hague

Sheppard D (2010) The International Criminal Court and "Internationally Recognized Human Rights": Understanding Article 21(3) of the Rome Statute. International Criminal Law Review 10:43–71

Slobogin C (1999) Why liberals should chuck the exclusionary rule. Univ Illinois Law Rev 363–446

Slobogin C (2013) A comparative perspective on the exclusionary rule in search and seizure cases. Vanderbilt Public Law Research Paper No. 13–21. http://papers.ssrn.com/sol3/papers.cfm?abstract_id=2247746. Accessed 14 May 2015

Sluiter G (2002) International criminal adjudication and the collection of evidence: obligations of states: obligations of states. Intersentia, Antwerpen

Sluiter G (2009) Human rights protection in the ICC pre-trial phase. In: Stahn C, Sluiter G (eds) The emerging practice of the International Criminal Court. Martinus Nijhoff Publishers, Leiden, pp 459–476

Ssenyonjo M (2013) The rise of the African Union opposition to the International Criminal Court; investigations and prosecutions of African leaders. Int Crim Law Rev 13:385–428

Stuart D (2010) Charter Justice in Canadian Criminal Law, 5th edn. Carswell, Toronto
Stein A (2007) Das Verbot der Folter im internationalen und nationalen Recht: unter Betrachtung seiner Durchsetzungsinstrumente und seines absoluten Charakters. Verlag Dr. Kovač, Hamburg
Triffterer O (2008) (ed) Commentary on the Rome Statute of the International Criminal Court: Observers' notes, article by article, 2nd edn. C.H. Beck et al., Baden-Baden
Vanderpuye K (2005) The International Criminal Court and discretionary evidential exclusion: toeing the mark? Tulane J Int Comp Law 14:127–177
Viljoen F (2012) International human rights law in Africa, 2nd edn. Oxford University Press, Oxford
Weigend T (2003) Is the criminal process about truth: a German perspective. Harv J Law Public Policy 26:157–173
Young (2011) "Internationally recognized human rights" before the International Criminal Court. Int Comp Law Q 60:189–208
Zahar A, Sluiter G (2008) International criminal law: a critical introduction. Oxford UniversityPress, Oxford
Zappalà S (2002) The rights of the accused. In: Cassese A, Gaeta P, Jones J (eds) The Rome Statute of the International Criminal Court: a commentary, vol 2. Oxford University Press, Oxford, pp 1319–135
Zappalà S (2003) Human rights in international criminal proceedings. Oxford University Press, Oxford

Chapter 5
Factors in the Balancing Exercise

Abstract Under Article 69(7) of the ICC Statute, not all legal violations committed during investigations lead to the exclusion of thereby tainted evidence. Instead, evidence is only excluded where such a violation has a specific negative impact on the proceedings of the ICC, namely because either the evidence lacks reliability or because its admission "*would be antithetical to and would seriously damage the integrity of the proceedings*". We have seen in Chap. 4 that the wording of Article 69(7) of the ICC Statute, while indicating a mandatory exclusionary rule at first sight, is ultimately a discretionary rule due to fact that these additional requirements were included in the provision. We have also seen in Chap. 4 that the exclusion of illicitly obtained evidence should be guided by the integrity theory, meaning the idea that the exclusion of evidence should serve the maintenance of the integrity of the Court. Under this theory, the exercise of the discretion granted under Article 69(7) of the ICC Statute requires the Court to strike a balance between the interests of '*due process*' and '*effective law enforcement*'. In order to guide this balance, this chapter will discuss a number of factors that may militate in favour of either one of these two poles.

Keywords Torture · Mandatory rule of exclusion · Good faith · Office of the prosecutor · Customary international law · Balancing of rights · Effective law enforcement · Discretion · Abuse of process doctrine · Lubanga

Contents

P. Viebig, *Illicitly Obtained Evidence at the International Criminal Court*,
International Criminal Justice Series 4, DOI 10.1007/978-94-6265-093-0_5

5.1 Introduction

In the previous chapter, we have determined the kind of violations that may trigger the ICC exclusionary rule. But as depicted before, the establishment of such a violation does not automatically lead to exclusion under Article 69(7) of the ICC Statute. Instead, evidence is only excluded where one of the additional requirements in Article 69(7)(a) or (b) is met. Given the greater contentiousness of these cases, we will concentrate on Article 69(7)(b), which is meant to exclude evidence even where its reliability is not at issue. As the ICC Pre-Trial Chamber stated in *Lubanga*, Article 69(7)(b) of the ICC Statute gives the judges the discretion "*to seek an appropriate balance between the Statute's fundamental values in each concrete case*".[1] Under the integrity theory, the exercise of this discretion demands striking a balance between the interests of 'due process' and 'effective law enforcement'.[2] In order to guide this balance, the following sections will discuss a number of factors that may militate in favour of either one of these two poles.

5.2 The Seriousness of the Crime

With respect to domestic criminal proceedings, the seriousness of the crime that the accused is charged with is a factor that is treated differently among the various legal systems reviewed. While the ECtHR takes it into account when assessing the fairness of the trials within the Member States to the ECHR,[3] there is disagreement among domestic courts about whether the seriousness of a crime increases the interest in effective law enforcement.

Despite the gradual restriction of its exclusionary rule, the U.S. Supreme Court has not developed an exception for particularly serious crimes. The more inclusionary approaches of German and English courts in turn have deemed the seriousness of the crime to be a valid criterion. Its consideration has, however, raised criticism within legal academia in these countries.[4] The critiques have followed the same line as the recent jurisprudence in Canada, where the majority of the

---

[1]*Prosecutor v. Lubanga* (Decision on the confirmation of charges), ICC (Pre-Trial Chamber), decision of 29 January 2007, para 84. Also see *Prosecutor v. Mbarushimana* (Decision on the confirmation of charges), ICC (Pre-Trial Chamber), decision of 16 December 2011, para 61.

[2]See Sect. 4.3.2.2.5.

[3]See *Jalloh v. Germany*, ECtHR, decision of 11 July 2006 (Application no. 54810/00), paras 119 and 122; see also Sect. 3.2.4.

[4]For Germany, see German Constitutional Court (BVerfG), decision of 31 January 1973, *BVerfGE* 34, p. 250; see also Sect. 3.3.1. For the English approach, see *Regina v. Khan*, Court of Appeal of England and Wales, decision of 15 June 1992, [1993] Crim. L.R. 54; see also Sect. 3.3.3.

judges has rejected the criterion.[5] These critics make allowance for the fact that the seriousness of the crime not only impacts on the public interest in its prosecution; it also raises the level of the penalty that the accused must expect in the event of a conviction. Naturally this also increases the interest of the individual in the exclusion of the evidence. As a consequence, the gravity of the crime could be seen as militating both in favour and against exclusion.

At the international level, the exceedingly grave character of international crimes might tip the scales. The international core crimes are considerably more serious than even the gravest of those crimes that are regularly judged by domestic courts. At the same time, under the rule of law, the punishment of convicted perpetrators cannot be increased proportionally. This difference to domestic proceedings could be relied upon to argue that at the international level, crime seriousness should be a factor in favour of exclusion.[6] We will see, however, that this argument cannot be sustained.

One may argue that teleological deliberations support the significance of the seriousness of a crime at the international level. As previously stated, the socio-pedagogical aim pursued by international criminal institutions requires not only respect for due process guarantees. It also demands not undermining the confidence within the international community in the validity of international criminal law and in effective prosecution of violations.[7] In this respect, one may also advance policy concerns. International crimes are serious in particular because of their dimensions in terms of territory and affected persons, as well as because of the particular identity of the possible perpetrators. This is also what makes international proceedings so costly. And it is also what makes it often so difficult to take suspects into custody. Accordingly, there is an increased need for justification where such proceedings fail. Finally, the socio-pedagogical purpose is closely intertwined with the solidarity with the victims of these serious crimes. The use of procedural tools that hamper the enforcement of international criminal law would be met with particular incomprehension in light of the immense suffering of the victims.

Deliberations of this nature have lead the ICTY to refer to the seriousness of the crimes when deciding on the exclusion of evidence. The tribunal has held that it would be inappropriate, *inter alia* in light of the seriousness of the crimes under its jurisdiction, to exclude relevant evidence only for procedural considerations. It considered that excluding evidence in such *cases "would constitute a dangerous obstacle to the administration of justice"*.[8]

---

[5] *Regina v. Grant*, Supreme Court of Canada, decision of 17 July 2009, [2009] 2 S.C.R. 353, para 84. See also Sect. 3.3.4.

[6] In favour, Scharf 2008, p. 169.

[7] See in particular Sect. 2.2.3.

[8] *Prosecutor v. Brđanin* (Decision on the Defence "Objection to Intercept Evidence"), ICTY (Trial Chamber), decision of 3 October 2003, para 7. Similar, see *Prosecutor v. Karadžić* (Decision on the accused's Motion to exclude intercepted conversations), ICTY (Trial Chamber), decision of 30 September 2010, para 10. See also Safferling 2012, p. 501.

Conversely, at the ICC, the Trial Chamber in the *Lubanga* case unequivocally declined to consider the seriousness of the crimes when applying Article 69(7)(b) of the ICC Statute. It argued that all of the crimes under the jurisdiction of the Court were serious but that this was no argument for the admissibility of evidence.[9] The Trial Chamber's consistency can be welcomed. Enforcement interests and solidarity with victims, as important as they are, cannot serve as an argument to generally disregard basic principles of procedural fairness.

This is particularly the case where the violation of human rights is concerned. The requirements of human rights law are minimum standards. Such basic principles cannot be circumvented even in order to prosecute the gravest crimes. This is further confirmed by the deliberations underlying the integrity rationale. We have opted above for a 'court-centred' version of the integrity theory.[10] From this perspective, the ICC must strive for the consistent application of the human rights values it was set up to promote. Given the limited mandate of the Court, this necessarily applies to alleged perpetrators of heinous crimes.

A comparison with the abuse of process doctrine is further instructive in this respect. This doctrine was one of the most controversially discussed procedural issues in the *Lubanga* case. The doctrine originates from common law and gives judges the power to stop a criminal process altogether where the rights of the accused have seriously been violated. Such a stay of proceedings has far more far-reaching consequences than the exclusion of single pieces of evidence. But even here, the seriousness of the crimes has not prevented the ICC judges from using this severe procedural sanction as an *ultima ratio*.[11]

If the ICC were to include crime seriousness in its balancing exercise, it would always have to admit the evidence. To rely solely on the concern for effectiveness and for the solidarity with victims would mean to concede exactly to the kind of 'public attitude' integrity we have dismissed earlier. Exclusionary rules for illicitly obtained evidence are exceptions to the general tendency in international criminal trials to admit most evidence. The Trial Chamber in *Lubanga* has emphasized this

---

[9] *Prosecutor v. Lubanga* (Decision on the admission of material from the "bar table"), ICC (Trial Chamber), decision of 24 June 2009, para 44.

[10] See Sect. 4.3.2.2.5.

[11] See *Prosecutor v. Lubanga* (Judgment on the Appeal of Mr. Thomas *Lubanga* Dyilo against the Decision on the Defence Challenge to the Jurisdiction of the Court pursuant to Article 19(2) (a) of the Statute of 3 October 2006), ICC (Appeals Chamber), decision of 14 December 2006. See also, *Prosecutor v. Lubanga* (Decision on the consequences of non-disclosure of exculpatory materials covered by Article 54(3)(c) agreements and the application to stay the prosecution of the accused, together with certain other issues raised at the Status Conference on 10 June 2008), ICC (Trial Chamber), decision of 13 June 2008; *Prosecutor v. Lubanga* (Redacted Decision on the Prosecution's Urgent Request for Variation of the Time-Limit to Disclose the Identity of Intermediary 143 or Alternatively to Stay Proceedings Pending Further Consultations with the VWU), ICC (Trial Chamber), decision of 8 July 2010.

exceptional nature of Article 69(7) of the ICC Statute.[12] The very reason to provide for such derogation rules is that, even in light of the gravity of allegations, the guarantees of procedural fairness must be adhered to.

5.3 The Importance of the Evidence

Another factor that one might think is relevant is the importance of the evidence for the outcome of the trial. This includes the question whether the evidence is the only sustainable evidence as well as the question of its probative value.

We have seen that, according to international case law, the notion of probative value pertains to the reliability and significance of the evidence.[13] Reliability is clearly relevant under subpara (a) of Article 69(7) of the ICC Statute. But is it also a consideration where exclusion is discussed under subpara (b)? And what about the significance of a piece of evidence? The ICC Trial Chamber in *Lubanga* rejected the impact of probative value as a factor for the balancing exercise in Article 69(7)(b) of the ICC Statute. It based its decision in particular on the lex specialis nature of the provision.[14] A discussion of the different views adopted at the national and international level supports the conclusion drawn by the ICC judges.

First of all, the jurisprudence of the ICTY is of no avail even though it refers to this factor. The tribunal has emphasized that a restrictive approach to the exclusion of evidence was warranted in particular because "*excluding what would appear to be on a prima facie basis relevant and important evidence" would mean to deny the tribunal "the possibility of having available evidence which would be otherwise difficult, if not impossible, to obtain*". When assessing this reference to the importance of a piece of evidence, it should however be borne in mind that the ICTY does not usually base its decisions on exclusion on Rule 95 of its Rules of Procedure and Evidence but on Rule 89(D).[15] In the quoted case, the appreciation of the probative value of the evidence also results from the express wording of this provision. We have seen however that the relationship between Rule 89(D) and Rule 95 should in fact be characterized by the *lex specialis* nature of the latter

---

[12] *Prosecutor v. Lubanga* (Decision on the admission of material from the "Bar Table"), ICC (Trial Chamber), decision of 24 June 2009, para 44.

[13] See Sect. 4.3.1.

[14] *Prosecutor v. Lubanga* (Decision on the admission of material from the "Bar Table"), ICC (Trial Chamber), decision of 24 June 2009, para 41; confirmed by *Prosecutor v. Katanga and Chui* (Decision on the Prosecutor's Bar Table Motions), ICC (Trial Chamber), decision of 17 December 2010, para 64.

[15] See Sect. 3.1.3.

provision.[16] This is exactly the conclusion that the *Lubanga* Trial Chamber rightly draws for Articles 69(4) and 69(7) of the ICC Statute in the decision mentioned at the outset.

The importance of the tainted evidence has, however, also been taken into consideration at the domestic level. The Germancorr Federal Supreme Court has attached value to the significance of the evidence for combating serious crimes.[17] The Canadian Supreme Court as well, in the last prong of its Section 24(2) test, considers how important the evidence is for the outcome of the trial. This includes the assessment of whether the evidence is the only or at least the decisive proof of the crime.[18] In both systems, the fact that the evidence was of particular importance has been considered militating in favour of admissibility. The same approach also underlies the jurisprudence of the European Court of Human Rights, which has asked whether the evidence was decisive for the conviction in the respective ECHR member state or whether it was merely used for corroboration.[19]

Interestingly, English courts have adopted exactly the opposite view. According to English case law, the significance of a piece of evidence militates in favour of exclusion. This jurisprudence relies on the argument that where evidence against a suspect is especially strong, investigators will be particularly tempted "*to do what the provisions are aimed to prevent*". Consequently, in such a case, "*the protection of the rules is most needed*".[20]

The English approach alludes to an important consideration that confirms the general irrelevance of this factor as supported by the ICC Trial Chamber. Contrasting the different domestic approaches reveals that the same problem arises here as with the factor of crime seriousness discussed above. Ultimately, the importance of a piece of evidence increases the interest of both parties in a decision favourable to them. This consideration is applicable to both domestic and international proceedings.

As a consequence, the impact of evidence on the outcome of the trial should be seen neither as militating against nor in favour of exclusion. Where the reliability of a piece of evidence is concerned, this aspect is solely relevant under Article 69(7)(a) of the ICC Statute. The significance of the evidence in turn can be taken into account under the general admissibility rule of Article 69(4) but not under the exceptional exclusionary rule in Article 69(7)(b) of the Statute.

---

[16]See Sect. 3.1.3.

[17]See Trüg 2003, p. 230; Rogall 1979, p. 29 et seq., see also Sect. 3.3.1.

[18]See *Regina v. Grant,* Supreme Court of Canada, decision of 17 July 2009, [2009] 2 S.C.R. 353, para 79. Also see Sect. 3.3.4.

[19]*Jalloh v. Germany*, ECtHR, decision of 11 July 2006 (Application no. 54810/00), para 121.

[20]*Regina v. Keenan*, Court of Appeal of England and Wales, decision of 26 April 1989, [1990] 2 Q.B. 54.

5.4 The Seriousness and Character of the Offence

5.4.1 The General Impact of the Seriousness of the Violation

Among the judicial systems reviewed, the seriousness of the violation is the least controversial among all the possible factors. This factor has been considered relevant by the ICTY,[21] as well as by the ECtHR.[22] At the national level, all of those systems that openly base their decision on a balancing exercise, namely the German, the English and the Canadian systems, consider this a relevant factor.[23] We have seen that the U.S. system does not openly balance the interests involved. Instead, it permits derivations from the theoretically mandatory exclusionary rule only by way of exceptions. Since there is no such exception for particularly serious violations, the U.S. system is the only one among the reviewed systems that does not enable its judges to assess the gravity of a violation as such.[24] As we will see, U.S. doctrine instead leaves room for related aspects such as the question whether the investigative authorities have acted in good faith. These aspects will be treated separately below.

The ICC, in its first case law on the application of Article 69(7) of the ICC Statute, has also referred to this factor. One commentator has asserted that the jurisprudence seems contradictory on this point.[25] In its decision on exclusion in *Lubanga*, the Trial Chamber held that "*the Statute does not 'quantify' the violation*", thereby claiming that even a non-serious violation could lead to the exclusion of evidence.[26] The judges relied on a historical approach. They held that the express limitation to 'serious violations' that earlier drafts had envisaged for the provision's chapeau, did not appear in the text finally adopted at the Rome Conference.[27] But at the same time, the decision, at a later point, considers the relevance of the fact that "*the violation was not of a particularly grave kind*".[28]

---

[21]See in particular *Prosecutor v. Brđanin* (Decision on the Defence "Objection to Intercept Evidence"), ICTY (Trial Chamber), decision of 3 October 2003, para 61; see also Sect. 3.1.4.

[22]See Sect. 3.2.4.

[23]On the English jurisprudence, see *Regina v. Keenan*, Court of Appeal of England and Wales, decision of 26 April 1989, [1990] 2 Q.B. 54; *Regina v. Absolam*, Court of Appeal of England and Wales, decision of 1 July 1988, [1988] Cr. App R. 332. See also Mellifont 2007, pp. 85–86. With respect to Canada, see *Regina v. Grant,* Supreme Court of Canada, decision of 17 July 2009, [2009] 2 S.C.R. 353, para 76. See also Stuart 2010, p. 318. On the German jurisdiction, see Sect. 3.3.1.

[24]On this systematic of the U.S. exclusionary rule, see Sect. 3.3.2.

[25]Alamuddin 2010, p. 301 et seq.

[26]*Prosecutor v. Lubanga* (Decision on the admission of material from the "Bar Table"), ICC (Trial Chamber), decision of 24 June 2009, para 35.

[27]*Prosecutor v. Lubanga* (Decision on the admission of material from the "Bar Table"), ICC (Trial Chamber), decision of 24 June 2009, fn. 67 to para 35.

[28]*Prosecutor v. Lubanga* (Decision on the admission of material from the "Bar Table"), ICC (Trial Chamber), decision of 24 June 2009, para 47.

This apparent contradiction can, however, be resolved by considering the scheme of Article 69(7). Under the chapeau of the provision, the seriousness of the violation is irrelevant. It is, however, a criterion that needs to be considered under the additional requirements, namely for the assessment of whether admitting the evidence would have an adverse effect on the integrity of the proceedings.

Admittedly, the decision in *Lubanga* is slightly misleading in this respect. At first sight, the previously made distinction is what the decision seems to come down to when it holds that "[i]*t is only in the second limb of the test that a requirement of a degree of 'seriousness' is introduced*". But the decision adds a rather confusing specification to the latter assertion. It states that the degree of seriousness introduced by the second prong "*is unconnected to the seriousness of the violation*".[29] This remark can be interpreted in two ways. Either the Chamber wanted to express that the fact that a violation was serious is irrelevant for Article 69(7) altogether. Or this statement only refers to the word 'violation' as contained in the chapeau of the ICC exclusionary rule. The latter interpretation of the decision seems preferable. Under the former, the Chamber would indeed be contradicting its later endorsement that the gravity of the violation is a factor relevant for the balancing exercise.

Ultimately, it is unlikely that the Chamber could have meant that the seriousness of the violation is not a factor to be considered at all. It seems in fact self-evident that the seriousness of the violation is relevant for the balancing exercise. In order to maintain the integrity of ICC proceedings, the weighting exercise under Article 69(7) is supposed to strike a balance between the interest of 'effective law enforcement' and 'due process'. The latter interests will obviously be affected to a greater degree depending on the extent to which a violation has interfered with specific rights and values.[30]

We will assume therefore that the seriousness of the violation is relevant for the balancing exercise. The problem is, however, that the details of this appraisal are unclear. In domestic discussions, this factor has been criticised most of all for its vagueness.[31] We have made a similar point for the jurisprudence of the *Ad hoc* tribunals.[32]

Admittedly, assessing whether a violation is particularly grave is an inherently subjective consideration. At the same time, the factor of seriousness can be specified at least to some degree. First of all, this factor must be distinguished from other criteria discussed below. To this effect, we will assume, first of all, that seriousness relates only to substantive aspects and not to the attitude of the

[29] *Prosecutor v. Lubanga* (Decision on the admission of material from the "Bar Table"), ICC (Trial Chamber), decision of 24 June 2009, para 35.

[30] Similar, Ambos 2010, p. 370. But see Edwards 2001, p. 339, who seems to reject the significance of whether the violation was serious.

[31] Slobogin 2013, p. 20 et seq.

[32] See Sect. 3.1.4.

investigators. This attitude will instead be treated under the heading of 'good faith'. Secondly, the specific actors involved in the measure will not be considered part of the question of seriousness but will be dealt with separately as well. Instead, seriousness will be understood as relating to the significance of the affected right and the extent to which the investigative measure has interfered with this right. The following sections will show that conclusions can be drawn in particular by looking at the most extreme cases at both ends of the scale.

5.4.2 Technical Mistakes

At the one end of the scale, the selective review of national and international jurisprudence carried out above suggests that the gravity factor is supposed to exclude in particular minor procedural mistakes, often referred to as 'technicalities'. This is a consideration that may be adopted for the ICC as well. The legitimacy of the proceedings would clearly suffer if adherence to formal rules would slavishly be regarded as indispensable at the expense of successful convictions. But what kind of cases does this involve?

A distinction can be made between the different categories of norms that may trigger the exclusionary rule. The notion of '*internationally recognized human rights*' contains broad principles instead of detailed regulations. As a consequence, minor deviations from widespread procedural practices will regularly not amount to a human rights violation. Violations of domestic law in turn are in principle irrelevant for the ICC exclusionary rule.[33] This includes both minor and more serious violations.

Accordingly, the question of 'technicalities' involves primarily cases where the initial violation pertains to the proper law of the ICC. But here, the low degree of regulation by the ICC proper law will have to be taken into account. We have seen that both the ICC Statute and the Rules of Procedure and Evidence concentrate on the regulation of essential procedural issues.[34] Moreover, according to the system of cooperation between the ICC and states, the main responsibility for investigations rests with the latter. This means that the ICC proper law contains only very few provisions setting out mere 'technicalities' and this is particularly true where the collection of evidence is concerned.

A small number of provisions which, depending on the circumstances of the case, may be qualified as 'technicalities' can be found in Chapter 5, section III of the ICC Rules of Procedure and Evidence. Examples pertain to the recording of certain statements and facts. Rule 111(2) of the RPE for instance requires that a record be made where a suspect is informed of his rights under Article 55(2)

[33] See Sect. 4.3.3.4.

[34] See Sect. 4.1.

of the ICC Statute. If the instruction as such is not disputed in the specific case, a violation of this rule might be considered a minor and thus negligible procedural mistake. A similar example would be Rule 112(1)(b) of the RPE, which demands for recording where the suspect waives his right to be questioned in the presence of counsel. Again, if the parties agree that the waiver was actually made, excluding a statement made under these circumstances would mean adhering to a technicality.

5.4.3 Automatic Exclusion for Particular Rights?—The Example of Torture

Conversely, on the opposite end of the scale, it has been established that a violation of certain 'super'-rights is generally so severe that exclusion is justified without the consideration of any further factors.[35] The assumption of such an automatic rule should be treated very carefully. As we have seen, excluding evidence requires a delicate balancing of interests that does not allow for inflexible bright-line rules. The following section will nevertheless demonstrate that a right may reach such a level of significance that other factors cannot outweigh its violation. To this end, a closer look will be given to the prohibition of torture. Torture is the most obvious example for a particularly grave violation. Accordingly, if the violation of any human rights norm is sufficiently grave to have such a dominant effect, this must be the prohibition of torture.

5.4.3.1 Mandatory Exclusion as an Internationally Recognized Human Right

As demonstrated above, the right not to be tortured is recognized almost universally.[36] This reflects the gravity of allegations of torture. In a number of domestic systems, this gravity has lead to the implementation of an automatic exclusionary rule where this prohibition is violated.[37] Among the systems reviewed in this research, automatic exclusion is recognized in both of the more inclusionary systems, the German and the English legal systems. In Germany, this derives from statutory law, namely from Section 136a of the German Code of Criminal Procedure. In the United Kingdom, the Supreme Court (formerly the House of Lords) has established the mandatory exclusionary rule through its jurisprudence.

[35]Alamuddin 2010, p. 303; Triffterer 2008—Piragoff, Article 69, para 71.

[36]See Sect. 4.3.3.5.3.

[37]See *A. and Others v. Secretary of State for the Home Department*, House of Lords, decision of 8 December 2005, [2005] UKHL 71, paras 37 and 38 with further references.

In the context of the fight against terrorism, following the September 11 attacks on the World Trade Center in 2001, the Court of Appeal claimed that where foreign states had passed over torture evidence to English authorities, this evidence could be admitted by UK Courts.[38] The House of Lords overruled this decision. The Lords held that it was a constitutional principle that evidence obtained by torture could never be received by a UK court, whatever the circumstances.[39]

At the international level, the problem has not yet come up in the practice of the international tribunals. The *Ad hoc* tribunals never had to decide upon the admissibility of torture evidence.[40] Their case law is therefore of little help. Some scholars have argued in favour of an automatic exclusion for the violation of certain rights, citing a number of quotes from the case law of both tribunals to support their argument.[41] These quotes, however, are of a very general nature and it doubtful whether they allow for such a conclusion. They rather seem to be the result of a lack of methodological depth in the said decisions. In particular, the respective decisions have failed to demonstrate in any way how their conclusions derive from the proper law of the tribunals.

More specific conclusions can be derived from international treaty law. Admittedly, under most of the conventions prohibiting torture, the admissibility of torture evidence remains unregulated. Two legal foundations exist in treaty law, however, that are valuable for this aspect of the construction of the ICC exclusionary rule.

Firstly, the European Charter of Human Rights provides a basis for the mandatory exclusion of torture evidence. Admittedly, the Charter does not set forth any explicit exclusionary rule for torture evidence. In particular, Article 3 of the Charter does not address the procedural consequences of a violation.[42] Moreover, we have seen that the ECtHR has generally been very reticent in its assessment of the inadmissibility of evidence.[43] The ECtHR has, however, treated violations of

[38]*A. and others v Secretary of State for the Home Department*, Court of Appeal of England and Wales, decision of 11 August 2004, [2004] EWCA Civ 1123.

[39]*A. and Others v. Secretary of State for the Home Department*, House of Lords, decision of 8 December 2005, [2005] UKHL 71, see in particular para 51. For a comprehensive discussion of this decision, see Thienel 2006, p. 401 et seq.

[40]Klamberg 2013, p. 402.

[41]See for instance Alamuddin 2010, p. 303, who quotes *Prosecutor v. Nchamihigo* (Decision on the Prosecutor's Application to Admit into Evidence the Transcript of the Accused's Interview as a Suspect and the Defence's Request to Hold a Voir Dire), ICTR (Trial Chamber), decision of 5 February 2007, para 21: "*It is well settled that a statement taken from a suspect would not be admitted into evidence at his trial if its rights during the investigation were not respected*". Similarly, see McKeever 2010, p. 627, who quotes *Prosecutor v. Delalić et al.*, (Decision on Hazim Delic's Motions Pursuant to Rule 73), ICTY (Trial Chamber), decision of 1 September 1997, para 15: "*The principle that confessions made by accused persons in the absence of their volition and arising from threats, inducement or hope of favour by persons in authority is inadmissible in evidence is well settled* [...]".

[42]Ambos 2010, p. 383.

[43]See Sect. 3.2.2.

the torture prohibition differently from other violations. While repeating their basic, generally reluctant, position, the European judges have held that violations of Article 3 generally affect the fairness of the trial as a whole. Their reasoning is essentially based on the significance of the torture prohibition in international law. The judges have held that Article 3 protects one of the most fundamental values of society and have concluded that torture evidence should never be relied upon.[44] We have seen that neither the ECHR nor the jurisprudence of its monitoring body is directly binding for the ICC. However, both the prohibition of torture and the right to a fair trial clearly fall into the category of '*internationally recognized human rights*'. Both Articles 3 and 6 of the Charter shape these rights and may therefore be referred to under Articles 69(7) and 21(3) of the ICC Statute. Their interpretation by the ECtHR in turn is relevant for the ICC as 'persuasive authority'.

Secondly, another international treaty is even more important for the interpretation of the ICC exclusionary rule. Beyond the regional ECHR regime, the widely recognized UN Convention against Torture (UNCAT)[45] also prohibits the use of torture evidence. The Convention goes in fact a step further than the ECHR. It explicitly sets forth an automatic exclusionary rule. While the already mentioned Article 2 of UNCAT is applicable only to the collection of the evidence, Article 15 provides for its subsequent exclusion from trial. It stipulates that all States Parties to the Convention "[...] *shall ensure that any statement which is established to have been made as a result of torture shall not be invoked as evidence in any proceedings, except against a person accused of torture as evidence that the statement was made.*" Like the ECHR, the provisions of UNCAT are not directly binding on the ICC since the Court, as an international organisation, cannot be party to the Convention. But given its widespread recognition, Article 15 of UNCAT is also evidence of the '*internationally recognized human right*' not to be tortured. It can therefore be used as an interpretative tool for Articles 69(7) and 21(3) of the ICC Statute.

[44] *Jalloh v. Germany*, ECtHR, decision of 11 July 2006 (Application no. 54810/00), para 105: [I]*ncriminating evidence—whether in the form of a confession or real evidence—obtained as a result of acts of violence or brutality or other forms of treatment which can be characterised as torture—should never be relied on as proof of the victim's guilt, irrespective of its probative value.*" See also *Gäfgen v. Germany*, ECtHR, decision of 1 June 2010 (Application no. 22978/05), para 167. The adverse effect of statements gained under torture on trial fairness can also be based on the right against self-incrimination, see Ambos 2010, p. 384; Thienel 2006, p. 404. This right is not explicitly mentioned in Article 6 of the ECHR. It appears however in Article 14(3)(g) of the ICCPR and has been held to be implied in the general right to a fair trial under Article 6(1) of the Charter, see Thienel 2006, p. 356.

[45] Convention against Torture and Other Cruel, Inhuman or Degrading Treatment or Punishment, signed on 10 December 1984, entered into force on 26 June 1987, available at http://www.un.org/documents/ga/res/39/a39r046.htm (last visited: October 2013).

5.4.3.2 Mandatory Exclusion as Part of Customary International Law

Beyond this the mandatory exclusion of torture evidence has even grown into a rule of customary international law. Accordingly, it is binding on the ICC under Article 21(1)(b) of the ICC Statute. International custom is generally considered to require the determination of a consistent state practice that is based on a corresponding opinio juris.[46] It can reasonably be argued that both of these elements exist with respect to the mandatory exclusion of torture evidence. The determination of such a customary rule is based in particular on Article 15 of UNCAT and its background.[47]

At the outset, we must note that a problem for the establishment of customary law is that the line between its two constituent elements has become increasingly blurred. It is often difficult to discern whether the acts of a state qualify as state practice or as its *opinio juris*.[48] It is contentious, for instance, whether treaties and conventions constitute state practice or whether they are the expression of the belief in a legal obligation.[49] The same question arises where states vote in favour of a resolution, for instance, at the UN General Assembly.

For the mandatory nature of the exclusion of torture evidence, the determination of a respective opinio juris has been based on the mandate of the drafters of UNCAT. Indeed, this mandate, provided by the UN General Assembly (GA), seems to focus on the codification of customary law.[50] This implies that states in the GA acted out of the belief that the rules laid down in the Convention already existed as international custom. Another GA resolution repeats the wording of Article 15 of UNCAT and may therefore also be considered evidence of such an *opinio juris*.[51]

A consistent state practice could, in light of the above, be established by simply referring to the act of ratifying or at least of signing UNCAT or of voting in favour of the above-mentioned GA resolutions. If however one considers these acts as belonging to opinio juris, the determination of state practice becomes more difficult. Many states have domestically implemented automatic rules of exclusion in cases of torture.[52] But these rules will often contain no explicit reference to

[46]See Werle 2012, para 154. See also Sect. 2.3.2.2.

[47]Thienel 2006, p. 365.

[48]Werle 2012, para 157.

[49]Roberts 2001, p. 757.

[50]See GA Resolution 32/62 of 8 December 1977, available at http://www.un.org/Depts/dhl/resguide/r32.htm (last visited: October 2013).

[51]UN GA Res. 59/182, para 6, available at http://www.un.org/ga/search/view_doc.asp?symbol=A/RES/59/182&Lang=E (last visited: October 2013). Altogether, see Thienel 2006, p. 365.

[52]Thienel 2006, p. 365. See also Association Against Torture, 'APT Background Paper on the Exclusionary Rule', *Background Bulletin*, 2012, available at: http://www.apt.ch/en/evidence-obtained-through-torture/ (last visited: October 2013).

international law. It is controversial whether, in such a case, state behaviour may be regarded as sufficient for customary international law.[53] Moreover, there is not yet any comprehensive survey of the way states have implemented automatic exclusionary rules for torture in domestic law, let alone how such rules have been applied by courts. This may refute the establishment of a consistent state practice.

Modern approaches to international custom focus, however, on the determination of an opinio juris. The traditional approach to custom used to determine customary rules through an inductive process, which primarily examined the particular instances of state practice. Modern approaches are more deductive. Custom is mainly inferred from the mere recognition of a legal rule through statements. Instances of inconsistent state practice are not supposed to have any impact on the existence of a rule as such, as long as they are treated as breaches of this custom.[54]

This is in fact a development of considerable importance for international criminal and human rights law since these legal areas suffer from a notorious lack of compliance.[55] Such problems of implementation also exist with respect to the prohibition of torture. We will address in the next section some of the attempts to curtail the prohibition of torture evidence. Applied to the present issue, the modern understanding of customary law allows a focus on the evidence for opinio juris to determine a mandatory exclusionary rule for torture evidence.

In addition, the customary status of the exclusionary rule is ultimately also supported by the interpretation of the right to a fair trial by the ECtHR.[56] The ECHR as such cannot be used as evidence for either state practice or opinio juris because its text does not contain any express exclusionary rule for torture evidence. Indirectly, the jurisprudence of international courts can, however, be indicative of the existence of customary law.[57] We have seen that the European judges have derived from Articles 6 and 3 of the Convention that torture evidence is always inadmissible. This jurisprudence of the ECtHR can be referred to as ‘persuasive authority’ that reflects the customary law status of a mandatory exclusionary rule for torture evidence.

5.4.3.3 An Exception to the Mandatory Exclusionary Rule?

The previous sections have demonstrated that, as a general rule, torture evidence must be excluded under Article 69(7) of the ICC Statute on the basis of the gravity

[53] Werle 2012, para 156.

[54] For a good example of this approach, see *Nicaragua v. The United States of America* (Case concerning military and paramilitary activities in and against Nicaragua), ICJ, decision of 27 June 1986, see in particular para 186 on the problem of inconsistent state behaviour.

[55] For international criminal law, see Werle 2012, para 159.

[56] Thienel 2006, p. 365.

[57] Werle 2012, p. 155.

of the violation alone. The question remains whether this quasi-automatic rule is absolute. Are ICC judges generally precluded from admitting such evidence, even in exceptional situations and regardless of any other considerations?

A case litigated before the Extraordinary Chambers in the Courts of Cambodia (ECCC) is interesting for this discussion. The judges had to decide on a defence motion that requested the exclusion of a number of witness statements. These statements had been made during interrogations at the notorious Khmer Rouge prison and torture facility S-21 and they concerned biographical information that victims of the facility had given at the beginning of their interrogation. The evidence was not therefore intended to be used against the victims of torture but against the leaders of their torturers.

The information was crucial to the prosecution's case because it was the only evidence of the command structure of the Khmer Rouge. During their regime, the Khmer Rouge had pursued a policy of intense secrecy. As a consequence, there was only very little documentation on its leadership. Of that scarce evidence, large parts were destroyed in face of the Vietnamese invasion in 1979. The archives of S-21, however, remained intact because they could not be destroyed in time before the arrival of the Vietnamese.[58]

The co-investigating judges acknowledged the binding nature of Article 15 UNCAT for the ECCC.[59] At the same time, they decided to exceptionally admit the said statements into evidence. The case is interesting for this research because it poses the question whether this decision indicates that, under certain circumstances, torture evidence is admissible in trials concerning international crimes.

Article 15 UNCAT does indeed allow the exceptional use of torture evidence. The scope of this exception however is extremely limited. The use of such evidence is only allowed against the torturer himself and only "*as evidence that the statement was made*". This exception is meant to make the prosecution of the international crime of torture possible. It ensures that evidence can be submitted that is required to prove that the crime of torture was committed. At the same time, the exception does not allow for a consideration of the content of torture evidence under any circumstances whatsoever.[60]

The judges of the ECCC did not dispute that the evidence in question did not meet the requirements of this exception. In their order however, they nevertheless admitted the statements, arguing that in light of the background of these

---

[58]On the history of the Khmer Rouge torture evidence, see Scharf 2008, p. 136 et seq.

[59]*Prosecutor v. IENG Thirith* (Order on the use of statements which were or may have been obtained through torture), ECCC (Office of the Co-investigating judges), decision of 28 July 2009. Other than for the ICC, UNCAT is directly applicable as a treaty to the ECCC. The ECCC formally remain part of the Cambodian domestic legal order and as such, they are bound by Cambodian law, see Zahar and Sluiter 2008, pp. 12 and 280. Cambodia has ratified the Convention in 1992, see the respective entry in the United Nations Treaty Collection, available at http://treaties.un.org/Pages/ViewDetails.asp?src=TREATY&mtdsg_no=IV-9&chapter=4&lang=en (last visited October 2013).

[60]McKeever, p. 617.

statements, Article 15 UNCAT could not be interpreted restrictively. The judges based their decision on teleological considerations. They claimed that a restrictive interpretation would be inconsistent with the object and purpose of UNCAT. Article 15 UNCAT had to be read in light of Article 31(3) of the VCLT, which means "*in good faith*". The Chamber's approach assumes therefore that while the prohibition of torture is absolute, exclusion of evidence tainted by torture is possible in exceptional cases.[61]

The decision has been criticized intensively. An assessment of these criticisms shows that there are several reasons why this case cannot serve as an example for the ICC. The discussion of this decision rather reveals that there are in fact no circumstances that could justify the admission of torture evidence by the ICC beyond the limited exception set forth in Article 15 of UNCAT.

The ECCC judges emphasized two aspects in their decision. Firstly, they referred to two purposes of exclusion, namely the deterrence rationale and the purpose of safeguarding the reliability of evidence. They held that in the particular case, these purposes did not require the exclusion of the evidence and that, as a consequence, its admission was justified.[62] Secondly, they emphasized that the statements would not be used against the person who was subjected to torture. Instead, it was supposed to serve as evidence against those accused of torture. The judges claimed that the latter should not be allowed to "*use the law designed to prevent torture to shield themselves from liability*".[63]

The ECCC judges were certainly right in dismissing any deterrent effect. The violations were committed 30 years ago by the officials of a political system that is no longer in existence. Their deliberations do not, however, give adequate consideration to the fact that the international exclusionary rule in Article 15 of UNCAT is based *inter alia* on integrity concerns.[64] The legitimacy of a trial against torturers would be seriously damaged if the respective court would essentially base its conviction on torture evidence.[65] This is not only supported by the widespread ban of torture as detailed above. Torture is also a crime under international law. If the same issue would be assessed by the ICC, it would even be a crime under the

---

[61]*Prosecutor v. IENG Thirith* (Order on the use of statements which were or may have been obtained through torture), ECCC (Office of the Co-investigating judges), decision of 28 July 2009, paras 24 et seq. See also Safferling 2001, p. 503 et seq.

[62]*Prosecutor v. IENG Thirith* (Order on the use of statements which were or may have been obtained through torture), ECCC (Office of the Co-investigating judges), decision of 28 July 2009, paras 24 et seq. With respect to deterrence, the ECCC Order refers to the lapse of time passed since the events took place, see para 24. The reliability concerns in turn are rejected with the assurance that the judges would take into account the problematic origin of the statements when evaluating the evidence, see para 28. Following a rather civil law oriented approach, the question of reliability is thus basically deemed a problem of weight rather than of admissibility.

[63]*Prosecutor v. IENG Thirith* (Order on the use of statements which were or may have been obtained through torture), ECCC (Office of the Co-investigating judges), decision of 28 July 2009, para 24.

[64]Scharf 2008, p. 154.

[65]Ambos 2010, p. 381.

Court's own Statute.[66] It seems highly hypocritical to prosecute a behaviour as an international crime and to use at the same time the outcome of this very behaviour for an effective prosecution.

This brings us to the ECCC's second, teleological argument, namely that the rule is not intended to shield those responsible for acts of torture from liability. The driving force behind this claim is essentially a concern for effectiveness. It is indeed difficult to accept that Article 15 of UNCAT can be used to the advantage of persons responsible for large scale torture. But once more, concerns for effectiveness alone cannot be used to circumvent the most basic human rights principles.[67] If the ICC would follow this route, it would resort to a 'public attitude' version of the integrity rationale while we have seen that it should implement a 'court-centred' integrity rationale.[68]

5.4.3.4 Interim Result

In conclusion, the consideration of the integrity rationale suggests that torture evidence is automatically excluded only because of the gravity of such violations. This mandatory outcome is not open to any exceptions beyond the literal wording of Article 15 of UNCAT. In particular, this exception cannot be expanded solely for concerns of effectiveness.

The example of torture shows that, as a matter of principle, under Article 69(7) of the ICC Statute, certain rights can in fact be of such significance that their violation quasi-automatically warrants exclusion. The automatic nature of exclusion does not mean that the test prescribed by Article 69(7) of the ICC Statute does not apply. Rather, the violation has such a major impact that the requirements of this test are always satisfied.[69]

It is doubtful, however, whether the current status of international human rights law allows the drawing of such a conclusion for rights other than the protection against torture. This would demand that a right has acquired such an indisputable status under international human rights law that non-admissibility would be the only consequence of a violation. At this point, other rights that have been suggested to have such a status, such as the right to silence or the right to counsel, probably don't share the same status within the international community. This is not to say that this state of affairs cannot evolve. As depicted elsewhere, human rights law is a dynamic legal area.[70] The significance of certain rights may thus increase. The understanding of Article 69(7) of the ICC Statute will then develop in turn.

---

[66]See Article 7(1)(f); Article 8(2)(a)(ii), alt. 1; Article 8(2)(c)(I), alt. 4 of the ICC Statute.

[67]Similar, Ambos 2010, p. 381; McKeever 2010, p. 622.

[68]On this distinction, see Sect. 4.3.2.2.5.

[69]See Alamuddin 2010, p. 303.

[70]See Sect. 4.3.3.3.

5.5 The Actors Involved in the Collection of Evidence

The system of cooperation between the ICC and states is of particular significance to the assessment of the next factor. We have seen that many investigative measures for ICC proceedings, particularly those that are coercive, have to be carried out by national police. Accordingly, the first question that arises is whether investigative mistakes committed by domestic authorities have the same impact as mistakes under the responsibility of the ICC Prosecutor. The distribution of responsibilities within the ICC cooperation system implies that this question must be treated differently from the way national systems sometimes treat the collection of evidence by a foreign state in a horizontal cooperation system. A second question will then relate to how the involvement of so-called intermediaries impacts on the issue of admissibility.

With respect to the first question, the U.S. system provides an illustrative example that can be contrasted against the ICC exclusionary rule. In U.S. doctrine, a further exception is made to the exclusionary rule for evidence gathered abroad. Under the so-called '*international silver platter doctrine*', the exclusionary rule does not apply to violations committed by foreign authorities. This doctrine is once again based on the deterrence theory. It is argued that the application of the exclusionary rule would not be able to influence the behaviour of foreign authorities.[71] The only instance where this exception does not apply is where a violation "*shocks the conscience of American courts*."[72]

The '*international silver platter doctrine*' cannot simply be transferred to the ICC. Admittedly, the ICC has no control over state authorities either. This, however, is exactly one of the reasons why deterrence is not the primary rationale of the ICC exclusionary rule in general.[73] Under Article 69(7) of the ICC Statute, the matter must rather be considered from the perspective of the integrity theory. Closely linked is the fact that, ultimately, a simple transposition of the '*international silver platter doctrine*' would lead to a far more significant restriction of the ICC exclusionary rule when compared to the domestic level. Unlike for domestic trials, such cases do not only arise exceptionally as evidence is routinely gathered by an external entity.[74]

[71]For a detailed explanation, see *United States v. Lee*, United States Court of Appeals for the Second District, decision of 7 June 2013, No. 12-0088-cr. See also Ambos 2010, p. 373; Scharf 2008, p. 152 et seq.

[72]See *United States v. Fernandez-Caro*, United States District Court for the Southern District of Texas, decision of 2 September 1987, 677 F.Supp 893 (1987), with further references. This seems to be a further indication of the, albeit limited, recognition of integrity concerns for the U.S. exclusionary rule; see also Sect. 3.3.2.

[73]See Sect. 4.3.2.2.3.

[74]But see Gallant 1999, p. 719, who refers to the doctrine and suggests that the involvement of OTP could be the decisive factor for drawing a line between admissible and non-admissible evidence under Article 69(7) of the ICC Statute.

Turning to another domestic example, the Canadian Supreme Court has followed a similar line to the United States, even though its exclusionary rule is explicitly based on the maintenance of judicial integrity. Based on the argument that Canadian Charter rights only apply on Canadian territory, the Supreme Court has rejected requests to exclude evidence under Section 24(2) of the Charter where foreign authorities were involved. Similar to the jurisprudence of the U.S. Supreme Court, in these circumstances, exclusion is only possible in exceptional cases. This would be the case where evidence was gathered "*in violation of principles of fundamental justice*".[75]

Despite the Canadian adoption of the integrity theory, this example cannot be transferred to the ICC either. Not only would this lead to the insignificance of the ICC exclusionary rule in large parts, but the ICC cooperation system also clearly sets it apart from the horizontal relationship between sovereign states. We have seen earlier that there is a sufficiently strong connection between the ICC and domestic authorities involved in evidence gathering to endorse the integrity theory.[76] In fact, this connection is closer than the relationship between states and foreign investigative authorities. Under the ICC cooperation regime, states have to conduct many investigative measures for the ICC because the Court itself lacks its own enforcement mechanisms. The Court cannot, however, escape accountability for acts of domestic authorities simply because the necessary investigations have been outsourced through a deliberate choice of its States Parties. As a consequence, the integrity of the Court is also endangered where it gets involved with domestically gathered tainted evidence.

This corresponds to international case law. The ICC, like the *Ad hoc* tribunals, has held that evidence can be excluded even if it has been collected by national authorities. In this respect, national investigative activities are measured not against the respective domestic law but in view of their conformity with ICC proper law and with '*internationally recognized human rights*'. We have seen above that a violation of national law is not as such sufficient to trigger the application of the ICC exclusionary rule.[77] The abidance by national law in turn is no guarantee for the admissibility of evidence. This conclusion has also been drawn by the ICTY. In the case, the tribunal rightly held that "[t]*he Trial Chamber is governed by its Rules. Accordingly, any evidence to be admissible in proceedings before it must satisfy the law as provided in the Statute and Rules*."[78] Similarly, evidence introduced in ICC trials must meet the standards set forth by Article 69(7) of the ICC Statute, even where the measure was conducted by national

[75]*Regina v. Harrer*, Supreme Court of Canada, decision of 19 October 1995, [1995] 3 S.C.R. 56, para 13. On the application of the Canadian Charter where Canadian officials are involved in enforcement measures abroad, see Rennie and Rothschild 2009, p. 127 et seq.

[76]See Sect. 4.2.2.2.5.

[77]See Sect. 4.3.3.4.

[78]*Prosecutor v. Delalić et al.* (Decision on Zdravko Mucic's Motion for the Exclusion of Evidence), ICTY (Trial Chamber), decision of 2 September 1997, paras 46 et seq.

authorities. In principle, this includes cases where the national authorities have not acted on behalf of the Prosecutor.[79] In such cases, however, the applicability of the ICC exclusionary rule is limited to instances of '*internationally recognized human rights*'. As we have seen before, independent investigations of sovereign states are not subject to the standards of the ICC proper law, even if the respective state is a State Party to the ICC Statute.[80]

But while a violation by national authorities generally suffices to meet the requirements of the chapeau of Article 69(7), there is reason to make further distinctions under its subpara (b), depending on the actors involved in an investigative measure. The identity of these actors influences the degree to which violations can be attributed to the Court. Three situations can be distinguished: either domestic forces have carried out the measure on their own; or they have conducted the measure on the request or in the presence of OTP staff; or the international investigators themselves were in control of the measure. The greater the extent to which OTP staff was involved, the more intense is the connection with the Court. Conversely, where domestic authorities act without the involvement of the Prosecutor, this would call for lowering the degree of attribution. While the Court cannot free itself from any responsibility for domestic mistakes, admitting evidence gathered by means of an illicit act committed by its own prosecutor would deeply affect its integrity.[81]

The idea that the participation of international investigators in rights violations is more serious than independent violations by domestic officials has also been alluded to in the case law of the *Ad hoc* tribunals.[82] And in the *Lubanga* case, the ICC Trial Chamber seems to have drawn the same conclusion for Article 69(7) of the ICC Statute. Here, OTP personnel was present, but did not control the controversial search. The judges explicitly found this to be a factor militating against the exclusion of the disputed evidence.[83]

Alongside the question of the involvement of national authorities, a second question arises with respect to the above-mentioned involvement of so-called intermediaries in ICC investigations.[84] In principle, the ICC must be held accountable for the conduct of private persons on which it relies in its investigations. Similar to the reliance on national authorities, the integrity of the Court is endangered where it uses evidence tainted by the illicit behaviour of intermediaries. As a

[79]See Alamuddin 2010, p. 301.

[80]See Sect. 4.3.3.1.

[81]Alamuddin 2010, p. 301. See also Gallant 1999, p. 719; Sluiter 2002, p. 226.

[82]See for instance *Prosecutor v. Mrkšić* (Decision Concerning the Use of Statements Given by the Accused), decision of 9 October 2006; *Prosecutor v. Barayagwiza* (Decision), ICTR (Appeals Chamber), decision of 3 November 1999, para 61. See also Alamuddin 2010, p. 301; Sluiter 2002, p. 226.

[83]*Prosecutor v. Lubanga* (Decision on the admission of material from the 'Bar Table'), ICC (Trial Chamber), decision of 24 June 2009, para 47.

[84]See Sect. 4.2.

consequence, where such persons violate the rights of the accused or the rights of other individuals, in particular of the witnesses they contact, this may theoretically trigger the ICC exclusionary rule. This applies all the more to those intermediaries who have, according to more recent practice, been provided with contracts and that are thus bound to the ICC on a verifiable legal basis.[85] As with the involvement of national authorities, the fact that an intermediary, and not a member of the OTP, has committed the violation may, however, impact on the weight to be attached to such a violation. The relevance of this factor would then depend on the specific bonds between the OTP and the intermediary, namely on the intensity of its involvement in the investigations, as well as on the legal terms of this involvement, in particular on the existence and the terms of a contract with the ICC.

In practice, however, is seems unlikely that, in cases where intermediaries commit a violation, evidence will often be excluded under Article 69(7) of the ICC Statute. This is due to the actual circumstances of the involvement of intermediaries in the investigations. First of all, intermediaries have not been authorised to participate in the actual questioning of witnesses.[86] The questioning, however, is where the rights of victims and witnesses are most likely to be violated. Intermediaries rather play a role in the preliminary phases: They establish the contact between the witnesses and the OTP, they collect the witnesses from their homes and organise meetings with the ICC investigators.[87]

What is more, past investigations have shown that intermediaries are more likely to convince victims that it is in their own interest to give false statements than to violate the victims' rights by applying pressure.[88] Manipulating witnesses in this way must certainly be considered a violation in terms of Article 69(7) of the ICC Statute, in particular with view to Article 70(1)(c) of the ICC Statute, as well as to the general fair trial rights of the accused. In such cases, however, the more important aspect will clearly be the deliberate decision of the witness herself to give false testimony. It thus seems more straightforward, instead of discussing the more complicated application of the ICC exclusionary rule, to simply not accord any evidentiary weight to the respective statements. Accordingly, the Trial Chamber, in the *Lubanga* case simply considered that where an intermediary has suborned a witness into giving false testimony, the respective statements were unreliable. As a consequence, the Chamber held that these statements were unable to establish beyond a reasonable doubt that the accused had committed the crime he was charged with.[89]

---

[85]On such contracts, see *Prosecutor v. Lubanga* (Judgment pursuant to Article 74 of the Statute), ICC (Trial Chamber), decision of 14 March 2012, paras 203, 204.

[86]*Prosecutor v. Lubanga* (Judgment pursuant to Article 74 of the Statute), ICC (Trial Chamber), decision of 14 March 2012, para 185.

[87]*Prosecutor v. Lubanga* (Judgment pursuant to Article 74 of the Statute), ICC (Trial Chamber), decision of 14 March 2012, para 191.

[88]Given the prospect of relocation for victims, there is a danger that witnesses may be motivated to give false testimony by pointing out the financial benefits, see Buisman 2013, p. 60 et seq.

[89]*Prosecutor v. Lubanga* (Judgment pursuant to Article 74 of the Statute), ICC (Trial Chamber), decision of 14 March 2012, para 191.

5.6 Good Faith

The next question is whether the attitude of prosecutors of international crimes towards a violation impacts on the decision about exclusion. Does is make a difference whether the responsible authorities disregarded rights deliberately or whether they made a mistake?

Without further explanation, the ICTY, in its case law, has considered good faith on the part of the investigating authorities to be a factor militating against exclusion.[90] At the national level, the attitude of investigators has also been deemed significant. It has been considered relevant in all of the domestic systems reviewed in this research, albeit to varying degrees. In the German,[91] as well as in the English legal system,[92] good faith is but one factor among others in a comprehensive balancing exercise. Bad faith usually leads to exclusion in these systems. Good faith in turn does not always result in admissibility. In contrast, both in Canada[93] and in the United States,[94] evidence is almost automatically admissible where investigators have acted in good faith.

In principle, it seems obvious that the mental element of the violation is also relevant for Article 69(7)(b) of the ICC Statute. At the same time, some further distinctions are necessary to assess the concrete impact of this factor.

The fact that we have adopted the integrity rationale as the decisive rationale for the ICC, does not fundamentally prevent us from taking into account good faith as a relevant factor. Admittedly, the prevalence of the deterrence theory is the reason that such great significance is attached to this factor in the United States. The reasoning goes as follows: Where investigators are not aware of their illicit behaviour, striving for deterrence will mostly become void, leaving only the possibility to raise awareness among investigators in order to avoid negligent mistakes. Once more, this reasoning, which is based on deterrence, falls short for the ICC

---

[90] *Prosecutor v. Haraqija and Morina* (Decision on Haraqija and Morina's Second Request for a Declaration of Inadmissibility and Exclusion of Evidence), ICTY (Trial Chamber), decision of 24 November 2008, para 20, 26; *Prosecutor v. Haraqija and Morina* (Judgment), ICTY (Appeals Chamber), decision of 23 July 2009, para 28; *Prosecutor v. Brđanin* (Decision on the Defence "Objection to Intercept Evidence"), ICTY (Trial Chamber), decision of 3 October 2003, para 63. See also Sect. 3.1.4.

[91] See Sect. 3.3.1.

[92] See *Regina v. Walsh*, Court of Appeal of England and Wales, decision of 13 July 1989, [1990] 91 Cr. App R. 161; *Regina v. Alladice*, Court of Appeal of England and Wales, decision of 8 May 1988, [1988] WL 624104. See also Mellifont 2007, p. 86. See also Sect. 3.3.3.

[93] See *Regina v. Grant,* Supreme Court of Canada, decision of 17 July 2009, [2009] 2 S.C.R. 353, para 75; see also Sect. 3.3.4.

[94] See *United States v. Leon*, United States Supreme Court, decision of 5 July 1984, 468 U.S. 897 (1984). See also *Arizona v. Evans*, United States Supreme Court, decision of 1 March 1995, 514 U.S. 1 (1995); more recently *Herring v. United States,* United States Supreme Court, decision of 14 January 2009, 07-513 (2009); see also Sect. 2.3.2.

because deterrence is not the decisive rationale behind Article 69(7)(b) of the ICC Statute. Integrity concerns, however, also justify the consideration of an investigator's attitude. This is demonstrated most clearly by the Canadian example, which also attaches great importance to this factor and which, as we have seen, is mainly based on the integrity theory. Honest mistakes clearly threaten the integrity of a court less than deliberate misbehaviour.[95]

Beyond that, there is reason not to apply the good and bad faith distinction categorically. The establishment of good faith should not directly result in the admission of tainted evidence. The Canadian and American systems should not be taken as an example in this respect. The recent jurisprudence of the Canadian Supreme Court attaches such an excessive importance to good faith that it almost amounts to an automatic rule. The new approach to Section 24(2) of the Canadian Charter has in fact been criticized in particular because of its focus on the mental element of the violation. This focus does not do justice to the broad discretion allocated to the judges under Section 24(2).[96] The same would be true for Article 69(7) of the ICC Statute. We have seen that the provision grants wide discretion to the ICC judges. Consequently, the establishment of good faith on the part of the authorities does not preclude the judges from concluding that the integrity of the proceedings is endangered by other characteristics of a specific case. The adoption of the integrity rationale warrants for a comprehensive balancing of interests which proscribes any sort of bright-line rule.

Conversely, where the authorities have acted in bad faith, admitting the respective evidence will considerably increase the danger of damage to a court's integrity. It is imaginable in cases of bad faith that the evidence will be admitted nonetheless, for example in cases of technical mistakes. But it seems likely that the negative effect of bad faith will regularly be greater than the exonerating effect of good faith.

A closer look reveals, however, that any meaningful consideration of the good faith and bad faith distinction requires further distinctions. The first question is whether bad faith only describes intentional conduct or whether negligence on the part of the investigating authorities is sufficient. Regarding searches and seizures, the German Supreme Court, for instance, in its case law on exigent circumstances, only considers exclusion to be appropriate where the investigators have "*deliberately or arbitrarily*" disregarded the requirement of a search warrant.[97] Negligence, on the other hand, does not warrant exclusion.[98] Under U.S.[99] and Canadian[100] law, however, negligence is sufficient to establish a case of bad faith.

[95]Similar Alamuddin 2010, pp. 231 and 305.

[96]Eberdt 2011, pp. 73 and 82.

[97]German Federal Supreme Court (BGH), decision of 12 April 2005, *Neue Juristische Wochenschrift* 2005, p. 1917 et seq.

[98]Meyer-Goßner 2013, Section 98, para 7.

[99]*United States v. Leon*, United States Supreme Court, decision of 5 July 1984, 468 U.S. 897 (1984).

[100]*Regina v. Harrison*, Supreme Court of Canada, decision of 17 July 2009, [2009] 2 S.C.R. 494, para 22.

For the ICC, this question cannot be answered entirely, apart from the factor discussed in the previous section. The assessment of the different sorts of attitudes depends to a great deal on the actors involved in an investigative measure. Once again, the maintenance of integrity imposes higher demands on the international prosecutor than it does where national authorities have collected the evidence.

In principle, it cannot generally be precluded that a grossly negligent mistake impacts on the integrity of the proceedings. Again, any categorical preclusion would impede on the judicial discretion accorded by Article 69(7) of the Statute. This is particularly the case where international investigators were in charge, where they were present during the measure or where they requested it. The OTP itself is part of the ICC and thus part of an institution striving for legitimacy. This requires a rather high degree of diligence on the part of its staff. The well-trained staff of the Prosecutor can ultimately also be expected to be able to comply with these demands. At the same time, negligence would naturally have a minor impact when compared to a deliberate mistake. Where the often less well-trained domestic authorities have committed a negligent mistake, the exclusion of evidence remains a possible consequence as well. But in such a case, important other factors will probably have to militate in favour of exclusion.

A related question is whether ignorance must pertain to the factual circumstances or whether good faith might also result from a misjudgment of the legal situation. Does it make a difference whether a police officer has searched the wrong person or whether he was simply misled in his legal assessment of the existence of exigent circumstances? Once again, there is no consensus at the domestic level. The Canadian Supreme Court has held that it is possible to exclude evidence where investigators have made legal mistakes. It argued that "*ignorance of Charter standards must not be rewarded or encouraged and negligence or wilful* [sic] *blindness cannot be equated with good faith*".[101] In Germany, on the other hand, a violation that results from a legal mistake does not amount to a reason for exclusion.[102]

For the ICC, we can draw on the previous findings. Ignorance of the law can never be deliberate, accordingly these are always cases of negligence. In this context, the difference between the standards that should be applied to the ICC Office of the Prosecutor when compared to national authorities is becoming even bigger. OTP staff should be well-educated in the law of criminal procedure and human rights law, and awareness of the legal standards to be met during the collection of evidence can be expected. The same standard cannot be expected from the staff of national authorities, in particular since evidence gathering often takes place in post-conflict states with little experience with rule of law standards.

---

[101]*Regina v. Grant,* Supreme Court of Canada, decision of 17 July 2009, [2009] 2 S.C.R. 353, para 75. For a similar assessment with respect to domestic exclusionary rules in general, see Slobogin 2013, p. 19.

[102]Meyer-Goßner 2013, Section 98, para 7.

References

Alamuddin A (2010) Collection of evidence. In: Khan K, Buisman C, Gosnell C (eds) Principles of evidence in international criminal justice. Oxford University Press, Oxford, pp 231–305

Ambos K (2010) The transnational use of torture evidence. Isr Law Rev 42:362–397

Buisman C (2013) Delegating investigations: lessons to be learned from the Lubanga judgment. Northwest J Int Hum Rights 11:30–82

Eberdt B (2011) Impaired exclusion: exploring the possibility of a new bright line rule of good faith in impaired driving offences. Rev Curr Law Law Reform 16:65–83

Edwards G (2001) International human rights law challenges to the new International Criminal Court: the search and seizure right to privacy. Yale J Int Law 26:323–412

Gallant K (1999) Individual human rights in a new international organization: the Rome Statute of the International Criminal Court. In: Bassiouni C (ed) International criminal law, Vol. II: procedural and enforcement mechanisms, 2nd edn. Transnational Publishers, New York, pp 693–723

Klamberg M (2013) Evidence in international criminal trials: confronting legal gaps and the reconstruction of disputed events. Martinus Nijhoff Publishers, Leiden

McKeever D (2010) Evidence obtained through torture before the Khmer Rouge tribunal unlawful pragmatism? J Int Crim Justice 8:615–630

Mellifont K (2007) The derivative imperative: how should Australian criminal trial courts treat evidence deriving from illegally or improperly gained evidence? Professional doctorate thesis, Queensland University of Technology. http://eprints.qut.edu.au/16388/1/Kerri_Mellifont_Thesis.pdf. Accessed 14 May 2015

Meyer-Goßner L (2013) Strafprozessordnung, 56th edn. C.H. Beck, Munich

Rennie J, Rothschild R (2009) The Canadian Charter of Rights and Freedoms and Canadian officials abroad. Supreme Court Law Rev 47:127–146

Roberts A (2001) Traditional and modern approaches to customary international law: a reconciliation. Am J Int Law 95:757–791

Rogall K (1979) Gegenwärtiger Stand und Entwicklungstendenzen der Lehre von den strafprozessualen Beweisverboten. Zeitschrift für die gesamte Strafrechtswissenschaft 191:1–44

Safferling C (2001) Towards an international criminal procedure. Oxford University Press, Oxford

Safferling C (2012) International Criminal Procedure. Oxford University Press, Oxford

Scharf M (2008) Tainted provenance: when, if ever, should torture evidence be admissible? Washington Lee Law Rev 65:129–172

Slobogin C (2013) A comparative perspective on the exclusionary rule in search and seizure cases. Vanderbilt Public Law research paper no. 13-21. http://papers.ssrn.com/sol3/papers.cfm?abstract_id=2247746. Accessed 14 May 2015

Sluiter G (2002) International criminal adjudication and the collection of evidence: obligations of states: obligations of states. Intersentia, Antwerpen

Stuart D (2010) Welcome Flexibility and Better Criteria form the Supreme Court of Canada for exclusion of evidence obtained in violation of the Canadian Charter of Rights and Freedoms. Southwestern J Int Law 16:313–332

Thienel T (2006) The admissibility of evidence obtained by torture under international law. Eur J Int Law 17:349–367

Triffterer O (2008) (ed) Commentary on the Rome Statute of the International Criminal Court: observers' notes, article by article, 2nd edn. C.H. Beck et al., Baden-Baden

Trüg G (2003) Lösungskonvergenzen trotz Systemdivergenzen im deutschen und US-amerikanischen Strafverfahren. Mohr Siebeck, Tübingen

Werle (2012) Völkerstrafrecht, 3rd edn. Mohr Siebeck, Tübingen

Zahar A, Sluiter G (2008) International Criminal Law: A critical introduction, Oxford University Press, Oxford

Chapter 6
The Relation Between the Violation and the Evidence

Abstract Article 69(7) of the ICC Statute, the main provision dealing with the exclusion of evidence, sets out a number of different requirements. The previous chapters have included approaches to the interpretation of these individual requirements. An important question left for the construction of the ICC exclusionary rule pertains to the relation between these requirements, more particularly to the relation between the legal violation committed during an investigation and the evidence whose admissibility is at stake. This chapter examines this relation, showing in particular that this relation not only pertains to the question of causality but also includes a normative dimension. This examination raises a number of questions that have likewise occurred in domestic debates. This includes for instance the question of whether an exclusionary rule should apply to derivative evidence, which would mean that a system of criminal procedure would apply some version of the so-called '*fruits of the poisonous tree doctrine*'. A related question pertains to situations where a person is interrogated several times and where a violation committed at an earlier occasion may require the exclusion of statements made during a later interrogation. Finally, a further problem concerns the handling of hypothetical considerations in cases where it would have been possible for investigators to collect the tainted evidence in a legally sound way.

Keywords Causality · Fruits of the poisonous tree doctrine · Remoteness · Derivative evidence · Torture · Consecutive statements · Hypothetical course of investigations · *Conditio sine qua non* · US Supreme Court

Contents

P. Viebig, *Illicitly Obtained Evidence at the International Criminal Court*,
International Criminal Justice Series 4, DOI 10.1007/978-94-6265-093-0_6

6.1 Causality and Normative Restriction

Some attempts at an interpretation of the different elements set out by Article 69(7) of the ICC Statute have been made in the previous chapters. An important question left for the construction of the ICC exclusionary rule pertains to the relationship between these requirements. In its chapeau, Article 69(7) of the ICC Statute requires that the evidence must have been "*obtained by means*" of the violation. The first issue this addresses is the nature of the link by which the emergence of the evidence must generally be tied to the initial violation. We will see, however, that requirements for the relationship between the violation and the evidence do not only arise from the chapeau of the provision. In a second step, this relationship may also affect the determination of whether the additional requirements in Article 69(7)(b) of the Statute are met.

To start with we will look at the basic demands that the chapeau places on this relationship. Is exclusion only warranted where the evidence would not have been gained 'but for' the violation? Or would it suffice instead that there is, for instance, a temporal connection because the violation coincided with the discovery of the evidence? These questions are relevant in those cases where the investigators have acted in an illegal way at the time of the collection of the evidence but where it was not this illegality by which the evidence was brought forth. Cases would include, for example, the seizure of items immediately after an illegal arrest or interrogation, or the disproportionate use of force when entering a premise in order to search it.

Once more, different solutions to this problem have been found in domestic systems. Among the domestic systems reviewed so far, the Canadian system has adopted the widest approach to the connection requirement. Canadian judges have argued that Section 24(2) of the Canadian Charter of Rights and Freedoms does not require a strict causal connection in the sense of a 'but for' or '*conditio sine qua non*' test. It has been held that a temporal or systematic connection was sufficient for the evidence to have been "*obtained in a manner*" in terms of Section 24(2). An example of the resulting jurisprudence concerns the right to counsel. Where investigators conduct a search but do not issue a warning on the right to counsel at its outset, physical evidence found subsequently can be excluded from trial under Canadian case law. In the respective case before the Canadian Supreme Court, it was clear that the evidence had not been obtained 'but for' the violation. The items found during the search would have been gathered independently of whether a warning were to be given. The concomitance of the violation and the evidence gathering, however, was deemed sufficient by the Court to apply the exclusionary rule.[1]

Other systems have applied a much stricter interpretation of the connection requirement. In Germany, causality in the sense of a '*condito sine qua non*' test is considered a fundamental requirement for exclusion. This requirement is in fact deemed so basic that there has been little legal discussion about it.[2] Under U.S. law, the establishment of a 'but for' causality may not always be sufficient for the exclusionary rule to apply. It is, however, considered the minimum requirement.[3]

English law in turn is ambivalent. The requirement of causality depends on the applicable norm. Strict causality has been required at least for confessions.[4] Under the modern statutory framework, it has been held that this follows from the wording of Section 76(2) of PACE. This provision requires that the evidence was obtained "*by oppression*" or "*as a consequence of anything said or done*".[5] The wording of the fair trial exclusionary rule under Section 78 of PACE in turn does not suggest that strict causality is necessarily required. In fact, this general exclusionary rule does not stipulate any requirements at all with respect to the means of evidence collection. It rather focuses on the consequences for trial fairness.[6] The rule only demands that trial fairness would be affected "*having regard to all the circumstances, including the circumstances in which the evidence was obtained*". As a consequence, the question of causation does not arise where the determination of an initial violation is concerned. However, for later purposes, we can already note that the relationship between the violation and the evidence has not

---

[1] *Regina v. Strachan,* Supreme Court of Canada, decision of 15 December 1988, [1988] 2 S.C.R. 980, para 46. Similar, see *Regina v. Therens*, Supreme Court of Canada, decision of 23 May 1985, [1985] 1 S.C.R. 613, para 66, where the admissibility of a breathalyser test was at stake which, as well, had been obtained subsequent to a violation of the right to counsel. See also Stuart 2010a, p. 580 et seq.

[2] Schröder 1992, p. 76 and p. 77. In the context of coercion under Section 136a of the StPO, see German Federal Supreme Court (BGH), decision of 31 May 1968, *Neue Juristische Wochenschrift* 1968, paras 1838 et seq. See also Meyer-Goßner 2013, Section 136a, para 28.

[3] See *Hudson v. Michigan*, United States Supreme Court, decision of 15 June 2006, 547 U.S. 586 (2006): "*Our cases show that but-for causality is only a necessary, not a sufficient, condition for suppression*". Also see Ambos 2010, p. 141; Cammack 2010, p. 642. Critical with respect to the decision in *Hudson* and in favour of a standard of mere "*contributory causation*", see Alschuler 2008, p. 1741 et seq.

[4] Ashworth 1977, p. 723.

[5] *Regina. v. Goldenberg*, Court of Appeal of England and Wales, decision of 18 May 1988, [1989] 88 Cr. App R. 285.

[6] Ashworth and Redmayne 2010, p. 349.

been considered altogether irrelevant. At least where there is no causal connection in the strict sense, this has been considered significant for the determination of whether admitting the evidence would have "*an adverse effect on the fairness of the proceedings*".[7]

Finally, from a human rights perspective, the European Court of Human Rights has claimed that "*it considers it decisive that there is a causal link*" between the evidence and the violation.[8] This seems to refer to a test of 'but –for' or '*conditio sine qua non*' causality and not to include mere temporal or contextual connections.

Turning to the ICC, the starting point for the analysis must once again be the wording of Article 69(7) of the ICC Statute.[9] The formulation "*obtained by means of*" clearly indicates that there must be a link between the evidence and the violation. This link must be one of causality.[10] A closer look reveals that a mere temporal or systematic connection would not suffice. A comparison with the wording of Section 24(2) of the Canadian Charter of Rights and Freedoms is particularly helpful. Differences between the provisions suggests that the Canadian Charter allows for a broader conception than the ICC Statute. The words "*in a manner*" in Section 24(2) may be understood as including a broader set of circumstances than "*by means of*". Moreover, in this context, one of the main arguments used by the Canadian Supreme Court does not apply to the ICC Statute. In order to support their broad approach, the Canadian judges have referred to the French version of the provision, which employs the expression "*obtenus dans des conditions*". In comparison, the French version of the ICC Statute uses the wording "*obtenus par un moyen*". This wording places a focus on the relationship to the improper behaviour as such rather than on the overall circumstances. In fact, the wording of Article 69(7) of the ICC Statute resembles much more the English provision on confessions in Section 76(2) of PACE, in particular the expression "*by oppression*" which, as we have seen, also stipulates a strict causal connection.

As a consequence, it will be argued here that, as a basic requirement, the connection between the violation and the evidence must be one of strict causality, conforming to the 'but for' or 'conditio sine qua non' test. This is the starting point for the assessment of the connection between the violation and the evidence. As mentioned at the outset, however, the evaluation of this connection does not end here. In other words, where the connection is one of strict causality, this does not necessarily mean that its specific nature is an indicator that the evidence should be excluded. As we will see, depending on the circumstances of the case, normative considerations may lead to different results. The next chapters will demonstrate that under subpara (b) of Article 69(7) of the ICC Statute, the seemingly boundless

---

[7]See *Regina v. Alladice*, Court of Appeal of England and Wales, decision of 8 May 1988, [1988] WL 624104; see also Birch 1989, p. 108.

[8]*Gäfgen v. Germany*, ECtHR, decision of 1 June 2010 (Application no. 22978/05), para 171.

[9]See Sect. 2.2.2.

[10]Alamuddin 2010, p. 241; Triffterer 2008—Piragoff, Article 69, para 59.

scope of violations included through the 'but for' causality requirement must be restricted. While the expression "*obtained by means of*" sets a causality requirement, the supplementary prong in Article 69(7)(b) of the ICC Statute stipulates *inter alia* a further normative prerequesite for the link between the violation and the evidence. As we will see, this ultimately reflects the situation in many domestic systems.

6.2 An International '*Fruit of the Poisonous Tree Doctrine*'?

The question of the link between the evidence and the violation is especially relevant in a particular kind of case. These cases have been illustrated by way of a well-known metaphor first used by the U.S. Supreme Court in the case of *Nardone v. United States*, namely the principle of the 'fruit of the poisonous tree'.[11] In a criminal trial, contentious evidence may be 'primary' evidence, meaning evidence that has been gathered directly through a violation. Such is the case, for instance, where the evidence is a coerced confession or a physical piece of evidence found during an illegal search, such as weapons or incriminating documents. To stay with the metaphor, such primary evidence would be the 'tree'. But the question of admissibility may also be raised where the 'fruits' of this 'tree' are concerned. This describes the 'secondary' evidence that was only discovered indirectly, as a result of the primary evidence. The most immediate example would be the case where a suspect is coerced into making a confession which leads the investigators to physical evidence such as a weapon or a grave.

The question that arises is whether Article 69(7) of the ICC Statute extends to such 'secondary' or 'derivative' evidence. If for instance, in the course of domestic investigations, a suspect or a witness is subjected to torture or any other form of improper coercion and then reveals the whereabouts of a mass grave, would evidence such as pictures of the site or expert analyses of the corpses be admissible into evidence? We will see that this question is not one of causality but one that depends on normative considerations. As a consequence, there is no categorical answer to this question in that derivative evidence would generally have to be excluded or generally admitted. Answers must rather be found on a case-by-case basis. This requires once more a weighing of the different interests involved. We have previously looked at a number of factors that tend to be relevant for the balancing exercise under Article 69(7)(b) of the ICC Statute. Where a case concerns derivative evidence, a further factor comes into play. The fact that the relationship between the violation and the derivative evidence is more remote than for direct evidence is an additional criterion for consideration.

[11]*Nardone v. The United States*, United States Supreme Court, decision of 11 December 1939, 308 U.S. 338 (1939).

Given the complexity of the issue, we will look a little closer at the solutions found in the different systems reviewed in the previous chapters. Only against this background will the above-mentioned proposal on how the ICC should deal with derivative evidence become plausible.

6.2.1 Domestic Approaches

At the national level, the issue of derivative evidence is treated rather heterogeneously. Some common denominators that may foster the development of an approach at the international level can, however, be identified.

6.2.1.1 United States

U.S. law provides an example for a comprehensive extension of the exclusionary rule to derivative evidence. Under the now long-established doctrine of the 'fruit of the poisonous tree', the exclusionary rule is generally applicable to derivative evidence. The U.S. Supreme Court has recognized this extension of the rule as early as 1920.[12] In its later case law, the Supreme Court judges further justified the 'fruits doctrine'. They claimed that by generally admitting derivative evidence, the Court would "invite the very methods deemed inconsistent with ethical standards and destructive of personal liberty."[13] In other words, the judges were of the view that to generally admit such evidence would promote illicit investigative measures. Conversely, the decision for exclusion must be based on its purported influence on the way investigative measures are used. This ultimately reflects the familiar rationale of deterrence.

But even the comprehensive U.S. 'fruits doctrine' is not without its limits. Up to now, the extent to which derivative evidence is covered by the exclusionary rule remains highly controversial.[14] Three of the previously mentioned exceptions to the exclusionary rule developed by the U.S. Supreme Court aim in particular at restricting the broad scope of the exclusionary rule caused by its applicability to derivative evidence, namely the 'independent source doctrine', the doctrine of

---

[12]See *Silverthorne Lumber Co. v. United States*, United States Supreme Court, decision of 26 January 1920, 251 U.S. 385 (1920). On the recognition of the '*fruits of the poisonous tree doctrine*', see also Ambos 2010, p. 130; Harris 1991, p. 314 et seq.; Hessler 2000, p. 239 et seq.; LaFave et al. 2004, p. 509 et seq.

[13]*Nardone v. The United States,* United States Supreme Court, decision of 11 December 1939, 308 U.S. 338 (1939).

[14]Ambos 2010, p. 131.

'inevitable discovery' and the 'attenuation doctrine'.[15] We will see that, ultimately, the idea behind all of these doctrines is that, in the cases they address, the relationship between the violation and the evidence is less intense.[16] This constitutes the justification to depart from the strict mandatory rule on grounds of proportionality.[17]

6.2.1.2 Canada

A decision-making by means of exceptions such as under U.S. law has not been necessary under the broad Canadian exclusionary rule. The flexible wording of Section 24(2) of the Canadian Charter of Rights and Freedoms generally allows for the exclusion of both primary and secondary evidence. In principle, the Canadian Supreme Court has applied the same tests for both categories of evidence.

It took some time, however, before the Court provided guidance on the issue of derivative evidence. We have seen that decisions on exclusion initially depended a great deal on whether evidence was considered 'conscriptive', meaning that it had been created by the accused himself as a result of a Charter violation.[18] It was

[15]On these exceptions, see in particular Sect. 3.3.2.

[16]See also Harris 1991, p. 315.

[17]See LaFave et al. 2004, p. 510, who point out that restricting the exclusionary rule means to recognize that "[*c*]*omplete exclusion of fruits would be excessive in light of the obvious competing considerations: that exclusion of evidence thwarts society's interest in convicting the guilty.*". In addition, U.S. courts have considerably restricted the exclusionary rule by rejecting its applicability to the so-called 'Miranda doctrine', which pertains to the right to be properly cautioned on one's right to silence and on the right to legal counsel and which was established by *Miranda v. Arizona*, United States Supreme Court, decision of 13 June 1966, 384 U.S. 436 (1966). This restriction in turn is based on the constitutional basis of the U.S. exclusionary rule. 'Miranda' rights are not themselves considered constitutional rights but only prophylactic measures. Accordingly, any failure to comply with them does not result in a violation of the suspect´s constitutional rights. The Supreme Court has argued that such a violation alone would however be able to provide a basis for the application of the constitutionally based exclusionary rule to derivative evidence. To this effect, first *Michigan v. Tucker*, United States Supreme Court, decision of 10 June 1974, 417 U.S. 433 (1974) and *Oregon v. Elstad*, United States Supreme Court, decision of 4 March 1985, 470 U.S. 298 (1985). For a more recent decision, see *United States v. Patane*, United States Supreme Court, decision of 28 June 2004, 02-1183 (2004). Also see LaFave et al. 2004, p. 526 et seq. For a critical assessment, see Cammack 2010, p. 650 et seq; Trüg 2003, p. 431 et seq. This jurisprudence can clearly not be transferred to the ICC Statute. Article 55(2) of the ICC Statute expressly sets forth a right of the suspect to be properly cautioned. Besides, there is no basis in Article 69(7)(b) of the ICC Statute for such an exception.

[18]*Regina v. Collins*, Supreme Court of Canada, decision of 9 April 1987, [1987] 1 S.C.R. 265, para 37. See also Part III C IV.

only after some time that the Court clarified that all kinds of derivative evidence, including real evidence, could be considered 'conscriptive' evidence.[19]

Under the Court's revised jurisprudence in turn, derivative evidence is evidently seen as falling under Section 24(2) of the Charter. When the Canadian Supreme Court in 2009 established its new approach to Section 24(2) in *Regina v. Grant*, it was in fact confronted with a case that concerned derivative evidence.[20] The Court ascertained the derivative nature of the evidence. It then pointed out explicitly that Section 24(2) of the Charter had overruled the practice under common law to admit derivative evidence as a matter of principle. The new test that it developed for its balancing exercise was directly applied to the derivative evidence in question, which was finally admitted for reasons other than its derivative nature.[21]

In Grant, not only did the judges not refuse to apply Section 24(2) to derivative evidence; this specific feature of the evidence was in fact not considered relevant at all for the decision. Earlier case law, however, suggests that the intensity of the connection between the evidence and the violation might very well be susceptible to assessment under Canadian law. We have seen that, as a starting point, Canadian law does not demand a strict causal connection between the violation and the evidence. However, under its initial framework for exclusion, the Canadian judges have considered the connection between the violation and the evidence relevant for the balancing of interests. This jurisprudence recognizes that where the link between the evidence and the violation is too tenuous, this may influence the inquiry into whether admission would "*bring the administration of justice into disrepute*" in terms of Section 24(2).[22] This evidently concerns derivative evidence in particular, which by its nature is linked less closely to the violation. In such cases, the remoteness of the violation must be taken into account as a factor in the balancing of the different interests involved.[23] In *Grant*, there were sufficient other reasons beyond the remoteness of the violation that already militated against exclusion. If the case were different, there seems no reason in principle however, why the deliberations under the former framework should not be transferable to the Supreme Court's new approach.

---

[19]At least the admission of derivative real evidence was generally considered fair in *Regina v. Collins* based on the argument that its existence as such did not depend on the involvement of the accused. It was only in its later case law that the Canadian Supreme Court unequivocally applied the 'conscriptive' test to derivative real evidence as well, excluding this evidence where it had ultimately been discovered through a suspects's involuntary contribution; see, *Regina v. Burlingham*, Supreme Court of Canada, decision of 18 May 1995, [1995] 2 S.C.R. 206, para 27. See also Mark D. Wiseman 1997, p. 440.

[20]*Regina v. Grant,* Supreme Court of Canada, decision of 17 July 2009, [2009] 2 S.C.R. 353. For a summary of the facts of the case, see also Stuart 2010b, p. 321.

[21]*Regina v. Grant,* Supreme Court of Canada, decision of 17 July 2009, [2009] 2 S.C.R. 353, in particular paras 116 et seq.

[22]See *Regina v. Strachan,* Supreme Court of Canada, decision of 15 December 1988, [1988] 2 S.C.R. 980, paras 46 and 47. See also Penney 2003, p. 126.

[23]See *Regina v. Therens*, Supreme Court of Canada, decision of 23 May 1985, [1985] 1 S.C.R. 613, para 66. Also see Stuart 2010a, p. 581.

6.2.1.3 Germany

We have seen that both the American and the Canadian Supreme Court have adopted approaches which, as a general principle, include derivative evidence into the scope of application of their respective exclusionary rule. The examples of the more inclusionary systems in Germany and in the United Kingdom in turn will demonstrate that this must not necessarily be the point of departure of a modern system of criminal procedure.

The German judiciary has generally looked unfavourably on the extension of the rules on exclusion to derivative evidence. The arguments that the German Federal Court of Justice (BGH) advances in this respect are essentially influenced by concerns of criminal policy.[24] The BGH has repeatedly held that a single procedural error cannot paralyse an entire criminal investigation.[25] The exclusion of derivative evidence has thus been rejected primarily on grounds of efficiency and not based on methodological deliberations.[26] This is also supported by the fact that the Court has applied the exclusionary rule to secondary evidence in exceptional cases.[27]

The BGH's refusal to adopt a version of the U.S. 'fruits of the poisonous tree doctrine' has been approved by some legal academics. It has been argued in particular that, in contrast to American law, the deterrence rationale does not govern the exclusion of evidence in Germany.[28] A number of scholars in Germany today would, however, support the extension of the exclusionary rule to derivative evidence.[29] Admittedly, the details of such a German 'fruits doctrine' remain contentious.[30] But it can be noted that it is not only supported by those in Germany that would favour deterrence as a theoretical basis. Scholars have also

---

[24]Muthorst 2009, p. 207.

[25]German German Federal Supreme Court (BGH), decision of 22 February 1978, *Neue Juristische Wochenschrift* 1978, p. 1390; German Federal Supreme Court (BGH), decision of 24 August 1983, *Neue Juristische Wochenschrift* 1984, p. 2772; German Federal Supreme Court (BGH), decision of 28 April 1987, *Neue Juristische Wochenschrift* 1987, p. 2525. See also Effer-Uhe 2008, p. 339; Kühne 2010, p. 558.

[26]Ambos 2010, p. 147.

[27]So far, the BGH has recognized the so-called '*Fernwirkung*', meaning an extension of the exclusionary rule to derivative evidence, only where a violation of the rules on the interception of telecommunications by the German intelligence agencies in the so-called G10 law (*Gesetz zu Beschränkung des Brief-, Post- und Fernmeldegeheimnisses*, as amended and promulgated on 13 August 1968, last amended on 31 July 2009) was concerned. See German Federal Supreme Court (BGH), decision of 18 April 1980, *Neue Juristische Wochenschrift*, 1980, p. 1700. In difference to the concept of '*Fernwirkung*', see the notion of '*Fortwirkung*', which applies more broadly in the case of consecutive statements; see fn. 940.

[28]Meyer-Goßner 2013, *Einleitung*, para 57.

[29]See Ambos 2010, p. 147, with further references.

[30]Effer-Uhe 2008, p. 399.

pointed to the detrimental effect that a general admission of tainted derivative evidence has on the integrity of criminal proceedings.[31]

6.2.1.4 England and Wales

Even though it would be possible to exclude derivative evidence under the procedural framework of PACE, the English approach is rather restrictive as well. This is particularly the case for derivative real evidence.

A relatively clear distinction is made in English law between the treatment of derivative physical evidence and derivative confessions. While derivative physical evidence will only be excluded in exceptional cases, the exclusion of derivative confessions is much more likely. This distinction follows from the general principles that characterise the English approach to exclusion. As explained above, English law is still influenced by the common law approach to evidence.[32] In accordance with the traditional approach under common law, stronger emphasis is placed on the reliability of evidence than on other values. As a consequence, where derivative evidence consists of physical evidence, it is unlikely to be excluded. Physical evidence regularly exists independently of the initial violation. Accordingly, a violation will usually have no impact on the quality of the evidence.[33]

Where the primary evidence is a confession, this assumption is confirmed by Section 76 of PACE. We have already seen that the entire section is based on reliability concerns only.[34] It corresponds to this assessment that under its para 4, secondary evidence discovered as a result of a confession is admissible as a matter of law.[35] Admittedly, the wording of Section 76(4) of PACE applies to both secondary statements and secondary real evidence. It will, however, be decisive primarily for cases of real evidence. The reason is that, as we will see below, secondary statements will often be inadmissible due to considerations other than Article 76(4).[36]

The wording of Section 78 of PACE in turn would allow for its application to derivative evidence. In principle, the consideration of values other than reliability is guaranteed by this discretionary exclusionary rule. Accordingly, where the collection of the primary evidence affects such values, derivative real evidence may very well be subject to exclusion under this provision.[37] We have seen, however, that the current jurisprudence on Section 78 of PACE continues to be

---

[31]Amelung 1991, p. 2539; Dencker 1977, p. 78 et seq.

[32]See Sect. 3.3.3.

[33]Mellifont 2007, p. 88.

[34]See Mellifont 2007, p. 77; Stone 1995, p. 10. See also Sect. 3.3.3.

[35]Choo 2013, p. 344.

[36]See Sect. 6.3.1.

[37]Choo 2013 p. 344.

influenced by the traditional common law approach. English Courts have adopted an inclusionary approach which remains sceptical towards the exclusion of evidence based on values other than reliability. It thus seems that real evidence will be excluded only in egregious cases.[38]

6.2.2 The Approach of the European Court of Human Rights

The ECtHR recently had the opportunity to address the exclusion of derivative evidence in the well-known case of *Gäfgen v. Germany*. In this case, the applicant had been convicted by a German Regional Court for the kidnapping and murder of a young boy. During the investigation, he had been arrested as a suspect. At the time, the whereabouts of the child were still unknown to the police. When questioning him, the interrogators had still hoped to be able to save the boy's life. The suspect, who in fact had already killed his victim and hidden the body near a pond, refused to reveal where he was holding the child. The responsible German deputy chief of police ordered his subordinate to threaten the suspect with "*pain he would never forget*". As a result of this threat, the suspect confessed and led the police to the body.

In the subsequent trial, the testimony made directly under the impression of the threat was excluded. However, the prosecution also introduced as evidence the boy's corpse and clothing, the autopsy record, as well as tyre tracks made by the defendant's car found near the pond. A motion by the defendant to exclude this derivative real evidence was rejected. Thereupon, the defendant reiterated his previous confession and was subsequently convicted and sentenced to life imprisonment.[39]

After his domestic appeals had been rejected, the former defendant brought his case to the European Court of Human Rights. He claimed *inter alia* that his rights under Articles 3 and 6 of the ECHR had been violated by the use of both the real evidence and the later confession he had made during the trial. The European judges noted that there was no real consensus among the ECHR's member states on the scope of the exclusionary rule.[40] In its own assessment, the Court did not find that admitting the evidence constituted a violation under the Charter.[41] At the same time, it did not generally reject the idea that tainted derivative evidence might have to be excluded in domestic criminal proceedings. In fact, the judges

---

[38]Mellifont 2007, p. 87.

[39]For a summary of the facts and procedural history, see Sauer and Trilsch 2011, p. 314.

[40]See *Gäfgen v. Germany*, ECtHR, decision of 1 June 2010 (Application no. 22978/05), para 69.

[41]See Safferling 2012, p. 503, who criticises the ECtHR for not having strictly implemented the '*fruit of the poisonous tree doctrine*'.

recognised that there was a causal link between the derivative evidence and the violation[42] and that in such a case, admitting derivative evidence could in principle amount to a violation of Charter rights.[43]

In order to understand why the Court did not decide that the applicant's Charter rights had been violated in this specific case, we have to consider, once more, the particular context of its decisions. We have assessed the special character of the Court as a human rights monitoring body earlier in this research.[44] The Court's rejection in Gäfgen was due to its general reticent approach to the review of evidentiary issues, which is a result of its particular character. Applying its holistic approach to the case at hand, the ECtHR found that admitting the real evidence did not amount to a violation of the applicant's right to fair trial. It argued in particular that his conviction was essentially based on the new confession he had made during the trial. The real evidence in turn had been used merely for corroboration purposes.[45]

In summary, it can be noted that, despite its holistic approach, the European Court of Human Rights has recognized in principle the extension of exclusionary rules for illegally gained evidence to derivative evidence. The fact that it did not hold in Gäfgen that excluding the evidence would have been necessary is merely a result of the Court's holistic approach and of the fact that, in that case, the applicant later confessed a second time.

6.2.3 The International Level—the Scope of Article 69(7) of the ICC Statute

So far, none of the international courts and tribunals have clearly defined the scope of their respective exclusionary rule. Consequently, no indication for a possible conception for international criminal proceedings may be drawn from the

[42]See *Gäfgen v. Germany*, ECtHR, decision of 1 June 2010 (Application no. 22978/05), para 171: "*For the purposes of its own assessment under Article 6, it considers it decisive that there is a causal link between the applicant's interrogation in breach of Article 3 and the real evidence secured by the authorities as a result of the applicant's indications* [...]. *In other words, the impugned real evidence was secured as a direct result of his interrogation by the police that breached Article 3*."

[43]*Gäfgen v. Germany*, ECtHR, decision of 1 June 2010 (Application no. 22978/05), para 178: "*The repression of, and the effective protection of individuals from, the use of investigation methods that breach Article 3 may therefore also require, as a rule, the exclusion from use at trial of real evidence which has been obtained as the result of any violation of Article 3, even though that evidence is more remote from the breach of Article 3 than evidence extracted immediately as a consequence of a violation of that Article.*" See also Jackson and Summers 2012, p. 193; Sauer and Trilsch 2011, p. 316.

[44]See in particular Sect. 3.2.6.

[45]*Gäfgen v. Germany*, ECtHR, decision of 1 June 2010 (Application no. 22978/05), para 179. On the admissibility of this new confession, see Sect. 6.3.1.

example of the *Ad hoc* tribunals. Given both the scarce case law on exclusion at the international level in general and the contentiousness of this particular issue even for domestic proceedings, this is hardly surprising.

With the previous approaches in mind, two general issues arise for the ICC rule: The first is the general scope of the rule. This concerns the question whether the previously made assertion that this rule applies to derivative evidence can be justified. The second main issue will be whether and how the connection between the evidence and the violation can be considered a valid factor when balancing the different interests.

6.2.3.1 The ICC Exclusionary Rule and 'Fruits'—General Applicability

It has been explained above that the words "*obtained by means of*" in Article 69(7) of the ICC Statute set a causality requirement. This causality requirement demands a 'but for' or 'conditio sine qua non' test. Accordingly, the violation must be an indispensable condition for the derivative evidence to be at the disposal of the investigating authorities.

Derivative evidence meets this test. This can best be illustrated through the example mentioned at the outset of the chapter: In the course of a coercive interrogation, the suspect reveals the whereabouts of a mass grave. The Office of the Prosecutor later relies on physical evidence such as pictures of the grave to reach a conviction. It is evident that the coercion was an indispensable condition. Without it, the suspect would not have made the revelation and the grave would therefore not have been found. In other words, 'but for' the coercion, the pictures would not have been at the disposal of the prosecution.

However, in order for reliable derivative evidence to be covered by the ICC's exclusionary rule, this evidence must also be able to fulfil the additional requirements set out in the rule's second prong. Where the reliability of the evidence is not at stake, its admission must be able to impair the integrity of the proceedings. There is nothing on a level of principle that would prevent derivative evidence from having an adverse effect on the integrity of the proceedings. Where the primary evidence undermines the Court's integrity, it seems at least possible that this adverse effect also extends to evidence derived thereof.

It has been held before that the ICC should apply a 'court-centred' understanding to integrity. Integrity in this sense demands the consistency of judicial decisions that is required to create growing public respect for a judicial institution.[46] If the prosecution were permitted to rely on secondary evidence where the primary evidence is excluded, it would at least partly be able to introduce the very same information that the non-admissibility of the primary evidence excluded from trial. In the previously mentioned example it would, for instance, prove the

[46]See Sect. 4.3.2.2.4.

existence of the mass grave not through the primary confession but through the pictures made as a consequence of its later discovery. This kind of contradiction would likely to expose the ICC to criticism for being inconsistent. It would probably raise the suspicion that its judges unduly circumvent procedural protections to the advantage of the prosecution.[47]

As an interim finding, it can thus be concluded that no fundamental arguments oppose the exclusion of derivative evidence, neither with respect to causality nor to the other requirements of Article 69(7)(b) of the ICC Statute.

This is in line with the reasoning behind the different approaches reviewed above. Internationally, the scope of exclusionary rules may be contentious. But categorical arguments are not usually advanced to reject the rule's application to derivative evidence. Even systems such as Germany, which largely disapprove of an extensive understanding of the exclusionary rule, argue on the basis of the effectiveness of criminal prosecution rather than on considerations of principle.

No considerations of principle are apparent at the level of international criminal prosecution either. While effectiveness concerns have an impact here as well, this is a question to be assessed on a case-by-case basis. Moreover, restrictions for real evidence as they are made in practice under English law are not compatible with the overall purpose of Article 69(7)(b) of the ICC Statute. We have seen before that the provision is not directed at the kind of reliability concerns that govern English case law.[48]

On the whole, the test for secondary evidence is therefore basically the same as for primary evidence, namely whether, in the particular case, admitting the evidence would have a negative bearing on the Court's integrity. At the same time, we will see that in the case of derivative evidence, the ensuing balancing exercise is particularly influenced by an additional factor that has not been considered so far, namely by how remote the evidence is from the violation. The next paragraph will demonstrate how this factor sets normative restrictions to the seemingly boundless scope of the exclusionary rule under the 'but for' causality test. Given that these normative restrictions are relevant in particular for derivative evidence, they will first be dealt with in this context. Section 6.2.3.2 below, however, will briefly address their relevance with respect to primary evidence.

6.2.3.2 Normative Restrictions

The 'but for' or 'conditio -sine qua non' causality test brings a large number of cases within the scope of the exclusionary rule. Proportionality, however, dictates that this scope must be restricted. The following paragraph will demonstrate how such a restriction can be achieved by taking into account how intensely or loosely

---

[47]For a similar argument at the domestic level, see *Regina v. Burlingham*, Supreme Court of Canada, decision of 18 May 1995, [1995] 2 S.C.R. 206.

[48]See Sect. 4.3.2.2.1.

the violation and the evidence are connected in the specific case. We will see that by assessing the respective connection, the scope of the ICC exclusionary rule, which has so far only been causally determined, can be restricted on the basis of normative deliberations.

The strength of the connection between the violation and the evidence has also been taken into consideration by domestic courts. The particularities of the ICC system of international prosecution suggest that it may even have a particularly strong impact at this level. We will first recall some ideas on proportionality in the context of exclusion that have been advanced in domestic systems. These ideas will then be assessed against the background of international criminal prosecutions.

To reject the 'fruits' theory as a whole, opponents at the national level have relied on the concern for the effectiveness of crime prosecution. To take just one example, the German Federal Court of Justice has held that isolated procedural mistakes were not to impede entire investigations.[49] This reference to effectiveness is grounded on proportionality concerns. While exclusion as such is deemed necessary in a modern legal system, this objection is supposed to set limits on its detrimental effects.

With respect to the ICC, we have relied on legitimacy concerns to argue that considerations of effectiveness should not be used routinely by an international criminal institution to set aside human rights guarantees. At the same time, we have seen that the effective implementation of international criminal law also has a major impact on such an institution's legitimacy.[50] Acknowledging that it is necessary to set limits on the exclusionary rule is at the very heart of the general idea of balancing the different interests involved. This must also guide the matter at hand. While the exclusion of derivative evidence by the ICC cannot be rejected as a matter of principle, the significance of effective criminal proceedings still points to a proportionality concern that cannot be disregarded altogether.

The need to comply with the limits set by proportionality is also recognized by those systems that do in fact accept the extension of the exclusionary rule to derivative evidence. At the same time, those systems offer ideas on how to steer a middle course by restricting the causally determined scope of an exclusionary rule on normative grounds.

We have seen that the construction of exceptions as carried out by the U.S. Supreme Court is ultimately based on the principle of proportionality. We must now look in particular at the so-called 'attenuation doctrine'. The exceptions of the 'independent source doctrine' and of the 'inevitable discovery doctrine' allude to the logical question of causality. The 'attenuation doctrine' in turn introduces a

---

[49] German Federal Supreme Court (BGH), decision of 22 February 1978, *Neue Juristische Wochenschrift* 1978, p. 1390; German Federal Supreme Court (BGH), decision of 24 August 1983, *Neue Juristische Wochenschrift* 1984, p. 2772; German Federal Supreme Court (BGH), decision of 28 April 1987, *Neue Juristische Wochenschrift* 1987, p. 2525. See also Sect. 3.3.1.

[50] See in particular Sect. 2.2.3.

more normative element to the analysis. In contrast to the other two exceptions, the 'attenuation doctrine' does not focus on the logically determined existence or non-existence of a connection between the evidence and the violation. Instead, where the connection has become "*so attenuated as to dissipate the taint*", a value-based assessment demands that the evidence must be admitted.[51] Where, for example, the defendant was arrested subsequent to an illegal search and then revealed the identity of another suspect, a statement that this suspect later makes of his own accord would be admissible under the 'attenuation doctrine'.[52]

The basic idea that remoteness is a factor for consideration is useful for the construction of the ICC exclusionary rule. The jurisprudence of the U.S. Supreme Court must nonetheless be treated with caution. Not only has the 'attenuation doctrine' been criticised at the domestic level for being too unclear;[53] more importantly, the differences between the U.S. and the ICC exclusionary rules must be given due consideration.

Firstly, the systematic approach of the ICC must naturally be different. Where the link between the evidence and the violation is too remote, this cannot simply lead to the non-applicability of the ICC exclusionary rule by means of an exception. Instead, this consideration must be included in the balancing exercise under Article 69(7)(b) of the ICC Statute. But even more important are the differences in terms of substance. Unlike Article 69(7) of the ICC Statute, the American exclusionary rule is primarily based on deterrence. The notion of "*the dissipation of the taint*" has consequently been clarified as marking "the point at which the deterrent effect of the exclusionary rule no longer justifies its costs".[54] This test cannot be guiding as such for the ICC exclusionary rule, which is based on integrity concerns.

But the fact that remoteness is also a relevant factor under an integrity oriented exclusionary rule is illustrated by the Canadian case law. It is clear from this case law as well that the consideration of the intensity of the connection between the gathering of the evidence and the violation serves to limit exclusion on a normative basis. We have seen that a broad understanding has been applied to the wording "*obtained in a manner*", as set forth by Section 24(2) of the Canadian Charter of Rights and Freedoms. It has not even been understood as requiring a logically

[51]See Ambos 2010, p. 510, who highlights the similarities with the normative attribution of criminal responsibility through the German doctrine of '*Zurechnungslehre*' (which could be translated by: '*doctrine of attribution*'). On the different doctrines, see also Sect. 3.3.2.

[52]See Ambos 2010, p. 139.

[53]Ambos 2010, p. 142; LaFave et al. 2004, p. 510.

[54]LaFave et al. 2004, p. 510.

based connection in terms of strict causality.[55] The remoteness of the evidence from the violation has, however, been considered under the evaluative inquiry into whether the admission of the respective evidence may "*bring the administration of justice into disrepute*".[56]

A similar conclusion may be drawn for the ICC. While the expression "*obtained by means of*" establishes a causality requirement, the additional prong in Article 69(7)(b) of the ICC Statute demands a further normative evaluation. This can be achieved by taking into account remoteness as another factor in the balancing exercise. Naturally, this factor is most relevant where derivative evidence is concerned. In such a case, the connection is *per se* less intense. Depending on the case, however, it may also play a role for the admissibility of primary evidence.

With the primacy of the integrity rationale in mind, the test defined for the American 'attenuation doctrine' can be reformulated for the ICC: Exclusion is not warranted under Article 69(7)(b) where the connection between the evidence and the violation is so remote that the damage to the integrity of the proceedings no longer justifies the cost of exclusion.

6.2.3.3 Determining Remoteness

The remoteness factor, however, presents some difficulty in its application. The normative nature of this factor makes it particularly susceptible to the subjective views of the bench responsible for the decision. We have seen that it is the nature of subjective evaluations that no definite standards can be established.[57] Nevertheless, it is possible, once more, to develop some reference points.

In domestic settings, it has also proven difficult to find exact criteria that would define when evidence is too remote from the violation to trigger the respective exclusionary rule. The U.S. Supreme Court has argued that this evaluation cannot be based on single considerations. It is instead subject to a multi-factored analysis.[58] This finding does not follow from the deterrence rationale but from the normative nature of the remoteness test. The same conclusion can be drawn for an integrity based exclusionary rule. The relevant criteria applied by domestic courts

---

[55] Even more broadly than Article 69(7) of the ICC Statute has been understood here, see Sect. 6.1. See also Stuart 2010a, p. 580 et seq.

[56] See *Regina v. Strachan*, Supreme Court of Canada, decision of 15 December 1988, [1988] 2 S.C.R. 980, paras 46 and 47. Also see Penney 2003, p. 126. Note that this consideration goes further than the English approach, which only considers the existence of a causal connection when it assesses whether admitting the evidence "*would have such an adverse effect on the fairness of the proceedings*" in terms of Section 78 of PACE; see Sect. 6.1.

[57] See Sect. 4.3.2.2.5.

[58] See United States Supreme Court, decision of 26 June 1975, 422 U.S. 590 (1975). Also see Trüg 2003, p. 457.

include, but are not limited to, the lapse of time between the violation and the gathering of the derivative evidence, as well as the presence of any intervening circumstances. These two criteria have been addressed by both the U.S. and the Canadian Supreme Court,[59] and will be relevant for the ICC exclusionary rule as well. Their consideration with respect to ICC proceedings even reveals that the peculiarities of the ICC system emphasize the particular significance of the remoteness factor at this level.

The most evident consideration is the temporal element. The time passed between the discovery of the evidence and the violation does clearly not interrupt the causal connection. It does, however, give rise to normative considerations. Where the chain of events is particularly long, the connection between the violation and the collection of the evidence is evidently less intense. This is not any different at the international level than at the national level. In fact, the relevance of this criterion increases at the international level due to the factual situation in which international proceedings regularly take place. Given both the temporal and the geographical dimension of international crimes, investigations usually take several years. When compared to the average domestic investigation, it is more likely therefore that there is a considerable lapse of time between the initial violation and the gathering of a derivative piece of evidence.

The consideration of intervening circumstances in turn has been relevant in domestic cases mostly in one particular case constellation. This is where the primary evidence leads the investigators to a new witness. Both the U.S. and the Canadian Supreme Court have held that, in such a case, the deliberate decision of the witness to talk to the investigators or to testify in court attenuates the connection to the extent that her statements are no longer tainted.[60] The U.S. Supreme Court has held that witnesses who are willing to talk to the authorities should be treated differently from inanimate evidence. It has argued that their free will makes it more likely that they have been discovered by legal means.[61]

The generality of this argument, which converges the 'attenuation doctrine' with the 'inevitable discovery doctrine', may be called into question. The assumption that a witness might theoretically have been found by legal means seems rather speculative. As we will see under the 'inevitable discovery doctrine' as well, hypothetical deliberations are only valid where they are based on a solid factual ground.[62] The intervening effect of a deliberate decision of a witness to speak to the authorities may, however, be endorsed for different reasons. Again, the causal

---

[59]See for instance *Brown v. Illinois*, United States Supreme Court, decision of 26 June 1975; *Regina v. Goldhart*, Supreme Court of Canada, decision of 4 July 1996, [1996] 2 S.C.R. 463, paras 40, 45.

[60]*United States v. Ceccolini*, United States Supreme Court, decision of 21 March 1978; *Regina v. Goldhart*, Supreme Court of Canada, decision of 4 July 1996, [1996] 2 S.C.R. 463, para 42.

[61]*United States v. Ceccolini*, United States Supreme Court, decision of 21 March 1978.

[62]See Sect. 6.4.2. For a critical assessment of this jurisprudence, see also LaFave et al. 2004, p. 525.

connection is not interrupted. The voluntary decision of a third person adds, however, a further condition for the discovery of the evidence. As a result, its origin is divided.

Of course, such a condition only has an independent effect where this intervening circumstance was not simply caused by the initial violation. Consequently, the degree to which the decision of the witness was influenced by the initial violation must be assessed. The implications of a decision to give a statement to investigators or to testify in court will be greater where this decision is the consequence of a detached reflection and of a desire to cooperate as opposed to where the witness feels compelled to cooperate as a result of the violation. The latter will be more likely, for instance, where the primary evidence incriminates the witness herself.[63]

In this context, the very assumption that many witness statements are deliberate has been called into question for procedural reasons. This is because witnesses in domestic proceedings have the duty to tell the truth and can often be compelled to appear for that purpose.[64] This argument however is applicable to ICC proceedings only to a limited extent. Unlike both in domestic systems and the Statutes of the *Ad hoc* tribunals, the ICC Statute does not provide the Court, let alone the Office of the Prosecutor, with subpoena powers in respect of witnesses. Witnesses can not therefore be compelled to speak to OTP investigators or to testify before the Court.[65] As a consequence, where the second statement has been made to ICC officials, the intervening nature of such a statement is even more plausible for ICC proceedings when compared to other procedural systems. The only instance where this criticism is in fact worth considering is where a witness has been compelled under domestic law. Depending on the circumstances of the individual case, such compulsion to give a statement may in fact influence the determination of a deliberate choice.

Finally, we should note that the aforementioned case constellation might be particularly interesting for our consideration of derivative evidence given the general significance of witness testimony in ICC proceedings. While the Nuremberg court could heavily rely on documentary evidence, modern conflicts tend not to produce many documents. As has been the case in previous modern international tribunals, the ICC is therefore highly dependent on eyewitness testimony.[66] Consequently, the case constellation of witness evidence is one of the most likely cases of derivative evidence that the Court may be confronted with at some point.

---

[63]Similar, *Regina v. Goldhart*, Supreme Court of Canada, decision of 4 July 1996, [1996] 2 S.C.R. 463, para 42.

[64]Trüg 2003, p. 456.

[65]Even though Article 64(6)(b) of the ICC Statute allows the Chambers to "*require the attendance and testimony of witnesses*", the lack of enforcement powers and in particular the unavailability of sanctions prevents that witnesses be compelled to appear; for a detailed assessment, see Sluiter 2009, p. 592 et seq.

[66]See Combs 2010, p. 12; Sluiter 2009, p. 591.

The previous assessment notwithstanding, there is a further instance where intervening circumstances may be considered in the context of international proceedings. This deliberation rests once more on the distribution of responsibilities within the ICC cooperation regime. We have seen that different actors can be involved in international investigations. This includes the Office of the Prosecutor and the national authorities, sometimes of more than one state. The case may arise where the national police of a certain state have committed the initial violation and have then submitted information to the international Prosecutor or to the authorities of another state. These actors would then be put in the position to obtain secondary evidence and may do so in a perfectly legal way. It may be argued that the violation is dissipated to some degree due to the intervening legal behaviour of other authorities.

Clearly, the point may be made that the subsequent legal behaviour of these authorities only means that these authorities are not committing any additional violation. But once more, the argument is not that the causal chain of events is interrupted. It rests on the normative argument of the degree to which investigatory violations committed by national authorities can be attributed to the ICC. We have already seen that even for primary evidence this attribution is somewhat diminished when compared to acts of the Office of the Prosecutor.[67] Where different actors are involved in a chain of events before the derivative evidence reaches the ICC, its integrity will be less affected than if it directly cooperates with those actors immediately responsible for human rights violations. This is consequently a consideration which, through the factor of remoteness, may be included into the balancing exercise.

6.2.3.4 Derivative Torture Evidence

Finally, a comment seems necessary on the fundamental question of the use of derivative torture evidence. The consideration of remoteness as an argument to reject exclusion must be handled very carefully where torture is concerned. For primary evidence, we have found that the elementary nature of the prohibition of torture requires that violations be treated particularly strictly.[68] Where derivative evidence is concerned, teleological considerations indicate that a high standard is required from the ICC also in these cases.

The absolute character of the torture prohibition has led human rights monitoring bodies to demand that a broad range of evidence must be excluded. The wording of the international exclusionary rule in Article 15 of the UN Torture Convention does not specify whether it is meant to cover fruits. The Committee against Torture, however, which monitors the implementation of the Convention, has recommended that both primary and secondary evidence be excluded under

---

[67]See Sect. 5.4.

[68]See Sect. 5.4.3.

the provision.[69] The same conclusion can be drawn from the jurisprudence of the ECtHR on Article 3 of the ECHR. In the case of *Gäfgen v. Germany* summarised above, the European judges, while ultimately finding that admitting the evidence in that case did not amount to a violation of the ECHR, quite unequivocally held that, in light of the absolute nature of the torture prohibition, admitting evidence gained by means of torture would always amount to a violation of the Convention. In this case, however, the contentious behaviour of the German police was classified not as torture but as degrading and inhuman treatment.[70] We have seen that at another point in the decision, the judges recognized, in principle, the application of the exclusionary rule to derivative evidence.[71] Taken together, it can be assumed that the ECtHR would have required the exclusion of the secondary evidence had it been confronted with derivative evidence that the Court would have assessed as having been obtained by torture instead of inhuman and degrading treatment.[72]

In light of its legitimacy concerns, the ICC should come to a similar conclusion and exclude evidence linked to torture on a large scale. More specifically, even where the connection between the evidence and the violation is rather remote, the Court should either exclude derivative torture evidence on an absolute basis or at least conclude that there is a strong presumption that the admission of such evidence is "*antithetical to and would seriously damage the integrity of the proceedings*".

6.3 Consecutive Statements

We will now give some additional consideration to the treatment of a particular instance of evidence, which also begs the question of the connection between the violation and the emergence of the evidence, but which cannot easily be equated with the cases of derivative evidence considered above.

---

[69]See Committee against Torture, *Concluding observations of the Committee against Torture on Germany*, para 193: "*The Committee recommends that further legislative attention be paid to the strict enforcement of article 15 of the Convention and that all evidence obtained directly or indirectly by torture be strictly prevented from reaching the cognizance of the deciding judges in all judicial proceedings.*", UN Doc. A/53/44 of 11 May 1998, available at: http://www.unhchr.ch/tbs/doc.nsf/%28Symbol%29/A.53.44,paras179–195.En?OpenDocument (last visited: October 2013).

[70]See *Gäfgen v. Germany*, ECtHR, decision of 1 June 2010 (Application no. 22978/05), paras 166 and 167.

[71]See *Gäfgen v. Germany*, ECtHR, decision of 1 June 2010 (Application no. 22978/05), para 171.

[72]Jackson and Summers 2012, p. 193. For a critical assessment of this distinction, see Sauer and Trilsch 2011, p. 318.

This is the case where a person, usually a suspect, has made a number of consecutive statements. The first statement, in this situation, is tainted by a violation and must be excluded. If the suspect subsequently testifies again, this time under legally sound conditions, the question arises whether the previous taint continues to impact on the admissibility of his later statements.

It seems worth taking a closer look at this problem. We will see that this question has already come up in international case law. Moreover, we have mentioned above the general significance of oral evidence in international criminal proceedings. And finally, the complexity of international crimes and of the related proceedings means that the need for repeated questioning is even more likely at this level.

In the situation described in the previous paragraph, the exclusion of the second statement has been called for at the national level based on two different lines of thought.

On the one hand, it has been justified due to the continuing effect of the initial violation. In the individual case, this violation might be so severe that it is reasonable to assume that, at the time of the second questioning, the defendant is still acting under its coercive effect. Where, for instance, the life of the defendant has been threatened at the outset, one may assume that this threat, even though not repeated prior to a second interview, still influences the defendant at that time.

On the other hand, exclusion has also been justified by relying on the continuing effect of the first statement. Scholars at the national level have termed this most figuratively the 'cat out of the bag' theory. This notion is based on the assumption of a psychological compulsion flowing from the delivery of the first statement. The idea is that the suspect is likely to feel bound by what he has previously told the authorities and will therefore feel compelled to repeat it.

Whether cases of consecutive statements should generally be treated as part of the 'fruits of the poisonous tree doctrine' is a matter of terminology. It is debatable to some extent whether consecutive statements should be subsumed under the terms 'primary' and 'secondary' or 'derivative' evidence that were previously used for categorization.

Where the discussion on exclusion is based on the continuing effect of the initial violation, the classification is rather easy. Here, the statement is directly tainted by the initial violation. Under these conditions, the second statement is in fact primary evidence.

Where, on the other hand, the justification for exclusion is based on the continuing effect of previously having talked to the authorities, the categorization is less clear. In contrast to derivative evidence in the usual sense, the first statement has not led investigators to new pieces of evidence. Instead, the connection that possibly exists between the statements arises from the psychological impact of having testified before. Accordingly, this kind of evidence can be considered derivative evidence, but it may also be seen as primary evidence or simply as a category of its own. The following deliberations will use the term 'secondary' evidence instead of 'derivative', in order to indicate that this kind of evidence is not, in the strict sense, derived from the primary statement.

Where a situation involving consecutive statements arises, courts at the national level sometimes seem to rely on both of the above-mentioned lines of thought to exclude the second statement, while at times they have preferred only one. Which line of reasoning is followed by a national court depends, on the one hand, on the facts of the particular case, which may indicate whether the respective person was influenced by the violation or by the fact of having testified before. On the other hand, it also depends on whether a particular jurisdiction accepts the premise of the second line of thought. While the first assumption, namely that the violation itself may continue to influence the suspect, is rather straightforward, we will see that the idea of a psychological connection between two statements has generally been called into question at the national level.

The first line of thought, the continuing effect that may derive from the initial violation, need not be discussed in more detail. This idea can always be turned to where the facts of a case give rise to the assumption that the violation still impacts on the suspect. The discussion will concentrate instead on the more debatable issue, whether, in addition, the judges at the ICC could also rely on the psychological impact of having testified before. Three general questions govern this issue. The first is whether there is a psychological effect, flowing from the fact that a suspect has testified before, which could impact on later statements. The second issue pertains to the nature and intensity of this connection. This concerns the question of how intense the link must be for a continuing effect to exist in the first place. And finally, the question arises whether this connection can subsequently be interrupted. In other words: is there a way to eliminate the psychological impact of having testified before and thus a way to heal the existing taint?

Before discussing a possible handling of consecutive statements under Article 69(7)(b) of the ICC Statute, a short overview will be given of how the issue is dealt with in other systems. This overview will demonstrate that the questions outlined above emerge in every system.

6.3.1 Consecutive Statements in Domestic Proceedings

It has been argued above that, as a matter of principle, the scope of Article 69(7)(b) of the ICC Statute extends to derivative evidence. This does not *per se* suggest a generous handling of the issue of consecutive statements. A look at domestic systems reveals that the solutions found for this particular situation do not necessarily follow from whether a system applies a generally broad or narrow understanding of the scope of its exclusionary rule. In fact, the domestic systems have, rather surprisingly, found answers that sometimes even take the opposite direction from their handling of the 'fruits' theory.

We have seen that in the more inclusionary systems in England and Germany, the exclusion of 'fruits' in general is treated rather restrictively.[73] Secondary confessional evidence, however, is excluded more often than real evidence.

Under English law, this finding extends to confessional evidence of any kind. It follows from the primary significance that is attached to the reliability of evidence. When compared to real evidence, which regularly exists independently from a violation, the reliability of statements is affected more easily. This also influences the way in which consecutive statements are treated.

In Germany in turn, the more frequent exclusion of confessional evidence follows precisely the way in which the problem of consecutive statements is handled. Under German case law, this problem is expressly treated as an issue that is separate from the 'fruits of the poisonous tree doctrine'.[74]

To some degree, both German and English courts have recognized the existence of a psychological connection between consecutive statements. In addition, the jurisprudence of these systems contains deliberations on the nature of the relationship considered necessary to assume that a first statement impacts on a subsequent one. Moreover, the possibility of this effect being interrupted is recognized.

The German Federal Supreme Court (BGH) has discussed the issue of consecutive statements in particular with respect to the right to be properly cautioned.[75] It has recognized that, where such a violation taints a primary statement, this can also affect the admissibility of a later statement. This will be the case where the defendant only testifies again because he believes that he is bound by what he has previously said.[76] The Court thus applies the above-mentioned 'cat out of the bag theory' to these cases. In this context, the German case law accords a major significance to whether an additional caution has been issued before the second statement was made. This caution must contain the indication that the previous statement is not admissible as evidence.[77]

Where such an additional caution was provided, the second statement is not excluded. Where, in turn, no such caution was given, exclusion still depends on an overall balancing exercise. Here, a main consideration in assessing the remaining psychological impact of the previous testimony has been whether the content of the statements was identical. Where this has been the case, the BGH has been

---

[73]See Sects. 6.2.1.3 and 6.2.1.4.

[74]In Germany, the '*fruits of the poisonous tree doctrine*' is commonly treated under the heading of '*Fernwirkung*', whereas the question of '*consecutive statements*' is considered under the heading of '*Fortwirkung*'.

[75]See Section 136(1)(2) of the German Code of Criminal Procedure (StPO).

[76]See for instance German Federal Supreme Court (BGH), decision of 18 December 2008, *Neue Juristische Wochenschrift* 2009, p. 1427.

[77]This explanation is dealt with in German doctrine under the term of '*qualifizierte Belehrung*', which might be translated by: '*additional caution*'.

more inclined to exclude the second testimony, considering that the interrogated person would more likely assume a connection between the interviews.[78]

In addition to the right to be properly cautioned, the issue of consecutive statements has also been discussed by the BGH where the initial testimony was obtained through coercion.[79] Here, the jurisprudence of the BGH is however rather opaque and thus not fruitful for the present research.[80]

Similar solutions have been found by English courts. English judges have recognized a continuing effect flowing from a previous statement. To justify the exclusion of secondary statements, English courts have relied *inter alia* on the psychological effect that presumably flows from the fact that the defendant had talked to the authorities before.[81] The courts have adopted a more comprehensive approach than their colleagues in Germany and English case law does not seem to make a distinction between different violations. Both where the right to be cautioned was concerned[82] and in cases of other violations,[83] English judges have excluded secondary confessions under both Sections 76 and 78.[84]

What remains somewhat unclear are the conditions under which English courts will assume a continuing effect. According to case law, such an effect does not exist in every case of consecutive statements. It is rather a matter of fact and

---

[78]*See German Federal Supreme Court (BGH), decision of 18 December 2008, Neue Juristische Wochenschrift* 2009, p. 1427.

[79]See Section 136a of the StPO.

[80]*See German Federal Supreme Court (BGH),* decision of 9 March 1995, *Neue Juristische Wochenschrift 1995,* p. 2047. The BGH seems to focus on the remaining coercive effect of the violation itself. It has excluded secondary statements based on the assumption that the violation continued to impact on the defendant's mind. But without explicitly saying so, the judges also seem to have attached some significance to the impact of having testified before. The case-law at least considers the lapse of time between the statements, as well as their similarity in content. The main difference to the cases of a failure to caution however pertains to whether and how the continuing effect on the second statement can be interrupted. The BGH has not decided so far whether this might require an additional caution. It has contented itself to observe the inconsistency of its own case-law; see German Federal Supreme Court (BGH), decision of 18 December 2008, *Neue JuristischeWochenschrift* 2009, p. 1427 (BGHSt 53, 112). See also Beulke 2012, para 142; Meyer-Goßner 2013, Section 136a, para 30.

[81]See *Regina v. McGovern*, Court of Appeal of England and Wales, decision of 18 May 1990, [1991] Crim. L.R. 124; *Regina v. Neil*, Court of Appeal of England and Wales, decision of 29 November 1993, [1994] Crim. L.R. 441. In addition, English courts have also relied on the fact that the initial oppression continued to operate, see *Regina v. Glaves*, Court of Appeal of England and Wales, decision of 29 January 1993, [1993] Crim. L.R. 685.

[82]See *Regina v. Neil*, Court of Appeal of England and Wales, decision of 29 November 1993, [1994] Crim. L.R. 441.

[83]*Regina v. McGovern*, Court of Appeal of England and Wales, decision of 18 May 1990, [1991] Crim. L.R. 124; *Regina v. Glaves*, Court of Appeal of England and Wales, decision of 29 January 1993, [1993] Crim. L.R. 685.

[84]See also Choo 2013, p. 344.

degree.[85] In their decisions, English judges have focussed on whether, in a particular case, the continuing effect had subsequently been interrupted. This has been held to be the case where "*the arrangements for the subsequent interview gave the accused a sufficient opportunity to decide whether to repeat or retract what was previously said, or say nothing.*"[86] However, the exact requirements for such a cure of previous procedural flaws remain unclear. In particular, English judges have not clearly established the necessity of an additional caution. In the literature, an interruption where the suspect was given the opportunity for full discussion with a solicitor has been discussed.[87] The case law, in turn, remains ambiguous.[88]

The view that the psychological situation is altered once a suspect has given a first statement has also been supported in Canadian case law. The so-called 'cat out of the bag theory' has in fact been applied rather generously by Canadian courts. In doing so, the jurisprudence of the Canadian Supreme Court once more relies on the integrity rationale as set forth in Section 24(2) of the Charter. The Canadian Supreme Court has held in this respect that a secondary statement "*might not be admitted if its admission would have the same effect as admitting the proximate evidence*", namely to "*bring the administration of justice into disrepute*".[89] On this basis, Canadian courts have excluded secondary statements for instance where a previous statement had been obtained in violation of the right to counsel.[90]

---

[85]*Regina v. Glaves*, Court of Appeal of England and Wales, decision of 29 January 1993, [1993] Crim. L.R. 685.

[86]*Regina v. Neil*, Court of Appeal of England and Wales, decision of 29 November 1993, [1994] Crim. L.R. 441. See also Choo 2013, p. 343.

[87]Mellifont 2007, p. 81.

[88]In *Regina v. Neil*, Court of Appeal of England and Wales, decision of 29 November 1993, [1994] Crim. L.R. 441, the defendant was interviewed twice. The Court of Appeal excluded his second statement even though it had been properly conducted, albeit without a previous opportunity to seek legal advice. It claimed that "*the circumstances of the second interview were insufficient to provide a safe and confident opportunity of withdrawing those admissions*". In contrast, in *Regina v. Singleton*, Court of Appeal of England and Wales, decision of 14 February 2002, [2002] EWCA Crim. 459, the judges, while confirming the authoritative decision on derivative statements in *Neil*, admitted a statement even though earlier testimony of the defendant was held to be inadmissible. The Court argued that "*the appellant plainly had ample opportunity to decide whether or not to volunteer a repetition of what he had earlier said*", even though no intervening circumstances were apparent. See also Mellifont 2007, p. 78 and p. 88.

[89]See *Regina v. Burlingham*, Supreme Court of Canada, decision of 18 May 1995, [1995] 2 S.C.R. 206.

[90]See *Regina v. Burlingham*, Supreme Court of Canada, decision of 18 May 1995, [1995] 2 S.C.R. 206: "*Appellant's statement [...] too was derivative evidence flowing from his confused state of mind stemming from the s. 10(b) violations and the critical decisions made in the absence of counsel. It was not mere windfall evidence for the Crown. Nothing would have been said had appellant not been improperly conscripted by the police to provide evidence against himself.*"Also see *Regina v. I. (L.R.) and T. (E.)*, Supreme Court of Canada, decision of 16 December 1993, [1993] 4 S.C.R. 504; *Regina v. Plaha*, Court of Appeal for Ontario, decision of 26 August 2004, paras 51 et seq.

In Canada, the exclusionary rule does not apply, however, where the connection between the statements is too remote.[91] This finding must once more be established on a case-by-case basis. One main consideration has been the lapse of time between the interviews. In addition, a number of contextual aspects have been assessed as indicators for a connection between two statements, such as the identity of the persons conducting the interviews, whether these interviews were all held in the same place or whether the defendant was confronted with statements he had made earlier.[92]

Moreover, it has been recognized that the connection can subsequently be loosened. This may be through the grant of legal advice between the interviews or by means of an additional caution on the non-admissibility of previous statements. The evaluation does not, however, focus solely on such events. This is where the generous application of the 'cat out of the bag theory' is most evident. Canadian courts have at times excluded evidence despite the fact that the defendant was given the opportunity to consult a lawyer in between several interviews.[93] They have held that this fact alone was not decisive but that its impact had to be evaluated on a case-by-case basis.[94] The same approach has been taken to the purportedly intervening effect of an additional caution. While this circumstance is taken into account, unlike in Germany, it is only one among other considerations and does not as such guarantee that the evidence is admitted.[95]

Finally, despite the generally broader conception of the exclusionary rule under U.S. law, a particularly inclusionary approach to consecutive statements has been taken by the U.S. Supreme Court. In general, the Supreme Court judges have rejected the application of a 'cat out of the bag' approach.[96] The effect that having talked to the authorities before might have on the mindset of the defendant has been deemed negligible. The link between the statements by way of a psychological compulsion is regarded as "*speculative and attenuated at best*".[97]

---

[91] *Regina v. Wittwer*, Supreme Court of Canada, decision of 5 June 2008, [2008] 2 S.C.R. 235, paras 21. See also Stuart, *Charter Justice in Canadian Criminal Law*, p. 584 et seq.

[92] *Regina v. Wittwer*, Supreme Court of Canada, decision of 5 June 2008, [2008] 2 S.C.R. 235, paras 21 and 22. *Regina v. Plaha*, Court of Appeal for Ontario, decision of 26 August 2004, paras 48 et seq.

[93] *Regina v. I. (L.R.) and T. (E.)*, Supreme Court of Canada, decision of 16 December 1993, [1993] 4 S.C.R. 504; *Regina v. Caputo*, Court of Appeal for Ontario, decision of 4 March 1997.

[94] *Regina v. Plaha*, Court of Appeal for Ontario, decision of 26 August 2004, para 47.

[95] *Regina v. R. (D.)*, Supreme Court of Canada, decision 27 April 1994, [1994] 1 S.C.R. 881; *Regina v. Plaha*, Court of Appeal for Ontario, decision of 26 August 2004, para 47.

[96] See *United States v. Bayer*, United States Supreme Court, decision of 9 June 1947, 331 U.S. 532 (1947). While the Court recognized that once a defendant has made a statement he "*can never get the cat back in the bag*", it refused to exclude the second testimony on this basis: "*But this Court has never gone so far as to hold that making a confession under circumstances which preclude its use perpetually disables the confessor from making a usable one after those conditions have been removed*".

[97] *Oregon v. Elstad*, United States Supreme Court, decision of 4 March 1985, 470 U.S. 298 (1985).

In light of this perspective, it is not surprising that this jurisprudence has also generally rejected the necessity for investigators to caution the suspect on the inadmissibility of his previous testimony.[98] Instead of focussing on the link between the statements, the emphasis in such cases has regularly been solely on the impact of the violation itself on later statements.[99] The focus is always on whether the voluntariness of the later statement is affected by this violation.[100]

There is one instance, however, where U.S. case law has in effect taken into account the psychological effect flowing from a previous statement, albeit explicitly. This pertains to the so-called 'Miranda' rights, which guarantee under U.S. law the right of a suspect to be properly cautioned on his right to silence and to legal counsel.[101] With respect to consecutive statements, the Supreme Court has applied the exclusionary rule in cases of a special kind of 'Miranda' violations. This concerns a particularly contentious interrogation technique.[102] The practice consists of first eliciting a statement from the suspect without cautioning him at all. Subsequently, the suspect is given the usual 'Miranda' warning and is then questioned a second time on the same issue and thereby confronted with his previous statements. The reason the Supreme Court makes such an exception lies once more in the deterrence rationale. The judges´ motive for excluding consecutive statements gained through this two-phase interrogation technique was clearly to deter a police technique that had gained increasing popularity and that has even been taught by police training units.[103]

According to the Supreme Court, the mid-interrogation warning is ineffective where, under the specific circumstances, the suspect is not able to voluntarily choose whether to confess or not.[104] Under U.S. case law as well, this decision is

---

[98]See *Oregon v. Elstad*, United States Supreme Court, decision of 4 March 1985, 470 U.S. 298 (1985).

[99]In order to determine whether the initial violation has a continuing effect, the test of the '*attenuation doctrine*' is applied. Accordingly, the question is whether the violation and the statement are sufficiently insulated from one another. On this case law, see LaFave et al. 2004, p. 529. On this test, see also Sect. 6.2.3.2.

[100]See *Lyons v. Oklahoma 1999,* United States Supreme Court, decision of 5 June 1944, 322 U.S. 596 (1944): "*The evidence in this case warranted the inferences that the effects of the coercion which initiated an earlier confession by the accused had been dissipated prior to his second confession, and that the latter was voluntary* […]."

[101]See *Miranda v. Arizona*, United States Supreme Court, decision of 13 June 1966, 384 U.S. 436 (1966).

[102]*Missouri v. Seibert*, United States Supreme Court, decision of 28 June 2004, 02-1371 (2004).

[103]This is not least evident from the fact that the judges also based their decision on the deliberate nature of the police conduct, see *Missouri v. Seibert*, United States Supreme Court, decision of 28 June 2004, 02-1371 (2004). See also Mellifont 2007, p. 119; Paterline 2004, p. 302, fn. 31.

[104]*Missouri v. Seibert*, United States Supreme Court, decision of 28 June 2004, 02-1371 (2004): "*For unless the warnings could place a suspect who has just been interrogated in a position to make such an informed choice, there is no practical justification for accepting the formal warnings as compliance with Miranda, or for treating the second stage of interrogation as distinct from the first, unwarned and inadmissible segment.*" See also Paterline, p. 302.

made on a case-by-case basis. The Supreme Court has relied on the short amount of time passed between the two interrogations, as well as on the fact that the same police personnel had led the interrogation and that it had confronted the suspect with his previous statement. Accordingly, although the Court does not say so explicitly, it has ultimately taken into account the psychological impact flowing from the earlier statement through the factors it has considered relevant.

The assumption of a disconnection in such cases seems, however, more likely than it would be for instance under the broad approach adopted in Canada. This is in line with the general scepticism of U.S. case law towards the psychological connection between statements made at different times. Similar to Canadian case law, however, the failure of the police to instruct the suspect on the non-admissibility of his previous statements is considered only one relevant consideration for the effectiveness of the mid-interrogation warning. It has not been considered the decisive factor for the admissibility of a later statement.

To bring in a human rights perspective, the notion of a continuing effect flowing from psychological pressure is also supported by the European Court of Human Rights. We have seen that in the case of *Gäfgen v. Germany*, the Court did not find that admitting the real derivative evidence amounted to a violation of the ECHR. Its main reasoning was that the conviction was ultimately based on the new confession that the applicant had made during trial.[105] The consideration by the judges of this new testimony in turn concerns the admissibility of consecutive statements.

In this case, the European judges did not find that the confession was tainted in terms of the ECHR. But at the same time, they did not generally reject the idea that such a second confession could be the result of a psychological compulsion flowing from an earlier statement. They did find, however, that in this case, there had been no such continuing effect because the applicant had been sufficiently cautioned on the inadmissibility of his earlier statements. In the view of the Court, this meant that the causal chain between the violation and the confession had been interrupted.[106]

In summary, the idea of a psychological connection between consecutive statements has been endorsed, albeit to diverging degrees, in all of the national systems reviewed, as well as by the ECtHR. The rather sceptical U.S. Supreme Court has at least in essence acknowledged this effect under exceptional circumstances. The crucial question is to what extent secondary statements are excluded in the different systems. Solutions are commonly found on a case-by-case basis. To this effect, the main considerations have been the time passed between the interrogations, the identity of investigation personnel and the statements´ similarity in content. Moreover, to varying degrees, the possibility of healing previous taints by breaking the connection between the different statements has

[105] See Sect. 6.2.2.

[106] *Gäfgen v. Germany*, ECtHR, decision of 1 June 2010 (Application no. 22978/05), para 179. For a critical assessment, see Sauer and Trilsch 2011, p. 319.

been recognized. Such possibilities have included the assistance of legal counsel and the issuance of a caution on the non-admissibility of previous statements. Mostly, these events have been included in the overall balancing exercise instead of considering one of them as decisive for the admissibility of secondary statements.

6.3.2 The Case Law of the ICTY

That the problem of consecutive statements may also become relevant in international proceedings is illustrated by a motion for exclusion that the ICTY had to decide on in the case. In this case, the suspect had been arrested in Austria. Both the domestic police and ICTY investigators had conducted interviews with him within a couple of days. At the first interview, conducted by the Austrian police, the defendant was not assisted by counsel because, under Austrian law, he had no corresponding right. At the second interview, which was with the ICTY investigators, he was cautioned on his right to remain silent and to be assisted by counsel. The suspect chose to speak to the investigators and did not want counsel to assist him.

At trial, the defence raised a motion against the admission of both of these interviews. It argued *inter alia* that the interviews had to be assessed together because they had to be seen "*as a continuing part of the entire process*". It contended in particular that, in view of the different legal background of each interview, the international investigators had had the duty to explain the defendant's rights more clearly to him.[107]

The tribunal found that the first interview conducted by the Austrian police was inadmissible because the right of the defendant to legal counsel as set forth in the ICTY Statute had been violated.[108] It did not, however, exclude the subsequent interview conducted by the tribunal's own investigators. It rejected in particular the assertion that the two interviews should be assessed together. In doing so, it did not reject the idea discussed above that consecutive statements might be related by a psychological connection. The test applied by the tribunal did not actually consider this idea. The judges confined their reasoning to whether the interrogations had to be treated as one single interview.[109] This argument was dismissed. As a consequence, the judges did not find the later statements to be tainted by what had happened before.[110]

[107]*Prosecutor v. Delalić et al.* (Decision on Zdravko Mucic's Motion for the Exclusion of Evidence), ICTY (Trial Chamber), decision of 2 September 1997, paras 3 and 7.

[108]*Prosecutor v. Delalić et al.* (Decision on Zdravko Mucic's Motion for the Exclusion of Evidence), ICTY (Trial Chamber), decision of 2 September 1997, para 55.

[109]See also Sluiter 1999, p. 242.

[110]See also Brady 2001, p. 292.

The reasoning that the tribunal applied to establish that the interrogations were conducted separately is partly reminiscent of the reasoning applied by domestic courts to argue against the existence of a psychological connection. While the tribunal recognised that there had been a contiguity of time and environment for both interviews, it raised a number of arguments to support their disconnectedness. These included the fact that different persons were involved in the interrogations and that the interviews had not been conducted at the same time. Finally, the different purposes pursued by the interrogators were taken into account, namely that the Austrian police had the goal of extraditing the defendant, while the ICTY investigators had interviewed him as a suspect in an international criminal case.[111] However, to ask whether two interrogations are in fact one is a test that naturally falls short of assessing whether there is a psychological connection. To establish that two interrogations are separate events is clearly less demanding.

Since they did not assume that there had initially been a connection between the interviews, it is not surprising that the ICTY judges did not search for a way to disrupt a link between the interviews. Accordingly, they did not accept the argument that the caution issued by the international investigators should have included more than merely reading to the defendant the rights he had during the second interrogation. Similarly, they found no fault with the fact that the defendant had not been assisted by counsel between the interviews. Instead, the judges considered it sufficient that the defendant had waived his right to counsel at the time of the second questioning.[112]

The assumption of a psychological link might actually have to be rejected in this case, even by proponents of a 'cat out of the bag' theory. The fact in particular that different investigators interrogated the defendant and that the interrogations evidently had different purposes would probably lead to the assumption that the interviews were sufficiently disconnected. The test applied in the decision raises doubts, however, about whether the idea of a mere psychological connection would have been considered sufficient by the ICTY judges had the circumstances been different.

6.3.3 Approach Under Article 69(7) of the ICC Statute

The right affected by repeated questioning is the right to silence. We have seen above that this right is not only an internationally recognized human right, it is also protected at the investigation stage most explicitly by Articles 55(1)(a) and

[111] *Prosecutor v. Delalić et al.* (Decision on Zdravko Mucic's Motion for the Exclusion of Evidence), ICTY (Trial Chamber), decision of 2 September 1997, paras 39 and 40.

[112] *Prosecutor v. Delalić et al.* (Decision on Zdravko Mucic's Motion for the Exclusion of Evidence), ICTY (Trial Chamber), decision of 2 September 1997, paras 58 et seq.

55(2)(b) of the ICC Statute.[113] With respect to the treatment of the question whether there is a psychological connection between consecutive confessions, the first question that arises is how the issue is to be subsumed under Article 69(7) of the ICC Statute.

As stated above, the connection between the evidence and a violation is relevant for two elements of Article 69(7). The expression "*obtained by means of*" stipulates a 'but for' causality requirement. In addition, the prerequisite of an adverse effect on integrity under Article 69(7)(b) may demand a further normative limitation. Where the evidence is too remote from the violation, it cannot be attributed to the Court in a way that would entail the negative consequences for its integrity necessary under this subparagraph.

Our previous discussion of an ICC version of the 'fruits of the poisonous tree doctrine' has revealed that for derivative evidence in general, the problem is not the causal connection between the violation and the evidence. The main question is whether the connection was sufficiently intense to meet the normative requirements of subpara (b) of Article 69(7).[114]

The question for consecutive statements in turn affects the issue of causality. It is disputable whether, under the 'cat out of the bag theory', a secondary statement is causally connected to the violation. We have seen that, according to this theory, the connection between consecutive statements is based on a purported psychological effect of the first statement. Applying a 'but for' test to this reasoning would mean asking whether the suspect would have testified had he not been influenced by the continuing effect that his earlier statement had on his mind. In order to argue that a later statement was 'obtained by means of' a violation, we must therefore establish the existence, in general and in the specific case, of such a psychlogical impact.

It will be proposed here that the ICC should generally endorse the so-called 'cat out of the bag theory'. Unlike the U.S. Supreme Court, which usually rejects this idea as 'speculative', the ICC should acknowledge the general possibility that a suspect might not be able to exercise an independent choice where he has previously talked to the authorities.

Article 55(1) of the ICC Statute protects the right of a person "*to not be compelled to incriminate himself or herself*". As a consequence, no person can be put under pressure to renounce her right to silence. Pressure during investigations may also result from having made revelations in a previous interrogation.[115] To reject this idea altogether is a misinterpretation of the psychological situation of the affected person. Once she has presented a certain version of the events to the

---

[113]See Sect. 4.3.3.5.2.

[114]See Sect. 6.2.3.2.

[115]Muthorst 2009, p. 283.

authorities, a person might feel bound to stick to this version. She might even repeat a statement made earlier merely in order to present some consistency to her interrogators.[116]

We have seen that this idea has, on the whole, been recognized in the domestic legal orders reviewed in this research. The particularities of international prosecutions could even be seen as adding to a person's confusion. The defence in the ICTY *Delalić* case rightly argued that it was confusing for the defendant to be subjected, within a short period, to different procedures that involved different civil rights and obligations.[117] Irrespective of whether the tribunal was right to reject this allegation in the case before it, the diverging degrees to which procedural rights are protected in different legal orders may be confusing for an interrogated person. This is in particular the case for the right to silence, whose protection, as we have seen, varies considerably among the different legal systems.[118] It can be added that, when compared to the ICTY, the danger of confusion increases at the ICC, whose operation and jurisdiction involves states with far more diverse legal backgrounds.

The reluctant position supported in U.S. case law, on the other hand, seems once more to be owed to the desire to limit the consequences of its otherwise wide exclusionary rule.[119] We have seen that the U.S. Supreme Court has recognized a connection between consecutive statements in exceptional cases. This indicates that its rejection is based on concerns for procedural effectiveness rather than on fundamental considerations. It is certainly a defensible policy choice within a given system to favour effectiveness in this particular case constellation. This choice, however, need not be the same in another system. The special concern of the ICC for its integrity once more suggests that a particularly sensitive handling of possible violations of due process rights should be favoured. The enornmous significance of the right to silence in international law in general, as well as in the ICC proper law, argues all the more for making allowance for the special psychological situation of a person who that is subjected to several interrogations.

The next issues pertain to the requirements that must be met to determine the existence of a continuing effect in the specific case and to the conditions for a subsequent healing of previous mistakes. Under Article 55(1) of the ICC Statute, the question is whether a person was compelled to give a statement. In other words, has there been any exercise of pressure? The decisive question with respect to the aforementioned issues is a subjective one. There is no pressure, and thus no continuing effect, where, from the point of view of the interrogated person, her new interrogation is sufficiently disconnected from the former interview.

---

[116]Mellifont 2007, p. 80.

[117]See *Prosecutor v. Delalić et al.* (Decision on Zdravko Mucic's Motion for the Exclusion of Evidence), ICTY (Trial Chamber), decision of 2 September 1997, para 16.

[118]See Sect. 4.3.3.5.2.

[119]Trüg 2003, p. 434.

The previous review of national and international case law gives some indication of a number of considerations that are relevant in determining whether a continuing effect ever existed. First of all, the temporal aspect is crucial. If either the violation or the previous interrogation occurred long before the later statement, it is unlikely that either one will still impact on an interrogated person. Likewise, the identity of investigative personnel will influence whether an interrogated person experiences the different interviews as closely intertwined. To a lesser degree, the place where the interviews took place might also have an impact. Finally, an important factor will be the nature of the questions. This may overlap with the equally relevant question whether, from the point of view of the interrogated person, both interviews had a similar purpose.

We have previously seen that, in international investigations, events are often less closely connected than in domestic investigations.[120] Accordingly, in international investigations, consecutive interviews will more often be made under circumstances that suggest to an interrogated person that her different interviews are separate events. This may result from the often greater number of actors involved in international investigations when compared to domestic investigations, their usually longer duration, as well as from the higher probability that different interrogations pursue different purposes.

But is it possible to interrupt a connection between two statements, where a psychological impact of a previous testimony must be assumed, despite the above? This assumption would have consequences for the practical work of the Court, in particular of OTP investigators. The investigators would have the opportunity to secure secondary statements by making sure that the necessary conditions for a healing of previous mistakes are met.

Two different possibilities have emerged from the case law of the domestic systems reviewed above. These are the issuance of an additional caution and the intermediate access to legal counsel. The common idea behind both possibilities is that the interrogated person must be put back in a position where she is aware of the fact that she is free to decide whether or not she wants to speak to the authorities.

This idea can be transferred to the ICC system. Whether the necessary information is transmitted to the interrogated person through counsel or through the authorities is, in principle, without significance. There is reason, however, to assume that the issuance of an additional caution is a more practicable solution and a better guarantee for equal treatment of affected persons than the assignment of counsel. The content of an additional caution would be subject to the control of the OTP. The international Prosecutor would have the opportunity to assess the non-admissibility of previous statements under the law of the ICC before

---

[120] For this discussion with respect to the remoteness between the violation and the emergence of the evidence as a factor in the general balancing exercise, see Sect. 6.2.3.3.

questioning a person a second time and to make sure that a standardized caution that would guarantee the admissibility of secondary statements is given to the suspect.

The OTP regulations in their present form include the general instruction to inform a person of their rights under Article 55(1) and (2). They fail, however, to elaborate on the content of the respective cautions.[121] Specifications, including on additional cautions, would be advisable. Where, in turn, national authorities conduct the second or subsequent interviews, they cannot be obligated to follow such instructions under the ICC cooperation regime. They should, however, be informed of any previous illegalities and recommended to give the same additional cautions provided to them by the OTP.

In conclusion, the ICC judges, when confronted with consecutive statements, may not only rely on the continuing effect of the initial violation. They may also argue that the interrogated person was unduly pressured by the fact of having testified before. The OTP, in turn, has the opportunity to guarantee the admissibility of secondary statements, in particular by providing an additional caution indicating the inadmissibility of the previous testimony.

6.4 Hypothetical Course of Investigations

One last question must be addressed with respect to the relationship between the violation and the emergence of evidence. The respective consideration is of a hypothetical nature. Domestic courts have admitted tainted evidence where the circumstances suggest that this evidence would ultimately have been discovered absent the actual violation. Based on this logic, a court might, for instance, admit the statement of a witness whose identity was discovered through the suspect's unlawful interrogation, if the interrogators would ultimately have come across this witness in the course of their investigations. Another example would pertain to the judicial warrant required in many systems to lawfully search private premises. Where an investigator conducts a search without such a warrant, evidence collected in this search could still be admitted if, at the time of the search, one of his colleagues has already requested a warrant and would thus have been able later on to make the same discovery in a lawful manner.

As we will see, these kinds of deliberations have been made at the domestic level for both primary and derivative evidence. We will further see that similar considerations can impact on the admissibility of evidence under Article 69(7)(b) of the ICC Statute.

---

[121] See Regulations 40(c) and 41(1) of the *Regulations of the Office of the Prosecutor* of 23 April 2009, available at http://www.icc-cpi.int/en_menus/icc/legal%20texts%20and%20tools/official%20journal/Pages/regulations%20of%20the%20otpasp (last visited: October 2013).

6.4.1 The Validity of Hypothetical Considerations

6.4.1.1 The Use of Hypothetical Considerations in Domestic Proceedings

The use of this concept in the doctrine of the U.S. Supreme Court has already been mentioned.[122] In its landmark decision in *Nix v. Williams*, the Supreme Court recognized the so-called 'inevitable discovery doctrine'. In this case, the police induced the defendant, who was suspected of having murdered a young girl, into guiding them to the location of the girl's body. In doing so, the officers unequivocally violated the defendant's right to legal counsel. The Supreme Court judges nevertheless approved the admission of the body into evidence. They found that, at the time of its discovery, a search of the area around the respective site had already been planned and that the body would thus ultimately have been found.[123]

From a doctrinal perspective, the '*inevitable discovery doctrine*' is based on the idea that where tainted evidence could have been gained through lawful means, there is no link in terms of a '*but for*' causality between the evidence and the violation.[124]

From a practical point of view, this exception is yet another example for a proportionality-driven restriction of the initially broad U.S. exclusionary rule. While the exclusionary rule is supposed to deter the police from violating the rights of the defendant, the '*inevitable discovery doctrine*' is meant to avoid that the latter ultimately profits from such acts. Conversely, it is claimed that the prosecution, while "*not to be put in a better position than it would have been in if no illegality had transpired*" should also not be put in a "*worse* [...] *position than they would have been in if no police error or misconduct had occurred.*"[125]

We have seen that under U.S. case law, the exclusionary rule is generally understood as extending to derivative evidence. It is this wide understanding in particular that has called for its restriction in the first place.[126] At the same time, this does not mean that the exceptions developed by the U.S. Supreme Court are necessarily limited to derivative evidence. The '*inevitable discovery doctrine*' for

---

[122]See Sect. 3.3.2.

[123]*Nix v. Williams*, United States Supreme Court, decision of 11 June 1984, 467 U.S. 431 (1984).

[124]See *Hudson v. Michigan*, United States Supreme Court, decision of 15 June 2006, 547 U.S. 586 (2006): "*In this case, of course, the constitutional violation of an illegal manner of entry was not a but-for cause of obtaining the evidence. Whether that preliminary misstep had occurred or not, the police would have executed the warrant they had obtained, and would have discovered the gun and drugs inside the house.*"

[125]See *Nix v. Williams*, United States Supreme Court, decision of 11 June 1984, 467 U.S. 431 (1984). See also Harris 1991, p. 317; Hessler 2000, p. 266.

[126]Beulke 1991, p. 667.

instance applies to primary evidence as well.[127] Examples would include statements forced from the defendant who would have testified in any case or the example mentioned above of evidence seized by means of a warrantless search where a warrant would have been obtained.[128]

The '*inevitable discovery doctrine*' has been criticized on the basis of two main considerations. On the one hand, it has been argued that rather than diminishing the significance of the violation, the existence of legal options would in fact make the police more culpable for choosing illegal means.[129] A related point of criticism is based on the deterrence rationale. It has been argued that the doctrine of '*inevitable discovery*' would encourage police shortcuts because it would reduce incentives to abide by lawful investigative methods. A policeman might be tempted to get hold of evidence readily available through illegal means if he was aware that this evidence would eventually be discovered and thus admissible under the '*inevitable discovery doctrine*'.[130] The Supreme Court in *Nix v. Williams* rejected such arguments, claiming that an officer had little to gain from shortcuts given the risk that the evidence would nevertheless be excluded, as well as the personal risk of departmental discipline and civil liability.[131]

For the further discussion of this factor, we must note that even in the U.S., the deterrence rationale is not the basis for this exception to the exclusionary rule. Both the Supreme Court and commentators have discussed the implication of the deterrence rationale for the '*inevitable discovery doctrine*'.[132] This discussion, however, is not directed at justifying this exception.[133] Quite the opposite: it is aimed at finding out whether the deterrence rationale precludes hypothetical considerations.

The U.S. doctrine of '*inevitable discovery*' has influenced the discussion on the relevance of hypothetical considerations beyond U.S. borders.[134] The decision in *Nix v. Williams* has repeatedly been referred to in *inter alia* the German legal literature.[135] The German Federal Court of Justice (BGH) deems it legitimate to rely on hypothetical assumptions. It has partly justified its previously described rejection of the '*fruits doctrine*' on this basis. The German judges argued that in

---

127 Trüg 2003, p. 454.

128 Ambos 2010, p. 137, fn. 843.

129 Slobogin 2013, p. 19.

130 LaFave et al. 2004, p. 513.

131 See *Nix v. Williams*, United States Supreme Court, decision of 11 June 1984, 467 U.S. 431 (1984). Also see Hessler 2000, p. 269.

132 LaFave et al. 2004, p. 513. Critical with respect to the implications for deterrence for instance Trüg 2003, p. 455.

133 Slobogin 2013, p. 7.

134 On the strong influence on the Spanish exclusionary rule for instance, see Thaman 2013, p. 377.

135 Beulke 1991, p. 666.

the event of derivative evidence, it was hardly ever possible to determine whether the evidence would not have been discovered through legal means.[136]

Furthermore, hypothetical considerations have also been advanced in Germany where the admissibility of primary evidence was concerned. The BGH has, for instance, admitted into evidence a blood sample that had been taken by a medical assistant rather than by a fully qualified doctor, as required by the StPO, the German Code of Criminal Procedure.[137] The Court, in this bellwether ruling, considered that the public interest in effective prosecution prevailed *inter alia* because the investigators would have had the opportunity under the provisions of the StPO to legally obtain the blood sample.[138] A similar example is the case of warrantless searches. In German case law, a warrantless search has not led to the inadmissibility of seized evidence where the legal requirements for the issuance of a warrant were fulfilled and where the warrant could hypothetically have been obtained by the authorities.[139]

These latter rulings demonstrate that hypothetical considerations are relied upon by the BGH in a rather generous way. Both cases show that the BGH sets rather low requirements for the degree of probability that must be met in order to justify the reliance on hypothetical assumptions. In the second case in particular, the BGH went well beyond the jurisprudence of the U.S. Supreme Court. Under similar circumstances, namely where a warrant had not yet been requested, the Supreme Court has rejected the compensation of a missing search warrant. Instead, the U.S. judges only admit evidence gathered in this way where a warrant has already been requested.[140]

Another difference to the jurisprudence of U.S. courts is once more the methodological approach under German law. The consideration of how investigations

---

[136]German Federal Supreme Court (BGH), decision of 28 April 1987, *Neue Juristische Wochenschrift* 1987, p. 2525. See also Rogall 1988, p. 389.

[137]Section 81(a) of the German Code of Criminal Procedure (StPO) stipulates: "(1) *A physical examination of the accused may be ordered for the purposes of establishing facts which are of importance for the proceedings. For this purpose, the taking of blood samples and other bodily intrusions which are effected by a physician in accordance with the rules of medical science for the purpose of examination shall be admissible without the consent of the accused, provided no detriment to his health is to be expected.*" On this case, see also Jahn and Dallmeyer 2005. On the consideration of a hypothetical course of events in German criminal law, see also Trüg 2003, p. 286, on Section 81(a) cases, see p. 289 et seq.

[138]German Federal Supreme Court (BGH), decision of 17 March 1971, *Neue Juristische Wochenschrift* 1971, p. 1097.

[139]German Federal Supreme Court (BGH), decision of 15 February 1989, *Neue Zeitschrift für Strafrecht*, 1989, p. 375, at p. 376. In this case, which caused great media attention in Germany, the defendant, 28 year old Monika Weimar, was accused of having murdered her two young daughters. During the investigations, the police first conducted a search of her house. This first search was covered by a legally sound search warrant. The investigators subsequently sealed the premises and issued a protocol of the search. The next day however, they reopened the house and searched it again without having obtained a further warrant for this second search. The BGH still decided to admit the respective evidence.

[140]Hessler 2000, p. 275 et seq.

might hypothetically have proceeded is not treated as an exception to the rule as it is under the U.S. exclusionary rule.[141] Instead, German judges rather refer to it as one factor among others in the general balancing exercise they conduct in order to determine whether evidence must be excluded.[142] The importance attached to this factor however cannot easily be determined because the German case law on hypothetical considerations is inconsistent. Actually, while the German legal academia, for the most part, approves of the reference to hypotheses in general,[143] this inconsistency has been widely criticized.[144]

Hypothetical assumptions are also made in the English system under Section 78 of PACE. As in Germany, these assumptions are taken into account as a factor in the balancing of interests. We have seen that physical evidence is only ever rarely excluded under English law.[145] It does not therefore come as a surprise that examples of the use of hypothetical considerations in English case law regularly pertain to the exclusion of confessions. One example concerns violations of the right to legal advice under Section 58 of PACE. English courts have asked whether the willingness of an interrogated person to speak to the police would have been affected if this right had been respected. They have rejected requests to exclude statements where this was answered in the negative because it was evident that the person would have talked in any event. The judges held that the evidence would not, under these circumstances, "*have such an adverse effect on the fairness of the proceedings that the court ought not to admit it.*"[146] Where, on the other hand, the alternative discovery remained uncertain, the courts have excluded the respective evidence.[147] This jurisprudence has been criticized for being speculative by construing events *ex post*.[148]

Finally, hypothetical considerations also play a role in the case law of the Canadian Supreme Court. In the context of its integrity based approach to exclusion, the question has been discussed under the heading of 'discoverability'. The fact that evidence could have been discovered through lawful means had a major impact under the Court's initial jurisprudence on Section 24(2) of the Canadian Charter of Rights and Freedoms. Where such 'discoverability' was established, the general bright-line rule for conscriptive evidence and evidence derived thereof no

---

[141]Trüg 2003, p. 287.

[142]Jahn and Dallmeyer 2005, p. 301.

[143]Trüg 2003, p. 286.

[144]Jahn and Dallmeyer 2005, p. 298; Rogall 1988, p. 389.

[145]See Sect. 6.2.1.4.

[146]*Regina v Alladice*, Court of Appeal for England and Wales, decision of 8 May 1988, [1988] WL 624104.

[147]*Regina v. Walsh*, Court of Appeal for England and Wales, decision of 13 July 1989, (1990) 91 Crim. App R. 161.

[148]Choo 2013, p. 343.

longer applied. 'Discoverable' evidence was categorically admitted.[149] When the Canadian Supreme Court in 2009 abandoned its former legal framework for exclusion, it revised not only the category of conscriptive evidence but also that of 'discoverable' evidence. The Court ruled that discoverability should no longer be decisive for admissibility. It did not, however, dismiss the significance of hypothetical assumptions altogether. It only gave up its former strict categorization. Similar to the approach of the German and the English judiciary, it found that hypothetical considerations should be treated as one factor in its new balancing exercise.[150]

6.4.1.2 Approach Under Article 69(7)(B) of the ICC Statute

We have seen that the recourse to hypothetical considerations has been acknowledged in all of the domestic systems reviewed. It will be proposed here that the same conclusion should guide decisions under the ICC Statute. We will see that the main problem in this context is the degree of probability that such hypotheses must meet. To this effect, some additional recourse to domestic solutions will be necessary.

First, however, the dogmatic categorization of hypothetical considerations shall be addressed. We have differentiated between the causal link that ties a piece of evidence to a violation on the one hand and normative evaluations on the other.[151] While the former describes the logical connection, the latter determines through a value-based assessment to what extent the intensity of this connection, as a balancing factor, impacts on whether exclusion is warranted. Under Article 69(7) of the ICC Statute, this would mean that if the existence of hypothetical means of evidence gathering removes the necessary causal link, the evidence would not have been "*obtained by means of*" the respective violation. If this were, however, a normative question, hypothetical considerations could be included in the balancing exercise under subpara (b).

At the domestic level, the relevance of hypothetical considerations has partly been endorsed based on the assumption that in the respective situations, there is no causal connection between the violation and the discovery of the evidence. The

[149] *Regina v. Stillman*, Supreme Court of Canada, decision of 20 March 1997, [1997] 1 S.C.R. 607, para 102. For a short review of the former approach, see *Regina v. Grant,* Supreme Court of Canada, decision of 17 July 2009, [2009]. On the former jurisprudence in general, see Sect. 3.3.4. See also Jonathan Dawe and Heather McArthur, 'Charter Detention and the Exclusion of Evidence After Grant, Harrison and Suberu', *Supreme Court Law Review*, 51 (2010), p. 416; Stuart 2010a, p. 600 and p. 601.

[150] *Regina v. Grant,* Supreme Court of Canada, decision of 17 July 2009, [2009] 2 S.C.R. 353, paras 121 et seq. On the new approach regarding discoverability, see also Dawe and McArthur, p. 416 et seq; Stuart 2010a, p. 600 and p. 601.

[151] See in particular Sect. 6.1.

argument is that even if the violation had not been committed, the evidence would still have emerged. It would simply have been discovered in the course of those events that are hypothetically added to the situation. Accordingly, there would be no causal link in the sense of a '*conditio sine qua non*' or '*but for*' causation.[152] This is the path followed *inter alia* by the U.S. Supreme Court.[153]

It can be doubted, however, that this is the methodologically sound justification for hypothetical considerations in either domestic or international proceedings. It has rightly been objected that a de facto existing connection cannot be replaced based on hypothetical assumptions.[154] In other words, while the argument raised above assesses the causal connection on a hypothetical basis, it must actually be determined solely on the basis of those events that have in fact taken place. For the ICC exclusionary rule, the wording of Article 69(7) seems to supports this view. The '*but for*' causality requirement is established by the words "*obtained by means of*". This expression, in addition to the French version "*obtenus par un moyen*", suggests that the actual course of events rather than a hypothetical one is decisive for this assessment.

Another idea that has also been endorsed at the domestic level, is more instructive. Hypothetical considerations should be considered at the normative level of the inquiry. Here, the Canadian case law can serve as a model. Under this case law, 'discoverability' plays a role in determining whether admitting the evidence "*would bring the administration of justice into disrepute*" in terms of Section 24(2) of the Canadian Charter of Rights and Freedoms. A similar approach was adopted by the English judiciary when it held that in such cases the evidence does not "*have such an adverse effect on the fairness of the proceedings*" in terms of Section 78 of PACE.[155]

Admittedly, unlike the ICC exclusionary rule, the exclusionary rules in both of these systems do not presuppose a 'but for' causality. It is possible, however, to require 'but for' causality in general and still claim that the consideration of hypothetical assumptions does not pertain to this requirement. In this

---

[152]With respect to the U.S. rule, see Ambos 2010, p. 135, with further references. With respect to the German discussion, see Rogall 1988, p. 387, with further references.

[153]*Hudson v. Michigan*, United States Supreme Court, decision of 15 June 2006, 547 U.S. 586 (2006). On this jurisprudence, see also Alschuler 2008, p. 1809.

[154]Beulke 1991, p. 660. See also *Hudson v. Michigan*, United States Supreme Court, decision of 15 June 2006, 547 U.S. 586 (2006), dissenting opinion Justice Breyer et al.: "*The majority first argues that "the constitutional violation of an illegal manner of entry was not a but-for cause of obtaining the evidence." But taking causation as it is commonly understood in the law, I do not see how that can be so. [...] Although the police might have entered Hudson's home lawfully, they did not in fact do so. Their unlawful behavior inseparably characterizes their actual entry; that entry was a necessary condition of their presence in Hudson's home; and their presence in Hudson's home was a necessary condition of their finding and seizing the evidence.*"

[155]See *Regina v. Alladice*, Court of Appeal of England and Wales, decision of 8 May 1988, [1988] WL 624104.

understanding, causality simply depends on the actual facts of a case and the causal relationship is not altered by adding hypothetical facts to the equation.[156] At the same time, hypothetical assumptions are then relevant as a normative consideration.

Applied to the ICC exclusionary rule, it can be argued that, while the causal link is not affected, the possibility that another investigative measure could have procured the evidence impacts on whether admitting it "*would seriously damage the integrity of the proceedings*" in terms of Article 69(7)(b) of the ICC Statute. In other words, the assumption is that the integrity of ICC proceedings would be in less jeopardy if alternative means seem possible.

This is justified by the fact that where this is the case, the violation was less important for the evidentiary situation that finally exists at the stage of court proceedings. This interpretation is also more easily compatible with the approach to the ICC exclusionary rule taken so far. Including hypothetical considerations in the balancing exercise avoids this aspect alone becoming decisive in the respective case constellations. This prevents once more the establishment of a bright-line rule alien to the discretionary nature of the ICC exclusionary rule.

Moreover, this would also allow the taking into account of some general criticisms raised at the domestic level. It has rightly been argued that where investigators choose to use illegal means even though legal options are at hand, this makes their behaviour all the more offensive.[157] Under a balancing approach, this can, however, be taken into account when assessing the weight of this factor. Where the investigators have acted in bad faith, less weight would be attached to hypothetical considerations.

6.4.2 The Probability Standard

The next question involves the degree of probability that must be met by such hypotheses. The issue can once more be illustrated through fictitious examples.

In the first example, OTP requests that national authorities question a suspect. This questioning is conducted without access to legal assistance and thus clearly in breach of Article 55(2)(c) of the ICC Statute. The suspect thereupon reveals details on the command structure of a certain state. Later, during the trial, the suspect expressly states that he had been willing to reveal this information, irrespective of the presence of legal counsel. In this case, it can be said almost with certainty that the evidence would have existed either way.

In contrast, the following example would be more difficult to assess. Here, the evidence on the command structure does not consist of statements made by the

[156]For such an approach in the German debate, see Roxin and Schünemann 2012, p. 148; Rogall 1988, p. 391.

[157]Slobogin 2013, p. 19.

suspect but of documentary evidence. The documents were found in the course of a warrantless search conducted by domestic police forces. At the time of the search, the international prosecutor had contacted the national authorities to request that they apply for a search warrant and subsequently search the premises on this basis. Now, would the documents also be admissible in light of the mere possibility that the request would have been granted and that the warrant would have been issued?

Again, a short description of the domestic approaches to this specific question is in order. In domestic systems, while the validity of hypothetical considerations is mostly acknowledged, the issue of probability is highly contentious.

The standard applied by the Germany judiciary is rather low. The German BGH only demands the abstract possibility that the evidence could have been gathered through other means. For the proof of this possibility, the German judges have not even requested that concrete facts suggest its probability. This jurisprudence has been criticised for being speculative[158] and for overly prioritising prosecutorial interests in efficiency.[159]

In the other systems reviewed, the standard is stricter. As the phrase 'inevitable discovery' suggests, U.S. courts demand that the evidence would 'ultimately' or 'inevitably' have been found through legal means.[160] The U.S. Supreme Court has requested that a 'preponderance of the evidence' must suggest that the evidence would have been discovered.[161] This probability must be established on the basis of verifiable, historical facts, not on mere speculation.[162] English courts seem to apply a similar standard. As stated before, it has not been found sufficient under

[158]Harris 1991, p. 320.

[159]Trüg 2003, p. 288 et seq.

[160]Trüg 2003, p. 455. This has been found to be the case in particular where the evidence would have been found through a routine procedure. An example for a routine procedure under U.S. law would be the so-called 'inventory search', meaning a search that is regularly conducted upon arrest or when the police seizes a vehicle. The notion of the 'inventory search' is an exception to the 4th amendment warrant requirement. According to the jurisprudence of the U.S. Supreme Court, the police may search vehicles and persons immediately upon arrest or the impoundment of a vehicle without a warrant being necessary. In addition, 'inevitability' has been acknowledged where the investigative procedure that is supposed to have alternatively provided the evidence had been initiated prior to the violation. Altogether, see Ambos 2010, p. 135 et seq; LaFave et al. 2004, p. 514.

[161]For more details on this and other standards of proof under the U.S. law of evidence, see fn. 1038.

[162]See *Nix v. Williams*, United States Supreme Court, decision of 11 June 1984, 467 U.S. 431 (1984): "*By contrast, inevitable discovery involves no speculative elements, but focuses on demonstrated historical facts capable of ready verification* [...]." Critical with respect to this standard, see Ambos 2010, p. 138; Hessler 2000, p. 261 et seq.

English case law that the alternative discovery remained uncertain.[163] This suggests that the probability standard requires something more than the mere possibility demanded by German courts. Similarly, the Canadian Supreme Court has stated that the judge must be able to determine the 'discoverability' of the evidence through alternative means with some confidence.[164]

Returning to Article 69(7)(b) of the ICC Statute, it will be argued here that the kind of normative restrictions that hypothetical assumptions call for demand a high degree of probability. Where no definite conclusion can be made, there is no room for the assumption that the impact of a violation on the integrity of ICC proceedings is reduced. In the case of a mere possibility, no legally relevant statement can in fact be made about an alternative means of evidence gathering. The mere possibility of an alternative, equally successful, investigative measure does not therefore influence the significance of the violation for the final evidentiary situation.

Accordingly, the ICC judges would have to make the determination that the alternative discovery of evidence would have occurred, not that it might have occurred or that it could have occurred.[165] Anything else is likely to draw the criticism of speculation that has also been raised at the domestic level. A high probability standard is also decisively supported by the integrity approach to exclusion. The criticism of speculation would probably be combined with the suspicion that the Court, on a weak factual basis, uses an argument that unilaterally favours the concern for effective prosecution. Such a reproach would considerably impact upon the integrity of ICC proceedings.

Naturally, in practice, virtual certainty can never be established in a criminal trial.[166] This, however, is not only the case for hypothetical assumptions. Admittedly, certitude can be gained more easily with respect to events that have in fact taken place. By their very nature, hypothetical considerations are always a matter of assumptions. Some amount of uncertainty may, however, also exist with respect to historical facts. This is so in any case of non liquet, where the judge remains in doubt about the historical facts of a case.

Below, the problem of cases of *non liquet* will be addressed with respect to the exclusion of evidence in general. The proposition will be made that the standard of proof for the ICC should be the above-mentioned 'preponderance of evidence'

---

[163]*Regina v. Walsh*, Court of Appeal for England and Wales, decision of 13 July 1989, (1990) 91 Crim. App R. 161: "[W]*e can see nothing in this case which could properly lead the court to the conclusion* [...] *that it was likely that the appellant would have made the admissions in any event. The very highest it could be put, to our minds, was that it was perhaps uncertain whether or not the presence of a solicitor would have made any difference.*"

[164]See *Regina v. Grant*, Supreme Court of Canada, decision of 17 July 2009, [2009] 2 S.C.R. 353, para 122.

[165]For the same line of thought with respect to the U.S. exclusionary rule, see LaFave et al. 2004, p. 515.

[166]See Beulke 1991, p. 671, who supports however a higher standard that would correspond to the '*no reasonable doubt standard*'.

standard.[167] This concerns, of course, historical facts. But there is no reason why the same standard should not be used to deal with the uncertainty that always remains in cases of hypothetical considerations. To apply the same standard as for historical events avoids the criticism of speculation.

At the same time, we will see that a higher standard, such as a 'beyond reasonable doubt' standard, is not appropriate as a general standard of proof for the ICC exclusionary rule.[168] For hypothetical considerations in turn, there is also no justification to extend the probability standard even beyond the standard that we will apply under Article 69(7) of the ICC Statute to the proof of verifiable historical facts.

6.4.3 Hypothetical Considerations and Judicial Warrants

A particularly controversial case in domestic proceedings is where a necessary search warrant is compensated by hypothetical assumption. The situation in question has been alluded to above. An item is seized in the course of a warrantless search. Can this item be admitted into evidence based on the allegation that a warrant would have been issued in any event? In light of the contentiousness of this issue in domestic debates, it seems worth adding some deliberations on a possible solution in ICC proceedings.

Beyond searches, the problems described here are of course also relevant for other coercive measures that usually require judicial consent. For domestic proceedings, these problems tend, however, to be discussed with respect to searches. The reason is simply that searches are measures that are carried out on a very regular basis in the course of criminal investigations. In ICC investigations, even though they are not conducted on the same regular basis as in domestic proceedings, searches can also be an important means of investigation. This is suggested by the fact that one of the first decisions concerning Article 69(7) of the ICC Statute was concerned with a search.[169] The following deliberations will therefore concentrate on this procedural tool. The results can, however, be transferred to other coercive measures such as the interception of telecommunication, which, as the case law of the ICTY demonstrates, is a coercive measure that can also play an important role in international investigations.[170] This is, of course, as long as one requires judicial consent for such measures.

---

[167]See Sect. 7.6.

[168]See Sect. 7.6.

[169]See *Prosecutor v. Lubanga* (Decision on the confirmation of charges), ICC (Pre-Trial Chamber), decision of 29 January 2007, para 84. See also Sect. 1.2.

[170]See for instance *Prosecutor v. Milosević* (Final Decision on the Admissibility of Intercepted Communications), ICTY (Trial Chamber), decision of 14 June 2004; *Prosecutor v. Brđanin* (Decision on the Defence "Objection to Intercept Evidence"), ICTY (Trial Chamber), decision of 3 October 2003.

This part of the research is itself based on a theoretical assumption. The requirement of a search warrant was not included in the ICC Statute. The following deliberations are therefore only reasonable if one assumes that a search warrant is necessary in investigations for the ICC despite this lack of regulation.

We have discussed earlier in this research whether a warrant requirement follows from the internationally recognized human right to privacy. The conclusion was that a search warrant should be requested for domestically conducted searches where such a requirement does not exist under the law of the respective state. In addition, it should also be requested where the ICC prosecutor himself exceptionally carries out a search on his own. In both instances, a warrant issued by the ICC would guarantee that there is at least one level of judicial supervision.[171] Just like in state proceedings, this raises the question whether hypothetical considerations may be included in decisions on exclusion where no warrant was issued. In the following paragraphs, we will assess the arguments discussed with respect to domestic proceedings against the background of international criminal investigations.

In domestic law, courts have partly relied on hypothetical considerations to compensate for the lack of a search warrant. The German jurisprudence can once more be mentioned as an example for a rather extensive reliance on hypothetical considerations in this regard. Items seized in the context of a warrantless search are regularly admitted based on the argument that a warrant would have been issued at the time of the search. Exclusion is considered necessary in such cases only where the authorities have acted in bad faith, namely where they have consciously bypassed or grossly misinterpreted the warrant requirement.[172]

In the United States in turn, there is no uniform case law on the matter. The Supreme Court has not yet ruled on the applicability of the 'inevitable discovery doctrine' to cases of warrantless searches. Some lower courts have found no problem with applying the doctrine. Others, however, have refrained from admitting evidence in such circumstances, referring to the particular significance of the warrant requirement. An illustrative example is where one court held that admitting evidence on this basis "*would tend in actual practice to emasculate the search warrant requirement of the Forth Amendment.*"[173] Scholars have also pointed to the deterrence rationale to dismiss hypothetical considerations in these cases. It has been argued that there would be no incentive to apply for a judicial warrant if, after the search, investigators could simply claim that they would have been able to get judicial consent.[174]

---

171 See Sect. 4.3.3.5.3.

172 See German Federal Supreme Court (BGH), decision of 18 April 2007, *Neue Juristische Wochenschrift* 2007, 2269 with further references. See also Eisenberg 2011, p. 935.

173 *Unites States v. Griffin*, United States Court of Appeals, 6th Circuit, decision of 21 April 1974, *502 F.2d 959 (1974)*. For an overview of the jurisprudence, see Alschuler 2008, p. 1806 et seq.

174 Ambos 2010, p. 136. On this critique with respect to the U.S. rule, see also LaFave et al. 2004, p. 513, who claim however that this is not directed against the '*inevitable discovery doctrine*' as such but only against its "*application in a loose and unthinking fashion*". Critical with respect to the '*hypothetical search warrant*' also Trüg 2003, p. 456, with further references.

This argument cannot be decisive in ICC proceedings since we have seen that deterring investigators is not a central consideration for the application of the ICC exclusionary rule. But the partial refusal of U.S. courts to apply the 'inevitable discovery doctrine' where a search warrant is missing reflects a very basic point of criticism that goes beyond deterrence. This objection has not only been raised in the United States. Scholars both in Germany and in the United States have pointed to the fundamental importance of a preventive judicial review of coercive measures and of searches in particular. It has been argued that admitting evidence under these circumstances would result in a clear judicial disregard of the legislative intent.[175]

While this is a valid argument in domestic systems, this criticism cannot, however, be transposed as such to ICC proceedings. The warrant requirement supported above does not rely on a clear legislative intent. Quite the opposite: the drafters of the ICC statute refrained from including a proposed provision on the right to privacy that contained a warrant requirement.[176] The assumption that, under specific circumstances, a warrant requirement can still be deduced from the right to privacy does not make it part of the legislative intent. The situation may be different if, at some point, the suggestion advanced in the literature to amend the ICC Statute and to provide for an express warrant requirement is followed.[177] De lege lata, however, the legislative intent argument cannot be relied upon to argue that compensating the lack of a search warrant is any more problematic than the application of hypothetical considerations to any other case.

A final remark shall be made with respect to the integrity theory. We have seen before that a 'court-centred' integrity rationale involves judicial decisions being consistent.[178] One could therefore object that it would be inconsistent for the ICC to demand a warrant in general but not also to exclude evidence where this requirement has not been complied with. This ostensible discrepancy, however, is only a result of the general non-mandatory nature of the ICC exclusionary rule.

Beyond the general criticism outlined above, it has been doubted whether the high probability standard previously required for hypothetical considerations in general can ever be met in cases of missing warrants. This is because the assumption that a warrant would have been issued is meant to outweigh the lack of a judicial decision. Judicial decisions, however, that are made on a discretionary basis, as it is the case with search warrants, are inherently subjective. Consequently, it has been held that the outcome of such a decision is impossible to predict. This would mean that it can never be determined with any certainty whether the issuance of a warrant was probable.[179]

---

[175]Alschuler 2008, p. 1808; Ambos 2010, p. 136; Beulke 1991, p. 673.

[176]See Edwards 2001, p. 349 et seq. See also Sect. 4.3.3.5.3.

[177]Edwards 2001, p. 412.

[178]See Sect. 4.3.2.2.5.

[179]Beulke 1991, p. 374.

Assertions on the hypothetical issuance of a warrant must in fact be treated with utmost caution. They are not however precluded as such. It seems possible in a given case to claim that there is no reasonable doubt that a warrant would have been issued and consequently that the probability standard identified for the ICC has been met. We must keep in mind that it is quite often the case that facts cannot be established with certainty in a criminal trial, be they of a subjective or an objective nature. At the same time, in some cases, it will be so likely that a judge would have issued the warrant that the standard can be regarded as fulfilled. This can be assumed in particular in cases where the legal requirements for the issuance of a search warrant are undoubtedly met.[180]

Admittedly, this is a borderline case with respect to the probability standard. This finding calls for caution in particular where the probability of the issuance of a warrant is not the only difficult determination to be made. Caution is required above all in those cases where, at the time of the discovery of the evidence, the investigating authorities had not even applied for the issuance of a search warrant. In such cases, a further level of subjective decisions is added, this time the decision to be taken by the investigators themselves to request judicial consent. This renders the hypothetical development of the events even more uncertain.

At the domestic level, U.S. courts have demanded that, in such a case, the prosecution must demonstrate that there had been an "*active pursuit*" of the warrant. This means that the investigative measure must have been at least initiated prior to the violation.[181] It would imply that the application for the search warrant must already have been issued before the warrantless search is conducted. Such a requirement would naturally diminish the risk of speculation.[182] We will not enter here into a detailed discussion of the "*active pursuit*" requirement. This would go well beyond the scope of this study. On a preliminary basis, it would, however, seem reasonable to adopt an equivalent to the "*active pursuit*" notion in ICC proceedings to avoid the criticism of speculation.

In conclusion, hypothetical considerations in ICC proceedings do not seem to be inappropriate *per se*, as a normative consideration, where the lack of a judicial warrant is concerned. Assumptions on the hypothetical course of events should, however, only be made very carefully in these cases and should take into account, in particular, the subjective decisions that precede the issuance of a warrant.

---

[180]In favour of the possibility of such a determination also Trüg 2003, p. 456.

[181]Ambos 2010, p. 136 et seq.; LaFave et al. 2004, p. 514.

[182]Harris 1991, p. 317. For a critique of the '*active pursuit*' requirement in U.S. case law, see Hessler 2000, p. 272 et seq., who contends that the requirement is too formalistic to be applied to the multiple fact patterns that can arise with respect to violations of the 4th amendment.

References

Alamuddin A (2010) Collection of evidence. In: Khan K, Buisman C, Gosnell C (eds) Principles of evidence in international criminal justice. Oxford University Press, Oxford, pp 231–305

Alschuler A (2008) The exclusionary rule and causation—Hudson V. Michigan and his Ancestors. Iowa Law Rev 93:1741–1818

Ambos K (2010) Beweisverwertungsverbote: Grundlagen und Kasuistik—Internationale Bezüge Ausgewählte Probleme. Duncker & Humblot, Berlin

Amelung K (1991) Grundfragen der Verwertungsverbote bei beweissichernden Hausdurchsuchungen im Strafverfahren. Neue Juristische Wochenschrift 40:2533–2540

Ashworth A (1977) Excluding evidence as protecting rights. Crim Law Rev 3:723–735

Ashworth A, Redmayne M (2010) The criminal process, 4th edn. Oxford

Beulke W (1991) Hypothetische Kausalverläufe im Strafverfahren bei rechtswidrigem Vorgehen von Ermittlungsorganen. Zeitschrift für die gesamte Strafrechtswissenschaft 103:657–680

Beulke W (2012) Strafprozessrecht, 12th edn. C.F. Müller, Heidelberg

Birch D (1989) The pace hots up: confessions and confusions under the 1984 Act. Crim Law Rev 95:95–116

Brady H (2001) The system of evidence in the Statute of the International Criminal Court. In: Lattanzi F, Schabas W (eds) Essays on the Rome Statute of the International Criminal Court, Vol. 1. Il Sirente, Ripa Fagnano Alto 2001, pp 279–302

Cammack M (2010) The rise and fall of the constitutional exclusionary rule in the United States. Am J Comp Law 58:631–658

Choo A (2013) England and wales: fair trial analysis and the presumed admissibility of physical evidence. In: Thaman S (ed) Exclusionary rules in comparative law. Springer, Dordrecht, pp 331–354

Combs N (2010) Fact-finding without facts: the uncertain evidentiary foundations of international criminal convictions. Cambridge University Press, Cambridge

Dencker F (1977) Verwertungsverbote im Strafprozess: ein Beitrag zur Lehre von den Beweisverboten. Carl Heymanns Verlag, Cologne

Edwards G (2001) International human rights law challenges to the new International Criminal Court: the search and seizure right to privacy. Yale J Int Law 26:323–412

Effer-Uhe D (2008) Die Entwicklung der Lehre von den Beweisverboten. Jura – Juristische Ausbildung 5:335–340

Eisenberg U (2011) Beweisrecht der StPO: Spezialkommentar, 7th edn. C.H. Beck, Munich

Harris K (1991) Verwertungsverbot für mittelbar erlangte Beweismittel: Fernwirkungsdoktrin in der Rechtsprechung im deutschen und amerikanischen Recht. Strafverteidiger 7:313–322

Hessler S (2000) Establishing inevitability without active pursuit: defining the inevitable discovery exception to the fourth amendment exclusionary rule. Mich Law Rev 99:238–278

Jackson J, Summers S (2012) The internationalisation of criminal evidence: beyond the common law and civil law traditions. Cambridge University Press, Cambridge

Jahn M, Dallmeyer J (2005) Zum heutigen Stand der beweisrechtlichen Berücksichtigung hypothetischer Ermittlungsverläufe. Neue Zeitschrift für Strafrecht 6:297–304

Kühne H (2010) Strafprozessrecht: Eine systematische Darstellung des deutschen und europäischen Strafverfahrensrecht, 8th edn. C.F. Müller, Heidelberg

LaFave W, Israel J, King N (2004) Criminal procedure, 4th edn. West Academic Publishing, St Paul

Mellifont K (2007) The derivative imperative: How should Australian criminal trial courts treat evidence deriving from illegally or improperly gained evidence? Professional Doctorate thesis, Queensland University of Technology. http://eprints.qut.edu.au/16388/1/Kerri_Mellifont_Thesis.pdf. Accessed 14 May 2015

Meyer-Goßner L (2013) Strafprozessordnung, 56th edn. C.H. Beck, Munich

Muthorst O (2009) Das Beweisverbot: Grundlegung und Konkretisierung rechtlicher Grenzen der Beweiserhebung und der Beweisverwertung im Zivil-. Straf- und Verwaltungsverfahren, Mohr Siebeck, Tübingen

Paterline M (2004) New challenge to Miranda: evaluating the effectiveness of mid-interrogation Miranda warnings and the admissibility of subsequent confessions: Missouri v. Seibert. Duquesne Law Rev 43:299–315

Penney S (2003) Taking deterrence seriously: excluding unconstitutionally obtained evidence under section 24(2) of the Charter. McGill Law J 49:105–144

Rogall K (1988) Hypothetische Ermittlungsverläufe im Strafrecht—ein Beitrag zur Lehre der Beweiserhebungs- und Beweisverwertungsverbote. Neue Zeitschrift für Strafrecht 9:385–393

Roxin C, Schünemann B (2012) Strafverfahrensrecht: Ein Studienbuch, 27th edn. C.H.Beck, Munich

Sauer H, Trilsch M (2011) Gäfgen v. Germany. Am J Int Law 105:313–319

Schröder S (1992) Beweisverwertungsverbote und die Hypothese rechtmäßiger Beweiserlangung im Strafprozess. Duncker & Humblot, Berlin

Slobogin C (2013) A Comparative Perspective on the Exclusionary Rule in Search and Seizure Cases. Vanderbilt Public Law Research Paper no. 13–21. http://papers.ssm.com/sol3/papers.cfm?abstract_id=2247746. Accessed 14 May 2015

Sluiter G (1999) Commentary: Prosecutor v. Mucić, exclusion of evidence. In: Klip A, Sluiter G (eds) Annotated leading cases of international criminal tribunals, Volume I: The International Criminal Tribunal for the Former Yugoslavia 1993–1998. Antwerpen, Intersentia, pp 242–243

Sluiter G (2009) I beg you, please come testify—the problematic absence of subpoena powers at the ICC. New Crim Law Rev 12:590–608

Stone R (1995) Exclusion of Evidence Under Section 78 of the Police and Criminal Evidence Act: Practice and Principles. http://www.worldlawbook.com/attachments/312.pdf. Accessed 14 May 2015

Stuart D (2010a) Charter justice in Canadian criminal law, 5th edn. Carswell, Toronto

Stuart D (2010b) Welcome flexibility and better criteria from the Supreme Court of Canada for exclusion of evidence obtained in violation of the Canadian Charter of Rights and Freedoms. Southwestern J Int Law 16:313–332

Thaman S (2013) Fruits of the poisonous tree in comparative law. Southwestern J Int Law 16:333–384

Triffterer O (2008) (ed) Commentary on the Rome Statute of the International Criminal Court: observers' notes, article by article, 2nd edn. C.H. Beck, Baden-Baden

Trüg G (2003) Lösungskonvergenzen trotz Systemdivergenzen im deutschen und US-amerikanischen Strafverfahren. Mohr Siebeck, Tübingen

Wiseman M (1997) The derivative imperative: an analysis of derivative evidence in Canada. Crim Law Quart 39:435–492

Chapter 7
Procedural Aspects

Abstract In the previous chapters, this work has developed an approach to the exclusion of illicitly obtained evidence by interpreting Article 69(7) of the ICC Statute in light of domestic and international law of criminal procedure. The present chapter addresses the practical implementation of the previous findings. It considers a number of procedural aspects that influence the implementation of the exclusionary rule in the context of ICC trials. This includes the determination of those procedural actors endowed with the right to file a motion for exclusion as well as the questions whether ICC judges are obliged to provide a ruling on the question of admissibility, in which parts of the proceedings the exclusionary rule applies and whether motions for exclusion must comply with a particular timing. Finally, a crucial question pertaining to the standard as well as to the burden of proof that applies if the facts of a case including tainted evidence remain contentious.

Keywords Burden of proof · Standard of proof · Procedural scope · *Proprio motu* power · Article 69(4) of the ICC Statute · Rule 63(3) · Timing

Contents

P. Viebig, *Illicitly Obtained Evidence at the International Criminal Court*,
International Criminal Justice Series 4, DOI 10.1007/978-94-6265-093-0_7

7.1 Introduction

This last section will address a number of procedural aspects that influence the practical implementation of the exclusionary rule in ICC trials. This includes a determination of the right of the different actors to invoke the ICC exclusionary rule as well as of its scope of application, an evaluation of whether motions must comply with a particular time frame and, finally, an assessment of the standard and burden of proof that applies in such cases. The way domestic legal systems treat these questions sometimes differs considerably. More so than for the issues addressed so far, the degree to which a system has incorporated inquisitorial or adversarial features into its procedural law plays a role for the solution it finds to these questions. For the ICC as well, the particular interplay of civil law and common law elements that characterize the compromise laid down in its Statute must be given due consideration.

7.2 The Right to Challenge the Admissibility of Evidence

In ICC proceedings, the general power to challenge the admissibility of evidence is set forth in Article 64(9) of the ICC Statute. This provision grants the Trial Chamber the discretion to rule on the admissibility of evidence on "*application of a party or on its own motion*". Accordingly, unlike in adversarial trials, the ICC judges are not dependent on the parties to challenge evidence but may rule on exclusion *ex officio*. This corresponds to the overall comparatively powerful role of ICC judges. Unlike in traditional adversarial systems, ICC proceedings are not characterized by a pure party process. The ICC proper law is the result of a diplomatic compromise. As such, it does not contain any clear commitment to either the inquisitorial or the adversarial system. Unlike in adversarial systems, the judges are not merely arbiters in a party process: They are generally vested with the authority and the duty to exercise control over the proceedings.[1] They can intervene actively in the proceedings by taking evidence[2] and examining witnesses in their own right.[3]

[1]See in particular Article 64(8)(b) of the ICC Statute, which allocates a broad power to the presiding judge, who may decide in large parts on the structure of the trial.

[2]See Article 64(6)(b) of the ICC Statute.

[3]See Rule 140(2)(c) of the ICC RPE. These broad judicial powers are in fact a general feature of international criminal proceedings; see Tochilovsky 2010, p. 164 et seq. This is *inter alia* reflected in the way the power to challenge evidence has been conceived in such proceedings. The ICTY for example has followed the same approach than the one laid down in the ICC Statute. The tribunal has stated that it considered its Trial Chamber to be the "*guardian and guarantor of the procedural and substantive rights of the accused*". It concluded that it had to intervene *ex officio* to exclude evidence that it deemed inadmissible, see *Prosecutor v. Martić* (Decision Adopting Guidelines on the Standards Governing the Admission of Evidence), ICTY (Trial Chamber), decision of 19 January 2006, para 11. See also *Prosecutor v. Delalić et al.* (Decision on the Prosecution's Motion for the Redaction of the Public Record), ICTY (Trial Chamber), decision of 5 June 1997, para 59. Further see Gaynor et al. 2013, p. 1030.

It is likely, however, that in practice, discussions of the ICC exclusionary rule will often be triggered by the parties. In addition to the prosecution and the defence, victims, too, may file a motion for exclusion. Admittedly, the wording of Article 64(9) of the Statute does not explicitly include victims. It merely refers to the parties, which as such only includes the prosecution and the defence. According to ICC case law, however, victims also have the right to challenge the admissibility of evidence. To this effect, the judges have relied in particular on the fact that they had the right under Article 69(4) to rule on admissibility of their own motion. They have held that, when exercising this *proprio motu* power under Article 69(4), nothing was keeping them from taking into account victims' views.[4]

7.3 The Duty to Rule on Admissibility

The next question is whether the Court's judges have a duty under the ICC proper law to take a decision on admissibility. Article 64(9) of the ICC Statute is complemented by Rule 63 of the ICC Rules of Procedure and Evidence. In principle, Rule 63(2) grants a wide discretion to the judges to decide whether to assess the admissibility of evidence or not. Where the general admissibility rule in Article 69(4) of the ICC Statute is concerned, there has, however, been extensive debate on the limits of this discretion. The discussion revolved around the question whether ICC Chambers are compelled to rule on the admissibility of evidence on a case-by-case basis or whether they have the freedom instead to admit on a *prima facie* basis a large amount of evidence even before it is submitted.[5] Where the admissibility of

---

[4]See *Prosecutor v. Lubanga* (Decision on victims participation), ICC (Trial Chamber), decision of 18 January 2008, para 109 "[T]*here is no provision within the Rome Statute framework which prohibits the Trial Chamber from ruling on the admissibility or relevance of evidence having taken into account the views and concerns of the victims, in accordance with Articles 68(3) and 69(4) of the Statute*". See also *Prosecutor v. Katanga and Chui* (Décision Relative aux Modalités de Participation des Victimes au Stade des Débats sur le Fonds), ICC (Trial Chamber), decision of 22 January 2010, para 50. The decision was subsequently upheld by the Appeals Chamber, see *Prosecutor v. Lubanga* (Judgment on the appeals of the Prosecutor and the Defence against Trial Chamber I's Decision on Victims' Participation of 18 January 2008), ICC (Appeals Chamber), decision of 11 July 2008, para 94 et seq. Klamberg 2013, p. 360 et seq.; Gaynor et al. 2013, p. 1031.

[5]The *Lubanga* Trial Chamber had applied the former approach, see *Prosecutor v. Lubanga* (Decision on the admissibility of four documents), ICC (Trial Chamber), decision of 13 June 2008, para 26 et seq.; it was subsequently followed by the Trial Chamber in the *Katanga and Chui* case, see *Prosecutor v. Katanga and Chui* (Decision on the Prosecutor's Bar Table Motion), ICC (Trial Chamber), decision of 17 December 2010, paras 14 et seq. The Bemba Trial Chamber in turn argued that it had the power to generally admit evidence, see *Prosecutor v. Bemba* (Decision on the admission into evidence of materials contained in the prosecution's list of evidence), ICC (Trial Chamber), decision of 19 November 2010, para 8 et seq. The latter decision has however been reversed by the Appeals Chamber, see *Prosecutor v. Bemba* (Judgment on the appeals of Mr. Jean-Pierre Bemba Gombo and the Prosecutor against the decision of Trial Chamber III entitled "Decision on the admission into evidence of materials contained in the prosecution's list of evidence"), ICC (Appeals Chamber), decision of 3 May 2011, paras 2 et seq., 45 and 70. On this debate, see also Safferling 2012, p. 491.

illicitly obtained evidence is concerned, this question need not be considered. Rule 63(3) unequivocally establishes a duty on the part of the judges to rule on admissibility where Article 69(7) is concerned.[6] Thus, where the judges gain knowledge about facts that suggest that evidence was gathered in a way that may trigger Article 69(7), they are compelled to take a decision on the admissibility of the respective evidence.

7.4 The Procedural Scope of Application of the ICC Exclusionary Rule

Rule 63 of the ICC RPE also addresses the question at what stage of the proceedings the ICC exclusionary rule is applicable. In its first paragraph, Rule 63 clarifies that Article 69 of the ICC Statute is applicable in proceedings before all of the Court's Chambers. Such a clarification was necessary in light of an ambiguity in the Statute. Article 69 is included in Part 6 of the Statute, which pertains to the trial proceedings. At the same time, the wording of Article 69 refers to "*the Court*" and not to "*the Trial Chamber*". This ambiguity is resolved by Rule 63(1).[7] The Pre-Trial Chamber in the *Mbarushimana* case confirmed that Rule 63(1) ensures that motions for exclusion can be made at every stage of the proceedings, even very early on. Contrary to the view of the prosecution, the judges held that this even includes the stage of challenges against the admissibility of a case under Article 19 of the ICC Statute.[8]

7.5 The Timing of a Motion

Rule 64(1) of the ICC RPE deals with the correct timing for filing a motion for exclusion. According to this rule, motions for exclusion must be made at the time when the evidence is submitted. Under this provision, motions can only be made at a later date if the issues were not known at that time. In such a case, the issue must be raised immediately after the party has gained knowledge of it. The question is what the consequences are if a party does not comply with these

[6] This has also been recognized in the previously mentioned contentious decision by the Bemba Trial Chamber, see *Prosecutor v. Bemba* (Decision on the admission into evidence of materials contained in the prosecution's list of evidence), ICC (Trial Chamber), decision of 19 November 2010, para 18.

[7] Piragoff 2001, p. 350. For the confirmation hearing, see also Rule 122(9) of the RPE, which expressly extends the applicability of Article 69 to this particular stage of the proceedings; see also Miraglia 2008, p. 492.

[8] *Prosecutor v. Mbarushimana* (Decision on the Defence Request for Disclosure), ICC (Pre-Trial Chamber), decision of 27 January 2011, para 16.

requirements. It seems highly questionable that, as a consequence of Rule 64(1), later motions could simply be rejected.

Similar restrictions regarding the timing of motions for exclusion can be found in domestic systems. They usually have the consequence that the party is precluded from objecting to the admission of evidence if it does not abide by these time limits. Such restrictions regularly exist in systems with adversarial style proceedings, where the parties themselves are responsible for the presentation of evidence. Thus, in the United States, the exclusionary rule will generally only be considered if the defence has filed a motion to suppress the tainted evidence before a certain point in the proceedings.[9] A failure to make an objection at the right time usually precludes the invocation of the exclusionary rule. Sometimes, U.S. courts retain the discretion to nevertheless entertain the motion, a power, however, that courts mostly use in a restrictive way.[10]

While such a restriction is ultimately a consequence of the party process, limitations like these are also known in more inquisitorial style systems. In Germany, for example, in a number of instances, the defence must object to the admission of tainted evidence before a certain point in the proceedings.[11] According to the jurisprudence of the German Federal Supreme Court (BGH), the defendant cannot otherwise invoke the exclusionary rule. This jurisprudence has, however, been heavily criticized. One of the reasons is precisely its incoherence with the role of judges in an inquisitorial trial. In civil law systems such as Germany, the judges bear the responsibility for the taking of evidence *ex officio*. The jurisprudence of the BGH has been assailed because it transfers this responsibility to the defence in a way that is alien to this system.[12]

Applied to the international level, this criticism indicates why it also seems questionable for ICC proceedings that the parties could be effectively precluded from invoking the exclusionary rule. We have seen that ICC proceedings are not governed by a pure party process and that ICC judges are not confined to the role of arbiters but play an active part in the proceedings. This powerful judicial role seems incompatible with the assumption that untimely motions for exclusion should be precluded.

---

[9]Today, such objections must mostly be raised before trial in a suppression hearing by way of a pre-trial motion. Only some states in the U.S. have kept an older rule, whereby such motions can be made during trial. According to this so-called '*contemporaneous objection rule*', the defence has to file a motion at the time the prosecution seeks the admission of the evidence, see LaFave et al. 2004, p. 499 et seq.; Trüg 2003, p. 460.

[10]LaFave et al. 2004, p. 501; Trüg 2003, p. 460.

[11]See German Federal Supreme Court (BGH), decision of 27 February 1992, BGHSt 38, 214; German Federal Supreme Court (BGH), decision of 12 January 1996, BGHSt 42, 15. According to this jurisprudence, Section 257 of the German Code of Criminal Procedure (StPO) determines the moment by which motions for exclusion may be filed. This would be the moment directly after the respective evidence has been examined at trial. See also Eisenberg 2011, p. 144 et seq.; Meyer-Goßner 2013, Section 136, para 25.

[12]Beulke 2012, p. 310 et seq.; Trüg 2003, p. 283.

It is instructive in this respect to return to the case law addressed above that argued in favour of a right of victims to challenge the admissibility of evidence.[13] We have seen that in this jurisprudence, the ICC judges, beyond the plain wording of Article 69(4) of the ICC Statute, have relied upon their *proprio motu* powers under this provision to justify the consideration of the motions made by victims. Where a party does not comply with the time limit set by Rule 64(1), a very similar consideration could justify nevertheless taking into account the motion filed by that party. Here as well, the Chamber would retain the discretion to deal with the matter *ex officio* and could use this power to accept the party's challenge to the admissibility of the respective evidence. Where illicitly obtained evidence is concerned, they would in fact have a duty to do so. As we have seen, Rule 63(3) of the RPE compels the judges to take a decision on admissibility where they gain knowledge about facts that suggest the application of Article 69(7). Ultimately, this duty reflects the responsibility of ICC judges for the guarantee of a fair trial. This responsibility cannot be transferred to the parties by precluding motions for exclusion where they have not complied with the correct time limits.

7.6 The Burden and Standard of Proof

A final, practically important, question needs to be addressed. This question pertains to the burden and standard of proof that applies to the ICC exclusionary rule. So far, we have only considered cases on the basis that the facts were clear. In practice, however, the facts of a case are often disputed between the parties. So what happens, for instance, if the defendant claims that he was forced to give a statement to the investigators while the prosecution denies these allegations? The matter is treated very differently in the domestic and international systems that we have reviewed so far. An overview of the different approaches is instructive for the development of a proper solution for the ICC.

In common law systems, the presentation of evidence is exclusively in the hands of the parties.[14] In these systems, the notion of the burden of proof describes first of all the responsibility of a party to produce sufficient evidence. In addition, it includes the burden of persuasion that establishes against which party a trier of facts must resolve an issue if he is in doubt. Both of these elements of the burden of proof are regularly allocated jointly to the same party.[15]

Both parties in adversarial trials bear parts of the burden of proof. The details of the distribution of responsibilities depend on the facts that need to be determined. The main burden is on the prosecution, which must prove the guilt of the

[13] *Prosecutor v. Lubanga* (Decision on victims participation), ICC (Trial Chamber), decision of 18 January 2008, para 109. See also Sect. 7.2.

[14] Safferling 2012, p. 56.

[15] Buisman et al. 2010, p. 38; LaFave et al. 2004, p. 503.

accused. This is a consequence of the presumption of innocence and of the resulting principle '*in dubio pro reo*'. With respect to matters not directly related to guilt, there is a general rule that the proponent of the respective issue bears the burden of proof.[16] While this is the common principle of adversarial systems, there is no uniform approach among these systems to the allocation of the burden proof for those facts that might justify exclusion.

In the United States, there is a shared responsibility with respect to the exclusion of evidence that follows the general common law distribution of duties. Once more, the main burden is on the prosecution. In most instances, it must prove that there was no violation of the constitutional rights of the defendant.[17] For cases of indirect evidence in turn, the defence generally only needs to establish that the secondary evidence is related to the primary evidence. The prosecution then bears the burden of proving that one of the exceptions to the '*fruits of the poisonous tree doctrine*' applies.[18] The effect of placing most obligations on the prosecution, however, is somewhat attenuated by the standard of proof that the prosecution must comply with. Instead of requiring that the prosecution proves '*beyond a reasonable doubt*' that there is no reason for applying the exclusionary rule, the U.S. Supreme Court has established that the lower '*preponderance of evidence*' standard is sufficient. It is enough under this standard that the prosecution proves that the existence of the respective fact is more probable than its non-existence.[19] This is based once more on a weighing of interests that relies on the deterrence theory. The U.S. Supreme Court considers that to require a higher standard would not increase the deterrent effect in such a way as to justify the exclusion of possibly cogent evidence.[20]

As a common law system, the Canadian system also employs the notion of the burden of proof as depicted above. When it comes to the distribution of responsibilities, however, the situation under Canadian law is more or less the converse of what has been described for the United States. According to the Canadian Supreme Court, the defendant has the general duty to both produce the necessary evidence and to persuade the court of all facts required by Section 24(2) of the

[16]Roberts and Zuckerman 2010, p. 331.

[17]With respect to violations of the 5th amendment for instance, the prosecution has to prove that a confession was voluntary or that the investigators have complied with the *Miranda* requirements; see LaFave et al. 2004, p. 506 et seq. With respect to violations of the 4th amendment, only in the case of a warrant, the defendant has to prove that there was no probable cause. Otherwise, the prosecution needs to prove that the search was reasonable; see LaFave et al. 2004, p. 504.

[18]Altogether, see Trüg 2003, p. 462 et seq.

[19]Three main standards of proof exist under U.S. procedural law: the highest standard is the '*beyond a reasonble doubt*' standard that is required to prove a person's guilt in criminal cases. The lowest is the '*preponderance of evidence*' standard that mostly applies in civil cases. For some circumstances, the '*clear and convincing evidence*' standard applies, which lies somewhere between the two other standards. See LaFave et al. 2004, p. 508.

[20]See *Leon v. Twomey*, United States Supreme Court, decision of 12 January 1972, 404 U.S. 477 (1972). See also LaFave et al. 2004, p. 508 et seq.; Trüg 2003, p. 464.

Canadian Charter of Rights and Freedoms.[21] Only exceptionally is the burden of proof shifted to the prosecution.[22]

The standard of proof, however, is not exceedingly high. The defendant only needs to persuade the judges '*on a balance of probabilities*', which equates the '*preponderance of evidence*' standard introduced above.[23] The same standard applies where the burden is shifted to the prosecution.[24] We have seen that, on a theoretical level, the Canadian exclusionary rule is comparatively strong. This picture is altered to some extent because the rule is watered down by the fact that the distribution of the burden of proof is rather unfavourable to the defendant. The low standard of proof that the defendant must meet, however, limits this effect.

Modern English law in turn somewhat deviates from a pure common law concept. On the one hand, Section 76(2) of PACE sets forth a traditional common law approach. For the admissibility of confessions, it explicitly places the burden on the prosecution. What is more, it even expressly lays down that the standard of proof in such cases must be '*beyond a reasonable doubt*'.[25] Section 78 of PACE on the other hand is rather alien to the traditional common law approach to decision-making. The provision grants a broad discretion to the judge to exclude evidence wherever it appears that admitting it would have an adverse effect on trial fairness. It has been established that "[t]*he concept of a burden of proof has no part to play in such circumstances*".[26] Instead, the judge has a duty to inquire into the matter on his or her own.[27] This is reminiscent of the traditional civil law approach as we will see in more detail below. But, in the end, this determination can only relate to the duty to present sufficient evidence, not to the duty of persuasion. Situations of *non liquet* may still arise where the judge remains in doubt about the facts.

---

[21]*R. v. Collins,* Supreme Court of Canada, decision of 9 April 1987, [1987] 1 S.C.R. 265, para 21. See also Choo and Nash 2007, p. 94. There is no case law that would suggest that this allocation of the burden of proof has changed under the approach to Section 24(2) of the Charter developed in 2009. On this approach, see Sect. 3.3.4.

[22]This would be the case for instance where the issue of discoverability is at stake. Where the prosecution claims that the evidence would have been discovered absent the violation, it must prove the facts that underlie this allegation, see *R. v. Burlingham,* Supreme Court of Canada, decision of 18 May 1995, [1995] 2 S.C.R. 206, p. 209 et seq.; *R. v. Bartle,* Supreme Court of Canada, decision of 29 September 1994, [1994] 3 S.C.R. 173, p. 179.

[23]*R. v. Collins,* Supreme Court of Canada, decision of 9 April 1987, [1987] 1 S.C.R. 265, para 21.

[24]*R. v. Burlingham,* Supreme Court of Canada, decision of 18 May 1995, [1995] 2 S.C.R. 206, p. 209 et seq.

[25]See Ma 1999, p. 285.

[26]*R. (on the application of Saifi) v. Governor of Brixton Prison),* Divisional Court, decision of 21 December, [2001] 1 W.L.R. 1134.

[27]On Section 78 and the burden of proof, see Doak and McGourlay 2012, p. 200.

An interesting discussion on this question can be found in the decision in the well-known case *A. and others* decided by the House of Lords (now the Supreme Court). Here, the majority placed the burden of persuasion on the defendant. It held that evidence allegedly obtained through torture should only be excluded if it is established on '*a balance of probabilities*' that the evidence was obtained through torture. According to the majority, the respective court should admit the evidence where it is left in doubt that this test is met.[28] There was disagreement among the judges, however, on the validity of this test. A minority among the judges argued that instead, the prosecution should have to demonstrate that there was '*no real risk*' that the evidence has been obtained through a violation.[29] Where the respective court was in doubt about the violation, it should exclude the evidence. This would ultimately have placed the burden of persuasion on the prosecution.[30] The minority argued that a defendant often has very few means of proving his allegation and that the majority's approach would consequently "*place on the detainee a burden of proof which, for reasons beyond his control, he can seldom discharge*."[31]

Beyond its instructive content, this jurisprudence indicates that there is no definite view on how to treat a situation of *non liquet* under English law. It must be noticed, however, that this case was not concerned with PACE but with general common law. Whether the majority would have applied the same distribution of responsibilities to Section 78 of PACE remains unclear. The use of the words '*it appears*' in Section 78 rather suggests the application of the '*no real risk*' standard applied by the minority.[32]

In civil law systems, the concept of placing an evidentiary burden on the parties is theoretically unknown. This pertains in particular to the responsibility of the parties to produce sufficient evidence. The defendant has no duty at all to collect evidence. The prosecutor, however, or in some systems the investigating judge, has the duty to collect evidence and to prepare a case. It is, however, the trial judge who ultimately bears the responsibility of conducting a proper investigation into the facts.[33] The consequence for the administration of the exclusionary rule is that it is also the judge who must inquire into facts to determine whether a violation was committed that might justify exclusion.

---

[28] *A. and Others v. Secretary of State for the Home Department*, House of Lords, decision of 8 December 2005, [2005] UKHL 71, paras 117 et seq, 138 et seq.; 156 et seq. and 172 et seq.

[29] *A. and Others v. Secretary of State for the Home Department*, House of Lords, decision of 8 December 2005, [2005] UKHL 71, paras 56, 80 and 98. For a direct comparison of both tests, see para 118 of the decision.

[30] Thienel 2006a, p. 407 et seq.

[31] *A. and Others v. Secretary of State for the Home Department*, House of Lords, decision of 8 December 2005, [2005] UKHL 71, para 80.

[32] Ambos 2010, p. 394.

[33] Buisman et al. 2010, p. 38 et seq.; Safferling 2012, p. 56. In German law, this duty is laid down in Section 244(2) of the German Code of Criminal Procedure.

But again, similar to what we have seen for English law, the possibility of a situation of *non liquet* remains, as the judge can always remain in doubt about the facts.[34] In this regard, the presumption of innocence and the principle '*in dubio pro reo*' are recognized in civil law systems as well.[35]

To take once again the example of German law, the result of the exercise of the jugde's large discetion to evaluate evidence under Section 261 of the German Code of Criminal Procedure must be that the judge is convinced of the guilt of the accused. If he is in doubt, the accused must be acquitted.[36] With respect to the exclusion of evidence, the matter is, however, different, at least under German law. Here, a situation of *non liquet* would result in the admission of the evidence. It is the prevailing view among German courts, as well as scholars, that the principle '*in dubio pro reo*' is only applicable to matters of substantive but not of procedural law. The underlying argument is that the presumption of innocence is simply the reverse side of the principle of guilt applicable in substantive criminal law.[37]

Critics have argued, however, that this ultimately imposes an adversarial-style duty on the defendant. Moreover, the same argument has been advanced as that by the minority of the English judges in the House of Lord's case *A. and others*, namely that the defendant will often have difficulties in providing proof of what happened during an investigation.[38]

As a next step of our inquiry, a human rights perspective shall be included. A consideration of the jurisprudence of the European Court of Human Rights demands once more that particular caution is given to the character of the ECtHR as a human rights monitoring body. As such, this court does not pass criminal judgments but deals with allegations against states. These allegations in turn may deal with criminal proceedings conducted by the domestic judiciaries. As a consequence, a distinction must be made between the allocation of the burden of proof in the ECtHR's own proceedings and its assessment of the same question with respect to domestic trials.

The way the ECtHR treats the burden of proof in its own proceedings does not directly pertain to the issue at hand. The principle '*in dubio reo*' does not apply in

[34]Ambos 2010, p. 393 et seq.; Trüg 2003, p. 291 et seq.

[35]See however Buisman et al. 2010, p. 38 et seq. on the differences regarding the standard and burden of proof among different civil law systems, as well as between civil and common law systems.

[36]Beulke 2012, p. 27.

[37]German Federal Supreme Court (BGH), decision of 28 June 1961, *Neue Juristische Wochenschrift* 1962, p. 1979 et seq. See also Meyer-Goßner 2013, Section 136a, para 143.

[38]Ambos 2010, p. 394; Trüg 2003, p. 293. For the even more problematic case of cross-border collection of evidence see the case of *El Motassadeq*, who was convicted by a German court in the context of the September 11 attacks on the World Trade Center. The court in this case found no proof for the allegation that witnesses had been subjected to torture. It therefore admitted summaries of their statements into evidence that had been obtained from the U.S. Department of Justice; see Hamburg Higher Regional Court (OLG), decision of 14 June 2005, *Neue Juristische Wochenschrift* 2005, 2326 et seq. See also Esser 2012, p. 153.

ECtHR cases in the first place. This tenet derives from the presumption of innocence that is only applicable in criminal cases.[39] The allocation of the burden of proof by the ECtHR is independent from this principle and depends on the characteristics of the case. As a general rule, an applicant bears the burden of proving '*beyond a reasonable doubt*' that his rights under the ECHR were violated.[40] This includes cases where the exclusion of evidence under Article 6 of the ECHR is concerned.

It is nevertheless interesting for our purposes to note the jurisprudence of the ECtHR in cases of injuries or death in police custody. The Court generally recognizes that the proof of a violation may follow from inferences and presumptions of facts. As a result, the judges have held that where an individual has been taken into police custody in good health but is injured at the time he is released, it is incumbent upon the respective state to provide plausible answers for the injuries.[41] While this jurisprudence is not as such transferable to criminal proceedings, it ultimately reflects a point already made, namely that it is often difficult for a defendant to provide full proof of what happened during a police investigation.

The question, however, that is more directly of concern for this research is how the ECtHR assesses the distribution of the burden proof in the context of domestic proceedings. We have seen that the ECtHR has repeatedly emphasised that the admissibility as well as the use of evidence is primarily a matter to be left to national regulation.[42] At the same time, the principle '*in dubio pro reo*', as a part of Article 6(2) of the ECHR, sets a general standard for the burden of proof.[43] The wording of the provision, however, clearly indicates that, under the Convention as well, this standard only applies to the question of guilt, not to procedural issues. The Court, however, has drawn conclusions for the burden of proof in procedural matters from the general right to a fair trial under Article 6(1) of the ECHR. We have seen that, under this right, a defendant must be given the possibility to effectively exercise his rights during a criminal trial.[44] This has had consequences for instance for the case law of the ECtHR on the law of evidence in cases of incitement. The Court has held that where the defendant justifies the exclusion of evidence based on the argument that he was incited to commit a crime, he must be able to effectively raise the issue at trial. It has concluded that in order for such a motion to be effective, the burden of proof for such violations must be on the

[39] Jens Meyer-Ladewig 2011, Article 38, para 19.

[40] Jens Meyer-Ladewig 2011, Article 38, para 22.

[41] See *Gäfgen v. Germany*, ECtHR, decision of 1 June 2010 (Application no. 22978/05), paras 69 and 92.

[42] See Sect. 3.2.2.

[43] Esser 2012, p. 512.

[44] See Sect. 3.2.4.

prosecution, provided that the allegations of the defendant are not wholly improbable.[45]

A look at the international level then again reveals that the ICTY has adopted an approach that benefits the defendant. The presentation of evidence at the Ad hoc tribunals follows a decidedly adversarial approach.[46] It does not therefore come as a surprise that the ICTY, in its case law, has endorsed the notion of the burden of proof as a whole and assumed a shared responsibility of both parties. This approach is naturally applicable to all questions of guilt but it has also been applied to the admissibility of evidence.

The burden of proof for all questions of admissibility has generally been placed on the party that seeks to introduce the respective evidence. Applied to the exclusion of evidence, this favours the defendant because it is regularly the evidence introduced by the prosecution that is attacked on the basis that it was gained illegally. In this case, the prosecution must prove '*beyond a reasonable doubt*' that the evidence was not obtained through improper means.[47] It is safe to say that when compared to all of the domestic systems reviewed above, the requirements placed on the prosecution by the ICTY are exceedingly high. The only system that places, at least partly, such high demands on the prosecution is the English system. Unlike under English law however, the jurisprudence of the ICTY does not even seem to limit the '*beyond a reasonable doubt*' standard to confessions.[48]

Turning to the ICC, the case law, so far, does not contain any general statement on the burden of proof for violations in terms of Article 69(7) of the ICC Statute. In the *Katanga* case, however, the Trial Chamber seems to have accepted a contention of the defence that the burden was on the Prosecutor to prove '*beyond a reasonable doubt'* that the defendant had voluntarily waived his right to be represented by counsel.[49] It seems therefore to follow the line of the ICTY. We

---

[45]*Ramanauskas v. Lithuania*, ECtHR, decision of 5 February 2008 (Application no. 74420/01), para 70. On the burden of proof in the context of incitement cases, see also Gaede and Buermeyer 2008, p. 286 et seq. The case of incitement is admittedly special in that some commentators do not treat it as a matter of procedural but rather of substantive law, see Gaede and Buermeyer 2008, p. 287.

[46]Klamberg 2013, p. 428 et seq.

[47]*Prosecutor v. Orić* (Order Concerning Guidelines on Evidence and the Conduct of Parties During Trial Proceedings), ICTY (Trial Chamber), decision of 21 October 2004, p. 5; *Prosecutor v. Martić* (Decision Adopting Guidelines on the Standards Governing the Admission of Evidence), ICTY (Trial Chamber), decision of 19 January 2006, para 9. See also *Prosecutor v. Delalić* (Decision on Zdravko Mucić's Motion for the Exclusion of Evidence), ICTY (Trial Chamber), decision of 2 September 1997, para 42. This jurisprudence also favours the defence in the—theoretically possible—case that the defence has introduced the evidence, whose exclusion is at stake. Other than the prosecution, the defence only needs to prove the admissibility of its evidence '*on a balance of probabilities'*.

[48]See *Prosecutor v. Orić* (Order Concerning Guidelines on Evidence and the Conduct of Parties During Trial Proceedings), ICTY (Trial Chamber), decision of 21 October 2004, p. 5, where the admissibility of documentary evidence is discussed.

[49]*Prosecutor v. Katanga and Chui* (Decision on the Prosecutor's Bar Table Motions), ICC (Trial Chamber), decision of 17 December 2010, para 56.

will see however that the contention that the prosecution always bears a burden of proof '*beyond a reasonable doubt*' is not plausible as a whole.

At the outset, we must once more make a distinction between the duty to present evidence and the burden of persuasion. In light of the fact that the judges at the ICC have the duty to inquire into the facts on their own, the duty to present evidence is not solely on the parties as would traditionally be the case in an adversarial system. The question that does arise, however, pertains to the burden of persuasion in case of a *non liquet*. As we have seen, this problem arises independently of whether a system's procedure is primarily adversarial or primarily inquisitorial.

The ICC Statute, in its Article 66(1) and (2), sets forth as a general principle that the Prosecutor has the onus of proving the guilt of the accused '*beyond reasonable doubt*'. This is combined with Article 67(1)(i) of the Statute which bars any reversal of the burden of proof. As an embodiment of the presumption of innocence, Article 66(1), however, expressly pertains only to the guilt of the accused. Where other issues are concerned, the discretion of the ICC judges is supposedly broader. The line followed by the Court has so far been to allocate the burden of the proof for questions other than guilt to the party that raises a motion before the Court.[50]

For our issue, the most likely case is that the defence requests the exclusion of the prosecution's evidence. The ensuing question would be whether the prosecutor bears the burden of persuasion as the party that seeks to introduce the evidence or whether this burden should be on the defence as the party that has raised the motion for exclusion.

A number of arguments suggest that the ICTY, as well as the domestic approaches in the United States and partly in the United Kingdom, should be followed in placing the burden of persuasion on the prosecution. This research has so far been guided by the integrity rationale, whereby the exclusion of evidence from ICC proceedings is justified with a view to maintaining the legitimacy of the Court. A high standard of fairness results from this rationale. Practical considerations suggest that it would hardly be compatible with this fairness standard to place the burden of proof on the defendant as the Canadian and German courts, and, partly, the English Supreme Court (formerly the House of Lords) do. We have addressed the criticism made with respect to domestic proceedings that the

[50] *Prosecutor v. Mbarushimana* (Decision on the "Defence Challenge to the Jurisdiction of the Court"), ICC (Pre-Trial Chamber), decision of 26 October 2011, para 20; *Prosecutor v. Ruto and Sang* (Judgment on the appeal of the Republic of Kenya against the decision of Pre-Trial Chamber II of 30 May 2011 entitled "Decision on the Application by the Government of Kenya Challenging the Admissibility" of the Case Pursuant to Article 19(2)(b), ICC (Appeals Chamber), decision of 30 August 2011, para 62; *Prosecutor v. Muthaura and Kenyatta* (Judgment on the appeal of the Republic of Kenya against the decision of Pre-Trial Chamber II of 30 May 2011 entitled "Decision on the Application by the Government of Kenya Challenging the Admissibility" of the Case Pursuant to Article 19(2)(b), ICC (Appeals Chamber), decision of 30 August 2011, para 61. See also Klamberg 2013, p. 127.

defendant often has very few means of investigating and proving the violation.[51] This is ultimately also reflected in the jurisprudence of the ECtHR on the proof of violations that have occurred in police custody.[52] Closely linked is also the argument occasionally made by the ECtHR that placing the burden of persuasion on the accused would have an adverse effect on the effective exercise of the rights of the defence, which would be unfair under Article 6(1) of the ECHR.[53]

These arguments are all the more true for ICC proceedings. As a consequence of the ICC cooperation regime, the Office of the Prosecutor regularly relies on evidence that has been collected by domestic authorities. The transnational nature of the investigative process makes it even more difficult for an accused to obtain evidence during the course of an investigative measure.[54] Moreover, the defence in ICC proceedings is generally at a structural disadvantage when it comes to investigating facts. While the Prosecutor acts in his official capacity as a representative of the ICC, it is regularly even more difficult for the defence to obtain the cooperation of states.[55]

We have seen, however, that under the integrity rationale, there is also the need to guarantee the effectiveness of the proceedings. This in turn calls for preventing the accused from simply relying on allegedly committed violations in order to escape his liability under the ICC Statute. The review of domestic systems indicates that a solution could be to limit the standard of proof to a certain degree. We have seen that under U.S. law, the standard of proof is not '*beyond a reasonable doubt*' but '*by a preponderance of evidence*'. Similarly, the minority in the case of *A. and others* held that the prosecution must prove that there is '*no real risk*' for the existence of a violation. While conversely applied to a burden that is placed on the defendant, the same mechanism is used by the Canadian Supreme Court. A similar approach could be applied by the ICC to attenuate the requirements placed on the prosecution. This would help to prevent evidence from having to be excluded due to almost every allegation made by the defendant.[56]

[51] See *A. and Others v. Secretary of State for the Home Department*, House of Lords, decision of 8 December 2005, [2005] UKHL 71, para 80.

[52] See *Gäfgen v. Germany*, ECtHR, decision of 1 June 2010 (Application no. 22978/05), paras 69 and 92.

[53] See *Ramanauskas v. Lithuania*, ECtHR, decision of 5 February 2008 (Application no. 74420/01), para 70.

[54] Ambos 2010, p. 394; Esser 2012, p. 153.

[55] See for instance Ambos 2007, p. 501; Jackson 2009, p. 26 et seq. On the rights and possibilities of the defence to collect evidence, see in more detail Klamberg 2013, p. 216 et seq.

[56] For the probability standard with respect to reliability, see however Sect. 4.3.2.3.

References

Ambos K (2010) Beweisverwertungsverbote: Grundlagen und Kasuistik—internationale Bezüge Ausgewählte Probleme. Duncker & Humblot, Berlin

Beulke W (2012) Strafprozessrecht, 12th edn. C.F. Müller, Heidelberg

Buisman C, Bouazdi M, Costi M (2010) Principles of civil law. In: Khan K, Buisman C, Gosnell C (eds), Principles of evidence in international criminal justice. Oxford University Press, Oxford, pp 7–95

Doak J, McGourlay C (2012) Evidence in context, 2nd edn. Routledge, Milton Park

Eisenberg U (2011) Beweisrecht der StPO: Spezialkommentar, 7th edn. C.H. Beck, Munich

Esser R (2012) Article 7 IPBPR and Art. 6 EMRK. In: Rosenberg L (ed) Die Strafprozessordnung und das Gerichtsverfassungsgesetz: StPO Band 11: EMRK/IPBPR, 26th edn. De Gruyter, Berlin

Gaede K, Buermeyer U (2008) Beweisverwertungsverbote und "Beweislastumkehr" bei unzulässigen Tatprovokation nach der jüngsten Rechtsprechung des EGMR. HRRS—Online-Zeitschrift für höchstrichterliche Rechtsprechung im Strafrecht 6:279–287

Gaynor F, Jackson J, Klamberg M, Tochilovsky V (2013) Appeals, reviews and reconsideration. In: Sluiter G, Friman H, Linton S, Zappalà S, Vasiliev S (eds) International criminal procedure: principles and rules. Oxford University Press, Oxford, pp 1051–1150

Klamberg M (2013) Evidence in international criminal trials: confronting legal gaps and the reconstruction of disputed events. Martinus Nijhoff Publishers, Leiden

LaFave W, Israel J, King N (2004) Criminal procedure, 4th edn. West Academic Publishing, St Paul

Meyer-Goßner L (2013) Strafprozessordnung, 56th edn. C.H. Beck, Munich

Meyer-Ladewig J (2011) Europäische Menschenrechtskonvention, 3rd edn. Nomos, Baden-Baden

Miraglia M (2008) Admissibility of evidence, standard of proof, and nature of the decision in the ICC confirmation of charges in Lubanga. J Int Crim Justice 6:489–503

Piragoff D (2001) Evidence. In: Lee R (ed) The International Criminal Court: elements of crimes and rules of procedure and evidence. Transnational Publishers, New York, pp 349–401

Roberts P, Zuckerman A (2010) Criminal evidence, 2nd edn. Oxford University Press, Oxford

Safferling C (2012) International criminal procedure. Oxford University Press, Oxford

Thienel T (2006) Foreign acts of torture and the admissibility of evidence: the judgment of the house of lords in A and others v. Secretary of State for the Home Department (No. 2). J Int Crim Justice 4:401–409

Tochilovsky V (2010) The nature and evolution of the rules of procedure and evidence. In: Khan A, Buisman C, Gosnell C (eds) Principles of evidence in international criminal justice. Oxford University Press, Oxford, pp 157–184

Trüg G (2003) Lösungskonvergenzen trotz Systemdivergenzen im deutschen und US-amerikanischenStrafverfahren. Mohr Siebeck, Tübingen

Chapter 8
Conclusion and Outlook

Abstract The final chapter of this book provides a short summary of the main findings of the present study. It recalls why rigid classifications and bright-line rules are not suitable for finding solutions to ICC cases related to illicitly obtained evidence and highlights the underlying conflict between effective law enforcement and due process rights. Furthermore, Chapter 8 recapitulates why the integrity rationale has been found to be the most compelling justification for the exclusion of evidence from trials at the ICC. The notion of integrity as it should be understood in ICC proceedings is summarized once more. In conclusion, the author emphasizes, in particular, the importance of a high fair-trial standard and calls for methodological consistency when dealing with the exclusion of evidence.

Keywords Due process · Effective law enforcement · Methodological consistency · Responsibility · Bright-line rule · Socio-pedagogical mandate

The most important lesson that one can learn from a closer examination of the many questions related to exclusionary rules is probably that these do not allow for simple answers. Deciding whether or not to exclude illicitly obtained evidence is a difficult judicial and, ultimately, also a difficult moral problem. The most immediate conclusion that we have drawn in this research is that such a decision cannot be made on the basis of categorical principles. Consequently, the ICC should not follow the policy of early common law systems of admitting all evidence as long as it is reliable. But neither should it, as some commentators have suggested, at least for human rights violations, automatically exclude all tainted evidence.[1] Moreover, it should not succumb to the temptation to establish the kind of bright-line rules which have sometimes been used at the domestic level to easily

[1]See Vanderpuye 2005, p. 130. Also see Zahar and Sluiter 2008, p. 382; Zappalà 2003, p. 152, who favour an automatic exclusionary rule at least in case of violations of internationally recognized human rights.

P. Viebig, *Illicitly Obtained Evidence at the International Criminal Court*,
International Criminal Justice Series 4, DOI 10.1007/978-94-6265-093-0_8

categorize whether evidence is admissible or not.[2] We have seen instead that in order to come to a just solution, decisions on exclusion must find a middle ground between the need for effective law enforcement on the one hand and the guarantee for due process on the other.

In this context, we have also come to another conclusion. The solution does not so much depend on how one characterizes the ICC system of criminal procedure according to the usual categories of comparative criminal law. The dividing line is not between civil and common law systems. Any system, irrespective of whether it has a more adversarial or more inquisitorial system of criminal procedure must find its own compromise between these two poles.

In case of the ICC, finding a maintainable compromise is of vital importance. We have detected as the central purpose of the Court its socio-pedagogical mandate. The ICC neither has the ability to truly deter future perpetrators of international crimes, nor will it be able to reintegrate into society the kind of perpetrators that already assume criminal liability for international crimes. Retribution as a sole purpose in turn does not suit any modern criminal court. As a consequence, building trust in the validity of international criminal and humanitarian law must be the central concern of this still young international criminal institution. This, however, implies that the ICC is perceived as a moral authority endowed with the legitimacy of a court that respects the rule of law.

The way a criminal court deals with illicitly obtained evidence is one of the many factors that make up how it is perceived. Article 69(7) of the ICC Statute draws the consequence for the Court and places the focus, besides reliability, on the impact that admitting evidence would have on the integrity of its proceedings. In doing so, it implements for the ICC a rationale for excluding evidence which is also discussed and increasingly advocated at the domestic level: the theory of integrity. Of course, this theory is not the only justification that has been advanced in domestic debates. But at least for the ICC, we have not only found that the integrity rationale corresponds to the Court's inherent need for legitimacy; we have also seen that other explanations discussed in domestic debates do not quite fit the particular situation of the ICC. The Court's proceedings are neither the right place to deter investigators from further violations nor to vindicate the rights of individuals that are affected by such violations.

As to the content of the notion of integrity, we have seen that this focus of the ICC exclusionary rule does not mean to simply subject the Court to public opinion. Public opinion is often too emotionally driven and does not sufficiently comply with the rule of law. Ultimately, such an understanding would not do justice to the overall socio-pedagogical purpose of the Court. Instead, integrity must be understood as requiring judicial decisions that do not contravene the very values the Court was set up to promote. As a consequence, ICC judges must at all

[2] An example here would be in particular the bright-line rule for '*conscriptive*' evidence initially established by the Canadian Supreme Court, see Sect. 3.3.4.

times apply a high standard when it comes to the fairness of its proceedings. This means in particular that the gravity of the crimes under the Court's jurisdiction cannot be relied upon as an argument to limit the guarantee for the individual and human rights of those persons that stand trial before the Court. It may seem bitter in the individual case not to be able to use evidence despite it being proof of a crime of this level of atrocity. This is, however, the price that the international community must pay in the worst case scenario if the ICC is to make any meaningful socio-pedagogical contribution. Of course, this only concerns the worst case scenario. Integrity does not mean that the interest of the international community in effective law enforcement should be disregarded altogether. We have seen that the integrity of an international criminal institution inherently suffers where this institution is not able to enforce the substantive criminal law under its jurisdiction. Consequently, even though the Court cannot simply subject its legitimacy to public opinion, it can and must take into account, when deciding on exclusion, the interest of the international community in general and of the victims in particular in the enforcement of international criminal law.

The tension that arises from the two poles 'due process' and 'effective law enforcement' must be solved through a balancing of interests. Naturally, one flaw of such decision-making is that it is subjective to a certain extent and therefore not entirely predictable. We have nonetheless found that the detriment caused to the principle of legal certainty can be attenuated by establishing a consistent body of case law and clear factors and criteria that judges must take into account when deciding on exclusion. In this research, we have been able to detect a number of such factors. The determination of these factors was guided both by the underlying integrity rationale and by the particularities of the system of international criminal justice.

In addition to factors such as the seriousness of the violation or the actors involved in the proceedings, which regularly play a role in cases of exclusion, we have also found that, depending on the circumstances of the case, the relationship between the violation and the evidence must be taken into account. Here, we have found that on a level of principle, the integrity rationale suggests a broad understanding of the ICC exclusionary rule. As a consequence, we have found that the ICC must, in principle, include derivative evidence in the scope of application of its exclusionary rule. We have, in other words, supported the development of the Court's very own version of the *'fruits of the poisonous tree doctrine'*. At the same time, we have found that in the single case, the specific relationship between the evidence and the violation can be included as a further factor in the balancing of interests. To this effect, we have relied on normative evaluations to limit the abundance of cases which, on principle, are covered by an exclusionary rule that extends to derivative evidence.

The discussion naturally does not end here. Quite the opposite: this research will hopefully contribute to raising a debate of increased methodological depth on the handling of illicitly obtained evidence by the ICC. Both the rationale for exclusion and the factors that we have filtered out in this research will certainly not find general acceptance. Looking at debates at the domestic level, which have lasted for decades and which still have not come to an end, it is rather to be expected that the question of how to deal with illicitly obtained evidence will trigger some amount of controversial debate at the international level as well.

The Court itself, in turn, would be well advised to create, over time, a coherent body of case law on its exclusionary rule. As mentioned above, such coherence is not only a question of judicial logic and sound methodology; it would guarantee some measure of legal certainty and enhance the conformity of the treatment of the different persons accused before the Court. Ultimately, this would help to avoid the criticism of arbitrariness that can be expected to come along with the subjective kind of decision-making implied by a balancing of interests. What is more, as for other issues, the development of a coherent body of case law will help to emancipate the Court from the jurisdiction of other institutions, both at the domestic and at the international level. This research was based on a decidedly comparative approach. Such an approach seemed sensible at a stage of development of the international law of evidence where both the ICC's case law and the academic discussion are still at their beginnings. It can be expected that the debate will become more self-contained as the case law and academic writing on the international law of evidence will increase.

But the further discussion of the ICC exclusionary rule will depend not only on the Court's methodological approach to the exclusionary rule. It will also depend on the future development of the relationship between the international law of criminal procedure and international human rights law. Despite its more detailed legal framework when compared to previous international criminal institutions, the ICC system of criminal procedure only contains very basic rules on how to conduct investigations. As a consequence, the interpretation of the ICC exclusionary rule is heavily dependent on the content one gives to the notion of '*internationally recognized human rights*'. Here as well, the integrity rationale suggests that the Court should be generous in its interpretation.

On the whole, the Court's first decisions on the exclusion of illicitly obtained evidence give cause for optimism.[3] So far, the ICC seems to be aware of its great responsibility for the respect of individual and human rights. It is to be hoped that the ICC, in the future, will improve the methodological consistency of its exclusionary rule and that it will continue to apply the high fair trial standard that is required not least by its own need for legitimacy. Only then can it do justice to its purpose and particular role as the first permanent international criminal court.

---

[3] See in particular *Prosecutor v. Lubanga* (Decision on the Admission of Material from the 'Bar Table'), ICC (Trial Chamber), decision of 24 June 2009 and *Prosecutor v. Katanga* (Decision on the Prosecutor's Bar Table Motions), ICC (Trial Chamber), decision of 17 December 2010, paras 55 et seq.

References

Ambos K (2007) The structure of international criminal procedure: "adversarial", "inquisitorial" or mixed? In: Bohlander M (ed) International criminal justice: a critical analysis of institutions and procedures. Cameron May, London, pp 429–503

Jackson J (2009) Finding the best epistemic fit for international criminal tribunals beyond the adversarial-inquisitorial dichotomy. J Int Crim Justice 7:17–39

Klamberg M (2013) Evidence in international criminal trials: confronting legal gaps and the reconstruction of disputed events. Martinus Nijhoff Publishers, Leiden

Vanderpuye K (2005) The International Criminal Court and discretionary evidential exclusion: toeing the mark? Tulane J Int Comp Law 14:127–177

Zahar A, Sluiter G (2008) International criminal law: a critical introduction. Oxford University Press, Oxford

Zappalà S (2003) Human rights in international criminal proceedings. Oxford University Press, Oxford

Erratum to: Illicitly Obtained Evidence at the International Criminal Court

Petra Viebig

Erratum to:
P. Viebig, *Illicitly Obtained Evidence at the International Criminal Court*, International Criminal Justice Series 4, DOI 10.1007/978-94-6265-093-0

A part of the Table of Cases was inadvertently published in Greek script instead of normal European script in the original version of this book.

The updated original online version for this book back matter can be found at
DOI 10.1007/978-94-6265-093-0

Petra Viebig (✉)
Public Prosecutor's Office, Staatsanwaltschaft Hamburg, Hamburg, Germany
e-mail: petra.viebig@googlemail.com

P. Viebig, *Illicitly Obtained Evidence at the International Criminal Court*,
International Criminal Justice Series 4, DOI 10.1007/978-94-6265-093-0_9

Bibliography

Acquaviva G, Combs N, Heikkilä M, Linton S, McDermott Y (2013) Trial Process. In: Sluiter G, Friman H, Linton S, Zappalà S, Vasiliev S (eds.) International Criminal Procedure:Principles and Rules, Oxford University Press, Oxford, pp 489-938.

Alamuddin A (2010) Collection of Evidence. In: Khan K, Buisman C, Gosnell C (eds) Principles of Evidence in International Criminal Justice. Oxford University Press, Oxford, pp 231-305.

Alschuler A (2008) The Exclusionary Rule and Causation - Hudson V. Michigan and his Ancestors, Iowa Law Review 93: pp 1741-1818.

Ambos K (2002) On the Rationale of Punishment at the Domestic and International Level. In: Marc Henzelin M and Roth R (eds), Le Droit Pénal à l'Épreuve de l'Internationalisation. Bruylant, Paris, pp 305-323.

Ambos K (2007) The Structure of International Criminal Procedure: "Adversarial", "Inquisitorial" Or Mixed?. In: Bohlander M (eds), International Criminal Justice: A Critical Analysis of Institutions and Procedures. Cameron May, London, pp 429-503.

Ambos K (2010) The Transnational Use of Torture Evidence. Israel Law Review 42: 362-397.

Ambos K, (2010) Beweisverwertungsverbote: Grundlagen und Kasuistik - Internationale Bezüge Ausgewählte Probleme. Duncker & Humblot, Berlin.

Ambos K, (2011) Art. 6 EMRK. In: Radtke H, Hohmann O (eds), Strafprozessordnung: StPO. Verlag Franz Vahlen, Munich, pp 2518-2535.

Amelung K (1990) Informationsbeherrschungsrechte im Strafprozeß. Dogmatische Grundlagen individualrechtlicher Beweisverbote. Duncker & Humblot, Berlin, 1990.

Amelung K (1991) Grundfragen der Verwertungsverbote bei beweissichernden Hausdurchsuchungen im Strafverfahren. Neue Juristische Wochenschrift 40: 2533-2540

Amelung K, Mittag M (2005) Beweislastumkehr bei Haussuchungen ohne richterliche Anordnung gemäß § 105 StPO. Neue Zeitschrift für Strafrecht 11:614-617.

Arsanjani M (1999) The Rome Statute of the International Criminal Court. The American Journal of International Law 93:22-43.

Ashworth A (1977) Excluding Evidence as Protecting Rights. Criminal Law Review, 3:723-735.

Ashworth A (2003) Exploring the Integrity Principle in Evidence and Procedure. In: Mirfield P, Smith R (eds), Essays for Colin Tapper, London, pp 107-125.

Ashworth A, Redmayne M (2010) The Criminal Process, 4th edn. Oxford, 2010.

Bantekas I (2006) Reflections on Some Sources and Methods of International Criminal and Humanitarian Law. International Criminal Law Review 6:121-136.

Becker S (2011) Preserving the Integrity of the Court Against Moral Defilement: People v. Wrice and the Question of Whether the Use of a Physically Coerced Confession Can Constitute Harmless Error - Lessons of Wisdom from International Law. DePaul Journal for Social Justice 5:3-29.

P. Viebig, *Illicitly Obtained Evidence at the International Criminal Court*, International Criminal Justice Series 4, DOI 10.1007/978-94-6265-093-0

Behrens H (1999) The Trial Proceedings. In: Roy S. Lee (ed) The International Criminal Court: The Making of the Rome Statute -Issues, Negotiations, and Results. Kluwer Law International, The Hague, pp 238-246.

Beling E (1903) Die Beweisverbote als Grenzen der Wahrheitserforschung im Strafprozess. Wissenschaftliche Buchgesellschaft, Breslau.

Berger M (2012) The Right to Silence in the Hague International Criminal Courts. University of San Francisco Law Review 47:1-54.

Beulke W (1991) Hypothetische Kausalverläufe im Strafverfahren bei rechtswidrigem Vorgehen von Ermittlungsorganen. Zeitschrift für die gesamte Strafrechtswissenschaft 103:657–680.

Beulke, W (2012) Strafprozessrecht, 12th edn. C.F. Müller, Heidelberg.

Bilz K (2012) Dirty Hands or Deterrence? An Experimental Examination of the Exclusionary Rule. Journal of Empirical Legal Studies 9:149–171.

Birch D (1989) The Pace Hots up: Confessions and Confusions Under the 1984 Act. Criminal Law Review 95:95-116.

Bitti G (2009) Article 21 of the Statute of the International Criminal Court and The Treatment of the Sources of Law in the Jurisprudence of the ICC. In: Carsten S, Goran S (eds), The Emerging Practice of the International Criminal Court. Martinus Nijhoff Publishers, Leiden, pp 285-304.

Boas G (2001) Creating Laws of Evidence for International Criminal Law: The ICTY and the Principle of Flexibility. Criminal Law Forum 12:41-90.

Böse M (2002) Die Verwertung im Ausland gewonnener Beweismittel im deutschen Strafverfahren.Zeitschrift für die gesamte Strafrechtswissenschaft 114:148–182.

Bothe M (1976) Die Bedeutung der Rechtsvergleichung in der Praxis internationaler Gerichte. Zeitschrift für ausländisches öffentliches Recht und Völkerrecht 36:280-299.

Bradley C (1982) The Exclusionary Rule in Germany. Harvard Law Review 96:1032-1066.

Bradley C (2010) Reconceiving the Fourth Amendment and the Exclusionary Rule. Law and Contemporary Problems 73:211-238.

Brady H (1999) The System of Evidence in the Statute of the International Criminal Court. In: Lattanzi F, Schabas W (eds) Essays on the Rome Statute of the International Criminal Court, Vol. 1. Il Sirente, Ripa Fagnano Alto, pp 279-302.

Buisman C (2013) Delegating Investigations: Lessons to be Learned from the Lubanga Judgment. Northwestern Journal of International Human Rights 11:30-82.

Buisman C, Bouazdi M, Costi M (2010) Principles of Civil Law. In: Khan K, Buisman C, Gosnell C (eds), Principles of Evidence in International Criminal Justice. Oxford University Press, Oxford, pp 7-95.

Burghardt B (2011) Die Rechtsvergleichung in der völkerstrafrechtlichen Rechtsprechung – von der Rechtsvergleichung als Mittel der Rechtsfindung zur diskursiv-vermittelnden Rechtsvergleichung. In: Beck S, Burchard C, Fateh-Moghadam F (eds) Strafrechtsvergleichung als Problem und Lösung. Nomos, Baden-Baden, pp 235-254.

Burghardt B, Geneuss J (2009) Der Präsident und sein Gericht. Zeitschrift für Internationale Strafrechtsdogmatik 4:126-142.

Caianiello M (2011) First Decisions on the Admission of Evidence at ICC Trials: A Blending of Accusatorial and Inquisitorial Models? Journal of International Criminal Justice 9:385-410.

Calvo-Goller N (2006) The Trial Proceedings Of The International Criminal Court: ICTY And ICTR Precedents. Martinus Nijhoff Publishers, Leiden, 2006.

Cammack M (2010) The Rise and Fall of the Constitutional Exclusionary Rule in the United States. American Journal of Comparative Law 58:631-658.

Cassese A (2003) The Influence of the European Court of Human Rights on International Criminal Tribunals - Some Methodological Remarks. In: Bergsmo A, Eide A (eds) Human Rights and Criminal Justice for the Downtrodden: Essays in Honour of Asbjørn Eide. Martinus Nijhoff Publishers, Leiden, pp 19-52.

Cassese A (2005) International Law, 2nd edn. Oxford University Press, Oxford, 2005.

Cassese A (2008) International Criminal Law, 2nd edn. Oxford University Press, Oxford, 2008.

Choo A (2013) England and Wales: Fair Trial Analysis and the Presumed Admissibility of Physical Evidence. In: Thaman S (ed), Exclusionary Rules in Comparative Law. Springer, Dordrecht et al., pp 331-354.

Choo A, Nash S (2007) Improperly Obtained Evidence in The Commonwealth: Lessons for England And Wales?. The International Journal of Evidence and Proof 11:75-105.

Combs N (2010) Fact-Finding Without Facts: The Uncertain Evidentiary Foundations of International Criminal Convictions. Cambridge University Press, Cambridge.

Combs N (2011) Evidence. In: Schabas W, Bernaz, N (eds), Routledge Handbook of International Criminal Law. London, pp 323-334.

Cryer R (2009) Means of Gathering Evidence and Arresting Suspects in Situation of State´s Failure to Cooperate'. In: Cassese A (ed) The Oxford Companion to International Criminal Justice. Oxford University Press, Oxford, pp 201-207.

Cryer R, Friman A, Robinson D, Wilmshurst W (2010) An Introduction to International Criminal Law and Procedure. 2nd edn. Cambridge University Press, Cambridge, 2010.

Currat P (2007) L'Interprétation du Statut de Rome. Revue québécoise de droit international 2:137-163.

Damaška M (2009) Problematic Features of International Criminal Procedure. In: Cassese A (ed) The Oxford Companion to International Criminal Justice. Oxford University Press, Oxford, pp 175-186.

Damaška M (2012) Reflections on Fairness in International Criminal Justice. Journal of International Criminal Justice 10:611-620.

Dawe J, McArthur H (2010) Charter Detention and the Exclusion of Evidence After Grant, Harrison and Suberu. Supreme Court Law Review 51:381-437.

Dencker F (1977) Verwertungsverbote im Strafprozess: Ein Beitrag zur Lehre von den Beweisverboten. Carl Heymanns Verlag, Cologne et al.

Dennis I (2010) The Law of Evidence, 4th edn. Sweet and Maxwell, London, 2010.

Dixon R (1997) Developing International Rules of Evidence for the Yugoslav and Rwanda Tribunals. Transnational Law & Contemporary Problems 7:81-102.

Doak J, McGourlay C (2012) Evidence in Context. 2nd edn. Routledge, Milton Park et al.

Douglas L (2006) The Didactic Trial: Filtering History and Memory into the Courtroom. European Review 14:513 – 522.

Eberdt B (2011) Impaired Exclusion: Exploring the Possibility of a New Bright Line Rule of Good Faith in Impaired Driving Offences. Review of Current Law and Law Reform 16:65-83.

Edwards G (2001) International Human Rights Law Challenges to the New International Criminal Court: The Search and Seizure Right to Privacy. The Yale Journal of International Law 26:323-412.

Effer-Uhe D (2008) Die Entwicklung der Lehre von den Beweisverboten. Jura – Juristische Ausbildung 5:335-340.

Eisenberg U (2011) Beweisrecht der StPO: Spezialkommentar, 7th edn. C.H. Beck, Munich.

Esser R (2008) EGMR in Sachen Gäfgen v. Deutschland (22978/05), Urt. v. 30.06.2008. Neue Zeitschrift für Strafrecht 12:657-662.

Esser R (2012) Article 7 IPBPR and Art. 6 EMRK. In: Rosenberg L (ed) Die Strafprozessordnung und das Gerichtsverfassungsgesetz: StPO Band 11: EMRK/IPBPR, 26th edn. De Gruyter, Berlin et al.

Fedorova M, Sluiter G (2009) Human Rights as Minimum Standards in International Criminal Proceedings. Human Rights & International Legal Discourse 3:9-56.

Fernández de Gurmedi S (2001). In: Lee R (ed) The International Criminal Court: Elements of Crimes and Rules of Procedure and Evidence. Transnational Publishers, New York, pp 235-258.

Friman H (1999) Rights of Persons Suspected or Accused of a Crime. In: Lee R (ed) The International Criminal Court: The Making of the Rome Statute: Issues, Negotiations, Results. Kluwer Law International, The Hague, pp 247-262.

Friman H (2003) Inspiration from the International Criminal Tribunals when Developing Law on Evidence for the International Criminal Court. Law and Practice of International Courts and Tribunals 2:373-400.

Gaede K (2009) Beweisverbote zur Wahrung des fairen Strafverfahrens in der Rechtsprechung des EGMR insbesondere bei verdeckten Ermittlungen. Juristische Rundschau 12:493-502.

Gaede K, Buermeyer U (2008) Beweisverwertungsverbote und "Beweislastumkehr" bei unzulässigen Tatprovokation nach der jüngsten Rechtsprechung des EGMR. HRRS - Online-Zeitschrift für höchstrichterliche Rechtsprechung im Strafrecht 6:279-287.

Gallant K (1999) Individual Human Rights in a New International Organization: The Rome Statute of the International Criminal Court. In: Bassiouni C (ed), International Criminal Law, Volume II: Procedural and Enforcement Mechanisms, 2nd edn. Transnational Publishers, New York, pp 693-723.

Gaynor F, Jackson J, Klamberg M, Tochilovsky V (2013) Appeals, Reviews and Reconsideration. In: Sluiter G, Friman H, Linton S, Zappalà S, Vasiliev S (eds.) International Criminal Procedure: Principles and Rules, Oxford University Press, Oxford, pp 1051-1150.

Glasser L (2003) The American Exlcusionary Rule Debate: Looking to England and Canada for Guidance. George Washington International Law Review 35:159-196.

Gosnell C (2010) Admissibility of Evidence. In: Khan A, Buisman C, Gosnell C (eds), Principles of Evidence in International Criminal Justice. Oxford University Press, Oxford, pp 375-442.

Gössel K (1981) Kritische Bemerkungen zum gegenwärtigen Stand der Lehre von den Beweisverboten im Strafverfahren. Neue Juristische Wochenschrift 13:649-656.

Gradoni L, Lewis D, Mégret F, Nouwen S, Ohlin J (2013) General Framework of International Criminal Justice. In: Sluiter G, Friman H, Linton S, Zappalà S, Vasiliev S (eds) International Criminal Procedure: Principles and Rules, Oxford University Press, Oxford, pp 39-130.

Gray R (2004) Evidence Before the ICC. In: McGoldrick D, Rowe P, Donnelly E (eds), The Permanent International Criminal Court: Legal and Policy Issues. Hart Publishing, Oxford et al., pp 287-314.

Greco G (2007) Victims' Rights Overview Under the ICC Legal Framework: A Jurisprudential Analysis. International Criminal Law Review 7:531-547.

Grover L (2010) A Call to Arms: Fundamental Dilemmas Confronting the Interpretation of Crimes in the Rome Statute of the International Criminal Court. European Journal of International Law 21:543-583.

Hafner G and Binder C (2004) The Interpretation of Article 21 (3) ICC Statute Opinion Reviewed, Austrian Review of International and European Law 9:163-190.

Harris K (1991) Verwertungsverbot für mittelbar erlangte Beweismittel: Fernwirkungsdoktrin in der Rechtsprechung im deutschen und amerikanischen Recht. Strafverteidiger 7:313-322.

Hay P (2011) US-Amerikanisches Recht, 5th edn. C.H. Beck, Munich.

Hessler S (2000) Establishing Inevitability Without Active Pursuit: Defining the Inevitable Discovery Exception to the Fourth Amendment Exclusionary Rule. Michigan Law Review 99:238-278.

Heyns C (2003) The African Regional Human Rights System: The African Charter. Penn State Law Review 108:670-702.

Ipsen K, Epping V, Heintschel von Heinegg W (2004) Völkerrecht, 5th edn. C.H. Beck, Munich.

Jackson J (2009) Finding the Best Epistemic Fit for International Criminal Tribunals Beyond the Adversarial–Inquisitorial Dichotomy. Journal of International Criminal Justice 7:17-39.

Jackson J, Summers S (2012) The Internationalisation of Criminal Evidence: Beyond the Common Law and Civil Law Traditions. Cambridge University Press, Cambridge.

Jäger H (1995) Markoverbrechen als Gegenstand des Völkerstrafrechts. In: Hankel G, Stuby G (eds) Strafgerichte gegen Menschheitsverbrechen: Zum Völkerstrafrecht 50 Jahre nach den Nürnberger Prozessen. Hamburger Edition, Hamburg, pp 325-354.

Jahn M, Dallmeyer J (2005) Zum heutigen Stand der beweisrechtlichen Berücksichtigung hypothetischer Ermittlungsverläufe. Neue Zeitschrift für Strafrecht 6: 297-304.

Kamardi C (2009) Die Ausformung einer Prozessordnung sui generis durch das ICTY unter Berücksichtigung des Fair-Trial-Prinzips. Springer, Berlin et al.

Kaul H, Kreß, C (1999) Jurisdiction and Cooperation in the Statute of the International Criminal Court: Principles and Compromises. Yearbook of International Humanitarian Law 2:143-175.

Kimani M (2009) Pursuit of Justice or Western Plot? International Indictments Stir Angry Debate in Africa. African Renewal. 23.3:12-15.

Klamberg M (2013) Evidence in International Criminal Trials: Confronting Legal Gaps and the Reconstruction of Disputed Events. Martinus Nijhoff Publishers, Leiden.

Kühne H (2010) Strafprozessrecht: Eine systematische Darstellung des deutschen und europäischen Strafverfahrensrecht, 8th edn. C.F. Müller, Heidelberg.

LaFave W, Israel J, King N (2004) Criminal Procedure, 4th edn. West Academic Publishing, St Paul.

Lepsius O (1997) Verwaltungsrecht unter dem Common Law: Amerikanische Entwicklungen bis zum New Deal. Mohr Siebeck, Tübingen.

Lister C (2005) What's in a Name? Labels and the Statute of the International Criminal Tribunal for the Former Yugoslavia. Leiden Journal of International Law 18:77-92.

Lubig S, Sprenger J (2008) Beweisverwertungsverbote aus dem Fairnessgebot des Art. 6 EMRK in der Rechtsprechung des EGMR. Zeitschrift für Internationale Strafrechtsdogmatik 9:433-440.

Ma Y (1999) Comparative Analysis of Exclusionary Rules in the United States, England, France, Germany, and Italy. Policing: An International Journal of Police Strategies & Management 22:280-303.

May R, Wierda M (2003) International Criminal Evidence. Transnational Publishers, New York.

McIntyre G, Defining Human Rights in the Arena of International Humanitarian Law: Human Rights in the Jurisprudence of the ICTY. In: Boas W, Schabas W (eds) International Criminal Law: Developments in the Case Law of the ICTY. Martinus Nijhoff Publishers, Leiden, pp 193-238.

McKeever D (2010) Evidence Obtained Through Torture Before the Khmer Rouge Tribunal Unlawful Pragmatism?. Journal of International Criminal Justice 8:615-630.

Mellifont K (2007) The Derivative Imperative: How Should Australian Criminal Trial Courts Treat Evidence Deriving From Illegally or Improperly Gained Evidence? Professional Doctorate Thesis, Queensland University of Technology. http://eprints.qut.edu.au/16388/1/Kerri_Mellifont_Thesis.pdf. Accessed 14 May 2015.

Meron T (2004) Evolution in the ICTY. Journal of International Criminal Justice 2:520-525.

De Meester K, Pitcher K, Rastan R, Sluiter G (2013) Investigation, Coercive Measures, Arrest and Surrender. In: Sluiter G, Friman H, Linton S, Zappalà S, Vasiliev S (eds.) International Criminal Procedure: Principles and Rules, Oxford University Press, Oxford, pp 171-380.

De Meester K (2009) Coercive Measures, Privacy Rights and Judicial Supervision in International Criminal Investigations: In Need of Further Regulation?. In: Sluiter K, Vasiliev S (eds) International Criminal Procedure: Towards a Coherent Body of Law. Cameron May, London, pp 273-309.

Meyer-Goßner L (2013) Strafprozessordnung, 56th edn. C.H. Beck, Munich.

Meyer-Ladewig J (2011) Europäische Menschenrechtskonvention, 3rd edn. Nomos, Baden-Baden.

Miller N (2002) An International Jurisprudence? The Operation of Across International Tribunals. Leiden Journal of International Law 15:483-526.

Miraglia M (2008) Admissibility of Evidence, Standard of Proof, and Nature of the Decision in the ICC Confirmation of Charges in Lubanga, Journal of International Criminal Justice 6:489-503.

Mitsch W (2008) Strafprozessuale Beweisverbote im Spannungsfeld zwischen Jurisprudenz und realer Gefahr. Neue Juristische Wochenschrift 32:2295-2301.

Møse E (2005) The ICTR: Experiences and Challenges. New England Journal of International and Comparative Law 12:1-16.

Mundis D (2001) From Towards: The Evolution of the ICTY Rules of Procedure and Evidence. Leiden Journal of International Law 14:367-382.

Muthorst O (2009) Das Beweisverbot: Grundlegung und Konkretisierung rechtlicher Grenzen der Beweiserhebung und der Beweisverwertung im Zivil-, Straf- und Verwaltungsverfahren. Mohr Siebeck, Tübingen.

Nasheri H (1996) The Exclusionary Rule: Differing Trends in Canada and the United States. Criminal Justice Review 21:161-180.

Nemitz J (2002) Strafzumessung im Völkerstrafrecht. Edition Iuscrim, Freiburg.

Nemitz J (2005) Die Hauptverhandlung unter besonderer Berücksichtigung des Beweisrechts. In: Kirsch S (ed) Internationale Strafgerichtshöfe. Nomos, Baden-Baden, pp 53-74.

Nerlich V (2009) The Status of ICTY and ICTR Precedence in Proceedings Before the ICC. In: Stahn C, Sluiter G (eds) The Emerging Practice of the International Criminal Court. Martinus Nijhoff Publishers, Leiden, pp 305-326.

Neubacher F (2006) Strafzwecke und Völkerstrafrecht. Neue Juristische Wochenschrift 14:966-970.

Nüse K (1966) Zu den Beweisverboten im Strafprozeß. Juristische Rundschau 8:281-288.

Orie A (2002) Accusatorial Versus Inquisitorial Approach in International Criminal Proceedings. In: Cassese A, Gaeta P, Jones J (eds) The Rome Statute of the International Criminal Court: A Commentary, Volume 2. Oxford University Press, Oxford, pp 1439-1495.

Osborn D (2000) Supressing the Truth: Judicial Exclusion of Illegally Obtained Evidence in the United States, Canada, England and Australia, Murdoch University Electronic Journal of Law 7. http://www.austlii.edu.au/au/journals/MurUEJL/2000/44.html. Accessed 14 May 2015.

Osmer J (1966) Der Umfang des Beweisverwertungsverbotes nach § 136a StPO. Doctoral Thesis, University of Hamburg, Hamburg.

Pakter W (1985) Exclusionary Rules in France, Germany, and Italy. Hastings International and Comparative Law Review 1:1-57.

Pampalk M, Knust N (2010) Transitional Justice und positive Komplementarität. ZIS - Zeitschrift für Internationale Strafrechtsdogmatik 11:669-675.

Paterline M (2004) New Challenge to Miranda: Evaluating the Effectiveness of Mid-Interrogation Miranda Warnings and the Admissibility of Subsequent Confessions: Missouri V. Seibert. Duquesne Law Review 43:299-315.

Pellet A (2002) Applicable Law. In: Cassese A, Gaeta P, Jones J (eds) The Rome Statute of the International Criminal Court: A Commentary, Volume 2. Oxford University Press, Oxford, pp 1051-1084.

Penney S (2003) Taking Deterrence Seriously: Excluding Unconstitutionally Obtained Evidence Under Section 24(2) of the Charter. McGill Law Journal 49:105-144.

Peskin V (2009) International Justice in Rwanda and the Balkans. Cambridge University Press, Cambridge.

Piragoff D (2001) Evidence. In: Lee R (ed) The International Criminal Court: Elements of Crimes and Rules of Procedure and Evidence. Transnational Publishers, New York, pp 349-401.

Potter S (1983) The Road to Mapp v. Ohio and Beyond: The Origins, Development and Future of the Exclusionary Rule in Search-and-Seizure Cases. Columbia Law Review 6:1365-1404.

Pradel J (2008) Droit Pénal Comparé, 3rd edn. Dalloz-Sirey, Paris.

Ransiek A (2002) Durchsuchung, Beschlagnahme und Verwertungsverbot. Strafverteidiger 10:565-571.

Rastan R (2008) Testing Co-operation: The International Criminal Court and National Authorities. Leiden Journal of International Law 21:431-456.

Redmayne M (2009) Theorizing the Criminal Trial. New Criminal Law Review 12:287-313.

Rennie J, Rothschild R (2009) The Canadian Charter of Rights and Freedoms and Canadian Officials Abroad. Supreme Court Law Review 47:127-146.

Roberts A (2001) Traditional and Modern Approaches to Customary International Law: A Reconciliation. American Journal of International Law 95:757-791.

Roberts P, Zuckerman A (2010) Criminal Evidence, 2nd edn. Oxford University Press, Oxford.

Rogall K (1979) Gegenwärtiger Stand und Entwicklungstendenzen der Lehre von den strafprozessualen Beweisverboten. Zeitschrift für die gesamte Strafrechtswissenschaft 191:1-44.
Rogall K (1988) Hypothetische Ermittlungsverläufe im Strafrecht - ein Beitrag zur Lehre der Beweiserhebungs- und Beweisverwertungsverbote. Neue Zeitschrift für Strafrecht 9:385-393.
Rogall K (1996) Über die Folgen der rechtswidrigen Beschaffung des Zeugenbeweises im Strafprozeß. Juristenzeitung 51:944-955.
Roxin C, Schünemann B (2012) Strafverfahrensrecht: Ein Studienbuch, 27th edn. C.H. Beck, Munich.
Rwelamira M (1999) Composition and Administration of the Court. In: Lee R (ed) The International Criminal Court: The Making of the Rome Statute: Issues, Negotiations, Results. Kluwer Law International, The Hague pp 153-174.
Rzepka D (2000) Zur Fairness im Deutschen Strafverfahren. Vittorio Klostermann, Frankfurt am Main.
Safferling C (2001) Towards an International Criminal Procedure. Oxford University Press, Oxford.
Safferling C (2009) Das Recht zu Schweigen und seine Konsequenzen. Zeitschrift für Internationale Strafrechtsdogmatik 13:784-794.
Safferling C (2012) International Criminal Procedure. Oxford University Press, Oxford.
Satzger H (2009) Der Einfluss der EMRK auf das deutsche Straf- und Strafprozessrecht – Grundlagen und wichtige Einzelprobleme. Jura - Juristische Ausbildung 31:759–768.
Sauer H, Trilsch M (2011) Gäfgen v. Germany. American Journal of International Law 105:313-319.
Schabas W (2003) Interpreting the Statutes of the Ad Hoc Tribunals. In: Vohrah et al. (eds) Man's Inhumanity to Man: Essays on International Law in Honour of Antonio Cassese. Kluwer International Law, pp 847-888.
Schabas W (2010) The International Criminal Court - A Commentary on the Rome Statute. Oxford University Press, Oxford.
Schabas W (2011) An Introduction to the International Criminal Court, 4th edn. Cambridge University Press, Cambridge.
Scharf M (2008) Tainted Provenance: When, If Ever, Should Torture Evidence Be Admissible? Washington and Lee Law Review 65:129-172.
Scheffer D (1999) The United States and the International Criminal Court. American Journal of International Law 93:12-22.
Schröder S (1992) Beweisverwertungsverbote und die Hypothese rechtmäßiger Beweiserlangung im Strafprozess. Duncker & Humblot, Berlin.
Schroeder F (2003) Die Gesamtprüfung der Verfahrensfairness durch den EGMR. Goltdammer's Archiv für Strafrecht. 5:293-298.
Schuon C (2010) International Criminal Procedure: A Clash of Legal Cultures. T.M.C. Asser Press, The Hague.
Seegers M (2005) Das Individualrecht auf Wiedergutmachung. LIT Verlag, Münster.
Shaw M (2008) International Law, 6th edn. Cambridge University Press, Cambridge.
Sheppard D (2010) The International Criminal Court and "Internationally Recognized Human Rights": Understanding Article 21(3) of the Rome Statute. International Criminal Law Review 10:43-71.
Slobogin C (1999) Why Liberals Should Chuck the Exclusionary Rule. University of Illinois Law Review 363-446.
Slobogin C (2013) A Comparative Perspective on the Exclusionary Rule in Search and Seizure Cases.Vanderbilt Public Law Research Paper No. 13-21. http://papers.ssrn.com/sol3/papers.cfm?abstract_id=2247746. Accessed 14 May 2015.
Sluiter G (1999) Commentary: Prosecutor v. Mucić, Exclusion of Evidence. In: Klip A, Sluiter G (eds) Annotated Leading Cases of International Criminal Tribunals, Volume I: The International Criminal Tribunal for the Former Yugoslavia 1993-1998. Intersentia, Antwerpen pp 242-243.

Sluiter G (2002) International Criminal Adjudication and the Collection of Evidence: Obligations of States: Obligations of States. Intersentia, Antwerpen.

Sluiter G (2009) I Beg You, Please Come Testify - The Problematic Absence of Subpoena Powers at the ICC. New Criminal Law Review 12:590-608.

Sluiter G (2009) Human Rights Protection in the ICC Pre-Trial Phase. In: Stahn C, Sluiter G (eds) The Emerging Practice of the International Criminal Court. Martinus Nijhoff Publishers, Leiden, pp 459-476.

Sluiter G (2010) Trends in the Development of a Unified Law of International Criminal Procedure. In: Stahn C, Van den Herik L (eds) Future Perspectives on International Criminal Justice. Asser Press, The Hague, pp 585-599.

Ssenyonjo M (2013) The Rise of the African Union Opposition to the International Criminal Court; Investigations and Prosecutions of African Leaders. International Criminal Law Review 13:385–428.

Staker C (2010) Interpretive Methodologies and the Use of Precedent in Cases Before International Criminal Courts. In: Khan A, Buisman C, Gosnell C (eds), Principles of Evidence in International Criminal Justice. Oxford University Press, Oxford pp 185-213.

Stein A (2007) Das Verbot der Folter im internationalen und nationalen Recht: Unter Betrachtung seiner Durchsetzungsinstrumente und seines absoluten Charakters. Verlag Dr. Kovač, Hamburg.

Stone R (1995) Exclusion of Evidence Under Section 78 of the Police and Criminal Evidence Act: Practice and Principles. www.worldlawbook.com/attachments/312.pdf. Accessed 14 May 2015.

Stuart D (2010) Charter Justice in Canadian Criminal Law, 5th edn. Carswell, Toronto.

Stuart D (2010) Welcome Flexibility and Better Criteria from the Supreme Court of Canada for Exclusion of Evidence Obtained in Violation of the Canadian Charter of Rights and Freedoms. Southwestern Journal of International Law 16:313-332.

Swoboda S (2012) Die Europäische Menschenrechtskonvention in Strafverfahren vor internationalen Gerichten. In: Höland A (ed) Wirkungen der Rechtsprechung des Europäischen Gerichtshofs für Menschenrechte im deutschen Recht. BMW Berliner Wissenschafts-Verlag, Berlin, pp 83-118.

Thaman S (2013) Fruits of the Poisonous Tree in Comparative Law. Southwestern Journal of International Law 16:333-384.

Thienel T (2006) Foreign Acts of Torture and the Admissibility of Evidence: The Judgment of the House of Lords in A and Others V. Secretary of State for the Home Department (No. 2). Journal of International Criminal Justice 4:401-409.

Thienel T (2006) The Admissibility of Evidence Obtained by Torture Under International Law. European Journal of International Law 17:349-367.

Tochilovsky V (2007) Jurisprudence of the International Criminal Courts and the European Court of Human Rights: Procedure and Evidence. Martinus Nijhoff Publishers, Leiden.

Tochilovsky V (2010) The Nature and Evolution of the Rules of Procedure and Evidence. In Khan A, Buisman C, Gosnell C (eds), Principles of Evidence in International Criminal Justice. Oxford University Press, Oxford pp 157-184.

Torres Chedraui A (2010) An Analysis of the Exclusion of Evidence Obtained in Violation of Human Rights in Light of the Jurisprudence of the European Court of Human Rights. Tilburg Law Review, 15:205-234.

Trechsel S, Summers S (2005) Human Rights in Criminal Proceedings. Oxford University Press, Oxford.

Triffterer O (2008) (ed) Commentary on the Rome Statute of the International Criminal Court: Observers' Notes, Article by Article, 2nd edn. C.H. Beck et al., Baden-Baden.

Trüg G (2003) Lösungskonvergenzen trotz Systemdivergenzen im deutschen und US-amerikanischen Strafverfahren. Mohr Siebeck, Tübingen.

Trüg G, Habetha J (2008) Beweisverwertung trotz rechtswidriger Beweisgewinnung – Insbesondere mit Blick auf die "Liechtensteiner Steueraffäre". Neue Zeitschrift für Strafrecht 9:481-492.

Vanderpuye K (2005) The International Criminal Court and Discretionary Evidential Exclusion: Toeing the Mark?. Tulane Journal of International and Comparative Law 14:127-177.
Villiger M (1985) Customary International Law and Treaties: A Study of Their Interactions and Interrelations, with Special Consideration of the 1969 Vienna Convention on the Law of Treaties. Martinus Nijhoff Publishers, Leiden.
Viljoen F (2012) International Human Rights Law in Africa, 2nd edn. Oxford University Press, Oxford.
Vogler R, Huber B (2008) Criminal Procedure in Europe. Duncker & Humblot, Berlin.
Volk K (2010) Grundkurs StPO, 7th edn. C.H. Beck, Munich.
Warnking V (2009) Strafprozessuale Beweisverbote in der Rechtsprechung des Europäischen Gerichtshofs für Menschenrechte und ihre Auswirkungen auf das deutsche Recht. Peter Lang, Frankfurt am Main.
Weigend T (2003) Is the Criminal Process About Truth: A German Perspective. Harvard Journal of Law & Public Policy 26:157-173.
Werle G (1997) Menschenrechtsschutz durch Völkerstrafrecht', Zeitschrift für die gesamte Strafrechtswissenschaft 109:808-829.
Werle G (2012) Völkerstrafrecht, 3rd edn. Mohr Siebeck, Tübingen.
Wigmore J (1922) Using Evidence Obtained by Illegal Search and Seizure. American Bar Association Journal 8:479-484.
Wiseman M (1997) The Derivative Imperative: An Analysis of Derivative Evidence in Canada. Criminal Law Quarterly 39:435-492.
Young R (2011) "Internationally Recognized Human Rights" Before the International Criminal Court. International & Comparative Law Quarterly 60:189-208.
Zahar A, Sluiter G (2008) International Criminal Law: A Critical Introduction. Oxford University Press, Oxford.
Zappalà S (2002) The Rights of the Accused. In: Cassese A, Gaeta P, Jones J (eds) The Rome Statute of the International Criminal Court: A Commentary, Volume 2. Oxford University Press, Oxford, pp 1319-13
Zappalà S (2003) Human Rights In International Criminal Proceedings. Oxford University Press, Oxford.

Table of Cases

International Jurisprudence

European Court of Human Rights

Gäfgen v. Germany, ECtHR, decision of 30 June 2008
 Application no. 22978/05
Gäfgen v. Germany, ECtHR, decision of 1 June 2010
 Application no. 22978/05
Harutyunyan v. Armenia, ECtHR, decision of 28 June 2007
 Application no. 36549/03
Jalloh v. Germany, ECtHR, decision of 11 July 2006
 Application no. 54810/00
Khan v. United Kingdom, ECtHR, decision of 12 May 2000
 Application no. 35394/97
Miailhe v. France, ECtHR, decision of 25 February 1993
 Application no. 12661/87
Ramanauskas v. Lithuania, ECtHR, decision of 5 February 2008
 Application no. 74420/01
Schenk v. Switzerland, ECtHR, decision of 12 July 1988
 Application no. 10862/84

Extraordinary Chambers in the Courts of Cambodia

Prosecutor v. IENG Thirith, (Order on the use of statements which were or may have been obtained through torture), Office of the Co-investigating judges, Decision of 28 July 2009 **002/19-19-2007-ECCC-OCIJ**

Inter-American Commission on Human Rights

Garcia v. Peru, Report No. 1/95 of 11 February 1995 **Case 11.0006**

An erratum of this chapter can be found under DOI 10.1007/978-94-6265-093-0_9

P. Viebig, *Illicitly Obtained Evidence at the International Criminal Court*,
International Criminal Justice Series 4, DOI 10.1007/978-94-6265-093-0

International Criminal Court

Prosecutor v. Al Bashir (Decision on the Prosecutor's Application for a Warrant of Arrest against Omar al Bashir), Pre-Trial Chamber, decision of 4 March 2009 **ICC-02/05-01/09-1**

Prosecutor v. Bemba (Decision on the admission into evidence of materials contained in the prosecution's list of evidence), Trial Chamber, decision of 19 November 2010 **ICC-01/05-01/08-1022**

Prosecutor v. Bemba (Judgment on the appeals of Mr Jean-Pierre Bemba Gombo and the Prosecutor against the decision of Trial Chamber III entitled "Decision on the admission into evidence of materials contained in the prosecution's list of evidence"), Appeals Chamber, decision of 3 May 2011 **ICC-01/05-01/08-1386**

Prosecutor v. Harun and Kushayb (Decision on the Prosecution Application under Article 58(7) of the Statute), Pre-Trial Chamber, decision of 27 April 2007 **ICC-02/05-01/07**

Prosecutor v. Katanga and Chui (Decision on the Defences' Applications for Leave to Appeal the "Decision on the admissibility for the confirmation hearing of the transcripts of interview of deceased witness 12"), Pre-Trial Chamber, decision of 22 May 2008 **ICC-01/04-01/07-496**

Prosecutor v. Katanga and Chui (Decision on the confirmation of charges), Pre-Trial Chamber, decision of 30 September 2008 **ICC-01/04-01/07-717**

Prosecutor v. Katanga and Chui (Decision on the Prosecutor's Bar Table Motions), Pre-Trial Chamber, decision of 17 December 2010 **ICC-01/04-01/07-2635**

Prosecutor v. Joseph Kony et al. (Decision on the Prosecutor's Position on the Decision of Pre-Trial Chamber II to Redact Factual Descriptions of Crimes in the Warrants of Arrest, Motion for Reconsideration, and Motion for Clarification), Pre-Trial-Chamber, decision of 28 October 2005 **ICC-02/04-01/05-60**

Prosecutor v. Lubanga (Judgment on the Prosecutor's Application for Extraordinary Review of the Pre-Trial Chambers I's 31 March Decision Denying Leave to Appeal), Appeals Chamber, decision of 13 July 2006 **ICC-01/04-168**

Prosecutor v. Lubanga (Decision on the Defence Request for Order to Disclose Exculpatory Materials), Pre-Trial Chamber, decision of 2 November 2006 **ICC-01/04-01/06**

Prosecutor v. Lubanga (Judgment on the Appeal of Mr. Thomas Lubanga Dyilo against the Decision on the Defence Challenge to the Jurisdiction of the Court pursuant to article 19 (2) (a) of the Statute of 3 October 2006), Appeals Chamber, decision of 14 December 2006 **ICC-01/04-01/06-772**

Prosecutor v. Lubanga (Decision on the Confirmation of Charges), Pre-Trial Chamber, decision of 29 January 2007 **ICC-01/04-01/06-803**

Prosecutor v. Lubanga (Decision Regarding the Practices Used to Prepare and Familiarise Witnesses for Giving Testimony at Trial), Trial Chamber, decision of 30 November 2007 **ICC-01/04-01/06-1049**

Prosecutor v. Lubanga (Decision on victims participation), Trial Chamber, decision of 18 January 2008 **ICC-01/04-01/06-1119**

Prosecutor v. Lubanga (Decision on the admissibility of four documents), Trial Chamber, decision of 13 June 2008 **ICC-01/04-01/06-1399**

*Prosecutor v. Lubanga (*Decision on the consequences of non-disclosure of exculpatory materials covered by Article 54 (3)(c) agreements and the application to stay the prosecution of the accused, together with certain other issues raised at the Status Conference on 10 June 2008), Trial Chamber, decision of 13 June 2008 **ICC-01/04-01/06-1401**

Prosecutor v. Lubanga (Judgment on the appeals of The Prosecutor and The Defence against Trial Chamber I's Decision on Victims' Participation of 18 January 2008), Appeals Chamber, decision of 11 July 2008 **ICC-01/04-01/06-1432**

Prosecutor v. Lubanga (Judgment on the appeal of the Prosecutor against the decision of Trial Chamber I entitled "Decision on the consequences of non-disclosure of exculpatory materials covered by Article 54(3)(e) agreements and the application to stay the prosecution of the accused, together with certain other issues raised at the Status Conference on 10 June 2008"), Appeals Chamber, decision of 21 October 2008 **ICC-01/04-01/06 OA 13**

Prosecutor v. Lubanga (Decision on the admission of material from the "bar table"), Trial Chamber, decision of 24 June 2009 **ICC-01/04-01/06-1981**

Prosecutor v. Lubanga (Redacted Decision on the Prosecution's Urgent Request for Variation of the Time- Limit to Disclose the Identity of Intermediary 143 or Alternatively to Stay Proceedings Pending Further Consultations with the VWU), Trial Chamber, decision of 8 July 2010 **ICC-01/04-01/06-2517**

Prosecutor v. Lubanga (Corrigendum to Redacted Decision on the Defence Request for the Admission of 422 documents), Trial Chamber, decision of 8 March 2011 **ICC-01/04-01/06**

Prosecutor v. Lubanga (Judgment pursuant to Article 74 of the Statute), Trial Chamber, decision of 14 March 2012 **ICC-01/04-01/06-2842**

Prosecutor v. Mbarushimana (Decision on the Defence Request for Disclosure), Pre-Trial Chamber), decision of 27 January 2011 **ICC-01/04-01/10-47**

Prosecutor v. Mbarushimana (Decision on the "Defence Challenge to the Jurisdiction of the Court"), Pre-Trial Chamber, decision of 26 October 2011 **ICC-01/04-01/10-451**

Prosecutor v. Mbarushimana (Decision on the confirmation of charges), Pre-Trial Chamber, decision of 16 December 2011 **ICC-01/04-01/10-465**

Prosecutor v. Muthaura and Kenyatta (Judgment on the appeal of the Republic of Kenya against the decision of Pre-Trial Chamber II of 30 May 2011 entitled "Decision on the Application by the Government of Kenya Challenging the Admissibility of the Case Pursuant to Article 19(2)(b))", Appeals Chamber, decision of 30 August 2011 **ICC-01/09-02/11-274**

Prosecutor v. Ruto and Sang (Judgment on the appeal of the Republic of Kenya against the decision of Pre-Trial Chamber II of 30 May 2011 entitled "Decision on the Application by the Government of Kenya Challenging the Admissibility of the Case Pursuant to Article 19(2)(b))", Appeals Chamber, decision of 30 August 2011 **ICC-01/09-01/11-307**

Situation in the Democratic Republic of the Congo (Judgment on the Prosecutor's Application for Extraordinary Review of the Pre-Trial Chamber I' 31 March 2006 Decision Denying Leave to Appeal), Appeals Chamber, decision of 13 July 2006 **ICC-01/04-168**

Situation in the Republic of Kenya (Decision Pursuant to Article 15 of the Rome Statute of the Authorization of an Investigation into the Situation in the Republic of Kenya), Pre-Trial Chamber, decision of 31 March 2010 **ICC-01/09-19**

International Criminal Tribunal for the Former Yugoslavia

Prosecutor v. Aleksoviski (Decision on Prosecutor's Appeal on Admissibility of Evidence), Trial Chamber, decision of 16 February 1999 **IT-95-14-1-T**

Prosecutor v. Blaškić (Judgment on the Request of the Republic of Croatia for the Review of the Decision of Trial Chamber II of July 1997), Appeals Chamber, decision of 29 October 1997 **IT-95-14-A**

Prosecutor v. Blaškić (Judgment), Trial Chamber, decision of 3 March 2000 **IT-95-14-T**

Prosecutor v. Delalić et al. (Decision on Hazim Mucić's Motions Pursuant to Rule 73), Trial Chamber, decision of 1 September 1997 **IT-96-21-T**

Prosecutor v. Delalić et al. (Decision on Zdravko Mucić's Motion for the Exclusion of Evidence), Trial Chamber, decision of 2 September 1997 **IT-96-21-T**

Prosecutor v. Delalić et al. (Decision on the Prosecution's Motion for the Redaction of the Public Record), Trial Chamber, decision of 5 June 1997 **IT-96-21-T**

Prosecutor v. Delalić et al. (Decision on the Motion of the Prosecution for the Admissibility of Evidence), ICTY (Trial Chamber), decision of 19 January 1998 **IT-96-21-T**

Prosecutor v. Delalić et al. (Decision on the Tendering of Prosecution Exhibits 104 - 108), Trial Chamber, decision of 9 February 1998 **IT-96-21-T**

Prosecutor v. Delalić et al. (Judgment) ICTY (Trial Chamber), decision of 16 November 1998 **IT-96-21-T**

Prosecutor v. Erdemović (Sentencing Judgment), Trial Chamber, decision of 29 November 1996 **IT-96-22-T**

Prosecutor v. Furundžjia (Sentencing Judgment), Trial Chamber, decision of 10 December 1998 **IT-95-17-1-T**

Prosecutor v. Furundžija (Judgment), Appeals Chamber, decision of 21 July 2000 **IT-95-17-1-A**

Prosecutor v. Haraqija and Morina (Decision on Haraqija and Morina's Second Request for a Declaration of Inadmissibility and Exclusion of Evidence), Trial Chamber, decision of 24 November 2008 **IT-04-84-R77.4-T**

Prosecutor v. Haraqija and Morina (Judgment), Appeals Chamber, decision of 23 July 2009 **IT-04-84-R77.4-A**

Prosecutor v. Karadžić and Mladić ("Mandat de perquisition"), Duty judge, under seal, 24 February 1998 (authorising the search of the headquarters of the Bratunac Brigade) **IT-95-18-I**

Prosecutor v. Karadžić and Mladić ("Mandat de perquisition"), Duty judge, under seal, 24 February 1998 (authorising the search of the headquarters of the Zvornik Brigade) **IT-95-18-I**

Prosecutor v. Karadžić (Decision on the accused's Motion to exclude intercepted conversations), Trial Chamber, decision of 30 September 2010 **IT-95-5-18-T**

Prosecutor v. Karadžić (Search warrant for the Public Security Center (CJB) Srpsko Sarajevo), Duty judge, under seal and *ex parte*, 11 September 2003 **IT-95-5-18**

Prosecutor v. Karadžić (Decision on the accused's requests for copies of search warrants), ICTY (Trial Chamber), decision of 29 August 2008 **IT-95-5-18-T**

Prosecutor v. Kordić and Čerkez (Decision Stating Reasons for Trial Chamber's Ruling of June 1999 Rejecting Defence Motion to Suppress Evidence), Trial Chamber, decision of 25 June 1999 **IT-95-14-2-T**

Prosecutor v. Kordić and Čerkez, Trial Chamber, Transcript of 2 February 2000 **IT-95-14-2-T**

Prosecutor v. Kupreškić et al. Trial Chamber, judgment of 14 January 2000 **IT-95-16-T**

Prosecutor v. Martić (Decision Adopting Guidelines on the Standards Governing the Admission of Evidence), Trial Chamber, decision of 19 January 2006 **IT-95-11-T**

Prosecutor v. Milosević (Final Decision on the Admissibility of Intercepted Communications), Trial Chamber, decision of 14 June 2004 **IT-02-54-T**

Prosecutor v. Mrkšić (Decision Concerning the Use of Statements Given by the Accused), Trial Chamber, decision of 9 October 2006 **IT-95-13-1-T**

Prosecutor v. Mrkšić et al. (Judgment), Trial Chamber, decision of 5 May 2009 **IT-95-13-1-T**

Prosecutor v. Mucić et al. (Judgment), Appeals Chamber, decision of 20 February 2001 **IT-96-21-A**

Prosecutor v. Orić (Oder Concerning Guidelines on Evidence and the Conduct of Parties During Trial Proceedings), Trial Chamber, decision of 21 October 2004 **IT-03-68-T**

Prosecutor v. Stakić (Provisional Order on the Standards Governing the Admission of Evidence and Identification), Trial Chamber, decision of 25 February 2002 **IT-97-24-T**

Prosecutor v. Tadić (Decision on the Prosecution's Motion Requesting Protective Measures for Victims and Witnesses), Trial Chamber, decision of 10 August 1995 **IT-94-1-T**

Prosecutor v. Tadić (Decision on the Defence Motion for Interlocutory Appeal on Jurisdiction), Appeals Chamber, decision of 2 October 1995 **IT-94-1-T**

International Criminal Tribunal for Rwanda

Prosecutor v. Bagosara and 28 others (Decision on the Admissibility of the Prosecutor's Appeal from the Decision of a Confirming Judge Dismissing an Indictment against Theoneste Bagosara and 28 Others), Appeals Chamber, decision of 8 June 1998 **ICTR-98-37-A**

Prosecutor v. Bagosora et al. (Decision on Exclusion of Evidence under Rule 95), Trial Chamber, decision of 27 January 2004 **ICTR-98-41-T**

Prosecutor v. Bagosora et al. (Decision on the Defence for Bagosora's Request to Obtain the Cooperation of the Republic of Ghana), Trial Chamber, decision of 25 May 2004 **ICTR-98-41-T**

Prosecutor v. Barayagwiza (Decision), Appeals Chamber, decision of 3 November 1999 **ICTR-97-19-A**

Prosecutor v. Karemera (Decision on Defence Oral Motions for Exclusion of Witness XMB's Testimony, for Sanctions against the Prosecution and for Exclusion Outside the Scope of the Indictment), Trial Chamber, decision of 19 October 2006 **ICTR-97-24-T**

Prosecutor v. Karemera (Decision on the Prosecution Motion for Admission into Evidence of Post-Arrest Interviews with Joseph Nzirorera and Mathieu Ngirumpatse), Trial Chamber, decision of 2 November 2007 **ICTR-97-24-T**

Prosecutor v. Karemera et al. (Decision on the Prosecutor's Motion for Amission of Certain Exibits into Evidence), Trial Chamber, decision of 25 January 2008 **ICTR-97-24-T**

Prosecutor v. Nchamihigo (Decision on the Prosecutor's Application to Admit into Evidence the Transcript of the Accused's Interview as a Suspect and the Defence's Request to Hold a Voir Dire), Trial Chamber, decision of 5 February 2007 **ICTR-01-63-T**

International Court of Justice

United Kingdom of Great Britain and Northern Ireland v. Albania (Corfu Channel Case),

ICJ, decision of 9 April 1949.

Effects of awards of compensation made by the U.N. Administrative Tribunal (Advisory Opinion), ICJ, decision of 13 July 1954.

Germany v. Denmark/Germany v. The Netherlands (North Sea Continental Shelf case), ICJ, decision of 20 February 1969.

Nicaragua v. The United States of America (Case concerning military and paramilitary activities in and against Nicaragua), ICJ, decision of 27 June 1986.

National Jurispruence

Canada

Regina. v. Bartle, Supreme Court of Canada, decision of 29 September 1994, [1994] 3 S.C.R. 173.

Regina v. Burlingham, Supreme Court of Canada, decision of 18 May 1995, [1995] 2 S.C.R. 206.

Regina v. Caputo, Court of Appeal for Ontario, decision of 4 March 1997.

Regina v. Collins, Supreme Court of Canada, decision of 9 April 1987, [1987] 1 S.C.R. 265.

Regina v. Genest, Supreme Court of Canada, decision of 26 January 1989, [1989] 1 S.R.C. 59.

Regina v. Goldhart, Supreme Court of Canada, decision of 4 July 1996, [1996] 2 S.C.R. 463.

Regina (on the application of Saifi) v. Governor of Brixton Prison, Divisional Court, decision of 21 December, [2001] 1 W.L.R. 1134.

Regina v. Grant, Supreme Court of Canada, decision of 17 July 2009, [2009] 2 S.C.R. 353.

Regina v. Harrer, Supreme Court of Canada, decision of 19 October 1995, [1995] 3 S.C.R. 56.

Regina v. Harrison, Supreme Court of Canada, decision of 17 July 2009, [2009] 2 S.C.R. 494.

Regina v. I. (L.R.) and T. (E.), Supreme Court of Canada, decision of 16 December 1993, [1993] 4 S.C.R. 504.

Regina v. Plaha, Court of Appeal for Ontario, decision of 26 August 2004.

Regina v. R. (D.), Supreme Court of Canada, decision 27 April 1994, [1994] 1 S.C.R. 881.

Hunter et al. v. Southam Inc., Supreme Court of Canada, decision of 17 September 1984 [1984] 2 S.C.R. 145.

Regina v. Stillman, Supreme Court of Canada, decision of 10 March 1997, [1997] 1 S.C.R. 607.

Regina v. Strachan, Supreme Court of Canada, decision of 15 December 1988, [1988] 2 S.C.R. 980.

Regina v. Therens, Supreme Court of Canada, decision of 23 May 1985, [1985] 1 S.C.R. 613.

Regina v. Wittwer, Supreme Court of Canada, decision of 5 June 2008, [2008] 2 S.C.R. 235.

Regina v. Wray, Supreme Court of Canada, decision of 26 June 1970, [1971] S.C.R. 272, 273.

England and Wales

A. and others v. Secretary of State for the Home Department, Court of Appeal of England and Wales, decision of 11 August 2004, [2004] EWCA Civ 1123.

A and Others v. Secretary of State for the Home Department, House of Lords, decision of 8 December 2005, [2005] UKHL 71.

Regina v. Absolam, Court of Appeal of England and Wales, decision of 1 July 1988, [1988] Cr. App. R. 332.

Regina v. Alladice, Court of Appeal of England and Wales, decision of 8 May 1988, [1988] WL 624104.

Regina v. Glaves, Court of Appeal of England and Wales, decision of 29 January 1993, [1993] Crim. L.R. 685.

Regina. v. Goldenberg, Court of Appeal of England and Wales, judgment of 18 May 1988, [1989] 88 Cr. App. R. 285.

Regina v. Keenan, Court of Appeal of England and Wales, decision of 26 April 1989, [1990] 2 Q.B. 54.

Regina v. Khan, Court of Appeal of England and Wales, decision of 15 June 1992, [1993] Crim. L.R. 54.

Regina v. Mason, Court of Appeal of England and Wales, decision of 21 May 1987, [1988] 1 W.L.R. 139.

Regina v. McGovern, Court of Appeal of England and Wales, decision of 18 May 1990, [1991] Crim. L.R. 124.

Regina v. Neil, Court of Appeal of England and Wales, decision of 29 November 1993, [1994] Crim. L.R. 441.

Regina v. Samuel, Court of Appeal of England and Wales, decision of 17 December 1987, [1988] Q.B. 615.

Regina v. Singleton, Court of Appeal of England and Wales, decision of 14 February 2002, [2002] EWCA Crim. 459.

Regina v. Walsh, Court of Appeal of England and Wales, decision of 13 July 1989, [1990] 91 Cr. App. R. 161.

Germany

German Federal Supreme Court (BGH), decision of 21 January 1958, *Neue Juristische Wochenschrift* 1958, p. 557.

German Federal Supreme Court (BGH), decision of 14 June 1960, *Neue Juristische Wochenschrift* 1960, p. 1580.

German Federal Supreme Court (BGH), decision of 28 June 1961, *Neue Juristische Wochenschrift* 1962, p. 1978.

German Federal Supreme Court (BGH), decision of 21 February 1964, *Neue Juristische Wochenschrift* 1964, p. 1139.

German Federal Supreme Court (BGH), decision of 31 May 1968, *Neue Juristische Wochenschrift* 1968, p. 1838.

German Federal Supreme Court (BGH), decision of 17 March 1971, *Neue Juristische Wochenschrift* 1971, p. 1097.

German Constitutional Court (BVerfG), decision of 31 January 1973, *Neue Juristische Wochenschrift* 1973, p. 891.

German Federal Supreme Court (BGH), decision of 14 March 1974, *Neue Juristische Wochenschrift* 1974, p. 1570.

German Federal Supreme Court (BGH), decision of 22 February 1978, *Neue Juristische Wochenschrift* 1978, p. 1390.

German Federal Supreme Court (BGH), decision of 18 April 1980, *Neue Juristische Wochenschrift*, 1980, p. 1700.

German Federal Supreme Court (BGH), decision of 24 August 1983, *Neue Juristische Wochenschrift* 1984, p. 2772.

German Federal Supreme Court (BGH), decision of 25 February 1985, *Neue Zeitschrift für Strafrecht* 1985, p. 262.

German Federal Supreme Court (BGH), decision of 28 April 1987, *Neue Juristische Wochenschrift* 1987, p. 2525.

German Federal Supreme Court (BGH), decision of 15 February 1989, *Neue Zeitschrift für Strafrecht* 1989, p. 375.

German Federal Supreme Court (BGH), decision of 27 February 1992, *Neue Juristische Wochenschrift* 1992, p. 1463.

German Federal Supreme Court (BGH), decision of 9 March 1995, *Neue Juristische Wochenschrift* 1995, p. 2047.

German Federal Supreme Court (BGH), decision of 12 January 1996, *Neue Juristische Wochenschrift* 1996, p. 1547.

German Constitutional Court (BVerfG), decision of 27 April 2000, *Neue Juristische Wochenschrift* 2000, p. 3557.

German Federal Supreme Court (BGH), decision of 13 January 2005, *Juristische Rundschau* 2005, p. 385.

German Federal Supreme Court (BGH), decision of 12 April 2005, *Neue Juristische Wochenschrift* 2005, p. 1917.

Hamburg Higher Regional Court (OLG), decision of 14 June 2005, *Neue Juristische Wochenschrift* 2005, p. 2326.

German Constitutional Court (BVerfG), decision of 30 June 2005, *Neue Zeitschrift für Strafrecht* 2006, p. 46.

German Federal Supreme Court (BGH), decision of 18 April 2007, *Neue Juristische Wochenschrift* 2007, 2269.

German Federal Supreme Court (BGH), decision of 20 December 2007, *Neue Juristische Wochenschrift* 2008, p. 1090.

German Constitutional Court (BVerfG), decision of 28 July 2008, *Neue Juristische Wochenschrift* 2008, p. 3054.

German Federal Supreme Court (BGH), decision of 18 December 2008, *Neue Juristische Wochenschrift* 2009, p. 1427.

United States

Arizona v. Evans, United States Supreme Court, decision of 1 March 1995, 514 U.S. 1 (1995).

– *Brown v. Illinois*, United States Supreme Court, decision of 26 June 1975, 422 U.S. 590 (1975).

Herring v. United States, United States Supreme Court, decision of 14 January 2009, 07-513 (2009).

Hopt v. Utah, United States Supreme Court, decision of 3 March 1884, 110 U.S. 574 (1884).

Hudson v. Michigan, United States Supreme Court, decision of 15 June 2006, 547 U.S. 586 (2006).

Leon v. Twomey, United States Supreme Court, decision of 12 January 1972, 404 U.S. 477 (1972).

Lyons v. Oklahoma, United States Supreme Court, decision of 5 June 1944, 322 U.S. 596 (1944).

Mapp v. Ohio, United States Supreme Court, decision of June 19 1961, 367 U.S. 643 (1961).

Massiah v. the United States, United States Supreme Court, decision of 8 May 1964, 377 U.S. 201 (1964).

Michigan v. Tucker, United States Supreme Court, decision of 10 June 1974, 417 U.S. 433 (1974).

Miranda v. Arizona, United States Supreme Court, decision of 13 June 1966, 384 U.S. 436 (1966).

Missouri v. Seibert, United States Supreme Court, decision of 28 June 2004, 02-1371 (2004).

Nardone v. The United States, United States Supreme Court, decision of 11 December 1939, 308 U.S. 338 (1939).

Nix v. Williams, United States Supreme Court, decision of 11 June 1984, 467 U.S. 431 (1984).

Silverthorne Lumber Co. v. United States, United States Supreme Court, decision of 26 January 1920, 251 U.S. 385 (1920).

Stone v. Powell, United States Supreme Court, decision of 6 July 1976, 428 U.S. 465 (1976).

Tehan v. United States, ex. Rel. Shott, United States Supreme Court, decision of 19 January 1966, 382 U.S. 406 (1966).

Terry v. Ohio, United States Supreme Court, decision of 10 June 1968, 392 U.S. 1 (1968).

United States v. Bayer, United States Supreme Court, decision of 9 June 1947, 331 U.S. 532 (1947).

Oregon v. Elstad, United States Supreme Court, decision of 4 March 1985, 470 U.S. 298 (1985).

United States v. Fernandez-Caro, United States District Court for the Southern District of Texas, decision of 2 September 1987, 677 F.Supp. 893 (1987).

Unites States v. Griffin, United States Court of Appeals, 6th Circuit, decision of 21 April 1974, 502 F.2d 959 (1974).

United States v. Lee, United States Court of Appeals for the Second District, decision of 7 June 2013, No. 12-0088-cr.

United States v. Leon, United States Supreme Court, decision of 5 July 1984, 468 U.S. 897 (1984).

United States v. Murray, United States Supreme Court, decision of 27 June 1988, 487 U.S. 533 (1988).

United States v. Patane, United States Supreme Court, decision of 28 June 2004, 02-1183 (2004).

United States v. Tejada, United States Court of Appeals, 7th Circuit, decision of 10 April 2008, 524 F.3d 809 (2008).

Weeks v. United States, United States Supreme Court, decision of 24 February 1914, 232 U.S. 383 (1914).

Legal Documents

International

African Charter on Human and Peoples' Rights, signed on 27 June 1981, entered into force on 21 October 1986; available at: https://www.achpr.org/instruments/achpr/ (last visited: October 2013).

American Convention on Human Rights, signed on 22 November 1969, entered into force on 18 July 1978; available at: http://www.cidh.org/Basicos/English/Basic3.American%20Convention.htm (last visited: October 2013).

Charter of the United Nations, adopted on 26 June 1945, entered into force on 24 October 1945, available at: http://www.un.org/en/documents/charter/ (last visited: October 2013).

Committee against Torture, *Concluding observations of the Committee against Torture on Germany*, UN Doc. A/53/44 of 11 May 1998, available at: http://www.unhchr.ch/tbs/doc.nsf/%28Symbol%29/A.53.44,paras.179-195.En?OpenDocument (last visited: October 2013).

Convention for the Protection of Human Rights and Fundamental Freedoms, adopted on 4 November 1950, entered into force on 3 September 1950, available at: http://www.echr.coe.int/Pages/home.aspx?p=basictexts&c=#n1359128122487_pointer (last visited: October 2013).

Human Rights Committee, General Comment no. 16 of 8 April 1988; available at: http://www.unhchr.ch/tbs/doc.nsf/%28Symbol%29/23378a8724595410c12563ed004aeecd?Opendocument (last visited: October 2013).

ICC Elements of Crimes, adopted on adopted on 9 September 2002, entered into force on 9 September 2002; available at: http://www.icc-cpi.int/en_menus/icc/legal%20texts%20and%20tools/official%20journal/Pages/elements%20of%20crimes.aspx (last visited: October 2013).

ICC Rules of Procedure and Evidence, adopted on 9 September 2002, entered into force on 9 September 2002; available at: http://www.icc-cpi.int/en_menus/icc/legal%20texts%20and%20tools/official%20journal/Pages/rules%20of%20procedure%20and%20evidence.aspx.

P. Viebig, *Illicitly Obtained Evidence at the International Criminal Court*, International Criminal Justice Series 4, DOI 10.1007/978-94-6265-093-0

ICTR Rules of Procedure and Evidence; all versions available at: http://www.unictr.org/tabid/95/default.aspx (last visited: October 2013).

ICTY Rules of Procedure and Evidence; all versions available at: http://www.icty.org/sid/136 (last visited: October 2013).

ILC, 'Report of the International Law Commission on the second part of its seventeenth session and on its eighteenth session', *Yearbook of the International Law Commission* (1963) II; available at: http://untreaty.un.org/ilc/publications/yearbooks/1963.htm (last visited: October 2013).

ILC, 'Report of the International Law Commission on the second part of its seventeenth session and on its eighteenth session', *Yearbook of the International Law Commission* (1966) II; available at: http://untreaty.un.org/ilc/texts/instruments/english/commentaries/1_1_1966.pdf (last visited: October 2013).

ILC, Summary records of the eighteenth session, *YBILC* (1966) I/2; available at: http://untreaty.un.org/ilc/publications/yearbooks/Ybkvolumes(e)/ILC_1966_v1_p2_e.pdf (last visited: October 2013).

International Covenant on Civil and Political Rights, signed on 16 December 1966, entered into force on 23 March 1976; available at: http://www.ohchr.org/EN/ProfessionalInterest/Pages/CCPR.aspx (last visited: October 2013).

ICC Preparatory Committee, *Report of the Preparatory Committee on the Establishment of an International Criminal Court,* Volume I, *Proceedings of the Preparatory Committee during March-April and August 1996,* U.N. Doc. A /51/22 of 13 September 1996.

Rome Statute of the International Criminal Court (ICC Statute), signed on 17 July 1998, entered into force on 1 July 2001; available at: http://www.icc-cpi.int/en_menus/icc/legal%20texts%20and%20tools/official%20journal/Pages/rome%20statute.aspx (last visited: October 2013).

Rome Statute, Official Records, Volume III; available at: http://untreaty.un.org/cod/icc/rome/proceedings/E/Rome%20Proceedings_v3_e.pdf (last visited: October 2013).

Staff Rules of the International Criminal Court, available at: http://www.icc-cpi.int/en_menus/icc/legal%20texts%20and%20tools/official%20journal/Pages/staff%20rules%20of%20the%20international%20criminal%20court%20%20annex%20to%20icc%20ai%202005%20003.aspx (last visited: October 2013).

Statute of the International Criminal Tribunal for the former Yugoslavia (ICTY Statute), last version of September 2009; available at: http://www.icty.org/sid/135 (last visited: October 2013).

Statute of the International Criminal Tribunal for Rwanda (ICTR Statute), last version of 31 January 2010; available at: http://www.unictr.org/Legal/StatuteoftheTribunal/tabid/94/Default.aspx (last visited: October 2013).

UN Doc. S/RES/827 of 25 May 1993; available at: http://www.un.org/en/ga/search/view_doc.asp?symbol=S/RES/827%281993%29 (last visited: October 2013).

UN Doc. S/RES/955 of 8 November 1994; available at: http://www.un.org/en/ga/search/view_doc.asp?symbol=S/RES/955%281994%29 (last visited: October 2013).

UNSC, Report of the Secretary-General pursuant to paragraph 2 of the Security Council Resolution 808 (UN Doc. S/225704) (1993), para. 106; available at: http://www.icty.org/x/file/Legal%20Library/Statute/statute_re808_1993_en.pdf (last visited: October 2013).

National

Canadian Constitution, adopted on 17 April 1982, entered into force 17 April 1982; available at: http://laws-lois.justice.gc.ca/eng/Const/page-15.html (last visited: October 2013).

Code C of the PACE Codes of Practice on "Detention, Treatment and Questioning of Persons by Police Officers"; available at: https://www.gov.uk/government/publications/pace-code-c-2012 (last visited: October 2013).

German Code of Criminal Procedure, *Strafprozessordnung* (StPO), as amended and promulgated on 7 April 1987, available in English at: http://www.gesetze-im-internet.de/englisch_stpo/index.html (last visited: October 2013).

Grundgesetz (German Basis Law), adopted on 23 May 1949, entered into force on 23 May 1949; available in English at: http://www.gesetze-im-internet.de/englisch_gg/index.html (last visited: October 2013).See Police and Criminal Evidence Act 1984 (PACE), in force since 31 October 1984, available at: http://www.legislation.gov.uk/ukpga/1984/60/contents (last visited: October 2013).

Police and Criminal Evidence Act 1984 (PACE), in force since 31 October 1984, available at: http://www.legislation.gov.uk/ukpga/1984/60/contents (last visited: October 2013).

United States Constitution, created on 17 September 1787, ratified on 21 June 1788; amended on 15 December 1791; available at: http://www.usconstitution.net/const.html (last visited: October 2013).

Index

P. Viebig, *Illicitly Obtained Evidence at the International Criminal Court*,
International Criminal Justice Series 4, DOI 10.1007/978-94-6265-093-0

J

K

L

M

MIX
Papier aus verantwortungsvollen Quellen
Paper from responsible sources
FSC® C105338

If you have any concerns about our products,
you can contact us on
ProductSafety@springernature.com

In case Publisher is established outside the EU,
the EU authorized representative is:
Springer Nature Customer Service Center GmbH
Europaplatz 3, 69115 Heidelberg, Germany

Printed by Libri Plureos GmbH
in Hamburg, Germany